Discard

The
Agatha Christie
WHO'S WHO

The
Agatha Christie
WHO'S WHO

Compiled by Randall Toye

A Jonathan-James Book

Holt, Rinehart and Winston
New York

Published by Holt, Rinehart and Winston, 383 Madison Avenue, New York, New York 10017.

Library of Congress Cataloging in Publication Data

Toye, Randall.
  The Agatha Christie who's who.

  "A Jonathan-James book."
  Bibliography:
  1. Christie, Agatha Miller, Dame, 1891–1976— Dictionaries, indexes, etc.   2. Christie, Agatha Miller, Dame, 1891–1976—Characters.
I. Title.
PR6005.H66Z49   1980   823'.912
80-14148
ISBN 0-03-057588-5

First Edition

Created and produced by
Jonathan-James Books
225 Duncan Mill Road
Don Mills, Ontario
Canada

Designed by Keith Abraham
Edited by Katherine Koller
Illustrations by Ron Berg
Jacket Painting by Tom Adams

Printed in the United States of America
10 9 8 7 6 5 4 3 2 1

Acknowledgements

When compiling a book of this kind, it's not so much what you know as who you know. The amount of material that had to be culled for characters and descriptions was enormous. With this in mind, I owe a debt of gratitude to Michael Atkins, Virginia Brisbin, Patrick Gaffney, Nairn Galvin, Suzanne Kilpatrick, Owen Mahoney, Wendi Restivo and Susan Welstead.

My special thanks must go to Judith Hawkins Gaffney, whose memory is incomparable and whose assistance was invaluable; to Claudia Marquis, who was in at the beginning; and to my editor, Katherine Koller, who did just what an editor is supposed to do.

I would also like to thank Elana Lore of *Ellery Queen's Mystery Magazine* and Cameron Hollyer of the Metropolitan Toronto Reference Library for supplying me with material I could not get elsewhere; Nick Harris of William Collins Sons & Co. Canada Ltd., for permission to reproduce the portrait of Agatha Christie by Tom Adams that appears on the dust jacket; and to Harold Ober Associates Incorporated for permission to reprint copyright material from the works of Agatha Christie.

To W.J.R.
My Partner in Crime

Introduction

I

By its very nature, a *Who's Who* must be selective, and in that respect this book conforms to the standard. An initial catalogue of over seven thousand listings drawn from sixty-six mystery novels and one hundred and forty-seven short stories has, with the greatest care, been pared down to just over two thousand characters. In doing so, it became necessary to eliminate all of the miscellaneous and historical names which, taken together, read like a telephone directory for a small town. It was also regretfully necessary to dispense with a gallery of minor characters who, though occasionally interesting for their description, had no more than a very peripheral connection with the story being told. The fact that these characters might have called to mind people of our own acquaintance did not, unfortunately, reserve them a place in a book which generally asked that the characters had some connection with the plot as a minimum requirement to justify an entry.

A very large complement of characters in the Christie canon does not actually appear in the stories and novels but is accorded a passing reference. This group includes such miscellaneous characters as cousins and aunts, postmistresses and innkeepers, and chauffeurs and cooks. Also in this category are Miss Jane Marple's "village parallels," people who have experienced situations similar to the one Miss Marple is currently investigating and who indirectly help her find the solution to the problem. These characters have no direct bearing on the story, and thus are not listed in the *Who's Who*. However, there is another group of characters made up of victims who have died before the action of the story begins and who, though they do not actually appear, are important to the plot and therefore warrant an entry.

Guided by these criteria of selection, the entries in the *Who's Who*, taken collectively, are designed to present, as completely as possible, the complexity and diversity of the world created by Agatha Christie. Victims, suspects, witnesses and heirs all deserve and receive an entry, as does an undergardener whose sole function was as a witness to a will. Murderers, although they are not identified as such, also receive full entries. Police superintendents, inspectors and constables are usually accorded an entry provided that they did more than merely stand guard in a doorway. Miss Christie's major sleuths, such as Jane Marple, Tuppence and Tommy Beresford, Ariadne Oliver, Parker Pyne and Hercule Poirot, all receive major entries, though in the case of Poirot a full-scale biography suggests itself as the only way to do justice to this great detective. The major supporting cast, which includes Colonel Arthur and Dolly Bantry, Albert Batt, Mr. Robinson, Mr. Goby, Superintendent Battle, Inspector Japp and Captain Arthur Hastings, is also discussed.

Taken separately, the entries, in the *Who's Who* are meant to reflect not only the importance of each character within the story, but also some particular characteristic or trait that makes them memorable. Quite often, this feature is observed and expressed by another character, and besides describing each other, the characters illuminate their own personalities, as does Colonel Abercrombie when he "looked at Poirot with an air of one considering some noxious insect," while Poirot thought that Abercrombie was one of those Englishmen "who are altogether so unpleasing and ridiculous that they should have been put out of their misery at birth."

The entries in the *Who's Who* are listed alphabetically by surname followed by first Christian name. A nickname or diminutive, if it is used frequently in the story, follows in parenthesis. In some cases, the name is followed by the designation AKA and then by one or more other names, indicating that the subject was "Also Known As" those identities. Where this occurs, all of the AKA identities are also entered separately and are cross-referenced to the main entry. The names are almost always followed by any genealogical relationships with other characters in the story, and the entry concludes with the novel or short story and story collection in which the character appears. Where a character appears in more than one work, the works are listed in chronological order by British publishing date. The titles of the works refer to the original British edition (with the exception of *Ten Little Niggers*, which is listed under its alternate title *And Then There Were None*); the corresponding American titles, where different, can be retrieved from the Bibliography. The works that feature Hercule Poirot, Arthur Hastings, Jane Marple and Ariadne Oliver are listed in Appendix A of the Bibliography. The entries for the other main characters, such as Tuppence and Tommy Beresford, Mr. Parker Pyne, Harley Quin and Mr. Satterthwaite, as well as those for lesser known repeating characters, conclude with a complete listing of book titles.

II

The world that Agatha Christie created and that generations of readers have come to love was a world in which the good triumphed and the bad did not. It was a world of subterfuge and villainy in which an often placid and conventional veneer was stripped away to reveal sentiments of avarice, jealousy and contempt. Murderers assumed a hundred disguises, from the paid companions of wealthy but often irritating elderly ladies to husbands and wives, sons and daughters, nieces and nephews, actors and actresses and lords and ladies. And it was a world in which men and women were eventually held accountable for their actions.

To populate this vast world of her creation, Agatha Christie, in common with most writers of fiction, drew upon her own experience to varying degrees. About the difficult task of originating and developing characters, she quickly learned, as she stated in *An Autobiography*, that "it is no good thinking about real people—you must create your characters for yourself. Someone you see in a tram or a train or a restaurant is a possible starting point, because you can make up something for yourself about them." But that elusive someone is often more than a starting point, and real people, including close acquaintants, occasionally had a way of intruding and leaving an undeniable mark on a fictional character. This was very clearly the case in *The Man in the Brown Suit*, Christie's fourth novel, in which she made a very conscious use of her friend Major Belcher.

Major Belcher had enlisted the aid of Archibald Christie, Agatha's first husband, as his assistant in the British Empire Mission. Together, Belcher, Archie and Agatha travelled to the Dominions to promote the forthcoming Empire Exhibition. *The Man in the Brown Suit* was Belcher's idea. Miss Christie acceded to Belcher's demand that he appear in the novel by creating the character of Sir Eustace Pedler to represent him. The original title of the book, *Mystery in the Mill House*, referred to Belcher's Mill House at Dornley, where the novelist and her husband had often dined, and it was in Sir Eustace Pedler's Mill House that the body of Anita Grünberg was discovered in *The Man in the Brown Suit*. Of Pedler, Christie wrote in *An Autobiography*: "He wasn't Belcher, of course, but he used several of Belcher's phrases, and told some of Belcher's stories. He, too, was a master of the art of bluff and could easily be sensed as an unscrupulous and interesting character. . . . It is, I think, the only time I have tried to put a real person whom I knew well into a book, and I don't think I succeeded. Belcher didn't come to life, but someone called Sir Eustace Pedler did." Whether or not she succeeded in her own mind, there can be little doubt that the likeable rogue Pedler is one of Christie's most interesting characters.

Other parallels from *The Man in the Brown Suit* are obvious. Major Belcher's secretary, a Mr. Bates, who looked like "he was going to cut your throat any moment," surfaces in Eustace Pedler's secretary, Guy Pagett, who had "the face of a fourteenth-century poisoner—the sort of man the Borgias got to do their odd jobs for them." And certain elements of Agatha Christie's own life emerge in Anne Beddingfeld, the heroine of *The Man in the Brown Suit*. Both had roots in quiet English towns, yet both were undeniably adventurous and seized upon the opportunity for travel when it presented itself. Just as Anne suffered from severe seasickness aboard the *Kilmorden Castle* en route to South Africa, so Agatha Christie was struck down by seasickness aboard the *Kildonan Castle* as she, her husband and Major Belcher made their way to South Africa, their first port-of-call.

It would be a mistake to place too much emphasis on these correspondences, but they do provide some insight into how Agatha Christie developed her characters. In *Appointment with Death*, to use a further example, the source for Lady Westholme is less obvious, but she begs to be compared with the real-life Lady Astor. Both were American by birth, both married British lords and both became the first woman Member of Parliament in the British House of Commons.

Occasionally, Agatha Christie found it convenient to rework characters from one story and put them into another. The most striking example of this occurs in the two short stories "The Mystery of the Baghdad Chest" from *The Regatta Mystery* and "The Mystery of the Spanish Chest" from *The Adventure of the Christmas Pudding*: Lady Alice Chatterton became Lady Abbie Chatterton; Edward Clayton became Arnold Clayton; Marguerita Clayton became Margharita Clayton; and Major Jack Rich became Major Charles Rich. Although such things are unusual, there are a few other interesting points about some characters. In the collection of Miss Marple stories titled *The Thirteen Problems*, Miss Marple's nephew Raymond West was romantically linked to a young artist named Joyce Lemprière. By "Miss Marple Tells A Story" from *The Regatta Mystery*, Raymond and Joyce have married, but Agatha Christie refers to Joyce as Joan West. In *Postern of Fate* we are told that Deborah, the daughter of Tuppence and Tommy Beresford, had three children aged fifteen, eleven and seven and that two of these children were twins. And Major John Despard of *Cards on the Table* is renamed Colonel Hugh Despard in *The Pale Horse*.

Other characters are repeated over a number of books, and although they age or marry or, in the case of police officers, achieve a higher rank, the character development is not very extensive. As well as such major characters as Hercule Poirot, Arthur Hastings, Tuppence and Tommy Beresford, Jane Marple, Mr. Parker Pyne, Harley Quin and Mr. Satterthwaite, supporting characters like Inspector Japp, Superintendent Battle, Colonel Race and Ariadne Oliver appear in the novels and short stories with a sustained regularity. On rare occasions, a character appears in the sagas of different sleuths. For example, both Felicity Lemon and Ariadne Oliver first appeared in *Parker Pyne Investigates,* but both went on to become staple characters in the Poirot novels. One of the more interesting and mysterious characters of this type is the well-travelled Mr. Robinson. A member of a financial syndicate called The Arrangers, Mr. Robinson played significant roles in a Poirot novel, *Cat Among the Pigeons*; a Marple novel, *At Bertram's Hotel*, a Tuppence and Tommy novel, *Postern of Fate*; and the intriguing *Passenger to Frankfurt*.

Yet the strangest case of all of a character appearing in more than one novel has to belong to the mystery of Julia Lancaster. In the Miss Marple novel *Sleeping Murder*, which was written in the early 1940s and not published until 1976, Gwenda and Giles Reed meet an unnamed elderly woman at Saltmarsh House, a sanatorium and rest home in Norfolk. She was "a charming-looking old lady with white hair" who came into the room holding a glass of milk. Three items in her conversation with

Gwenda Reed demand attention. She asks Gwenda the question: "Is it your poor child, my dear?" She mentions the time: "Half past ten—that's the time. It's always half past ten. Most remarkable." And she concludes: "Behind the fireplace. But don't say *I* told you." In the Tuppence and Tommy novel *By the Pricking of My Thumbs*, published in 1968, Tuppence meets a woman who identifies herself as Julia Lancaster at the Sunny Ridge nursing home. She was "an old lady with white hair . . . holding a glass of milk in her hand," and three elements about her conversation take us back to the woman of *Sleeping Murder*. Mrs. Lancaster says to Tuppence: "Excuse me, was it your poor child?"; "That's where it is, you know. Behind the fireplace"; and "Always the same time of day. . . . Ten past eleven. Yes, it's always the same time every morning."

There can be little doubt that this is the same character. Yet Julia Lancaster dies in *By the Pricking of My Thumbs*, and the mystery of the child, the fireplace and the time remains unsolved. What is the meaning of this passage, and why does it appear in two novels that were written over twenty years apart? That remains one more mystery for the readers of Agatha Christie to solve, a mystery for which you will have to rely on your own "little grey cells."

Randall Toye
Hamilton, 1980

AARONS, JOSEPH "If you want to know anything about the dramatic profession," said Poirot, "there is one person who knows all there is to know and that is my old friend, Mr. Joseph Aarons." Poirot and Aarons worked together in *Murder on the Links, The Big Four* and *The Mystery of the Blue Train.*

ABBOT, MR. A lawyer to the village of Wychwood, he became Luke Fitzwilliam's first major suspect in the multiple deaths. Abbot was out of town on Derby day, the day Lavinia Fullerton was slain in London. *Murder is Easy.*

ABBOT, MR. The grocer who sold Elinor Carlisle the fish pastes used in the sandwiches which were believed to have poisoned Mary Garrard. He was horrified at her query concerning ptomaine poisoning from his fish pastes. *Sad Cypress.*

ABDUL The servant who discovered Mrs. Boynton's body, he was included in Mahmoud's description of the natives: "all very stupid Bedouin—understand nothing." *Appointment with Death.*

ABERCROMBIE, COLONEL Mistakenly referred to as "Colonel Arrowbumby," he "looked at Poirot with an air of one considering some noxious insect. . . . Poirot, eyeing him with distaste, said to himself, 'In verity, there are some Englishmen who are altogether so unpleasing and ridiculous that they should have been put out of their misery at birth'." *One, Two, Buckle My Shoe.*

ABERNETHIE, HELEN Beloved sister-in-law of the late Richard Abernethie, she and her late husband Leo were childless, but some time after his death she had an affair with a Canadian and gave birth to a son, whose existence she hid from her husband's family for fear of censure. She was coshed on the head while trying to telephone Mr. Entwhistle regarding an incongruity in Cora Lansquenet's behaviour. *After the Funeral.*

ABERNETHIE, MAUDE "Deep-voiced, sturdy and thick-set" wife of the invalid Timothy Abernethie, she was considered "bossy and interfering." When she broke her ankle, Susan Banks arranged for Miss Gilchrist—out of a job since the murder of her employer, Cora Lansquenet—to take the position of cook-housekeeper for Mr. and Mrs. Timothy Abernethie. *After the Funeral.*

11

ABERNETHIE, TIMOTHY Husband of Maude Abernethie and only surviving brother of Richard Abernethie, he was a chronic invalid who allowed and encouraged his wife to perpetuate his helpless condition. He felt he should have been the heir to both his brother's vast estate and position as head of the family, and thought only "undue influence" prevented this. He considered Poirot to be a "damned little mountebank." *After the Funeral.*

ACKROYD, FLORA The daughter of Mrs. Cecil Ackroyd and Roger Ackroyd's niece, Flora, said James Sheppard, possessed "the real Scandinavian gold hair. Her eyes are blue—blue as the water of a Norwegian fiord, and her skin is cream and roses. She has square, boyish shoulders and slight hips." According to the terms of Roger Ackroyd's will, she inherited twenty thousand pounds. She became betrothed to Hector Blunt. *The Murder of Roger Ackroyd.*

ACKROYD, MRS. The widow of Roger Ackroyd's ne'er-do-well brother Cecil Ackroyd, she and her daughter Flora had lived in Canada, but when they moved to Fernly Park, they became dependent on the charity of Roger Ackroyd. According to James Sheppard, Mrs. Cecil Ackroyd had a handshake like "a handful of assorted knuckles and rings." *The Murder of Roger Ackroyd.*

ACKROYD, ROGER The master of Fernly Park is quite possibly the most famous victim in the history of detective fiction. Dr. James Sheppard said: "Ackroyd has always interested me by being a man more impossibly like a country squire than any country squire could really be. He reminds one of the red-faced sportsmen who always appeared early in the first act of an old fashioned musical comedy. . . . Of course, Ackroyd is not really a country squire. He is an immensely successful manufacturer of (I think) wagon wheels." He became secretly engaged to Mrs. Ferrars a few months prior to his death. Ack-royd knew Poirot as a private inquiry agent in London and may have had cause to make use of Poirot's professional services. *The Murder of Roger Ackroyd.*

ADAMS, CARLOTTA An actress, mimic and impersonator, she had "charm of a somewhat negative order" according to Hastings. Jane Wilkinson, impressed by Carlotta's impersonation of her, offered ten thousand dollars for a repeat performance at a dinner party. Carlotta was poisoned with veronal and was discovered dead after the party. She had at one point assumed the alias of Mrs. Van Dusen. *Lord Edgware Dies.*

ADAMS, DR. Physician attending Mrs. Pengelley, he was described by Hastings as "the typical genial red-faced country doctor of fiction. He received us politely enough, but at a hint of our errand, his face became purple." Poirot thought he was "obstinate as a pig." "The Cornish Mystery" from *The Under Dog.*

ADDISON, THOMAS The father of Lily Gilliat and Maria Horton and the husband of the deceased Pilar Addison, he was an old friend of Mr. Satterthwaite's from childhood days. Although he was colour-blind and gout-ridden, he was still a man of action who greatly enjoyed fishing. "The Harlequin Tea Set" from *Winter's Crimes 3.*

AFFLICK, JACKIE Married to Dorothy Afflick, Jackie Afflick "looked like the popular idea of a successful bookmaker." Dressed in "a rather violently checked suit," he had a coach tour business— "Afflick's Daffodil Coaches. Painted bright yellow. It's a vulgar world nowadays. . . . Horrible great butter-coloured brutes." The irrepressible Afflick met his wife Dorothy on a cruise and married her because of her socially prominent position. *Sleeping Murder.*

AKIBOMBO, MR. An African student living in Mrs. Nicoletis' youth hostel, he was "very superior and civilized—but there's a good old West African belief in magic very close to the surface." Usually very confused but "frightfully nice," he suffered from stomach upsets due to the strange food in England. His professor said Mr. Akibombo had muddled thought processes. *Hickory Dickory Dock.*

ALBERT The mechanic at The Hollow, he looked after the health of his friend Henrietta Savernake's beloved car, a Delage. After a "wholly technical conversation" with her concerning the car, he told her that it was "running a treat." *The Hollow.*

ALCADI An aeroplane pilot, he was "a dark-skinned, handsome young man" who flew Mrs. Calvin Baker, Torquil Ericsson, Andrew Peterson, Helga Needheim, Dr. Barron and Hilary Craven, in disguise as Olive Betterton, part of the way to the Brain Trust complex. Monsieur Leblanc described him as "Young, reasonably competent. No more. Badly paid." *Destination Unknown.*

ALDIN, MARY A distant cousin of Lady Tressilian's, she had been her paid companion for fourteen years. Her employer described her as "one of those selfless creatures whose lives are continually being sacrificed to those of other people. She has a really first-class brain—a man's brain—she had read widely and deeply and there is nothing she cannot discuss. And she is as clever domestically as intellectually." *Towards Zero.*

ALFRED Formerly the footman at Chimneys, he left after being offered a hundred-pound bonus and three times his salary to work for Mr. Mosgorovsky at the Seven Dials Club. Bundle Brent, who investigated the Club, recognized Alfred and persuaded him to aid her while she spied on the Seven Dials group. *The Seven Dials Mystery.*

ALFREDGE, MADAME "A Whitechapel Jewess with dyed hair and a voice like a corncake," she was proprietress of a clothing store and employer of Midge Hardcastle. A vitriolic, "small woman with a thick nose," she hoped that Midge would attract her "smart friends" and raise the quality of her clientele. Because of this fond hope, Madame Alfredge was overcome when Edward Angkatell came to the store looking for Midge. *The Hollow.*

ALI, ACHMED "Voluble and aggressive" Egyptian student living in Mrs. Nicoletis' youth hostel, with a large collection of "extremely pornographic literature and postcards," he saw perverted sexual urges in everything. *Hickory Dickory Dock.*

ALI, PRINCE The son of an Eastern potentate, he brought to London a famous ruby to be reset as a wedding present for the princess he was to marry. The gem was subsequently stolen from him by a woman he met on his journey. When Poirot first met the Prince, the young man was "clearly in a state of complete misery," "gazing down at his well-polished shoes, with an air of the utmost dejection on his coffee-coloured face." "The Theft of the Royal Ruby" from *Double Sin.*

ALICE A "little maid of all work" at St. Mary Mead, she was totally devoted to Katherine Grey, and said: ". . . Cut myself in little pieces for her, I would, any day." *The Mystery of the Blue Train.*

ALI YUSUF "Semi-Turk" accomplice of Raoul Menier and an accomplished jeweller, was arrested in Beirut for stealing artifacts from the American expedition at Tell Yarimjah in Iraq and for substituting copies for the originals. *Murder in Mesopotamia.*

ALI YUSUF, PRINCE, HERIDITARY SHEIK OF RAMAT Grandson of the tyrant Achmed Abdullah, husband of Alice Calder and father of their son, Allen, he was the twenty-five-year-old ruler of Ramat. He was trying to convert his sheikdom into a democratic "welfare state." He entrusted his old schoolfriend and pilot, Bob Rawlinson, with over half a million pounds' worth of jewels which he was to smuggle out of Ramat. He and Rawlinson were both killed in an assassination plot, contrived by their head mechanic Sergeant Achmed. *Cat Among the Pigeons.*

ALLABY, MR. A widower residing in Italy, Mr. Allaby was in London looking for a governess when he first met Joyce Lambert, who was kneeling over the prostrate form of her dog Terry. "He looked a little like a dog" and eventually hired Joyce to be his son's governess. "Next to a Dog" from *The Golden Ball.*

ALLEN, BARBARA *Née* Armitage, she was a woman of about twenty-seven with "a pretty, wistful, perhaps slightly stupid face." Earlier in her life, in India, she bore an illegitimate daughter who died shortly after birth. Engaged to Charles Laverton-West, MP, she was found dead of a bullet wound. "Murder in the Mews" from *Murder in the Mews.*

ALLENSON, CAPTAIN JIMMY "A handsome young fellow of thirty, with white teeth and an infectious smile," he had once saved Lady Cynthia Drage from dying of boredom in Cairo. He was shot while embracing Moira Scott in the Privy Garden at Greenways House. "The Shadow on the Glass" from *The Mysterious Mr. Quin.*

ALLERTON, MAJOR A guest at Styles, he was immediately disliked by Hastings, who called him: "A nasty fellow if ever I saw one! And all glossed over with this superficial charm of manner. The sort of fellow who would kill his grandmother." In the midst of a fling with Nurse Craven, he also attracted Hastings' daughter Judith. Without Poirot's intervention, Has-

tings might have killed him: "I knew instinctively Allerton was a rotter—and nine out of ten men would have agreed with me. Whereas nine women or possibly the whole ten would have fallen for him immediately." *Curtain.*

ALLERTON, MRS. Widowed mother of Tim Allerton, she was vacationing with her son on the S.S. *Karnak* at the time of Linnet Doyle's murder. Intensely affectionate towards her son, she reported hearing a splash the night of the murder and developed a friendship with Poirot during the voyage. *Death on the Nile.*

ALLERTON, TIM The son of Mrs. Allerton, he said that he was a writer, but "it was understood among his friends that inquiries as to literary output were not encouraged." His heart was captured by Rosalie Otterbourne and he proposed marriage to her with an eloquent, "Rosalie, would you—you know what I mean?" Luckily for him, she did. *Death on the Nile.*

ALLOWAY, LORD AKA Sir Ralph Curtis. The head of the newly formed Ministry of Defence, he was described by Poirot: "He has brains, resource, power. He is the strong man that England needs to guide her through these difficult days of reconstruction." Lord Alloway was being blackmailed by Mrs. Conrad, an enemy agent, over a scandal in his past. He sent Poirot an autographed photograph of himself the day he succeeded David MacAdam as Prime Minister of England. "The Submarine Plans" from *The Under Dog.*

ALTAMOUNT, LORD EDWARD Although he had retired from active participation in affairs of State and was seldom publicly seen, he was described by Stafford

Nye: "He stands for England. He still stands for England until he's buried in Westminster Abbey or a country mausoleum, whatever he chooses. He has *been* England, and he knows England, and I should say he knows the value of every politician and government official in England pretty well, even if he's never spoken to them." *Passenger to Frankfurt.*

ALTON Hastings described the butler: "One of the handsomest young men I have ever seen. Tall, fair, he might have posed to a sculptor for Hermes or Apollo. Despite his good looks there was something vaguely effeminate that I disliked about the softness of his voice." Alton stole one hundred pounds in francs from the dead Lord Edgware and then disappeared. There was an implication that he was Lord Edgware's lover. *Lord Edgware Dies.*

ALVERSTOKE, LORD A former Lord Chief Justice, he was deaf, infirm and almost blind, but even Mr. Aristides felt the threat of Lord Alverstoke: "His eyes . . . met the eyes of a man as old as himself, cold, legal eyes. This man, he knew, could not be bought." *Destination Unknown.*

AMALFI *See* **LEATHERN, SAMUEL.**

AMALFI, MARIA *See* **LEATHERN, EVE.**

AMBERIOTIS, MR. "A Greek gentleman of somewhat doubtful antecedents," Amberiotis was a spy in Germany and France and sometime after that began his career as a blackmailer. He was given an overdose of painkillers, adrenalin and procaine at the dentist's and became the second murder victim, but police were convinced that he shot his dentist, Henry Morley, after his appointment. *One, Two, Buckle My Shoe.*

AMERY, BLANCHE The twenty-four-year-old daughter of the Earl of Rustonbury and Lady Rustonbury, she discussed Bianca Capelli's plight with Edouard Bréon and Paula Nazorkoff and later re-

alized that Bianca Capelli was Miss Nazorkoff. "Swan Song" from *The Golden Ball.*

AMES, DR. ROBERT Robert Ames was "a capable-looking man of thirty-odd" who had once saved Rupert Bleibner from drowning. He accompanied the Men-her-Ra expedition in the capacity of staff doctor. "The Adventure of the Egyptian Tomb" from *Poirot Investigates.*

AMPHREY, MISS "The Amp" to her students, she "was a very successful headmistress. She combined discipline with modern ideas of self-determination." Having forced a fraudulent confession from Sylvia Battle through the use of a word-association test, Miss Amphrey sent for Superintendent Battle, Sylvia's father, who said: "That woman is a fool . . . that gimlet-eyed Amp of yours has had as pretty an example of unusual psychology shoved under her nose as any half-baked exponent of misunderstood theories could ask for." *Towards Zero.*

ANASTASIA, GRAND DUCHESS (ALEXA) The Grand Duchess Anastasia has the longest name in the Christie canon: the Grand Duchess Anastasia Sophia Alexandra Marie Helena Olga Elizabeth of Catonia. The niece of Prince Osric, she was directed to marry her cousin, Prince Karl, who, according to Lady Elizabeth Gaigh, was "a horribly pimply person." However, with Lady Elizabeth's assistance, Alexa eventually married her true love, Lord Roland Gaigh. "The Girl in the Train" from *The Golden Ball.*

ANCHOUKOFF, BORIS Maniacally faithful valet to Prince Michael Obolovitch, he said of his master: "I would have died for him! And since he is dead, and I still live, my eyes shall not know sleep, or my heart rest, until I have avenged him. . . . Not all at once will I kill him—oh no!—first I will slit his nose, and cut off his ears and put out his eyes, and then—then, into his black heart, I will thrust this knife." George Lomax, always wary of any action which was not strictly old-school British, criticized Anchoukoff: "Pure-bred Herzoslavakian, of course. . . . Most uncivilized people. A race of brigands." Later, Anchoukoff attached himself, doglike and with little explanation, to Anthony Cade. *The Secret of Chimneys.*

ANDERSEN, DR. The "Great Shepherd" of the Flock of the Shepherd in Devonshire, a combination of "heathen" (according to Miss Carnaby) eastern religious beliefs and primitive Christianity, attracted quite a number of lonely women enamoured of the handsome Dr. Andersen. His church encouraged converts to make out their wills in favour of the Flock. The women who joined subsequently succumbed to various fatal illnesses. "The Flock of Geryon" from *The Labours of Hercules.*

ANDERSEN, THELMA A Danish woman bearing a strong resemblance to Dagmar Ferrier, she was hired by Everett Dashwood, following Poirot's instructions, to impersonate Mrs. Ferrier in the company of the notorious Argentine dancer and gigolo, Ramon. "The Augean Stables" from *The Labours of Hercules.*

ANDERSON, COLONEL The Chief Constable who worked with Inspector Crome on the A.B.C. case, he was a pessimistic and irritable man. Poirot described him as a man of action, though not a great thinker. Anderson believed that the fourth murder, because it was out of sequence, was a mistake and that the intended victim was Roger Emmanuel Downes. *The A.B.C. Murders.*

ANDERSON, ESTHER *See* **WALTERS, ESTHER.**

ANDERSON, GRETA Although she began her career with the Gutemans as an *au pair* girl, she was also "a chaperone, a cicerone, a duenna and a governess" to Ellie Guteman. Michael Rogers said: "She was like a Brunnehilde, a super Valkyrie

with shining golden hair. She smelt and looked and tasted of sex." *Endless Night.*

ANDRAS, COUNT AKA No. 5, Five o'clock. Count Andras was attached to the Hungarian Embassy in London and was a dear friend of Gerald Wade's. Bundle Brent noted him as "an elegant, slender, young man wearing evening clothes of exquisite cut. The grace with which he moved was foreign rather than English." He was an aviator. Later, Bundle remarked: "He's got a queer way of speaking—a kind of venomous, lisping way—that I think I'd know again." *The Seven Dials Mystery.*

ANDRÉ A member of Edward Goring's group of subversives, he, along with a man named Juvet, posed as a Frenchman interested in archaeology but whose real purpose was to search Richard Baker's room at Expedition House for a secret message given to Baker by Henry Carmichael. *They Came to Baghdad.*

ANDRENYI, COUNTESS (H)ELENA MARIA *Née* Helena Goldenberg, she was the sister of Sonia Armstrong and the daughter of Linda Arden. Her exotic beauty was outstanding. She and her husband Count Rudolph Andrenyi, smudged the initial H of her first name with a grease stain on her passport so that she would not be implicated by the H on the monogrammed handkerchief discovered at the scene of the murder. *Murder on the Orient Express.*

ANDRENYI, COUNT RUDOLPH A Hungarian count and diplomat, he met his future wife, Helena Maria Andrenyi, while connected with the Hungarian Embassy in Washington, D.C. "The man wore English clothes of loose tweed, but he was not English. Though only the back of his head was visible to Poirot, the shape of it and the set of the shoulders betrayed him." *Murder on the Orient Express.*

ANDREW Grandson of Tuppence and Tommy Beresford, he was the fifteen-year-old son of Deborah, and brother of Janet and Rosalie. He was a lover of poetry, quoted verse with conscious erudition and planned to become a poet, but in his less poetical moments he was addicted to detective fiction. *Postern of Fate.*

ANDREWS, SQUADRON LEADER An R.A.F. man whom Colonel Monro said "had it all in hand," he flew the Colonel, Lord Edward Altamount, Horsham, Sir James Kleek and Mr. Robinson to Robert Shoreham's home in Scotland. Andrews had "done this sort of thing before more than once. Flying a plane of people out to an unlikely spot, with unlikely passengers, being careful to ask no questions except such as were of an entirely factual nature." *Passenger to Frankfurt.*

ANGELICA *See* **SHAPLAND, ANN.**

ANGELIQUE, SISTER MARIE A Belgian refugee during World War I, Sister Marie knew the history of the Guardian of the Crystal. She discovered that Dr. Rose was trying to make her reveal the nature of the Sixth Sign, but she was convinced that "many centuries must go by ere the world is ready to have the power of death delivered into its hand." When Dr. Rose's little cottage on the cliff was swept away by a landslide, both he and Sister Marie were killed. "The House of Death" from *The Golden Ball.*

ANGKATELL, DAVID Cousin to Edward Angkatell and heir to his fortune, David Angkatell had been an intellectual at Oxford. Lady Angkatell said: "One wishes they could put off being intellectual until they were rather older. As it is, they always glower at one so and bite their nails and seem to have so many spots and sometimes an Adam's apple as well. And either they won't speak at all or else are very loud and contradictory." *The Hollow.*

ANGKATELL, EDWARD The cousin of Lady Lucy Angkatell and the owner of Ainswick, the Angkatell's ancestral home, he was hopelessly in love with his cousin and childhood companion, Henrietta Savernake. After his suicide attempt he came to terms with the present, responded to Midge Hardcastle's love and demonstrated a new-found maturity. *The Hollow.*

ANGKATELL, SIR HENRY Husband to Lady Lucy Angkatell and owner of The Hollow, he hosted the weekend party at which Dr. John Christow was murdered. Quite overshadowed by his wife, he "looked old and tired, and his face was the face of a man who lives at close quarters with fear." *The Hollow.*

ANGKATELL, LADY LUCY Cousin and wife of Sir Henry Angkatell and over sixty years of age, she caught Poirot's eye: "She is old—her hair is grey—there are lines in her face. Yet she has magic—she will always have magic." Possessed of "disconcertingly rapid thought processes," she also had an extraordinarily pervasive charm which had caused "inconvenience, annoyance and bewilderment to everyone she met, but she was adored by all." *The Hollow.*

ANGUS Garrulous gardener at Littlegreen House, he was an ally of Charles Arundell's from the old days. Charles discussed the virtues of arsenic with Angus, who was also witness to Emily Arundell's revised will. *Dumb Witness.*

ANNESLEY, GERARD The unobtrusive husband of Mabelle Annesley, he had "a hungry despairing look." He did not hear his wife being strangled in the adjoining suite at Laidell. "The Bird with the Broken Wing" from *The Mysterious Mr. Quin.*

ANNESLEY, MABELLE The wife of Gerard Annesley, the mistress of Roger Graham, the friend of Madge Keeley and present with her husband at the Keeley's home, Laidell, she was the youngest member of the doomed Clydesley family. "She had the quality of enchantment. She might have been one of those creatures who are only half human—one of the Hidden People from the Hollow Hills. She made everyone else look rather too real. But at the same time, in a queer way, she stirred his pity. It was as though semi-humanity handicapped her. He sought for a phrase and found it. *A bird with a broken wing,* thought Mr. Satterthwaite." She had hopes of approaching happiness with Roger Graham but was strangled with a string from her ukulele. "The Bird with the Broken Wing" from *The Mysterious Mr. Quin.*

ANNETTE Assumed name of Jane Finn, she aided Tommy Beresford to escape from the Soho hideout of the Bolshevist gang. Tommy "decided at once she was one of the most beautiful girls he had ever seen. Her hair was a full rich brown with sudden glints of gold in it, as though there were imprisoned sunbeams struggling in its depths. There was a wild-rose quality about her face. Her eyes, set wide apart, were hazel that again recalled a memory of sunbeams." She spoke to him in a soft, broken English, but as he escaped she thrice shouted out the name "Marguerita." *The Secret Adversary.*

ANNIE When Poirot questioned Mrs. Todd's parlourmaid about the disappearance of Eliza Dunn, the cook, she said: "White slavers, sir, I've said so all along! Cook was always warning me against them. *Don't you sniff no scent, or eat any sweets—no matter how gentlemanly the fellow!'* I'm sure of it. As likely as not, she's been shipped to Turkey or one of them Eastern places where I've heard they like them fat!" Poirot, said Hastings, "preserved an admirable gravity" throughout Annie's monologue. "The Adventure of the Clapham Cook" from *The Under Dog.*

ANSELL, MR. Solicitor with the firm of Ansell and Worrall, he was "more easily intimidated than intimidating . . . anxious not to stand on his rights but instead to assist the police in every way possible" when questioned about Adele Fortescue's will. *A Pocket Full of Rye.*

ANSTRUTHER, MR. The brother of Kitty, he first heard the fascinating story of Sister Marie Angelique from William P. Ryan, an American newspaper correspondent. He later learned about the Hound of Death and the Sixth Sign from Sister Marie, who came to trust and confide in him. "The Hound of Death" from *The Golden Ball.*

ANTHONY, MRS. *See* **MERROWDENE, MARGARET.**

ANTOINE, MONSIEUR *See* **LEECH, ANDREW.**

ANTROBUS, DR. AKA Constantine or Dr. Claudius. Dr. Antrobus was the assumed name of an associate of Parker Pyne's who had a talent for acting. Constantine specialized in transferring the soul from one body to another. "The Case of the Rich Woman" from *Parker Pyne Investigates.*

APPLEBY, COLONEL He had complete confidence in the police force and thought that "desiccated old women are always the ones who go in for" anonymous letters. *The Moving Finger.*

APPLEDORE When Mr. Meadowes (alias Tommy Beresford) showed surprise that such an excellent servant as Appledore could be found in hard times, Commander Haydock mentioned the "remarkably low wages" for which Appledore was willing to work. *N or M?*

ARBUTHNOT, COLONEL Colonel Armstrong's best friend who saved his life during World War I and was currently serving in India, he was the only pipe smoker on board the Calais Coach and the pipe cleaner left at the scene of the murder was of the type he used. *Murder on the Orient Express.*

ARBUTHNOT, DR. GEORGE A taciturn physician, he was a friend of Lady Frankie Derwent's who assisted her in gaining access to the Bassington-ffrench household. When asked by Sylvia Bassington-ffrench why Frankie's own family was not to be notified, the quick-witted young physician informed her they were Christian Scientists. *Why Didn't They Ask Evans?*

ARCHDALE, BETTY "A pure cockney if every there was one," she was a parlourmaid for the George Bartons, she had "the close-to-the-door-when-there's-anything-interesting-going-on technique," and overheard Anthony Brown threaten to carve up Rosemary Barton's face. *Sparkling Cyanide.*

ARCHER, MRS. *See* **DAVIS, JESSE.**

ARDEN, ENOCH *See* **TRENTON, CHARLES.**

ARDEN, LINDA *See* **HUBBARD, MARTHA.**

ARDINGLY, DAVID An old friend of Mark Easterbrook's, he was "a remarkably clever young man" who "could only find relaxation with girls who were practically half-witted." *The Pale Horse.*

ARGUILEROS, KARL AKA Franz Joseph, he was reputed to have been the son of Adolf Hitler, and was the leader of the Youth Movement. According to Sir Stafford Nye, "he came forth out of the world of myth. Myth, heroes, resurrection, rebirth, it was all there. The hero spoke . . . with the arrogance of a young man who knows that he is vastly superior to any other person in the world." Franz Joseph was the assumed name of Karl Aguileros, whom Colonel Pikeaway explained was "a common or garden fraud, a rank imposter . . . carefully chosen for the part he was to play, groomed for stardom. In his early youth he was a professional actor—he was branded in the foot with a swastika—a story made up for him full of romantic details." *Passenger to Frankfurt.*

ARGYLE, CHRISTINA (TINA) An adopted daughter of Leo and Rachel Argyle, she was a "graceful dark half-caste child." Tina worked as a librarian in the County Library in Redmyn, visiting her parents on the weekends, and claimed to have loved her murdered adoptive mother. *Ordeal by Innocence.*

ARGYLE, HESTER An adopted daughter of Leo and Rachel Argyle's, she was an Irish beauty who deeply resented her omniscient, too-competent adoptive mother and ran away to join the theatre, flung herself into what she considered a proper grown-up affair and returned home unhappy. She felt that, if her fiancé Donald Craig really loved her, he would have staked his life on her innocence of her mother's murder instead of offering her sanctuary from guilt; because Dr. Calgary did believe in her and worked to prove her innocence, even though he knew her only slightly, she fell in love with him. *Ordeal by Innocence.*

ARGYLE, JACK (JACKO) The adoptive and delinquent son of Leo and Rachel Argyle, he was secretly married to Maureen Argyle. Leo Argyle thought "he was not clever enough to be successful in crime, even petty crime," although he was convicted of killing Rachel Argyle after having quarrelled with her about money. He died of pneumonia six months after he began serving his life sentence, and before his alibi could be proven. *Ordeal by Innocence.*

ARGYLE, LEO The widower of Rachel Argyle, he had been an Oxford Don, and had been attracted to the strong-principled American heiress Rachel Konstam by "her warmth of heart. Only, and there was the tragedy, that warmth of heart had not really been for him . . . in love with him, yes. But what she had really wanted from him and from life was children." After the discovery that Rachel could bear no children of her own, she began her adoption campaign and Leo slipped "into the background of Rachel Argyle's life. . . . He withdrew more and more into his library." He had fallen in love with his secretary, Gwenda Vaughan, but felt that a divorce or an affair were both out of the question, and he and Gwenda bore their love in unrequited inactivity. Both Leo and Gwenda were suspects in Rachel's murder. *Ordeal by Innocence.*

ARGYLE, MARY *See* **DURRANT, MARY.**

ARGYLE, MICHAEL (MICKY) Adopted by Leo and Rachel Argyle, he had never been able to accept that his real mother had off-handedly sold him to Rachel Argyle for a hundred pounds. Little Micky would have greatly preferred his squalid, noisy, crowded home, his beloved fish-and-chip suppers and his natural mother's long succession of "uncles" to the sterile prosperity of his adoptive home. Micky was in love with his adoptive sister, Christine. *Ordeal by Innocence.*

ARGYLE, RACHEL The wife of Leo Argyle, she was the adoptive mother of Mary Durrant, and of Michael, Christina, Hester and Jacko Argyle. Mr. Marshall said: "The great tragedy of her life was that she was unable to have children." She begged, borrowed, bought and in some cases, stole children to fulfil her need. She operated a wartime nursery at her home, Viper's Point, which she renamed Sunny Point. In Dr. MacMaster's opinion, "Her maternal obsession never really slackened. . . . Her whole mind, night and day, was on those children. . . . Far too much was done for them. The thing she didn't give them and that they needed, was a little plain, honest-to-goodness neglect. . . . Those children were pampered and spoon-fed and fussed over and loved and in many ways it didn't do them any good." Kirsten Lindstrom, the children's nurse, said she was "so sure of herself, benev-olent, tyrannical—a kind of living walking embodiment of MOTHER KNOWS BEST." Rachel Argyle's epitaph read, "Her children shall rise up and call her blessed." *Ordeal by Innocence.*

ARISTIDES, MR. The enormously wealthy and powerful financier described himself as a collector of brains: "One day the tired nations of the world will wake up and realize that their scientists are old and stale, and that the young brains of the world, the doctors, the research chemists, the physicists, the surgeons, are all here in my keeping. And if they want a scientist, or a plastic surgeon, or a biologist, they will have to come and buy him from *me!*" *Destination Unknown.*

ARISTOPOULOS An Athenian jeweller who reproduced accurate paste replicas of valuable gems, he was thought by Parker Pyne to be "quite a genius." "The Oracle at Delphi" from *Parker Pyne Investigates.*

ARMSTRONG, DR. EDWARD GEORGE An eminent Harley Street physician whose clientele were rich, bored women, he was accused of the death of Louisa Mary Clees and was the seventh murder victim on Indian Island. He had unsuccessfully operated on the Clees woman while drunk, and was pushed from a cliff and drowned in the sea. *And Then There Were None.*

ARRICHET, FRANÇOISE The old servant at Paul Renauld's Villa Geneviève upheld the common opinion regarding the English: they are mad and liable to do the most unaccountable things at any moment. *Murder on the Links.*

ARUNDELL, CHARLES The charming but rascally nephew of Emily Arundell, he was the son of Thomas Arundell and the notorious acquitted murderess Mrs. Varley. He once threatened Emily Arundell when she refused to lend him money: "Told her she was going about it the right way to get bumped off." He had also considered poisoning his aunt with arsenic. Poirot knew, however, that Charles' crimes would always be those of weakness. *Dumb Witness.*

ARUNDELL, EMILY The "dumb witness" of the story, Miss Arundell was a "well-preserved, handsome old lady" who survived one murder attempt, but later fell victim to phosphorus poisoning. In spite of her sense of family obligation, she left her estate to her companion, Wilhelmina Lawson, thereby disinheriting her nieces Theresa Arundell and Bella Tanios and nephew Charles Arundell. She wrote Poirot about the murder attempt, but the letter was mislaid and not posted until about two months after her death. *Dumb Witness.*

ARUNDELL, THERESA Wild, cynical, jaded niece of Emily Arundell, she "conveyed the impression . . . of being at least twice as much alive as most people. There hung about her the restrained energy of a whiplash." She told Poirot: "I want the best! The best food, the best clothes. . . . I want to live and enjoy . . . to give absurd, extravagant parties—I want everything that's going on in this rotten world—and I don't want it some day—I want it now!" *Dumb Witness.*

ASCANIO, SIGNOR A small thin man with a secretive and furtive glance in his eyes, he visited Count Foscatini on the evening prior to the Count's death and was suspected of his murder. "The Adventure of the Italian Nobleman" from *Poirot Investigates.*

ASCHER, ALICE The first victim of the A.B.C. murderer, she was slain by a blow to the back of the head as she leaned over for a package of cigarettes in the small tobacco shop that she kept in Andover. Estranged from her husband Franz Ascher, she was the aunt of Mary Drower. *The A.B.C. Murders.*

ASCHER, FRANZ An "unpleasant bit of goods," Ascher used to threaten his wife Alice regularly when drunk, but he was really afraid of her. He claimed to have been at the Red Dog pub drinking with his mates at the time of his wife's murder. *The A.B.C. Murders.*

ASHLEY, DIANA The beloved of both Elliot Haydon and his cousin Sir Richard Haydon, "was one of the notorious beauties of the season" and was "capricious in her favours." "The Idol House of Astarte" from *The Thirteen Problems.*

ASKEW, THOMAS The landlord of Anglers' Arms, he was "a stout genial person who permitted information to leak from him." *Why Didn't They Ask Evans?*

ASTOR, ANTHONY *See* **WILLS, MURIEL.**

ASTWELL, LADY NANCY The wife of Sir Reuben Astwell, she was described by Lily Margrave as "an awfully good sort, and frightfully kind, but she isn't—how can I put it? She isn't an educated woman." Lady Astwell believed in intuitions and "guidance," which would not allow her to accept the guilt of Charles Leverson for her husband's murder. "The Under Dog" from *The Under Dog.*

ASTWELL, SIR REUBEN The husband of Lady Nancy Astwell and a bad-tempered financier, Sir Astwell had quarrelled with his nephew, Charles Leverson, the night before he was killed. Earlier in life he had swindled Lily Margrave's brother, Humphrey Naylor, out of a gold mine. "The Under Dog" from *The Under Dog.*

ASTWELL, VICTOR The brother of the deceased Sir Reuben Astwell, he possessed a violent temper and was in love with Lily Margrave. "The Under Dog" from *The Under Dog.*

ATKINSON, COLONEL This garrulous old friend of Tommy Beresford's was nicknamed Moustachio-Monty. He offered Tommy advice: "Elderly ladies can sometimes give you useful information. Elderly ladies and children of five years old. All the unlikely people come out sometimes with a truth nobody had ever dreamed of." *Postern of Fate.*

ATLAS Drunken, horse-betting reporter with the *Dublin Sun,* he was urged by Poirot to bet on the horse Hercules: "I tell you this, Hercules cannot fail." The horse, a long shot, came in paying sixty-to-one odds. "Golden Apples of the Hesperides" from *The Labours of Hercules.*

AUSTIN, CELIA "Slow on the uptake" and "a bit of a bore," she worked in a hospital dispensary and lived in Mrs. Nicoletis' youth hostel. Under Valerie Hobhouse's coaching, she stole assorted articles from the other hostel residents to suggest that she had symptoms of kleptomania and thus attracted the attention of a psychiatric student Colin McNabb. The night she and Colin were engaged she died of morphine tartrate poisoning. *Hickory Dickory Dock*

AVERBURY, CLAUD AKA Claud Leason, the name given to Averbury by Jane Helier in her description of the plan to expose "Mary Kerr," whom Averbury had married after divorcing Jane Helier. "The Affair at the Bungalow" from *The Thirteen Problems.*

BABBINGTON, REVEREND STEPHEN
Husband to Margaret and father of four
sons, he died suddenly after drinking half
a cocktail at the home of Sir Charles Cartwright. Other than a trial run for the
murderer, there was no discernible motive for his death. *Three-Act Tragedy.*

BADCOCK, ARTHUR AKA Alfred Beadle.
As Arthur Badcock, he was the husband
of the murdered Heather Badcock, but as
Alfred Beadle he had been the first husband of Marina Gregg. Detective Inspector Frank Cornish thought that he looked
"like a chewed-out bit of string," but he
was looked upon with a romantic eye by
Mary Bain. *The Mirror Crack'd from Side
to Side.*

BADCOCK, HEATHER The wife of Arthur Badcock rescued Miss Marple from
a fall in front of her house, exclaiming:
"I've heard about you. You're the one
who does all the murders." Heather Badcock "thought always of what an action
meant to *her,* never sparing a thought of
what it might mean to somebody else,"
and had unwittingly contaminated the
pregnant Marina Gregg with German
measles. Mrs. Badcock died from poisoning at Miss Gregg's fête in honour of the

St. John's Ambulance Association. *The
Mirror Crack'd from Side to Side.*

BADGWORTHY, CHIEF INSPECTOR
"Inclined to breathe hard in moments of
professional strain," his biggest fear was
that Scotland Yard might take over from
the local Market Basing Police force in
the investigation of the murder of Prince
Michael Obolovitch. *The Secret of Chimneys.*

BAILEY, DONOVAN A friend to Jimmy
Faulkener and Mildred Hope, he maintained a friendly rivalry with Jimmy over
the love of Patricia Garnett and was married to Ernestine Grant for eight years.
With Jimmy, he discovered the dead body
of a woman in Patricia's apartment building. "The Third-Floor Flat" from *Three
Blind Mice and Other Stories.*

BAIN, MARY A neighbour of the Arthur
Badcocks, she was a widow with "gipsy
colouring that went with her dark hair
and eyes" who was determined to become the next Mrs. Badcock. *The Mirror
Crack'd from Side to Side.*

BAKER, MR. AND MRS. The couple who
did for Andrew Marsh at Crabtree Manor

23

and who were witnesses to one of his wills, Mr. and Mrs. Baker were "a pleasant couple, the man gnarled and pink-cheeked, like a shrivelled pippin, and his wife a woman of vast proportions and true Devonshire calm." "The Case of the Missing Will" from *Poirot Investigates.*

BAKER, MRS. CALVIN The liaison officer between Mr. Aristides' Brain Trust complex and the outside world, "no one could have mistaken Mrs. Calvin Baker for anything but a travelling American, comfortably off, with an inexhaustible thirst for precise information on every subject under the sun." Horrified, Hilary Craven thought she was "without either heart or conscience. She was the efficient instrument in the hands of a big unknown force." *Destination Unknown.*

BAKER, CHERRY The wife of Jim Baker, Cherry Baker was Miss Marple's young housekeeper-cook during the reign of the old dragon Miss Knight. When Miss Knight left St. Mary Mead, Cherry and her husband came to live with Miss Marple and look after her needs. *The Mirror Crack'd from Side to Side; Nemesis.*

BAKER, DAVID Norma Restarick's boyfriend, a painter, was called a "peacock" by Ariadne Oliver who thought he was "representative of the youth of today. He wore a black coat, an elaborate velvet waistcoat, skin-tight pants and rich curls of chestnut hair hung down on his neck. He looked exotic and rather beautiful, and it needed a few moments to be certain of his sex." Poirot pointed out that had he been living in the time of Van Dyke, no one would have disapproved of his clothes. *Third Girl.*

BAKER, JIM The husband of Cherry Baker, he liked to assemble model con-struction units, a hobby which caused his wife to remark: "To get any attention round here you have to be a super jet or a turbo prop." *The Mirror Crack'd from Side to Side.*

BAKER, RICHARD (OWL) An archaeologist and former schoolmate of Henry Carmichael's, Baker had saved Carmichael's life in Basrah, after which he was given a coded message. On the way to Murik to join Dr. Pauncefoot Jones' dig, he rescued Victoria Jones in the desert, of whom he said: "She must be one of those hysterical girls who say curates are in love with them or that doctors assault them." *They Came to Baghdad.*

BALDWIN, SUPERINTENDENT Superintendent with the Helmouth Police Station, he was a "large comfortable looking man" who worked on the Marlene Tucker murder case and the mystery of Hattie Stubbs' disappearance. *Dead Man's Folly.*

BALL, MR. The proprietor of the Black Swan Inn and the employer of Mary Stroud, he was "a large, slow-thinking, heavily-moving man" who "exhaled a strong odour of beer." *The A.B.C. Murders.*

BALSANO, GIUSEPPE The unfortunate waiter at the Luxembourg, he had looked after Rosemary Barton's birthday party table the night she died, and also served the party on the first anniversary of her death at which her husband George Barton also succumbed to cyanide poisoning. *Sparkling Cyanide.*

BANKS, GREGORY Weak, neurotic husband of Susan Abernethie Banks and a chemist by trade, he was "a 'yes' man" with a guilt complex from mixing a nearly lethal prescription for a customer who insulted him. So strong was his need for punishment that he confessed to the murders. *After the Funeral.*

BANKS, SUSAN ABERNETHIE Strong-willed daughter of Gordon Abernethie and wife of Gregory Banks, she had "a little too much personality for everyday life" and closely resembled her uncle Richard Abernethie: "She had the same kind of dominant personality that Richard had had, the same driving energy, the same foresightedness and forthright judgement." If she had been male, she probably would have inherited the position of head of the family. *After the Funeral.*

BANTRY, COLONEL ARTHUR The husband of Dolly Bantry and a close personal friend to Miss Marple and Chief Constable Melchett, Colonel Bantry could often be seen about Gossington Hall, his stately home in St. Mary Mead, with "his gun in his hand and his spaniel at his heels." In his library at Gossington Hall, the body of Pamela Reeves, disguised as Ruby Keene, was found. *The Thirteen Problems; The Body in the Library; Sleeping Murder.*

BANTRY, DOLLY "A tough and unbreakable old lady," Dolly Bantry was the wife of Arthur Bantry and Miss Marple's closest friend in St. Mary Mead. Her two passions in life were detective fiction and gardening. After the dead body was found in the library at Gossington Hall, she said to Miss Marple: "What I feel is that if one has got to have a murder actually happening in one's own house, one might as well enjoy it, if you know what I mean." After her husband's death, Mrs. Bantry sold Gossington Hall and travelled about visting her four children and nine grandchildren. She eventually settled in the East Lodge on the grounds of Gossington Hall. *The Thirteen Problems; The Body in the Library; The Mirror Crack'd from Side to Side; Sleeping Murder.*

BARKER, SISTER Nurse at the Carristown hospital, she "had a habit of looking at you and looking away almost immediately, leaving you with the feeling that you had been inspected in a very short space of time, and judgement pronounced upon you." *Nemesis.*

BARLEY, HARLEY The scarecrow in the fields of the Home Farm at Thomas Addison's Doverton Kingsbourne resembled Harley Quin. Timothy and Roland Gilliat sang a song about Mister Harley Barley for Mr. Satterthwaite: "Harley Barley stands on guard, Harley Barley takes things hard. Guards the ricks and guards the hay, keeps the trespassers away." "The Harlequin Tea Set" from *Winter's Crimes 3.*

BARLING, GREGORY An old family friend of the Lytcham Roches, he had been responsible for some financial schemes in which they had lost money, and he was in love with Diana Cleves. Diana, however, could not abide him: "That man's a crook. . . . I told the Old Man so, but he wouldn't listen—went on putting money into his rotten concerns." Hubert Lytcham Roche left his money to Diana on the condition that she marry Barling and no one else. "The Second Gong" from *Witness for the Prosecution.*

BARNABY, SIR GEORGE The widower of Lady Vivien Barnaby and the proprietor of Deering Hill, he was, according to Mr. Satterthwaite, "A man perpetually fussing over the little things of life. A man who wound his clocks every Friday afternoon, and who paid his own housekeeping books every Tuesday morning and who always saw to the locking of his own front door every night. A careful man." Barnaby was at a bridge party with some neighbours at the time of his wife's death. "The Sign in the Sky" from *The Mysterious Mr. Quin.*

BARNABY, LADY VIVIEN The murdered wife of Sir George Barnaby, Lady Vivien had loathed her elderly husband and was involved with Martin Wylde, who was subsequently tried for her murder. "The Sign in the Sky" from *The Mysterious Mr. Quin.*

BARNARD, MAJOR Mr. Lecky and Major Barnard played golf after the game between Anthony Sessle and Mr. Hollaby at Sunningdale. Barnard reported that Sessle spoke with a mysterious "woman in brown," and played golf like an entirely different man when he returned from the discussion. "The Sunningdale Mystery" from *Partners in Crime*.

BARNARD, MR. The husband of Mrs. Barnard and the father of Elizabeth and Megan Barnard, he had been an ironmonger until his retirement ten years before. Barnard considered his murdered daughter, Elizabeth, as "just a merry, happy girl—with a decent fellow that she was—well, we'd have called it walking out with in my young days," and was at a loss to understand why she was killed. *The A.B.C. Murders.*

BARNARD, MRS. The wife of Mr. Barnard and the mother of Elizabeth and Megan Barnard, she was of Welsh origin. Hastings noted that "she walked with the uncertain gait of a person who had had a great shock." *The A.B.C. Murders.*

BARNARD, ELIZABETH (BETTY) The second victim of the A.B.C. murderer. Betty Barnard was the daughter of Mr. and Mrs. Barnard, the sister of Megan Barnard and the fiancée of Donald Fraser. Twenty-three years old, she was found on a beach at Bexhill-on-Sea, strangled with her own knitted belt. A waitress at the Ginger Cat, Betty had an eye for men, and she was constantly stepping out with them much against the wishes of her fiancé. *The A.B.C. Murders.*

BARNARD, MEGAN The sister of Elizabeth Barnard and the daughter of Mr. and Mrs. Barnard, Megan became a member of Poirot's "Special Legion" created to solve the A.B.C. murders, and the great detective said that it was "unfortunate that she is so intelligent." *The A.B.C. Murders.*

BARNES, MRS. Joyce Lambert's landlady, Mrs. Barnes was "a big, formidable-looking woman. Beneath the exterior of a dragon she concealed an unexpectedly

warm heart." "Next to a Dog" from *The Golden Ball.*

BARNES, GEORGE The brother of Will Barnes, with whom he operated the ferry from Easterhead Bay to Saltcreek, George informed Superintendent Battle that Nevile Strange had gone across to Easterhead the night of Lady Tressilian's murder and had not come back again. *Towards Zero.*

BARNES, REGINALD AKA Albert Chapman. As a secret service agent for British Intelligence, Barnes was known under the code name QX 912. He assumed the alias of Albert Chapman, which was also used by Alistair Blunt. Barnes was considered "useful because he was an insignificant sort of chap—the kind whose face isn't easily remembered." *One, Two, Buckle My Shoe.*

BARNETT, INSPECTOR The "discreet soldierly-looking" inspector investigating the death of Benedict Farley. "The Dream" from *The Adventure of the Christmas Pudding.*

BARRACLOUGH, RAYMOND Debonaire film-lover and sex object, he was having an affair with Lady Cicely Horbury. Barraclough introduced Lady Cicely to Madame Giselle, who then blackmailed the lovers to prevent Lady Cicely from defaulting on her loan. A suggestive photograph of the lovers was printed by the newspaper *Sketch,* and Lady Cicely was eventually persuaded by Poirot to grant her husband a divorce. *Death in the Clouds.*

BARRETT, JANE Elderly and devoted maid to Lady Tressilian, "usually as calm as a battleship," she was prevented from hearing Lady Tressilian's bell one night owing to a barbiturate-induced coma after drinking her evening senna-pod tonic. *Towards Zero.*

BARRON, BARBARA *See* **STRAN-LEIGH, LADY.**

BARRON, BEATRICE AKA Alice Clayton. When the *Uralia* went down off the coast of New Zealand it was claimed that Beatrice had drowned, and the title of Lady Stranleigh passed to her sister Barbara. Beatrice, however, had not lost her life, only her memory, and was led to believe that she was Alice Clayton. She later died of a heart attack. "The Voice in the Dark" from *The Mysterious Mr. Quin.*

BARRON, DR. LOUIS A celebrated bacteriologist, he loved his work, but not for the sake of humanity; if he had to unleash from a tiny vial a virus that would destroy all human life, he would do so without hesitation. The undercover F.B.I. agent Andrew Peters said he'd "sell his grandmother to the knacker's yard to get equipment for his work." Dr. Barron joined Mr. Aristides to gain "Freedom from Fools." *Destination Unknown.*

BARROW, MISS Along with Miss Cooke, Miss Barrow was a private investigator hired by Mr. Rafiel before his death to watch Miss Marple on the Famous Houses and Gardens of Great Britain tour. The detectives acted as Miss Marple's "guardian angels" and saved her from a third murder attempt. *Nemesis.*

BARRY, MAJOR A retired army officer whose interest in gossip was a bit abnormal, Major Barry was a guest at the Jolly Roger Hotel when Arlena Marshall died. A man with "boiled gooseberry eyes," the Major was summed up by Poirot as "an admirer of women. A teller of long and boring stories." *Evil Under the Sun.*

BARTLETT, MISS *See* **COOKE, MISS.**

BARTLETT, MRS. "A big stout woman of middle age . . . she had a pleasant face and blue eyes." Aside from being his landlady, she was in love with Joe Ellis. *The Body in the Library.*

BARTLETT, GEORGE He had "an immense difficulty in saying what he meant," and was not tremendously popular with his fellow guests at the Majestic Hotel. He was the last person to see Ruby Keene alive. His beautiful Minoan 14 automobile was found on fire in an abandoned quarry with the remains of Ruby Keene inside. *The Body in the Library.*

BARTON, EMILY Last remaining daughter of the "old-fashioned Victorian monster" Mamma Barton, she was a sister and nurse to Agnes, Edith, Minnie and Mable Barton and tended them until they all died. "A charming creature . . . like a piece of Dresden," she rented a house to Jerry and Joanna Burton. Owing to tax problems, she experienced financial worries. *The Moving Finger.*

BARTON, GEORGE Rosemary Barton, fifteen years his junior, married him because, she told him, "You're nice and funny and sweet and you think I'm wonderful." Six months after his wife's death, he received anonymous letters telling him Rosemary had not committed suicide, as it first appeared, but had been murdered. He held a party at the Luxembourg at the same table where Rosemary had died a year before, thinking that his wife's murderer would give him or herself away; however, when George drank from his champagne glass, he fell dead from cyanide poisoning. *Sparkling Cyanide.*

BARTON, LADY LAURA The daughter of the late Earl of Carroway and sister of the current Earl and Member of the House of Lords, Lady Laura was an old, dear friend of the Kingston Bruce family. She had been staying with them when Mrs. Betts-Hamilton's irreplaceable pink pearl was stolen. A matter of a missing teaspoon labelled her as a kleptomaniac.

"The Affair of the Pink Pearl" from *Partners in Crime.*

BARTON, MARY Amy Durrant's cousin, Mary Barton was with Amy on holiday at the Metropole Hotel in Teneriffe on Grand Canary Island when Amy drowned. After Amy's death, Mary assumed her cousin's identity and travelled to Australia to inherit the family fortune. "The Companion" from *The Thirteen Problems.*

BARTON, ROSEMARY The sister of Iris Marle, the wife of George Barton, the cousin of Victor Drake and niece of Lucilla Drake, she was at the height of her beauty and a formidable but brainless woman when she died. "Rosemary's life was one of late mornings in bed, fork luncheons with other debutantes, dances most evenings of the week." She had inherited the entire fortune of her "Uncle" Paul Bennett, her mother's platonic lover and a family friend. In her brief life she managed to offend a number of people, any one of whom would have had sufficient motive for murder: her jealous husband George; Sandra Farraday, whose husband was one of Rosemary's lovers; Ruth Lessing, George Barton's devoted secretary, Stephen Farraday, MP, whose career was in jeopardy after a fling with Rosemary; and Anthony Browne, whose real identity she knew was Tony Morelli. *Sparkling Cyanide.*

BASSINGTON-FFRENCH, HENRY A J.P., he was the owner of Merroway Court, husband of Sylvia, the brother of Roger Bassington-ffrench and a morphine addict. He spent vast amounts of time shut up in his study and his death was considered suicide. *Why Didn't They Ask Evans?*

BASSINGTON-FFRENCH, ROGER AKA John Savage, he was the brother of Henry and brother-in-law of Sylvia Bassington-ffrench. The family ne'er-do-well, he was widely travelled and had never worked a day in his life. He had forged a will using the name John Savage, and once wrote: "I had always had two ambitions. I wanted to be the owner of Merroway, and I wanted to command an immense amount of money. A Bassington-ffrench played a great part in the reign of Charles II. Since then the family has dwindled down to mediocrity. I felt capable of playing a great part again." *Why Didn't They Ask Evans?*

BASSINGTON-FFRENCH, SYLVIA The wife of Henry and the adoring mother of Tommy Bassington-ffrench, she had a cool, impersonal, drawling voice and spoke with a calm, incurious and slightly American accent. Sylvia knew Lady Frances Derwent's cousins, the Draycotts, which facilitated the reception of Lady Frankie into the Bassington-ffrench home. Lady Frankie thought Sylvia "not quite happy. . . . There was an anxious expression in her eyes sometimes that did not argue a mind at peace with herself." *Why Didn't They Ask Evans?*

BASSINGTON-FFRENCH, TOMMY The son of Henry and Sylvia Bassington-ffrench, he had been the near-victim of several potentially fatal accidents: once, while on the swings with his uncle Roger— "you know, giving him high ones such as children love"—the branch had given way; spinal damage was feared but the child healed perfectly. The winter before, Tommy had nearly drowned. The boy worshipped his uncle Roger Bassington-ffrench. *Why Didn't They Ask Evans?*

BATANI The old native woman, described by Anne Beddingfeld as "hideous as sin," she was asked by Harry Rayburn to take care of Anne after her fall from Victoria Falls. Rayburn had once cured Batani of a deadly fever and was assured of her loyalty. *The Man in the Brown Suit.*

BATES, ANNIE The maid at Kings Lacey, she suspected that Desmond Lee-Wortley and the woman acting as his sister were going to poison Poirot, so she left a message warning him against eating

Christmas pudding. Poirot rewarded her with a vanity case. "The Theft of the Royal Ruby" from *Double Sin.*

BATEMAN, RUPERT (PONGO) The private secretary to Sir Oswald Coote, Pongo had attended school with Jimmy Thesiger, Ronny Devereux and Bill Eversleigh. "The words 'Life is real, life is earnest' might have been written specially for him," said Jimmy. Because of his light tread, he was delegated to hide the alarm clocks under Gerald Wade's bed. *The Seven Dials Mystery.*

BATESON, LEONARD (LEN) Plodding medical student who lived in Mrs. Nicoletis' youth hostel, he was a large, friendly Cockney, warm-hearted, generous and kind, but prone to flare-ups of temper. His father was confined for insanity but, since it was not of the hereditary kind, there was no barrier to his marriage to Sally Finch. *Hickory Dickory Dock.*

BATT, ALBERT Albert Batt appeared in all five of the Tuppence and Tommy Beresford books. He was the husband of Milly Batt (whose name changed to Amy in *Postern of Fate*), and the father of Charlie, Jean and Elizabeth. He was the fifteen-year-old lift boy at the residence of Mrs. Vandermeyer, a job he left to become the office boy at Tuppence's and Tommy's International Detective Agency. During the early years of World War II, in which he was too young to enlist, he operated the Duck and Dog pub in Kensington. After the war, he went back to Tuppence and Tommy and served as their butler. Albert, said Tuppence, "was not given to the exercise of deep reasoning. Like most Englishmen, he felt something strongly and proceeded to muddle around until he had, somehow or other, cleared up the mess." *The Secret Adversary; Partners in Crime; N or M?; By the Pricking of My Thumbs; Postern of Fate.*

BATT, ELSIE Miss Batt had been parlourmaid to the late Mrs. Craddock and told Sergeant O'Connor of Dr. Roberts' association with Mrs. Craddock—that he had innoculated her, and that he had access to Mr. Craddock's shaving brush. *Cards on the Table.*

BATTERSBY, MISS Seventy-year-old retired Headmistress of Meadowfield School, she had known Norma Restarick as a pupil there. Although she was semi-retired, coaching the senior girls about coping with the students' parents, she was "in full vigour and energy" according to Poirot. *Third Girl.*

BATTLE, SUPERINTENDENT The husband of Mrs. Battle and the father of their five children, the youngest of whom was Sylvia, and the uncle of Inspector James Leach, Superintendent Battle was a burly, stolid, impassive and determined Scotland Yard man who worked almost entirely on cases of a delicate political nature. In the Christie canon, Battle appears in four books of his own and one other in which he joined forces with Poirot, Ariadne Oliver and Colonel Race to solve the murder of Mr. Shaitana (*Cards on the Table*). He was "a big, square, wooden-face man" who made on-lookers feel that he was "carved out of wood . . . and that the wood in question was the timber out of a battleship." Anthony Cade said: "I've an impression that there are no flies on Superintendent Battle." Battle was a simple man who believed only what he saw with his own eyes. Among his mottoes were: "We never know as much as we'd like to know"; "Never display emotion"; "Anyone may be a criminal"; and "Never give in." *The Secret of Chimneys; The Seven Dials Mystery; Cards on the Table; Murder is Easy; Towards Zero.*

BATTLE, SYLVIA The sixteen-year-old daughter of Superintendent and Mrs. Battle, she was their youngest child and at Miss Amphrey's school near Maidstone. This tall, dark, angular girl falsely confessed to the thefts at her school, pitifully eager to halt Amphrey's suspicions and psychological tricks. *Towards Zero.*

BAUER, CARL AKA Dr. Charles Bower, he was a Russian spy sent to discover whether Mr. Blunt of the International Detective Agency was the real double agent Blunt or not. As Dr. Bower, he was to have consulted the Agency about secret papers, act as suspicious as possible and arouse Mr. Blunt's interest in the matter. "The Adventure of the Sinister Stranger" from *Partners in Crime*.

BAUER, JOHN Replacing Alfred as the new footman at Chimneys, he "apparently . . . was the perfect servant, well-trained, with an expressionless face. He had, perhaps, a more soldierly bearing than most footmen and there was something a little odd about the shape of the back of his head." Bundle Brent first thought him to be of Swiss extraction and then: "No, German! That martial carriage, and flat back to the head." *The Seven Dials Mystery*.

BAUERSTEIN, DR. A tall, bearded man who was staying in Styles St. Mary on the pretext of resting from a nervous breakdown, Dr. Bauerstein was one of the greatest living experts on poisons. Bauerstein, who had befriended Mary Cavendish, was eventually unmasked as a German spy. Poirot, oddly enough, called Bauerstein a patriot and admired him. *The Mysterious Affair at Styles*.

BAULT, FELICIE This Brittany peasant orphan was "one of the most famous figures in France. Scientists from all over the world came to see her. She had no less than four distinct personalities." She was unconscious of the change of existence of each different state: "Felicie One wrote French badly and haltingly, spoke no foreign languages, and was unable to play the piano. Felicie Two, on the contrary, spoke Italian fluently and German moderately. She could discuss politics and art and she was passionately fond of playing the piano. Felicie Three had many points in common with Felicie Two. She was intelligent and apparently well-educated, but in moral character she was

a total contrast. She appeared, in fact, an utterly depraved creature—but depraved in a Parisian and not a provincial way. She knew all the Paris *argot*, and the expressions of the chic *demi-monde*. Her language was filthy and she would rail against religion and so-called 'good people' in most blasphemous terms. Finally there was Felicie Four—a dreamy, almost half-witted creature, distinctly pious and professedly clairvoyant." Felicie also had remarkable physical strength. In their childhood, there had been a strange relationship between Felicie and Annette Ravel. After Annette died from consumption, Felicie took her own life by choking herself. "The Fourth Man" from *Witness for the Prosecution*.

BEADLE, ALFRED *See* **BADCOCK, ARTHUR.**

BEADON, BADGER The stammering, squinting best friend of Bobby Jones, he was "a nervous-looking young man with a curious lack of chin and an agreeable smile." He wrote "in an illiterate scrawl which reflected no credit on the expensive public school which had educated him" and assisted Bobby Jones and Lady Frankie Derwent in their investigation. *Why Didn't They Ask Evans?*

BEATRICE She was a "somewhat slatternly-looking maid" to Mr. and Mrs. Gardner, slipshod in her duties. Inspector Narracott "purposely did not hand his official card to the maid. The mere fact of his being a police officer, as he knew by experience, would render her awkward and tongue-tied." *The Sittaford Mystery*.

BECK, COLONEL Chief of the Special Branch and Colin Lamb's superior, he had a favourite topic of conversation: "Why nothing tastes of anything nowadays." He was very much interested in the crescent drawn on a piece of paper found in the agent Hanbury's pocket, and was attempting to trace connections of names such as Diana, Artemis or anything relating to a moon-goddess and "crescenty." *The Clocks.*

BEDDINGFELD, ANNE The daughter of a pedantic and eccentric anthropologist, Professor Beddingfeld, Anne eventually became the wife of Harry Rayburn after turning down offers of marriage from none other than Colonel Race and Sir Eustace Pedler. Calling herself "Anna the Adventuress," she often likened her life to the exploits of her favourite cinema heroine from *The Perils of Pauline.* She became entangled in a web of intrigue which took her to South Africa after she saw the "Man in the Brown Suit" in the Hyde Park Corner Tube Station. *The Man in the Brown Suit.*

BELL, MISS The youngest typist at Rex Fortescue's Consolidated Investments Trust, she mistook her employer's death throes for an epileptic fit and suggested putting a cork in his mouth. *A Pocket Full of Rye.*

BELL, SERGEANT Energetic and optimistic member of the Scotland Yard team investigating events at the Hickory Road hostel, he "looked rather like an eager greyhound." *Hickory Dickory Dock.*

BELLEVER, JULIET (JOLLY) "A gaunt elderly lady . . . she had an arrogant nose, a short haircut and wore stout well-cut tweeds." Jolly Bellever was Carrie Louise Serrocold's "nurse, dragon, watchdog, secretary, housekeeper and very faithful friend." *They Do It with Mirrors.*

BELLING, MRS. J. The licensed proprietress of the Three Crowns public house, "fat and excitable and so voluble that there was nothing to be done but to listen patiently until such time as the stream of conversation should dry up," she said: "There's many a little thing that I hear that never goes to the police." *The Sittaford Mystery.*

BELTANE, THE HONOURABLE EUSTACE The uncle of Lord Cronshaw, Eustace Beltane became the Sixth Viscount Cronshaw after his nephew's death. He was dressed as Punchinello at the Victory Ball. "The Affair at the Victory Ball" from *The Under Dog.*

BEN The son of Martha, the cook-housekeeper at the home of Lily Crabtree, Ben was described by his mother as a "bad one" who had been in jail twice. After the death of Lily Crabtree, Ben apparently left the country. "Sing a Song of Sixpence" from *The Listerdale Mystery.*

BENCE, MARGOT "Margot Bence, Personality Photographer" had been five when her natural mother had sold her "for a mess of pottage" to Marina Gregg, and nine when Marina Gregg's fascination with her had worn off. Margot, the official photographer at the reception for the St. John's Ambulance Association at Gossington Hall, was not recognized by Marina. *The Mirror Crack'd from Side to Side.*

BENNET, ALICE Carlotta Adams' loyal maid, she was "a neat, middle-aged woman with hair drawn tightly back from her face." She discovered Carlotta's body and called in Dr. Heath. *Lord Edgware Dies.*

BENSON, MRS. Anne Meredith, Mrs. Benson's paid companion, described her employer as a "disagreeable, self-righteous grenadier of a woman." Mrs. Benson died from eating hat paint which she had confused with Syrup of Figs. *Cards on the Table.*

BENT, CLIFFORD (CLIFF) The son of an oil magnate, Cliff Bent was the leader of the young men who visited Sir Stafford Nye in an attempt to interest him in their Youth Movement: "We want young men, a great many young men and we've got a great many young men who aren't revoluntionary, who aren't anarchistic, who will be willing to try and make a country run profitably. . . . We know about you and you're the sort of man we want." *Passenger to Frankfurt.*

BENTHAM, ALICE "Gooseberry-eyed housemaid" at Gull's Point, she discovered the comatose body of Jane Barrett the morning after Lady Tressilian's murder. Superintendent Battle referred to this intuitively observant woman as "the pop-eyed one" of the staff. *Towards Zero.*

BENTHAM, MILDRED An elderly lady from Somerset on the Famous Houses and Gardens of Great Britain tour, she was travelling with her companion Miss Lumley. Both of these ladies "were slightly crippled and often in pain from feet or backs or knees but were nevertheless of those whom age and ailments could not prevent from enjoying life while they still had it. Old pussies, but definitely not stay-at-home old pussies." *Nemesis.*

BENTLEY, JAMES Lodger and convicted murderer of Mrs. McGinty, he was described as "a deceitful fellow with an ungracious, muttering way of talking." Poirot was approached by Superintendent Spence, who was convinced of the man's innocence, to re-open investigation of the case some three weeks before Bentley was to have been hanged. *Mrs. McGinty's Dead.*

BERCY, SIR AMBROSE A charming, distinguished man, he was involved in a *crime passionelle* with his niece, Sylvia Keene, and Jerry Lorimer. "The Herb of Death" from *The Thirteen Problems.*

BERESFORD, BETTY The adopted daughter of Tuppence and Tommy Beresford, she was the natural daughter of Vanda Polonska, a penniless Polish refugee who had sold her daughter to the spy Millicent Sprot. After Mrs. Sprot was apprehended, Betty was taken into the Beresford home. After attending university, Betty went to Africa and did anthropological research. *N or M?; Postern of Fate.*

BERESFORD, DEBORAH The daughter of Tuppence and Tommy Beresford and the twin sister of Derek, Deborah married a man also named Derek by whom she had three children. Although we are told in *Postern of Fate* that two of these children were twins, their names and ages were: Andrew, 15; Janet, 11; and Rosalie, 7. During World War II, Deborah worked in the coding and code-breaking department of British Intelligence. After the death of her husband, she returned to live with her parents. *N or M?; By the Pricking of My Thumbs; Postern of Fate.*

BERESFORD, DEREK The son of Tuppence and Tommy Beresford and the brother of Deborah, he served in the Royal Air Force in World War II, and was recommended for a special citation. *N or M?*

BERESFORD, PRUDENCE COWLEY (TUPPENCE) The wife of Tommy Beresford and the mother of Derek, Deborah and the adopted Betty, she was the fifth daughter of Archdeacon Cowley of Little Missendell. Tuppence had "no claim to beauty, but there was character and charm in the elfin lines of her little face, with its determined chin and large, wide-apart grey eyes that looked mistily out from under straight black brows." During World War I, she worked in a hospital; after the war, out of a job, she and her childhood friend Tommy Beresford formed the Young Adventurers Ltd. Shortly afterwards, they started the International Detective Agency. Always pausing to admire her own ingenuity, she was given "full marks for industry, zero for modesty" by her husband. Mr. Carter found that she possessed "more intuition and less common sense" than Tommy. In later life, she and Tommy resided at The Laurels with a Manchester terrier named Hannibal. *The Secret Adversary; Partners in Crime; N or M?; By the Pricking of My Thumbs; Postern of Fate.*

BERESFORD, LIEUTENANT THOMAS (TOMMY) The husband of Tuppence Beresford and the father of Derek, Deborah and the adopted Betty, he was described by Mr. Carter as "an ordinary clean-limbed, rather blockheaded young Englishman. Slow in his mental processes. On the other hand, it's quite impossible to lead him astray through his imagination. He hasn't got any—so he's difficult to deceive." Tommy formed Young Adventurers Ltd. with Prudence Cowley, a childhood friend, who later became Tuppence Beresford, shortly after World War I (in which he had been twice wounded). With Tuppence he established the International Detective Agency and together they began their life work of solving crime. Tommy was affectionately referred to as "Carrots" or "Carrot Top" by his children, owing to his bright red hair. By the time of *Postern of Fate,* he and Tuppence were over seventy years old, and had retired to The Laurels. *The Secret Adversary; Partners in Crime; N or M?; By the Pricking of My Thumbs; Postern of Fate.*

BERESFORD, SIR WILLIAM Tommy Beresford's uncle, he was a misogynist who was delighted by Tuppence's pertness and maintained Tommy as his heir. *The Secret Adversary.*

BERNARD, DR. RALPH The GP at Marsdon Leigh who examined the body of Mr. Maltravers and cited the cause of death as internal hæmorrhage, he was an "elderly man, high-shouldered and stooping, with a pleasant vagueness of manner." Hastings called him "rather an old ass." "The Tragedy at Marsdon Manor" from *Poirot Investigates.*

BERNSDORFF, DR. BOB He diagnosed Rex Fortescue's mental ailment as G.P.I., General Paralysis of the Insane, and determined the cause of death to be taxine, an alkaloid found in yew-tree berries: "Really *most* interesting. . . . You've no idea, Neele, how tired one gets of the inevitable weed-killer. Taxine is a real treat. . . . Interesting for you, too, I should think. Varies the routine!" *A Pocket Full of Rye.*

BEROLDY, JEANNE *See* **DAUBREUIL, MADAME.**

BESSNER, DR. CARL A German doctor vacationing on the S.S. *Karnak,* he examined Linnet Doyle's corpse and the bullet wound in Simon Doyle's leg. Unwittingly, he revealed to Colonel Race the identity of "X." Much to Mr. Ferguson's dismay, Dr. Bessner was successful in his marriage proposal to Cornelia Ruth Robson. *Death on the Nile.*

BETTERTON, OLIVE She had been married to her second husband Thomas Betterton only six months when he disappeared, and she later died in a plane crash near Casablanca. Mrs. Betterton's persona was adopted by Hilary Craven in order to infiltrate the Brain Trust complex where Thomas Betterton worked. *Destination Unknown.*

BETTERTON, THOMAS CHARLES (TOM) The widower of Olive Betterton, he was also the widower of Elsa Mannheim, a scientific colleague whom he married in order to associate himself with her work on ZE Fission, and for the credit of which he poisoned her. He had then defected to work in Mr. Aristides' Brain Trust complex, but found himself unable to work in captivity. He knew that Hilary Craven was an impostor but he played along with her in hopes of escaping. *Destination Unknown.*

BETTS-HAMILTON, MR. Dyspeptic and subdued husband of Mrs. Betts-Hamilton, he only "emerged from his taciturnity to mention the value in dollars of the missing pearl." "The Affair of the Pink Pearl" from *Partners in Crime.*

BETTS-HAMILTON, MRS. With her husband, she was staying at the Kingston Bruces when she discovered that she was missing a pink pearl from her pendant. To avoid publicity, the Kingston Bruces called Tuppence and Tommy Beresford's International Detective Agency to solve the mystery. "The Affair of the Pink Pearl" from *Partners in Crime.*

BEX, MONSIEUR LUCIEN The Commissary of Police in charge of the Renauld case, Bex had worked with Poirot in 1909 in Ostend when the latter was still a member of the Belgian Police. *Murder on the Links.*

BIG CHARLOTTE *See* **VON WALDSAUSEN, THE GRÄFIN CHARLOTTE.**

BIGGS, ABRAHAM *See* **GRANT, ROBERT.**

BIGGS, ALFRED The "somewhat boneheaded" page boy at the dental offices of Henry Morley and Mr. Reilly, he consistently mispronounced the patients' names. Colonel Abercrombie was "Arrowbumpy," Miss Kirby was "Shirty" and Hercule Poirot was "Peerer." His preference for American detective fiction inspired Poirot to unravel a clue in the mystery—the time of the victim's death. *One, Two, Buckle My Shoe.*

BILL He was embarrassed when he and Joe, both "decent class workmen," told Inspector Parminter and Detective Sergeant Kane that they had seen the mysterious, heavily-clad man rush past them, and had found a notebook inscribed with two addresses and the music from "Three Blind Mice" which the man had dropped. During the interview, Bill "coughed and shuffled his feet with the sheepish air of one who has not done himself justice." "Three Blind Mice" from *Three Blind Mice.*

BILLINGSLEY, MR. Solicitor with the firm Billingsley, Horsethrop and Walter, he provided the police with information on Fortescue's erratic behaviour, the financial status of Fortescue's firm and the fact that Fortescue's wife Adele was to

inherit the fortune if she survived him for a month. *A Pocket Full of Rye.*

BIMBO A good-looking young man vacationing at Cannes, Bimbo was well on his way to becoming Lady Stranleigh's fifth husband. "The Voice in the Dark" from *The Mysterious Mr. Quin.*

BINDLER, HORACE He was well-known for his photographic collection of "monstrosities," and so Raymond West took him to view Greenshaw's Folly: " 'But my dear,' he cried, 'how wonderful.' His voice rose in a high screech of aesthetic delight, then deepened in reverent awe." While visiting the Folly, he witnessed Miss Katherine Dorothy Greenshaw's will. "Greenshaw's Folly" from *The Adventure of the Christmas Pudding.*

BINION, DR. AKA Commander Haydock, Binion was a dental surgeon and a friend of Commander Haydock's who often used the dentist's surgery for his own purposes. *N or M?*

BINNS, EDITH After Lady Hesketh-Dubois died, her maid Edith met Ariadne Oliver and told her that Lady Hesketh's hair had fallen out and that Zachariah Osborne had visited prior to Lady Hesketh's illness. Mark Easterbrook thought it may have been a case of thallium poisoning. *The Pale Horse.*

BIRELL, LOUISE AKA Louise Carpenter or Charpentier, Louise Birell was the woman for whom Andrew Restarick left his wife and child and with whom he went to live abroad for a year. Fifteen years later, when she learned that Andrew Restarick had returned to England, she wrote to him suggesting that they reunite for old times' sake. Norma Restarick, under a drug-induced delusion, believed herself the murderer of Louise Birell, who had died from defenestration. *Third Girl.*

BLACK, CAPTAIN As a guest at Marsden Manor, he told Mrs. Maltravers a strange story of suicide. "He was not ill-looking, with a lean deeply bronzed face that spoke of tropic climes." "The Tragedy at Marsdon Manor" from *Poirot Investigates.*

BLACKETT, MRS. "A small neat woman" who "lived in a neat little house and garden," she was interviewed by Miss Marple when the detective pretended to need water after a dizzy spell. Miss Marple found her most informative on the subject of Nora Broad, Mrs. Blackett's first cousin. This astute woman said: "I'm sixty-five and I know what's what and I know the way a girl looks and I think I know who it was, but I'm not sure." *Nemesis.*

BLACKLOCK, DR. The father of Charlotte and Letitia Blacklock, he was remembered as "a real old pig-headed bully, absolutely set in his ways, and convinced that everything he thought and said was right. Probably killed thousands of patients through obstinacy. He wouldn't stand for any new ideas or methods." *A Murder is Announced.*

BLACKLOCK, CHARLOTTE (LOTTY) The daughter of Dr. Blacklock, she impersonated her deceased sister, Letitia, in order to gain an inheritance from Randall Goedler, her sister's employer. Only Dora Bunner knew the real identity of this distinguished-looking woman in her sixties. *A Murder is Announced.*

BLACKLOCK, LETITIA (LETTY; BLACKIE) The deceased daughter of Dr. Blacklock and the sister of Charlotte Blacklock, she had been secretary, confidante and heiress to Randall Goedler. Belle Goedler said: "Letitia, you know, has really got a man's mind. She hasn't any feminine feelings or weaknesses. I don't believe she was ever in love with a man . . . she never knew any of the fun of being a woman." *A Murder is Announced.*

BLAIR, SUZANNE The wife of the Honourable Clarence Blair, she was Anne Beddingfeld's confidante and fellow adventuress. A roll of film, supposedly dropped by a steward onto her bed in the middle of the night, was discovered to contain diamonds. *The Man in the Brown Suit.*

BLAIRGOWRIE, DUKE OF Although famed as "a most haughty and inaccessible nobleman," the Duke of Blairgowrie had wed the daughter of a Chicago pork butcher. He approached Tommy Beresford, who as Mr. Blunt was disguised as a blind man, and convinced him to search for his missing sixteen-year-old daughter. He died after falling on an electrified knob-studded floor he had prepared for Tommy. "Blindman's Buff" from *Partners in Crime.*

BLAKE, BASIL The husband of Dinah Lee, Blake was the young man who found what was thought to be Ruby Keene's body in his home, Chatsworth Cottage, and knowing that he would be suspected of killing her, dumped the corpse in Colonel Arthur Bantry's library at Gossington Hall. Blake was the subject of much gossip in St. Mary Mead because of his "loose morals" and seemingly outrageous style of dress. *The Body in the Library.*

BLAKE, THE HONOURABLE ELVIRA Daughter of Bess Sedgwick and Lord Coniston, she was to inherit a trust fund when she reached the age of twenty-one. She questioned Colonel Luscombe, who acted as her godfather, guardian and trustee, about her financial affairs, which were complicated by her mother's bigamous marriages. Elvira was involved with Ladislaus Malinowski, the racing car driver, who was also having an affair with her mother. *At Bertram's Hotel.*

BLAKE, MEREDITH Neighbour of the Crales, he was a sensitive, romantic contrast to his brother, Philip. He was an amateur herbalist. Hemlock (coniine) was stolen from his laboratory and used to murder Amyas Crale. It appeared that he was in love with Caroline Crale, and he was suspected of the murder, but actually he was in love with Elsa Greer, who refused his offer of marriage after the trial. *Five Little Pigs.*

BLAKE, PHILIP Brother of Meredith Blake, he was Amyas Crale's best friend. Poirot thought he "looked rather like a contented pig." Although it appeared as though he hated Caroline Crale and blamed her for Amyas' death, Poirot discovered that Philip was in love with her. He and his brother discovered the missing coniine the day of the murder, but they did nothing about it in time to halt the crime. *Five Little Pigs.*

BLAKE, SUSAN Less talkative than her friend Pamela Lyall, with whom she was vacationing in Rhodes, she openly admitted to a "horrid side" of herself which enjoyed calamities. She thought Valentine Chantry was the most idiotic woman she had ever met. Her perfect tan was the envy of all her friends, and she successfully engaged Poirot to smear suntan lotion on her shoulder. "Triangle at Rhodes" from *Murder in the Mews.*

BLANCHE, ANGÈLE The new French mistress at Meadowbank, she was "slender and mouselike and not very noticeable, but she herself noticed everything." She had no control over her classes and hated teaching, which was hardly surprising considering she was without teaching qualifications and was impersonating her dead sister, the original Angèle. She was planning to save her money for a vacation on the Riviera but died before she could realize her dream. *Cat Among the Pigeons.*

BLAND, DETECTIVE INSPECTOR Gentle and "damned respectable" Chief Constable of the county, he was a capable man who, according to Poirot, "made a very fair and unprejudiced survey of the case." *Dead Man's Folly.*

BLAND, JOSIAH Husband of Valerie and later of Hilda Bland, he lived near the house where the murder victim was found. In the construction trade, he was "a very bad builder. . . . Uses pretty poor materials. Puts up the kind of houses that looks more or less all right until you live in them, then everything falls down or goes wrong." *The Clocks.*

BLAND, VALERIE The assumed name of Josiah Bland's second wife, Hilda Martindale, sister of Katherine Martindale, she "had all the airs of an invalid who accepts her invalidism with a certain amount of enjoyment." She assumed the name of her husband's first wife to collect an inheritance from Valerie's distant relatives in Canada. *The Clocks.*

BLATT, HORACE "It was Mr. Blatt's apparent ambition to be the life and soul of any place he happened to be in . . . he was puzzled at the way people seemed to melt and disappear when he himself arrived on the scene." A guest at the Jolly Roger Hotel, Blatt was suspected of smuggling heroine. *Evil Under the Sun.*

BLEIBNER, MR. The uncle of Rupert Bleibner, he was an American from New York who, along with Sir John Willard, was co-discoverer of the tomb of Men-her-Ra. He died at the site of the dig from what was at first supposed to be the ancient Curse of the Mummy's Tomb. "The Adventure of the Egyptian Tomb" from *Poirot Investigates.*

BLEIBNER, RUPERT The dissolute nephew of Mr. Bleibner, he was convinced by Robert Ames that he had contracted leprosy. On his return to New York, Rupert, distraught over his supposed affliction, committed suicide. He left a will naming Ames as his heir. "The Adventure of the Egyptian Tomb" from *Poirot Investigates.*

BLETCHLEY, MAJOR A crusty, irascible, opinionated man, he felt that "Women are all very well in their places, but not before breakfast." This spit-and-polish type was shocked at current military and moral effeminacy: " 'God, these young fellows nowadays make me sick. Hot baths—coming down to breakfast at ten o'clock or later. No wonder the Germans have been putting it over on us. . . . It's all this democracy,' said Major Bletchley gloomily. 'You can overdo anything!' " *N or M?*

BLIGH, GERTRUDE (NELLIE) AKA Mrs. Johnson. As Mrs. Johnson, she was employed by Sir Phillip Starke to pose as a distant relation to Julia Starke, to keep an eye on Lady Starke in the different rest homes she inhabited and to move her from one to another when Lady Starke's mental peculiarities began to surface. *By the Pricking of My Thumbs.*

BLONDIN, MONSIEUR GASTON Snobbish proprietor of "that modish little restaurant Chez Ma Tante," he condescended to speak with Poirot, who recalled an incident "wherein a dead body, a waiter, M. Blondin and a very lovely lady had played a part." Poirot first saw Jackie de Bellefort and Simon Doyle at Blondin's establishment. *Death on the Nile.*

BLORE, WILLIAM HENRY AKA Mr. Davis, he was formerly with the C.I.D. and since his retirement had operated a detective agency in Plymouth, and had been hired to protect Mrs. Owen's jewels on Indian Island. He was accused of causing the death of James Stephen Landor, and was the eighth victim of the Island murderer. His skull was crushed by a heavy white marble clock. *And Then There Were None.*

BLUNDELL, CALEB (POP) The father of Carol Blundell, he bragged that his daughter's earrings were worth eighty thousand dollars when in fact they were virtually worthless. "The Pearl of Price" from *Parker Pyne Investigates.*

BLUNDELL, CAROL The daughter of Caleb Blundell, she asked Parker Pyne to find her pearl earring, which she believed to be worth a fortune. "The Pearl of Price" from *Parker Pyne Investigates.*

BLUNT, ALISTAIR AKA Albert Chapman. Blunt was the legitimate husband of Gerda Grant and the bigamous consort of Rebecca Sanseverato, *née* Arnhold. He was "the head of the greatest banking firm in England. A man of vast wealth. A man who said yes and no to governments." Lacking emotion, he was "so essentially British." *One, Two, Buckle My Shoe.*

BLUNT, MAJOR HECTOR A big game hunter who, according to Sheppard, "has shot more wild animals in unlikely places than any man living," he was an old friend of Roger Ackroyd's and was at Fernly Park when Ackroyd died. "He talks little, and what he does say is said jerkily, as though the words were forced out of him unwillingly." Blunt was eventually betrothed to Flora Ackroyd. *The Murder of Roger Ackroyd.*

BLUNT, ADMIRAL PHILIP A member of Mr. Cedric Lazenby's Cabinet, Admiral Blunt lived up to his name: when Mr. Lazenby suggested he might pay a personal visit to Russia, Admiral Blunt replied, "You stick where you are, Prime Minister. . . . Don't you go arseing around with the Russkies again. All *they* want at present is to keep out of all this mess. They haven't had as much trouble there with the students as most of us have." *Passenger to Frankfurt.*

BLUNT, THEODORE The former manager of the International Detective Agency, Mr. Blunt had operated a kind of clearinghouse for international Communist spies. Mr. Carter asked Tommy Beresford to take on the persona of the absent Mr. Blunt, and to use the number "sixteen" as a password to identify Communist contacts. Tommy and Tuppence worked as double and occasionally treble agents for British Intelligence under the direction of Mr. Carter. *Partners in Crime.*

BODLICOTT, HENRY (CHUCK) He was a nervous young man who took over his murdered grandfather's work in Tuppence and Tommy Beresford's garden. He asked Tuppence if she were "the lady what caught spies or something in the last war," and when she admitted that she was, she earned not only his spaniel-like affection forever but his willingness to help in the Mary Jordan investigation. *Postern of Fate.*

BODLICOTT, ISAAC He was the town handy-man who loved meeting newcomers and was murdered by being coshed on the head for knowing too much. *Postern of Fate.*

BOLFORD, MR. Mr. Bolford was a partner in the tailoring firm of Bolford and Avory's, one of those tailors "who, while catering essentially for men, occasionally condescended to cut a suit for certain favoured members of the feminine sex." He said that the problem with England was that there was "no heart in things." *They Came to Baghdad.*

BOLLARD, MR. Co-owner of the respectable and well-established jewellery store Bollard and Whitley in Bond Street, he knew that Elvira Blake had stolen a diamond and sapphire bracelet but did not report the theft to the police. *At Bertram's Hotel.*

BOND, JAMES Unlike Ian Fleming's character, he was not a strong man and was continually redressing himself for his wrongs, but was valiantly attempting to cultivate a more "dynamic personality." While on holiday, he discovered the Rajah of Maraputna's missing emerald, and was celebrated for having unmasked the thief. "The Rajah's Emerald" from *The Golden Ball.*

BOND, SERGEANT PERCY Assistant to Inspector Kelsey in questioning the suspects after the murder of Grace Springer, he had a stringent fear since his childhood: "There's something about schoolmistresses that gives me the hump." *Cat Among the Pigeons.*

BONES, BILLY *See* **OSSINGTON, SIR WILLIAM.**

BONNINGTON, HENRY He took Poirot to dine at the Gallant Endeavour inn, where the detective's interest in the Gascoigne case was first aroused. One reason Mr. Bonnington liked the Gallant Endeavour was that Augustus John used to eat there. He hated sauces or what he considered "French kick-shaws" or anything which covered up food, and considered it suspicious; Poirot adopted this metaphor as his guide in the case. "Four and Twenty Blackbirds" from *The Adventure of the Christmas Pudding.*

BORROW, RICHARD (DICK) A "hard-working East-End parson," he had a "thin ascetic face and . . . star-gazing fanatical eyes." His friend, the millionaire Silas Hamer, gave all of his money to Borrow's mission. "The Call of the Wings" from *The Golden Ball.*

BOSCOMBE, MR. Poirot complimented Mr. Boscombe's salesmanship: "You felt at once that you were welcome in his gallery all day long if you liked without making a purchase. Sheerly, solely looking at those delightful pictures—though when you entered the gallery you might not have thought they *were* delightful. But by the time you went out you were convinced that delightful was exactly the word to describe them." *Third Girl.*

BOSCOWAN, EMMA *Née* Wing, she was a sculptress and the widow of the artist William Boscowan, who had painted "House by a Canal." Emma Boscowan verified that some unknown hand had added a small boat, named "Waterlily," to the canal in the painting. *By the Pricking of My Thumbs.*

BOSNER, FREDERICK His wife Louise discovered that he was a paid German spy, and that some of the information he leaked to Germany led to the sinking of an American transport ship, causing the loss of hundreds of lives. She turned him in. A few weeks later, a body identified as his was discovered in a train wreck. He survived the accident but with extreme facial damage, assumed the identity of the man who had died, and as Dr. Eric Leidner, built a reputation and finally remarried his wife Louise, who was not at all suspicious. *Murder in Mesopotamia.*

BOTT, POLICE CONSTABLE A policeman of "energetic steps" who swung "magnificently down on his beat," he discovered the poisoned Mrs. Nicoletis but, due to the pervasive odour of brandy on her, thought she was merely drunk and locked her up. *Hickory Dickory Dock.*

BOUC, MONSIEUR Belgian director of la Compagnie Internationale des Wagons Lits, he had a long-standing friendship with Hercule Poirot, dating from the time Poirot was the star of the Belgian police force. He hired Poirot to investigate the murder of Samuel Edward Ratchett, and suspected Antonio Foscarelli of the crime: "He has been a long time in America . . . and he is an Italian, and Italians use the knife! And they are great liars! I do not like Italians." *Murder on the Orient Express.*

BOURGET, LOUISE Maid to Linnet Doyle, she was a "vivacious Latin brunette" with "a kind of sharp cunning in her face" which did not endear her to Poirot. She was slain when she attempted to blackmail the person who murdered her mistress. *Death on the Nile.*

BOURNE, URSALA The sister of Mrs. Richard Folliott and the wife of Captain Ralph Paton, Roger Ackroyd's step-son, Ursala was dismissed from her position as parlourmaid at Ackroyd's Fernly Park on the day of her master's death. *The Murder of Roger Ackroyd.*

BOWER, DR. CHARLES AKA Carl Bauer, he consulted Tommy Beresford's International Detective Agency and used the code number "sixteen" to attract the in-terest of "Mr. Blunt." "The Adventure of the Sinister Stranger" from *Partners in Crime.*

BOWER, JOHN *See* **BAUER, JOHN.**

BOWERS, MISS For two years a nurse to Miss Van Schuyler, she accompanied her employer on the S.S. *Karnak,* where she informed Poirot of her patient's "little idiosyncracy"—kleptomania. Nurse Bowers summarized Miss Van Schuyler's character: "There's nothing serious the matter with her. She just likes plenty of attention, and she's willing to pay for it." *Death on the Nile.*

BOYD CARRINGTON, SIR WILLIAM (BILL) He had inherited a large country estate from his uncle, Sir Everard, and was staying at Styles temporarily. In spite of Hastings' complete approval of the man, Poirot maintained: "He repeats himself, he tells the same story twice—and what is more, his memory is so bad that he tells back to you the story that you have told him. A man of outstanding ability? Not at all. An old bore, a windbag—*enfin*—the stuffed shirt!" To Hastings, Poirot remarked: "Just the type you *would* admire!" *Curtain.*

BOYLE, MRS. A boarder at the Davis' guest house, Monkswell Manor, in Berkshire, she was a "large forbidding-looking woman with a resonant voice and masterful manner. Her natural aggressiveness had been heightened by a war career of persistent and militant usefulness." She had taken an immediate and acid dislike to Christopher Wren, the young architect, and he in turn repeatedly taunted her with murder threats. She was strangled to death during a snow storm. "Three Blind Mice" from *Three Blind Mice and Other Stories.*

BOYNTON, MRS. One of the most repellent characters in all of Christie's fiction, she had been a prison wardress because, in Dr. Gerard's opinion, "she loved tyranny" and "rejoices in the infliction of pain." She was Elmer Boynton's widow, the mother of Ginerva Boynton and the step-mother of Lennox, Carol and Raymond Boynton. Dr. Gerard said: *"What a horror of a woman!* Old, swollen, bloated, sitting there immovable—a distorted old Buddha—a gross spider in the centre of a web . . . small, black smouldering eyes they were, but something came from them—a power, a definite force, a wave of evil." She brushed aside her manifold bodily infirmities with the statement, "I don't give in to my body! It's the mind that counts!" She was murdered by an injection of digitoxin while on tour with her wretched family in Petra. *Appointment with Death.*

BOYNTON, CAROL The step-daughter of Mrs. Boynton, she was nervous, "watchful, alert, unable to relax." She said of her step-mother: "She's gone on being a wardress to us. That is why our life is just—being in prison." *Appointment with Death.*

BOYNTON, GINERVA (JINNY) The daughter of Elmer and Mrs. Boynton, she had an "unearthly smile that lifts the lips of the Maidens in the Acropolis at Athens—something remote and lovely and a little inhuman." *Appointment with Death.*

BOYNTON, LENNOX The son of Elmer Boynton, and the step-son of Mrs. Boynton, he was married to Nadine Boynton, one of Mrs. Boynton's "slaves," who was brought into the household for an express purpose: "The desire of a man for a mate was stronger than the hypnotic spell. But the old woman was quite aware of the power of sex." *Appointment with Death.*

BOYNTON, NADINE A distant American relation of Elmer Boynton's, she was the wife of Lennox Boynton, who had come to live with the Boynton's while she was earning a nursing degree at Mrs. Boynton's command. She tried to use the threat of running away with Jefferson Cope to shock her husband into severing the

chains his mother had bound around him. *Appointment with Death.*

BOYNTON, RAYMOND (RAY) The step-son of Mrs. Boynton and son of Elmer Boynton, he thought that murdering Mrs. Boynton would be "just like killing a mad dog—something that's doing harm in the world and must be stopped." *Appointment with Death.*

BRABAZON, ARCHDEACON An old friend of Elizabeth Temple's, he was unhappily convinced that he had been the cause of Verity Hunt's death because he had tried to talk her out of marrying Michael Rafiel, who had up to that point proven himself a thoroughly bad sort. *Nemesis.*

BRADBURN, CYRUS G. The American millionaire who purchased Ashley Grange from Eleanor Le Couteau, he made "no bones about paying the fancy price of sixty thousand pounds" because the house was filled with valuable and fine French relics and antiques. "At the Bells and Motley" from *The Mysterious Mr. Quin.*

BRADBURY-SCOTT, ANTHEA One of Colonel Bradbury-Scott's three peculiar nieces, she was sister to Clotilde Bradbury-Scott and Lavinia Glynne. Miss Marple compared her to "a mature Ophelia." *Nemesis.*

BRADBURY-SCOTT, CLOTILDE Another of Colonel Bradbury-Scott's nieces, Clotilde was a well-educated woman who spoke three languages. "Clotilde, Miss Marple thought, was certainly no Ophelia, but she would have made a magnificent Clytemnestra—she could have stabbed a husband in his bath with exultation. But since she had never had a husband, that solution wouldn't do. Miss Marple could not see her murdering anyone else but a husband." She had an overriding passion for her ward, Verity Hunt. *Nemesis.*

BRADLEY, C.R. A disbarred lawyer, he was described by Divisional Detective Inspector Lejeune: "He's a smooth dealer, and adept at never doing anything that we can pin on him. He knows every trick and dodge of the legal game. He's always just on the right side of the line. He's the kind of man who could write a book like those old cookery books, 'A hundred ways of evading the law'." *The Pale Horse.*

BRANDON, EILEEN With Jesse Davis, her job at Customer's Reactions Classified was to obtain householders' opinions about various products. She had found the job unsavoury, and had taken another job as a waitress in an expresso bar. *The Pale Horse.*

BRECK, DR. ALAN Dr. Breck was a physicist with the Harwell Atomic Institute. He analyzed specimens of uranium that had been brought to him by the late Sir Rupert Crofton Lee, and gave a report at the historic conference that took place in Baghdad. *They Came to Baghdad.*

BRENT, CLEMENT EDWARD ALISTAIR The Ninth Marquis of Caterham, Lord Caterham was the father of Eileen (Bundle), Dulcie (Guggle) and Daisy (Winkle). As the proprietor of the famous country seat Chimneys, Lord Caterham was often expected to fill the shoes of his deceased brother Henry, who had been Secretary of State for Foreign Affairs. However, "there was nothing that bored Lord Caterham more than politics—unless it was politicians." Lord Caterham's prevailing characteristic was "a wholly amiable inertia." *The Secret of Chimneys; The Seven Dials Mystery.*

BRENT, DAISY AND DULCIE Edward Brent, Lord Caterham's two younger children, they were "high-spirited young women of twelve and ten, and though their names might be Dulcie and Daisey . . . they appeared to be more generally known as Guggle and Winkle." *The Secret of Chimneys.*

BRENT, EDNA Employee of Miss Martindale's Cavendish Secretarial and Typing Bureau, a co-worker of Sheila Webb's and the second murder victim, she had a voice which was usually "breathy and slightly nasal," was fond of flashy red stiletto heels and was described as "rabbitty." Because one of her red stiletto heels had broken, she was unable to go out to lunch the day Sheila was sent to Miss Pebmarsh's, and therefore knew the particulars of the phone calls received at the Typing Bureau that morning. She was garrotted with a scarf in a telephone booth. *The Clocks.*

BRENT, LADY EILEEN (BUNDLE BRENT) The outspoken, curious, adventurous and intelligent daughter of Lord Caterham, she was the elder sister of Dulcie and Daisy, affectionately known as Guggle and Winkle. A popular society girl and a "red hot Socialist," she was infamous for driving at breakneck speeds. She became engaged to Bill Eversleigh, who once commented: "the grass never did grow under Bundle's feet." *The Secret of Chimneys; The Seven Dials Mystery.*

BRENT, EMILY CAROLINE "Enveloped in an aura of righteousness and unyielding principles, Miss Brent sat in her crowded third-class carriage and triumphed over its discomfort and its heat" on her way to Indian Island, where she was accused of the death of Beatrice Taylor. Although her death appeared to have been brought about by a bee sting, she, the fifth victim, had actually been drugged and injected with potassium cyanide. *And Then There Were None.*

BRENT, MARCIA, MARCHIONESS OF CATERHAM The widow of Alistair Brent's brother Henry, formerly the Eighth

Marquis of Caterham. "Lady Caterham was a large woman—large in every way. Her proportions were majestic, rather than ample." And, thinking of her niece Bundle Brent, "an unfortunate love affair, in Lady Caterham's opinion, was often highly beneficial to young girls. It made them take life seriously." *The Seven Dials Mystery.*

BRÉON, EDOUARD A famous retired French baritone, he "had a weakness for countesses," and was thus easily persuaded by Lady Rustonbury to take the place of the ailing Signor Roscari as the male lead, "Scarpia," in *Tosca.* When he was young, he had known Bianca Capelli, and had refused to intercede and save her lover from death. Bréon was murdered during the performance. "Swan Song" from *The Golden Ball.*

BRETT, DR. He examined the body of Barbara Allen and noticed that the gun was in the wrong position for her to have shot herself in the head. "Murder in the Mews" from *Murder in the Mews.*

BREWIS, AMANDA Secretary and housekeeper to Sir George Stubbs, she had a "pleasant mild face." Poirot admired her: "You seem, in this house, to have everything organized to perfection." An astute woman, she was in love with her employer and recognized that the seemingly vapid Lady Harriet Stubbs was "wanting in the top storey" only when she chose to be. *Dead Man's Folly.*

BREWSTER, EMILY When describing her to Colonel Weston, Poirot said, "She has a voice like a man's. She is gruff and what you call hearty. She rows boats and has a handicap of four at golf. . . . I think, though, that she has a good heart." Together with Patrick Redfern she discovered what at first was thought to be the body of Arlena Marshall. *Evil Under the Sun.*

BREWSTER, JIM A member of the Youth Movement, Jim Brewster "was a young man with beetle brows who frowned and to whom perpetual suspicion seemed to be second nature." *Passenger to Frankfurt.*

BREWSTER, LOLA An actress, she arrived at Marina Gregg's private party at Gossington Hall with the actor Ardwyck Fenn and "a new rust-red hair-do. The very latest Fiji Islander type." Twelve years previously, Lola had lost a husband, Robert Truscott, to Marina Gregg, and at the time threatened to shoot her. "That bitch needn't think she'll get away with it. If I don't shoot her now I'll wait and get her in some other way. I don't care how long I wait, years if need be, but I'll get even with her in the end." Soon after, she married Eddie Groves and subsequently took a pot-shot at him. *The Mirror Crack'd from Side to Side.*

BRICE-WOODWORTH, PATRICIA The daughter of the redoubtable General Lord Woodworth, and the fiancée of Gerald Tollington, she had the coolness and detachment of the very young "and took charge of the situation" when George Barton was poisoned. *Sparkling Cyanide.*

BRIDGET Em Lacey's great-niece, she was a black-haired girl of about fifteen with "enormous vitality." With Colin Lacey and Michael she plotted a Boxing Day surprise for Poirot—a staged murder mystery for him to solve. "The Theft of the Royal Ruby" from *Double Sin.*

BRILL, INSPECTOR The "soldierly and stolid" officer who was summoned to Hunterbury Hall to investigate the house and room in which Mary Gerrard died. He found a scrap of paper which turned out to be a fragment of a printed label, at first thought to be from a tube of morphine. At the trial he reeled off his evidence "with practiced ease." *Sad Cypress.*

BRISTOW, FRANK He was the talented young artist of "The Dead Harlequin." Because the Harlequin in the painting so strikingly resembled Harley Quin, Mr.

Satterthwaite purchased the painting. Bristow felt that the Charnley home, which figured in the painting, would "make a good People's Park." "The Dead Harlequin" from *The Mysterious Mr. Quin.*

BROAD, NORA The errant daughter of Nancy Broad, Nora was the town "good-time girl . . . a sly, sexy little village girl." Gossip explained her disappearance as a case of being pregnant and running away. In fact, Nora had been murdered. Her disfigured body was identified as that of Verity Hunt, another girl who was missing. *Nemesis.*

BROADRIBB, JAMES Senior partner of Broadribb and Schuster, Solicitors, he was the deceased Jason Rafiel's lawyer. Mr. Rafiel wrote: "Like the majority of the human race he is susceptible to the sin of curiosity." He treated Miss Marple with courtesy and thought her "The Provincial Lady. A good type. Fluffy old girl. May be scatty—may not. Quite a shrewd eye." *Nemesis.*

BROWN, MR. He was rumoured to be "The master criminal of this age." Mr. Brown was so elusive that not only was his real identity unknown to Mr. Carter of British Intelligence, but few of Brown's own followers knew him; some, like Boris Ivanovitch, thought him to be a phantom manufactured to frighten the lesser agents. The sinister Mr. Brown originated and financed most of the peace propaganda in Britain during World War I. *The Secret Adversary.*

BROWN, GERALDINE MARY ALEXANDRA A young girl convalescing from a broken leg, she observed tenants of Wilbraham Crescent through a pair of opera glasses and was able to give Colin Lamb several new angles on that block of houses. Her English translation of German phrases was not to be trusted. *The Clocks.*

BROWN, JOHN *See* **CRACKENTHORPE, CEDRIC.**

BROWN, LAURENCE An unstable and neurotic but conscientious man, he was hired by Aristide Leonides as private tutor for his grandchildren Josephine and Eustace Leonides. He had chosen to work in hospital rather than take a human life during the war, saying: "I'm very sensitive and highly strung. I—the very idea of killing is a *nightmare* to me." Sophia Leonides pointed out: "Why do men always think that a caveman must necessarily be the only type of person attractive to the opposite sex? Laurence has got sex appeal, all right." This slender, shrunken tutor and his would-be mistress Brenda Leonides were arrested for the murder of his employer and her husband, Aristides Leonides. *Crooked House.*

BROWNE, ANTHONY AKA Tony Morelli, he was a handsome young man with a shady past, alternately in love with Rosemary Barton and Iris Marle. He was a prime suspect in the murder of Rosemary Barton and proposed to Iris Marle. *Sparkling Cyanide.*

BRUN, MADEMOISELLE GENEVIÈVE *See* **MORY, ANGÈLE.**

BRYANT, DR. ROGER JAMES Melancholy and attractive specialist on diseases of the ear and throat, he was a passenger on board the *Prometheus* at the time of Madame Giselle Morisot's death. An avid flautist, he had brought his instrument on board the airplane, and he was therefore suspected of being the poison-dart shooter. *Death in the Clouds.*

BUCKLE, MRS. The mother of Marlene Buckle and an old acquaintance of Ariadne Oliver's, she believed that someone from outside the household had killed General and Lady Ravenscroft. She told Mrs. Oliver about Lady Ravenscroft's four wigs and mistakenly remembered Dolly

Jarrow's name as Mrs. Jerryboy. *Elephants Can Remember.*

BUCKLEY, REVEREND GILES Distant Yorkshire cousin of Nick Buckley, he was the husband of Jean Buckley and the father of the murdered Maggie Buckley. He retained his clerical image in his interview with Poirot by uttering such statements as "In the midst of life we are in death." *Peril at End House.*

BUCKLEY, JEAN Wife to Reverend Giles Buckley, she showed much more strength of character than he did after the murder of their daughter, Maggie. She sent Poirot a letter Maggie had written to her before the murder. *Peril at End House.*

BUCKLEY, MAGDALA (MAGGIE) Daughter of Reverend Giles Buckley and his wife Jean, she was of Nick Buckley's large group of Yorkshire cousins. Nick sent for her while his life was in danger, and she was shot while wearing Nick's old lacquer-red Chinese shawl. She was engaged to Captain Michael Seton, an aviator who was missing and presumed dead. *Peril at End House.*

BUCKLEY, NICK The favourite of her grandfather Nicholas and hence called after him, she was the cousin of Charles Vyse and of the Yorkshire Buckleys. Nick Buckley was passionately attached to End House, which she inherited upon her brother's death. Freddie Rice called her "the most heaven-sent little liar that ever existed." Poirot, however, found her a "scatterbrain" and "feather-head" because she professed not to have heard of him. During a meeting with Poirot, the third of five attempts was made on her life. *Peril at End House.*

BULLARD, LOUISA The housemaid at Deering Hill, just before Lady Barnaby's murder, she saw white smoke from a passing train that had "formed itself into the sign of a gigantic hand. A great white hand against the crimson of the sky. The fingers were crooked-like, as though they

were reaching out for something." Her testimony led to Martin Wylde's acquittal. "The Sign in the Sky" from *The Mysterious Mr. Quin.*

BULMER, SIR EDWIN Counsellor for the defence in the Elinor Carlisle murder trial, he was considered a bad choice by Peter Lord: "They've briefed Bulmer, K.C., the forlorn hope man; that's a give-away in itself!" *Sad Cypress.*

BULSTRODE, HONORIA Remarkable and capable Headmistress of Meadowbank, she was referred to as "The Bull" or "Bully" by her students. During her career "she had met and dealt with incipient disasters and turned them into triumphs. It had all been stimulating, exciting, supremely worthwhile." However, during her last few terms before retirement, Meadowbank was struck with irreparable calamity: several of the mistresses were murdered. *Cat Among the Pigeons.*

BUNNER, DORA (BUNNY) About sixty when she died of poisoning, Dora had "been painstaking but never competent at anything she undertook." She knew that Charlotte Blacklock was impersonating her deceased sister, Letitia Blacklock. *A Murder is Announced.*

BURCH, BESSIE Niece and heir of Mrs. McGinty and wife of Joe Burch, she was normally a "pleasant young woman," but Poirot found that "her natural distrust of foreign-looking gentlemen with black moustaches wearing large fur-lined coats was not to be overcome easily." *Mrs. McGinty's Dead.*

BURCH, JOE Husband of Bessie Burch, he was a painter. "He seemed anxious to appear co-operative. And that, Poirot reflected, was very faintly out of character." *Mrs. McGinty's Dead.*

BURGESS, WILLIAM Live-out manservant of Major Rich, he discovered the body of Arnold Clayton the morning after

Clayton's murder, and was at one time a suspect in the killing. "He had those pale blue, rather shifty eyes, that unobservant people often equate with dishonesty." "The Mystery of the Spanish Chest" from *The Adventure of the Christmas Pudding.*

BURGOYNE The manservant to Major Jack Rich, he noticed a stain on the rug which he traced to the stabbed body of Edward Clayton in his master's Baghdad chest. He related his tale to Poirot in an impersonal but precise manner, and was tipped by the detective for his aid. "The Mystery of the Baghdad Chest" from *The Regatta Mystery.*

BURNABY, MAJOR JOHN EDWARD He was the best friend of the murdered Captain Trevelyan, with whom he had skied and climbed mountains in Switzerland and gone big-game hunting and exploring in their youth. As elderly gentlemen, they confined their adventures to Tuesday and Friday get-togethers at which Burnaby worked crosswords and Trevelyan did acrostics. He was present at the séance during which the spirits directed the planchette to announce Trevelyan's murder and, although Burnaby felt psychic investigations were "Tommyrot!" he was visibly shaken at the message, and left the séance with Sergeant Graves and Dr. Warren and thereafter found Trevelyan's murdered body. *The Sittaford Mystery.*

BURNS, CHARLIE A shipping clerk, he won the love of Gillian West over his rival, Phil Eastney, by being "always pleasant, and good-tempered." "The Face of Helen" from *The Mysterious Mr. Quin.*

BURROWS, GODFREY Secretary for two years to the eccentric Sir Gervase Chevenix-Gore, Burrows had a slightly unreal mechanical smile, and was very much aware of his "sleek brushed-back hair and a rather obvious style of good looks." Definitely of an inferior social class, he was considered "not quite out of the top

drawer." "Dead Man's Mirror" from *Murder in the Mews.*

BURSHAW, MISS Second-in-command at Miss Pope's establishment for girls in Neuilly, she was "a grey-haired, fussy-looking woman" who was bringing a group of girls across the Channel to France when Winnie King's disappearance was discovered. "The Girdle of Hippolyta" from *The Labours of Hercules.*

BURTON, DR. The physician attending the poison victims at Thurnley Grange, he was a "tall, elderly man with bent shoulders and a kind but worried face." He determined that arsenic had been in the chocolates Lois Hargreaves had received, which caused serious illness to four persons, and speculated that the trouble was due to socialist agitation. On analyzing the poison fig paste sandwiches, Burton found they contained ricin, a vegetable toxin, which was also discovered in Dennis Radclyffe's cocktail. "The House of Lurking Death" from *Partners in Crime.*

BURTON, DR. He was a friend of Poirot's and a Fellow of All Soul's. He had "the habit of covering himself and everything round him with tobacco ash. In vain did Poirot surround him with ash-trays." He was appalled to learn that Poirot was considering retirement to raise vegetable marrows—"great swollen green things that taste of water"—and indicated that Poirot could better spend his time studying classical texts, which was Dr. Burton's own specialty. Following his suggestion, Poirot researched his namesake, and decided that he, like the original Hercules, would take on twelve more cases during the coming year especially chosen for their parallels to the Twelve Labours of Hercules. "Foreword," from *The Labours of Hercules.*

BURTON, JERRY He was brother to Joanna Burton, with whom he rented a house from Emily Barton in Lymstock. An intelligent, compassionate, gentle and

45

kind man who was temporarily convalescing, he fell in love with Megan Hunter
and ultimately married her. *The Moving
Finger.*

BURTON, JOANNA Sister of Jerry Burton, she also found her true love in Wyn-
stock, Dr. Owen Griffith, the village doctor.
She and Jerry received a poison-pen letter
which suggested they were not related at
all, but were living in sin. *The Moving
Finger.*

BURTON-COX, MRS. Perhaps the most
obnoxious woman in the entire Christie
canon, Mrs. Burton-Cox was widowed by
her first husband, Cecil Aldbury, and by
her second, Major Burton-Cox. She inherited a substantial sum of money from
each man, and was the adoptive mother
of Desmond Burton-Cox. She was "what
in French could have been called *une
femme formidable,* but who definitely had
not only the French variety of being formidable, but the English one of being supremely bossy." When she first met Poirot
at Adriadne Oliver's flat she mistook him
for a piano tuner, but when she realized
he was a professional detective, she escaped as quickly as possible. *Elephants
Can Remember.*

BURTON-COX, DESMOND The adopted
son of Mrs. Burton-Cox, he was Celia
Ravenscroft's fiancé. He was actually the
son of Kathleen Fenn and Cecil Aldbury,
Mrs. Burton-Cox's first husband. After
giving up Desmond to her dead lover's
wife, Kathleen Fenn became a successful
pop star and in vain tried to regain cus-
tody of her son. When she died, she left
him a fortune not to be revealed until he
was twenty-five. Wanting to dominate her
son and retain control over his money,
Mrs. Burton-Cox disapproved his pend-

ing marriage to Celia Ravenscroft. *Elephants Can Remember.*

BURY, COLONEL NED An old friend of
the Chevenix-Gore family, Colonel Bury
was a soldierly-looking elderly man. He
had been in love with Lady Vanda Chevenix-Gore for decades and contented
himself with "following her about like
a dog," spending most of his time with
her family. "Dead Man's Mirror" from
Murder in the Mews.

BUTLER, JUDITH The mother of Miranda Butler, Judith met and became
friends with Ariadne Oliver when they
were both touring Greece. Judith had "the
attributes of a water-spirit. She could have
been a Rhine maiden. Her long blond hair
hung limply on her shoulders, she was
delicately made-up with a rather long face
and faintly hollow cheeks, whilst above
them were big sea-green eyes fringed with
long eyelashes." *Hallowe'en Party.*

BUTLER, MIRANDA The precocious and
perceptive twelve-year-old daughter of
Judith Butler, she was like "a dryad or
some elf-like being." When Poirot commented that her name suited her, she replied: "Are you thinking of Shakespeare?"
Poirot found that "it was her gravity that
was so attractive. He wondered what
passed through her mind. It was the sort
of thing one would never know. She would
not say what she was thinking easily. He
doubted if she would tell you what she
was thinking, if you asked her. She had
an original mind, he thought, a reflective
mind. He thought too that she was vulnerable." Among her friends were Michael Garfield the architect and the
murdered Joyce Reynolds. *Hallowe'en
Party.*

CABOT, MR. AND MRS. ELMER
Impersonators from America who were
escaping with three thousand pounds from
a train robbery, they were on their way
from Bertram's Hotel to Paris when noticed by Chief Inspector Davy. *At Bertram's Hotel.*

CADE, ANTHONY AKA Gentleman Joe;
Jimmy McGrath; Nicholas Sergius Alexander Ferdinand Obolovitch; Nicholas v
of Herzoslavakia. This charming, boyish
and adventurous rake was "most peculiar
in his ideas, consorted with Socialists
and Republicans, and acted in a way
highly unbecoming to his position. He
was sent down from Oxford . . . for some
wild escapade." His friend, Jimmy
McGrath, introduced him into a web of
intrigue. He fell in love with Virginia
Revel, but she was not the same lady who
wrote the letters he was given. *The Secret
of Chimneys.*

CALDER, ALICE Wife of Ali Yusuf and
mother of their son Allen, she was "about
twenty-five, pleasant looking, with a kind
of fair, chocolate-box prettiness." She was
so certain of her husband's love that the
prospect of polygamy in Ramat did not
deter her. In addition, she did not become

hysterical at the sight of a fortune in unset
jewels he sent her. *Cat Among the Pigeons.*

CALGARY, DR. ARTHUR A geophysi-
cist recently returned from the Hayes
Bentley Expedition to the Antarctic, he
had been absent during Jacko Argyle's
trial for murder, and realized too late that
he was the only one who could provide
Jacko's alibi. Although Jacko had since
died in prison, Dr. Calgary was determined to clear his name and identify the
real murderer of Rachel Argyle. During
his investigation, Dr. Calgary fell in love
with Hester Argyle, Jacko's step-sister.
Ordeal by Innocence.

CAPEL, DEREK He shot himself when
he learned that the body of Eleanor Portal's husband, old Mr. Appleton, was going
to be exhumed for an autopsy. "The Coming of Mr. Quin" from *The Mysterious
Mr. Quin.*

CAPELLI, BIANCA AKA Paula Nazorkoff. Bianca Capelli was an opera singer
who, through Edouard Bréon, had "the
chance of big engagements, but she was
foolish." She had "the laugh of a child,
the digestion of an ostrich and the temper

47

of a fiend, and she was acknowledged to be the greatest dramatic soprano of her day." She sang "Tosca" during the performance at which Bréon, singing "Scarpia," was killed. "Swan Song" from *The Golden Ball.*

CARBURY, COLONEL Colonel Carbury, who prided himself on being a "tidy man," enlisted Poirot's aid in the Boynton case, which was becoming quite an untidy affair. Colonel Carbury's "tie was under his left ear, his socks were wrinkled, his coat was stained and torn. Yet Hercule Poirot did not smile. He saw, clearly enough, the inner neatness of Colonel Carbury's mind, his neatly docketed facts, his carefully sorted impressions." *Appointment with Death.*

CARDEW TRENCH, MRS. Mrs. Cardew Trench was the loquacious and insular Englishwoman staying at the Tio hotel in Baghdad who "had a hoarse voice of one who is in the habit of training and calling to sporting dogs." She also had "a mania for knowing all about everybody." *They Came to Baghdad.*

CARDIFF, PETER A painter protegé of Frances Cary's, he was, in Ariadne Oliver's eyes, "quite the dirtiest-looking young man she's ever seen. Oily black hair hung in a kind of circular bob down the back of his neck and over his eyes in front. His face apart from the beard was unshaven, and his clothes seemed mainly composed of greasy black leather and high boots." *Third Girl.*

CAREY, RICHARD He was an architect at the archaeological dig in Tell Yarimjah. Nurse Leatheran said of him: "To say a man is handsome and at the same time to say he looks like a death's head sounds a rank contradiction, and yet it was true." Poirot said he had "le sex appeal." He maintained a stormy relationship with Louise Leidner; although he loved her and was unable to resist her advances, he was so loyal to her husband that he was on the verge of a nervous breakdown. Poirot said: "In Mr. Carey I had found an ideal murderer" for the *crime passionelle. Murder in Mesopotamia.*

CARLILE, CHARLIE Lord Mayfield's confidential secretary for nine years, he discovered that the new bomber plans were missing. Leonie, Mrs. Vanderlyn's French maid, said: "I do not believe he has ever looked at a girl in his life, that one." "The Incredible Theft" from *Murder in the Mews.*

CARLISLE, ELINOR KATHERINE Niece of Mrs. Laura Welman and fiancée of Mrs. Welman's nephew Roderick, she was accused of murdering Mary Gerrard by serving her poisoned fish paste sandwiches. Mary had been diligently pursued by Roddy, who eventually agreed to break off his engagement with Elinor. Nevertheless, Elinor bestowed two thousand pounds on her rival, Mary, and named Roddy benefactor of her will. Poirot recognized Elinor's self-righteousness, pride and self-restraint, and also her "capacity for passion." *Sad Cypress.*

CARLO A member of the Comrades of the Red Hand, he was supposed to act as sentry, but was easily penetrable by Anthony Cade: "That fool Carlo goes his round with the tread of an elephant—and the eyes of a bat." *The Secret of Chimneys.*

CARLTON-SMITH, NAOMI The daughter of one of the Duchess of Leith's first cousins, and the fiancée of Alec Gerard, she was an artist who sketched Harley Quin as a harlequin in the middle of a kaleidoscopic snowstorm. Her wish to commit suicide dissolved when Gerard was cleared of the theft of Rosina Nunn's opal. "The World's End" from *The Mysterious Mr. Quin.*

CARMICHAEL, LADY An old friend of Poirot's, she was "a dear lady whose chief delight was exercising her tongue on the subject of her neighbours." She had a habit of hitting Poirot's knuckles with a paper-cutter to emphasize her point, but provided him with information on General Grant. "The Horses of Diomedes" from *The Labours of Hercules.*

CARMICHAEL, LADY The step-mother of Sir Andrew Carmichael and Sir William Carmichael's widow, she was thought by Dr. Edward Carstairs to have marked occult powers. Lady Carmichael's throat was lacerated by a cat's claws as she lay in her bed, and she subsequently died from shock at the sight of the recovered Sir Andrew Carmichael. "The Strange Case of Sir Andrew Carmichael" from *The Golden Ball.*

CARMICHAEL, SIR ANDREW The stepson of Lady Carmichael, and the son of the late Sir William Carmichael, Andrew Carmichael was the proprietor of Wolden in Herefordshire and the fiancé of Phyllis Patterson. Sir Andrew qualified as the most unusual protagonist in Christie's fiction. His spirit had been murdered with prussic acid, but his body remained alive and was inhabited by the spirit of a grey Persian cat. The shock of falling into a pond restored him. "The Strange Case of Sir Andrew Carmichael" from *The Golden Ball.*

CARMICHAEL, HENRY (FAKIR) "Henry Carmichael. British Agent. Age about thirty. Brown hair, dark eyes, five-footten. Speaks Arabic, Kurdish, Persian, Armenian, Hindustani, Turkish and many mountain dialects. Befriended by the tribesmen. Dangerous." On his way to Baghdad with the evidence of a secret weapon, he was killed. He left a "faded red knitted scarf" as a sign to Victoria Jones at the Tio Hotel, and a coded message with Richard Baker. Eventually, these messages found their way to Mr. Dakin, his supervisor at British Intelligence. *They Came to Baghdad.*

CARNABY, AMY "Fluttering" companion to Lady Milly Hoggin, and sister of the invalid Emily Carnaby, she had also worked for Lady Julia Hartingfield. She

was "devoted to dogs," and very attached to her sister. They had a Pekinese named Augustus which kept Emily company, and was "far more intelligent" and "much handsomer" than other Pekes. "The Nemean Lion" from *The Labours of Hercules.*

CARNABY, AMY A staunch member of the Church of England, she consulted Poirot about a friend who had fallen into the clutches of a questionable spiritual leader, Dr. Andersen. Poirot said she had "great determination and courage" and "good histrionic powers," besides being "one of the most successful criminals" he had ever encountered. "The Flock of Geryon" from *The Labours of Hercules.*

CARNABY, EMILY Invalid sister of Amy Carnaby, she lived alone with a Pekinese named Augustus. Her health prevented her from gaining or saving any money for the future. "The Nemean Lion" from *The Labours of Hercules.*

CARPENTER, MRS. Muzzy-headed but well-meaning chaperone and companion to Elvira Blake, "The Carpenter," was "a fussy-looking middle-aged lady wearing a rather unfortunate flowered violet hat." *At Bertram's Hotel.*

CARPENTER, ADELAIDE She was "just a big soft white purry person. One of those middle-aged pussies who always manage to dig themselves in comfortably somewhere." She was a *dame de compagnie* to the murdered Sylvia Keene, Sir Ambrose Bercy's niece. "The Herb of Death" from *The Thirteen Problems.*

CARPENTER, DICKIE He was a sailor who "belonged to that inarticulate order of young Englishmen who dislike any form of emotion, and who find it peculiarly hard to explain their mental processes in words." He died during an operation to mend a leg "that got messed up in that torpedo business." "The Gipsy" from *The Golden Ball.*

CARPENTER, EVE Formerly employed by Mrs. McGinty and *née* Selkirk, she had recently wed Guy Carpenter. She thought Poirot was a vacuum cleaner salesman or a domestic survey representative. Although extremely careful to do nothing to disrupt her husband's political position, her scent was in the air and her lipstick on a cup in the room where Laura Upward's body was discovered. *Mrs. McGinty's Dead.*

CARPENTER, LOUISE *See* **BIRELL, LOUISE.**

CARR, LADY ESTHER *See* **KING, MURIEL.**

CARRÈGE, MONSIEUR The Judge d'Instruction or Examining Magistrate in the Kettering case, Carrège prided himself on his most genial manner, and most delicately handled the questioning of Ada Beatrice Mason when she was found after the murder. *The Mystery of the Blue Train.*

CARRINGTON, LADY ADELINE *See* **CLAPPERTON, ADELINE.**

CARRINGTON, THE HONOURABLE FLOSSIE The wife of The Honourable Rupert Carrington and the daughter of Mr. Halliday, she was murdered and her jewels stolen on the *Plymouth Express.* "The Plymouth Express" from *The Under Dog.*

CARRINGTON, AIR MARSHAL SIR GEORGE The husband of Lady Julia Carrington and the father of Reggie Carrington, he was a guest at Lord Mayfield's country retreat in Sussex to review the plans for a new bomber. The Air Marshal aired his accumulated grievances to Poirot: "The lack of grit and stamina in the younger generation, the fantastic way in which mothers spoiled their children and always took their side, the curse of gambling once it got hold of a woman, the folly for playing for higher stakes than you could afford." "The Incredible Theft" from *Murder in the Mews.*

CARRINGTON, LADY JULIA She was the wife of Sir George Carrington and the mother of Reggie Carrington. "Her manner was abrupt and restless, that of a woman who lived on her nerves." Bridge was "the breath of life to her." "The Incredible Theft" from *Murder in the Mews.*

CARRINGTON, REGGIE The twenty-one-year-old son of Sir George Carrington and Lady Julia Carrington, Reggie was desperately in need of money and was infatuated with Mrs. Vanderlyn, but he had no qualms about surprising Leonie, Mrs. Vanderlyn's French maid, and kissing her rather dramatically on the staircase. "The Incredible Theft" from *Murder in the Mews.*

CARRINGTON, THE HONOURABLE RUPERT Married to Flossie Halliday Carrington, Rupert Carrington, said Hastings, had "pretty well run through his own money on the turf, and I should imagine old man Halliday's dollars came along in the nick of time." "The Plymouth Express" from *The Under Dog.*

CARRISBROOK, ZOE *See* **HAVERING, ZOE.**

CARRUTHERS, MISS A fellow guest at the Crown Hotel in Barnchester with Mr. and Mrs. Rhodes, she was "rather a horsy spinster who dropped her g's . . . wore mannish coats and skirts" and was one of the suspects in the murder of Mrs. Rhodes. "Miss Marple Tells a Story" from *The Regatta Mystery.*

CARRUTHERS, NURSE Preening and comfortable plump nurse to Emily Arundell during her last illness, she told Poirot that Wilhemina Lawson lied to Emily Arundell about the location of the recently revised will. *Dumb Witness.*

CARSLAKE, ALAN The brother of Neil Carslake, he was thought by his sister Sylvia to be "the one person who loved and needed her," and she fled to him when she could bear her husband's jealousy no longer. "In a Glass Darkly" from *The Regatta Mystery*.

CARSLAKE, SYLVIA The sister to Neil and Alan Carslake, she had been engaged to Charles Crawley, but later broke it off. Her husband, the anonymous narrator, was at first happy in his marriage, but soon his jealousy of her admirer Derek Wainwright drove her back to her childhood home, Badgeworthy, and her brother, Alan. "In a Glass Darkly" from *The Regatta Mystery*.

CARSON The butler at Gipsy Acres, he was married to Mrs. Carson, the cook. Carson and his wife had been hired as security agents by Andrew Lippincott to protect Ellie Guteman Rogers from kidnapping and violence. *Endless Night*.

CARSTAIRS, ALAN AKA Alex Pritchard, he was a Canadian, "rather a celebrity in his way ... a naturalist and big-game hunter and explorer." Mrs. Rivington thought he, like all Canadians, was touchy. He was not satisfied that John Savage's death had been suicide, but Carstairs' investigation ended with a fatal fall from a cliff. His body was first identified as Alex Pritchard's. *Why Didn't They Ask Evans?*

CARSTAIRS, DR. EDWARD An eminent psychologist, he discovered that Sir Andrew Carmichael had been murdered with prussic acid and that the spirit of a cat occupied his body. "The Strange Case of Sir Andrew Carmichael" from *The Golden Ball*.

CARSTAIRS, THE HONOURABLE JULIA. One of Ariadne Oliver's "elephants" who remembered the Ravenscroft tragedy quite well, she was visited by Mrs. Oliver at her residence in a "Home for the Privileged" at Hampton Court.

Although she was slightly deaf, she remembered voices better than faces. *Elephants Can Remember*.

CARTER, DETECTIVE SERGEANT An alias assumed by a member of the Patterson gang for the purpose of relieving Anthony Eastwood of his extensive collection of silver, old enamels and other valuables. "Mr. Eastwood's Adventure" from *The Listerdale Mystery*.

CARTER, A. AKA Lord Easterfield. As the Chief of British Intelligence, Mr. Carter had commissioned Tuppence and Tommy Beresford to do a number of jobs, the first of which was to track down Jane Finn. He was "a tall man with a lean, hawklike face and a tired manner." Tommy Beresford recognized Carter from Intelligence work in France during World War I, but not until *N or M?*, when Carter was a sick man, did he learn that Carter's real name was Lord Easterfield. *The Secret Adversary; Partners in Crime; N or M?*

CARTER, FRANK Fiancé of Gladys Nevill and a scoundrel who gained no one's affections, he had the looks of a murderer, and was in the habit of loitering at the dental offices where Gladys worked. Henry Morley disapproved of the match. Under the name of "Dunning" or "Sunbury," Carter landed a job as gardener to Alistair Blunt, and was arrested for the murder of Morley. *One, Two, Buckle My Shoe*.

CARTER, HARRY The husband of Mrs. Carter and father of Lucy Carter. His drinking mates said: "His language was a treat to hear. Didn't mince his words, Harry didn't." Mr. Abbot and Lord Easterfield, who said he was merely "a ruffian ... a drunkard and a man of evil tongue," had quarrelled with Carter before he was drowned. *Murder is Easy*.

CARTER, LUCY The daughter of Mrs. Carter and her late husband Harry, she was employed as a barmaid at her father's pub, the Seven Stars, and had been receiving the attentions of Mr. Abbot. Lucy had been riding with Rivers, Lord Easterfield's chauffeur, the same night Rivers was killed. *Murder is Easy.*

CARTER, STEPHEN A guest at Barton Russell's memorial dinner for his late wife Iris, he was "known as silent Stephen. Sort of man who says, 'I am not at liberty to state, etc., etc.'" As an old Etonian, he belonged to the class of people that Tony Chappell felt should have been drowned at birth. After the collapse of Pauline Weatherby, potassium cyanide was discovered in Carter's pocket. "Yellow Iris" from *The Regatta Mystery.*

CARTON, L.B. The husband of Anita Grunberg, he was referred to as "the Mothball man" by Anne Beddingfeld, who discovered a note, near the subway track where Carton died, which said: "17.122 Kilmorden Castle." Carton and his wife framed John Eardsley and his friend Harry Lucas for a robbery at De Beers diamond mines. *The Man in the Brown Suit.*

CARTWRIGHT, DR. A physician in Market Basing, Dr. Cartwright was called to Lord Caterham's country seat Chimneys on two occasions: once to examine the body of Prince Michael Obolovitch, and later to examine the corpse of Gerald Wade. *The Secret of Chimneys; The Seven Dials Mystery.*

CARTWRIGHT, SIR CHARLES A famous actor who had not been on stage for two years since his nervous breakdown, he assumed several role-types including: "Commander Vanstone," "Aristide Duval," "Lord Englemount" and "John Ellis." His given name was Charles Mugg, and he toyed with adopting the name, Ludovic Castiglione, but in the end he decided to appeal to the British love of alliteration: hence Charles Cartwright was his stage name. *Murder in Three Acts.*

CARVER, DR. "A world-renowned elderly archaeologist," he was a member of Parker Pyne's party travelling from Amman to Petra who developed a criminal fondness for Carol Blundell's pearl earrings, which he did not realize were fake. "The Pearl of Price" from *Parker Pyne Investigates.*

CARY, FRANCES Mrs. Ariadne Oliver encountered her in Peter Cardiff's art studio, where she was posing, David Baker joked, "as a desperate girl demanding an abortion." While abroad in Kenya, she met Robert Orwell and together they planned the impersonations of Andrew and Mary Restarick. *Third Girl.*

CASPAR, MR. This "beaming" foreigner was taking the same Famous Houses and Gardens of Great Britain tour as Miss Marple, who thought he was "very excitable" and "possibly a dangerous character," but attributed most of her opinions to foreign prejudice. *Nemesis.*

CASPEARO, SENORA DE "A handsome woman from Venezuela," she had a particular taste in men: "How ugly are old men! Oh how they are ugly! They should all be put to death at forty, or perhaps thirty-five would be better. Yes?" *A Caribbean Mystery.*

CASSELL, DR. Bundle Brent brought Ronny Devereux, whom she thought she had run down in her Hispano Suza, to this physician in Market Basing for treatment. He told her that she had not killed the victim by her reckless driving, but that the man had been shot. *The Seven Dials Mystery.*

CASSETTI *See* **RATCHETT, SAMUEL EDWARD.**

CASSON, MRS. One of Margery Gale's neighbours at Abbot's Mead, she was involved in psychic research. Margery said: "She is one of these silly women that runs a craze to death." She brought the medium Mrs. Lloyd to Abbot's Mead. "The Voice in the Dark" from *The Mysterious Mr. Quin.*

CASTIGLIONE, LUDOVIC *See* CART-
WRIGHT, SIR CHARLES.

CASTLE, MRS. The owner and proprietress of the Jolly Roger Hotel on Leathercombe Bay where Arlena Marshall was
murdered, she was "a woman of forty-
odd with a large bust, rather violent henna-
red hair and an almost offensively refined
manner of speech." *Evil Under the Sun.*

CASTLETON, HARRY *See* DUGUES-
CLIN, QUENTIN.

CATERHAM, LORD *See* BRENT, ALIS-
TAIR EDWARD, NINTH MARQUIS OF
CATERHAM.

CATERHAM, MARQUIS OF *See* BRENT,
ALISTAIR EDWARD, NINTH MARQUIS
OF CATERHAM.

CAUX, MONSIEUR The Commissary of
Police assigned to the Ruth Kettering
murder, he "blew out his chest impor-
tantly" when he introduced himself to
Katherine Grey. His ambition was to lay
the Comte de la Roche by his heels. *The
Mystery of the Blue Train.*

CAVENDISH, JOHN The husband of
Mary Cavendish, the brother of Lawrence
Cavendish and the step-son of Emily Inglethorp, Cavendish was a very important catalyst in the Christie canon; through
him, Hastings and Poirot became reac-
quainted after a hiatus of many years.
Cavendish met the wounded Hastings,
whom he had known since childhood in
World War I London, and invited him to
convalesce at Styles Court, while Poirot,
a Belgian refugee, was lodged in Leastways Cottage nearby. *The Mysterious
Affair at Styles.*

CAVENDISH, LAWRENCE About forty
years of age, Lawrence was the younger
brother of John Cavendish and Emily Inglethorp's step-son. According to John
Cavendish, Lawrence had "gone through
every penny he ever had publishing rotten verses in fancy bindings." Lawrence

became romantically involved with Cynthia Murdoch. *The Mysterious Affair at
Styles.*

CAVENDISH, MARY As the wife of John
Cavendish, she gave "the impression of
a wild untamed spirit in an exquisitely
civilized body" in Hastings' opinion.
Hastings imagined himself to be in love
with her, but she was also befriended by
Dr. Bauerstein, later revealed to be a German spy, which led to a good deal of
misunderstanding in the English upper-
class fashion, between Mary and her husband, John. Later, in "The Adventure of
the 'Western Star' " from *Poirot Investigates,* she counselled Lady Yardley to
seek Poirot's advice. *The Mysterious Affair at Styles.*

CAWTHORN, THE HONOURABLE VIR-
GINIA *See* REVEL, VIRGINIA.

CAYLEY, ALFRED The husband of Elisabeth Cayley, he was described by Major
Bletchley as "a kind of walking chemist's
shop." When Elisabeth returned from a
rubber of bridge in the garden one evening, he was "as a neglected invalid, enjoying himself a great deal, coughing in
a sepulchral manner, shivering dramatically and saying several times: '*Quite* all
right, my dear. I hope you enjoyed your
game. It doesn't matter about *me* at all.
Even if I *have* caught a severe chill, what
does it really matter? There's a war on!' "
N or M?

CAYLEY, ELISABETH Wife to the invalid Alfred Cayley; she was "an anx-
ious-faced woman who seemed to have
no other aim in life than to minister to
Mr. Cayley's wants." *N or M?*

CAYMAN, AMELIA The wife of Leo Cayman, she and her husband identified the

body of Alan Carstairs as being that of her brother, Alex Pritchard. Lady Frankie Derwent referred to her as "a painted-up raddled bitch." *Why Didn't They Ask Evans?*

CAYMAN, LEO AKA Edgar Templeton, this "hearty bounder" was the husband of Amelia Cayman. As Edgar Templeton, he posed as the husband of Rose Emily Templeton at Tudor Cottage. *Why Didn't They Ask Evans?*

CAZALET, DR. A "cheerful, round-faced little man with spectacles," Dr. Cazalet was a Harley Street physician called upon by Poirot to hypnotize Lady Nancy Astwell. "The Under Dog" from *The Under Dog.*

CELESTINE Mrs. Opalsen's personal French maid, she was arrested for stealing one of her mistress' pearl necklaces but was cleared by Poirot. "The Jewel Robbery at the 'Grand Metropolitan' " from *Poirot Investigates.*

CHADWICK, MISS Mistress at Meadowbank, she was often called "Faithful Chaddy." Inspector Kelsey judged her: "Good forehead, obstinate mouth, untidy grey hair, no trace of hysteria. The kind of woman, he thought, who could be depended upon in a crisis though she might be overlooked in ordinary everyday life." She died by throwing herself between Miss Bullstrode and an assassin. *Cat Among the Pigeons.*

CHALLENGER, COMMANDER GEORGE He and his physician uncle supplied Nick Buckley, Freddie Rice and her husband with cocaine. He was in love with Nick Buckley. *Peril at End House.*

CHANDLER, ADMIRAL CHARLES Father of Hugh Chandler, Admiral Chandler was from a family which had been active in naval service since the time of Sir Walter Raleigh. His best friend was Colonel George Frobisher. He had no hope that the "cursed foreigner" Poirot would

be able to save his son from the Chandler family curse, mental illness. "The Cretan Bull" from *The Labours of Hercules.*

CHANDLER, HUGH Beautiful, bull-like son of Admiral Charles Chandler and ex-fiancé of Diana Maberly, he left his two loves, the Navy and Diana, because he feared that he had inherited the family mental illness. He considered that suicide was his only alternative. Diana appealed to Poirot to prove the young man's sanity. "The Cretan Bull" from *The Labours of Hercules.*

CHANTRY, COMMANDER TONY Sixth husband of Valentine Chantry and bored with her after only six months of marriage, he fell in love with Marjorie Gold while vacationing in Rhodes with his wife. "Triangle at Rhodes" from *Murder in the Mews.*

CHANTRY, VALENTINE Formerly Valentine Dacres and recently wed to her sixth husband, Tony Chantry, she was dramatic and theatrical, talked constantly without apparent intelligence and flirted openly with the handsome Douglas Gold. She was killed by a form of strophanthin, a heart poison. "Triangle at Rhodes" from *Murder in the Mews.*

CHAPMAN, ALBERT See **BARNES, REGINALD** and **BLUNT, ALISTAIR.**

CHAPMAN, NIGEL AKA Nigel Stanley. A student of Bronze Age, Mediaeval and Italian history who lived at Mrs. Nicoletis' youth hostel, he was an *enfant terrible* with "all the charm of a spoiled child who has never grown up." *Hickory Dickory Dock.*

CHAPMAN, SYLVIA See **GRANT, GERDA.**

CHAPPELL, ANTHONY (TONY) A young friend of Poirot's who was "steeped in misery—wallowing in gloom," he was asked by Poirot: "Something perhaps to do with your baby having left you?" Having had "what the vulgar call words" with Pauline Weatherby, he was melodramatically considering poisoning himself before Poirot offered his aid. "Yellow Iris" from *The Regatta Mystery.*

CHARLES The "notorious and popular head waiter" at the Luxembourg, he had poured the fatal wine at Rosemary Barton's birthday party. "Gracefully bowing, Charles withdrew and darted like an angry dragonfly on some very inferior grade of waiter who was doing the wrong thing at a table near the window." *Sparkling Cyanide.*

CHARLTON, MR. Simeon Lee's lawyer and a partner in the firm Charlton, Hodgkins and Bruce, he was "an old-fashioned type of solicitor with a cautious blue eye." He disliked reading wills in the company of heirs because fights always occurred afterwards. *Hercule Poirot's Christmas.*

CHARNLEY, LADY ALIX AKA "Weeping Lady with the Silver Ewer," she had been married to Lord Reggie Charnley only one month before his alleged suicide, and bore his son after his death. Mr. Satterthwaite, whom she contacted in hopes that he would sell "The Dead Harlequin" by Bristow to her, described Lady Alix as "a Frozen Lady." "The Dead Harlequin" from *The Mysterious Mr. Quin.*

CHARNLEY, HUGO The brother of the deceased Lord Reggie Charnley and lover of Monica Ford, his hopes of coming into the family's estate had been dashed by the birth of a son to Lord Reggie and Lady Alix Charnley. "The Dead Harlequin" from *The Mysterious Mr. Quin.*

CHARNLEY, LORD REGGIE Returning from their honeymoon, he and his new wife Lady Alix had hosted a large fancy-dress ball to celebrate their homecoming when, in the words of Colonel Monckton, "just as the guests were starting to arrive Charnley locked himself into the Oak Parlour and shot himself . . . damned bad taste—to do a thing like that." Lord Reg-

gie had made love to Monica Ford, a governess, before his marriage and had impregnated her. "The Dead Harlequin" from *The Mysterious Mr. Quin.*

CHARPENTIER, LOUISE *See* **BIRELL, LOUISE.**

CHATTERTON, LADY ABBIE Wife of Lord Chatterton and a friend of Poirot's and of Margharita Clayton's, she enticed Poirot to a party so that Margharita could consult him about the death of her husband. "Lady Chatterton was one of the brightest jewels in what Poirot called *le haut monde.* Everything she did or said was news. She had brains, beauty, originality and enough vitality to activate a rocket to the moon." "The Mystery of the Spanish Chest" from *The Adventure of the Christmas Pudding.*

CHATTERTON, LADY ALICE "Lady Chatterton was one of Poirot's most ardent admirers. Starting from the mysterious conduct of a Pekinese, he had unravelled a chain which led to a noted burglar and housekeeper. Lady Chatterton had been loud in his praises ever since." Like her counterpart, Lady Abbie Chatterton from "The Mystery of the Spanish Chest," she arranged a meeting to introduce Poirot to a friend in distress. "The Mystery of the Baghdad Chest" from *The Regatta Mystery.*

CHECKHEATON, LADY MATILDA The great-aunt of Sir Stafford Nye, whom she called "Staffy," she was an indomitable Victorian with pronounced views on almost any subject. She was staunchly conservative, had a talent for sleuthing and was privy to confidential information from her powerful friends. She argued with Dr. Donaldson about having a wheelchair: "One has one's pride, you know, and while you can still hobble around with a stick or a little support, you don't really want to look absolutely a crock or bedridden or something. It'd be easier if I were a man . . . I mean one could tie up one's leg with one of those enormous bandages and padded things as though one had the gout. . . . Yes, a wheelchair." Lady Matilda's companion-secretary was Miss Amy Leatheran. *Passenger to Frankfurt.*

CHELLES, MONSIEUR *See* **VICTOR, KING.**

CHESTER, ADELA She informed Mr. Pyne that she lived for her son, Basil, and was extremely upset that he was ruining his life by being engaged to Betty Gregg. However, after her son fell in love with the exotic Dolores Ramona, Mrs. Chester began to see the English Betty in a more favourable light. "Problem at Pollensa Bay" from *The Regatta Mystery.*

CHESTER, BASIL The son of Adela Chester, he was tired of being stifled by his mother, yet he also clearly enjoyed his mother's constant attention. With her, he vacationed at Pollensa Bay, where he met Betty Gregg and Delores Ramona. 'Problem at Pollensa Bay" from *The Regatta Mystery.*

CHETWYND, GORDON Sir Stafford Nye, a comfortable seven minutes late for a meeting with Chetwynd, whom he thought had a "nicely suspicious mind," said: "Inclined to be a mean man, Mr. Chetwynd. A great one for making enemies in the wrong places." *Passenger to Frankfurt.*

CHEVENIX-GORE, SIR GERVASE FRANCIS XAVIER Brother of Anthony and Pamela Chevenix-Gore and married to Lady Vanda Chevenix-Gore, he divided the world between the Chevenix-Gores and everyone else. In order to perpetuate his family, he plotted to force his daughter Ruth to marry his nephew Hugo. Although "everything he touched turned to gold," Ruth said he "had the brains of a louse!" "Dead Man's Mirror" from *Murder in the Mews.*

CHEVENIX-GORE, RUTH Illegitimate daughter of Anthony Chevenix-Gore and Miss Lingard, she was adopted by Sir

Gervase and Lady Vanda Chevenix-Gore and was married to Captain Lake. Her black hair, well-chiselled features and beautiful colouring made her one of the loveliest girls Poirot had ever seen. "Dead Man's Mirror" from *Murder in the Mews.*

CHEVENIX-GORE, LADY VANDA ELIZABETH Daughter of Colonel Frederick Arbuthnot, wife of Sir Gervase Chevenix-Gore and adoptive mother of Ruth Chevenix-Gore, she was an elderly but still handsome, vague but clever woman with "a leaning towards the occult." She said she was a reincarnation of Queen Hatshepsut and of an Atlantan priestess. "Dead Man's Mirror" from *Murder in the Mews.*

CHICHESTER, REVEREND EDWARD *See* **MINKS, ARTHUR.**

CHILCOTT, MARY An old school friend of Lois Hargreaves', Mary had been staying at Thurnley Lodge when the poisonings occurred, made funeral arrangements after Lois was poisoned and had a steady countenance that did not reflect the agitation that she said she felt. "The House of Lurking Death" from *Partners in Crime.*

CHRISTOW, GERDA Plain but clever wife of Dr. John Christow, mother of Terence and Zena, and sister of Elsie Patterson, she was in every way the antithesis of her husband's former fiancée and present lover Veronica Cray. She absolutely worshipped her husband. Henrietta Savernake imagined Gerda as a sculpture: "a strange submissive figure, a figure offering up worship to an unseen deity— the face raised—blind, dumb, devoted— terribly strong, terribly fanatical." After her husband's murder, she was discovered holding a revolver. *The Hollow.*

CHRISTOW, DR. JOHN Husband to Gerda Christow, father of Terence and Zena Christow, he was a friend of the Angkatells'. His patients were rich hypochondriacs but his real professional interest was researching a cure for the rare Ridgway's disease. Formerly fiancé and presently lover of Veronica Cray, he was also having an affair with Henrietta Savernake, whose detachment he regarded as a challenge. Poirot discovered him shot dead near the swimming pool with his wife standing over him, holding a revolver. *The Hollow.*

CHRISTOW, ZENA Nine-year-old daughter of John and Gerda Christow, she was an extraordinarily talented card-reader and described her father's relationships with the people at The Hollow with amazing accuracy. She also predicted her father's death. *The Hollow.*

CHUDLEIGH, ROSE Rose Chudleigh had been the cook for the Templetons at Tudor Cottage and was witness to the will that Roger Bassington-ffrench forged when he posed as John Savage. She "lived in a small cottage that seemed to be overflowing with china dogs." *Why Didn't They Ask Evans?*

CINDERELLA (CINDERS) *See* **DUVEEN, DULCIE.**

CLANCY, DANIEL Creator of the fictional detective Wilbraham Rice, he was on board the *Prometheus* when Madame Giselle Morisot was murdered. He was by far Japp's favourite suspect: "These detective story writers, always making the police out to be fools, and getting their procedure all wrong. . . . Set of ignorant scribblers! This is just the sort of fool murder that a scribbler of rubbish would think he could get away with." *Death in the Clouds.*

CLAPPERTON, ADELINE The wife of John Clapperton, she was the widow of Lord Carrington for six months when she met Clapperton in the war hospital she managed. Left a great deal of money by her first husband, she never let Colonel Clapperton forget that she bought him, and that he depended upon her for every penny. She was found stabbed to death with a native knife on a boat tour docked

near Alexandria. "Problem at Sea" from *The Regatta Mystery.*

CLAPPERTON, COLONEL JOHN A former music hall entertainer who married Lady Carrington for her money, he was not highly respected by General Forbes during the war: "Joined up and was out in France counting tins of plum and apple. Huns dropped a stray bomb and he went home with a flesh wound in the arm." "Problem at Sea" from *The Regatta Mystery.*

CLARK, DR. CAMPBELL "Dr. Clark was in the forefront as a physical and mental specialist, and his last book, *The Problem of the Unconscious Mind,* had been the most discussed book of the year." He discussed Felicie Bault's schizophrenia and the relationship of body, soul and spirit with Canon Parfitt. "The Fourth Man" from *Witness for the Prosecution.*

CLARK, SERGEANT Sergeant with the local constabulary aiding Inspector Grange in his investigation of the death of John Christow, he discovered from the kitchenmaid, Doris Emmot, that Gudgeon, the butler, had been seen with a revolver on the day of the murder. *The Hollow.*

CLARKE, SIR CARMICHAEL The husband of Lady Charlotte Clarke and the brother of Franklin Clarke, Sir Carmichael was the third victim of the A.B.C. murderer. He received a blow to the head during his nightly stroll. He was a collector of Chinese art and lived near Devon. *The A.B.C. Murders.*

CLARKE, LADY CHARLOTTE She was the wife of Sir Carmichael Clarke and the sister-in-law of Franklin Clarke. After her husband's death, she sent for Poirot to investigate and dismissed Thora Grey. *The A.B.C. Murders.*

CLARKE, FRANKLIN The brother of Sir Carmichael Clarke and brother-in-law to Lady Charlotte Clarke, Franklin stood to inherit his brother's fortune when Lady

Clarke died. At his request Poirot formed the "Special Legion" to solve the A.B.C. murders. He also suggested that Poirot insert an advertisement in the newspapers which read: "A.B.C. Urgent. H.P. close on your track. A hundred for my silence. X.Y.Z." *The A.B.C. Murders.*

CLAYTHORNE, VERA ELIZABETH An efficient games mistress, she was accused of the murder of Cyril Ogilvie Hamilton in a cryptic message at Indian Island. She had been the first to realize the significance of the "Ten Little Indians" rhyme which hung in all the guestrooms. When all the other guests were dead except her and Philip Lombard, she did not hesitate to steal his revolver and shoot him, thinking that he, of course, was the Island killer. Her sanity impaired, she then hanged herself with the noose that dropped from the ceiling and became the tenth victim, complying with the last verse of the rhyme: "One little Indian boy left all alone; He went and hanged himself and then there were none." *And Then There Were None.*

CLAYTON, ALICE *See* **BARRON, BEATRICE.**

CLAYTON, ARNOLD The murdered husband of Margharita Clayton, his body was discovered in Major Rich's Spanish chest. "The Mystery of the Spanish Chest" from *The Adventure of the Christmas Pudding.*

CLAYTON, ELSIE The "lachrymose" daughter of Mrs. Rice with whom she was on holiday at Lake Stempka in Herzoslavakia, she met Harold Waring at the resort, who soon fell for her. Poirot maintained that she was "a most accomplished little actress. Everything is very pure—very innocent. She appeals, not to sex, but to chivalry." "The Stymphalian Birds" from *The Labours of Hercules.*

CLAYTON, MARGHARITA The wife of the murdered Arnold Clayton and the beloved of Major Charles Rich, Mrs. Clayton had "a kind of mediaeval simplic-

ity—a strange innocence that could be, Poirot thought, more devastating than any voluptuous sophistication." She had a tendency to inspire passion in men without trying. She consulted Poirot in an attempt to clear Major Rich of her husband's murder. The resemblance of Margharita Clayton to Marguerita Clayton of "The Mystery of the Baghdad Chest" is not accidental (*see* Introduction). "The Mystery of the Spanish Chest" from *The Adventure of the Christmas Pudding.*

CLAYTON, MARGUERITA Loved by Major Jack Rich, she was the widow of Edward Clayton, and had a beauty which attracted tragedy. She hoped that Poirot, whom she had met at Lady Alice Chatterton's fête, would clear her lover from any suspicion in the death of her husband. "The Mystery of the Baghdad Chest" from *The Regatta Mystery.*

CLEGG, EMMELINE She found happiness and peace within the Flock of the Great Shepherd and was described by her friend Miss Carnaby as foolish and credulous. Miss Clegg made a will leaving all of her estate to the movement, even though three other women with similar wills had died shortly after their bequests. "The Flock of Geryon" from *The Labours of Hercules.*

CLEGG, FREDA The daughter of the deceased John Clegg, she was bored and had gone to Parker Pyne looking for adventure. She became involved with Major Charlie Wilbraham, one of Pyne's clients. "The Case of the Discontented Soldier" from *Parker Pyne Investigates.*

CLEGG, JOE The second husband of Maureen Clegg, he had wanted her to divorce her first husband, Jacko Argyle, who was imprisoned for the murder of Rachel Argyle. He bridled at the suggestion that the verdict had been mistaken: "I've always understood . . . that an English trial was as fair a thing as can be." *Ordeal by Innocence.*

CLEGG, MAUREEN The widow of Jacko Argyle whose marriage to him had been a secret from his family until she was forced to supplicate for financial assistance, she began divorce proceedings while her husband was in prison. Soon after she married Joe Clegg. Dr. Calgary felt that "possibly . . . this pretty, silly child was more of a realist" than himself. *Ordeal by Innocence.*

CLEMENT, DENNIS Leonard Clement's sixteen-year-old nephew, he was fascinated with the subject of murder and attempted to carry out an amateur investigation. He fell in love with Lettice Protheroe and defended her peculiar habits. *Murder at the Vicarage.*

CLEMENT, GRISELDA The wife of Leonard Clement and the mother of David and Leonard, she was twenty years younger than her husband, "distractingly pretty and quite incapable of taking anything seriously." Her husband said that she "treats the whole parish as a huge joke arranged for her amusement." After the death of her husband, she continued to live in the shabby old vicarage in St. Mary Mead where she was a great friend to Miss Marple. *Murder at the Vicarage; The Body in the Library; 4.50 from Paddington.*

CLEMENT, LEONARD (LEN) The husband of Griselda Clement, the father of David and Leonard, and the uncle of Dennis Clement, he was the vicar in St. Mary Mead and lived next to Miss Marple's cottage. The body of Colonel Lucius Protheroe was discovered in his study. The activities of his wife, who was twenty years his junior, "more than ever convinced [him] that celibacy is desirable for the clergy," *Murder at the Vicarage; The Body in the Library.*

CLEVELAND, JANE AKA Miss Montresor. She was hired to impersonate the Grand Duchess Pauline of Ostrova. As a reporter from New York, Miss Montresor attended a bazaar at the Countess of Anchester's home and there changed clothing with the woman who purported to be the Grand Duchess Pauline. Little did Jane know that she was a stand-in for an attempted assassination victim. "Jane in Search of a Job" from *The Golden Ball.*

CLEVELAND, MORTIMER An investigator into subconscious phenomena and a member of the Psychical Research Society, "he was by nature peculiarly susceptible to atmosphere, and by deliberate training he had increased his own natural gift." While a guest of the Dinsmeads' he found an S.O.S. inscribed in the dust on his dressing table one morning. He discovered that a murder had been committed and prevented another, using a pocketful of test tubes he happened to be carrying. "S.O.S." from *Witness for the Prosecution.*

CLEVES, DIANA The adopted daughter of the Lytcham Roches', she was also their cousin, and was in love with Captain John Marshall, while she flirted with Geoffrey Keene and was loved by Gregory Barling. Under the terms of her adoptive father's will, the bewitching Diana would not inherit if she refused to marry Gregory Barling. Asked whether she was sorry to learn of her father's death she replied: "Of course. I'm modern, you know, M. Poirot. I don't indulge in sob stuff. But I was fond of the Old Man." "The Second Gong" from *Witness for the Prosecution.*

CLITHERING, SIR HENRY A former Commissioner of Scotland Yard and the uncle of Inspector Dermot Craddock, Clithering implicitly trusted all of Miss Marple's judgements and once capsulized her virtues with a terse, "She's the goods." He also said: "The old Pussies . . . what did I tell you? They hear everything. They see everything. And, unlike the famous adage, they speak all evil." *The Thirteen Problems; The Body in the Library; A Murder is Announced.*

CLOADE, FRANCES The wife of Jeremy Cloade, she was the daughter of the infamous crook Lord Edward Trenton. In order to raise money for her husband's business, she blackmailed David Hunter, who had prevented a loan from Rosaleen Cloade, by making him pay to silence "Enoch Arden." *Taken at the Flood.*

CLOADE, GORDON The brother of Jeremy Cloade, Lionel Cloade and Adela Marchmont, the uncle of Rowley Cloade and the husband of Rosaleen Cloade, he died instantly when his house on Campden Hill was bombed. Before his marriage he had been the archetype of the benevolent uncle, and his loss was felt by all his relatives. *Taken at the Flood.*

CLOADE, JEREMY The brother of Gordon Cloade, Lionel Cloade and Adela Marchmont, he was a solicitor with the firm of Cloade, Brunskill and Cloade, a firm considered not "brilliant . . . but very sound." *Taken at the Flood.*

CLOADE, KATHERINE (KATHIE) Dr. Lionel Cloade's wife was described by Poirot's valet George: "Good walking-shoes, brogues. A tweed coat and skirt—but a lace blouse. Some questionable Egyptian beads and a blue chiffon scarf." She wanted Poirot to prove that Rosaleen's marriage to Gordon Cloade was illegal so that the Cloade family would inherit Gordon's money. *Taken at the Flood.*

CLOADE, DR. LIONEL The brother of Gordon Cloade, Jeremy Cloade and Adela Marchmont, he was married to Katherine Cloade. He examined the body of "Enoch Arden" and testified to the cause and the time of death at the inquest. *Taken at the Flood.*

CLOADE, ROSALEEN The wife of Gordon Cloade, sister of David Hunter and the former wife of Captain Robert Underhay. *See* **CORRIGAN, EILEEN**. *Taken at the Flood.*

CLOADE, ROWLAND (ROWLEY) Gordon Cloade's nephew and Lynn Marchmont's

cousin and fiancé, he had long suffered guilt feelings over the deaths of Johnnie Vavasour and Major Porter. When Lynn Marchmont broke their engagement, he attempted to strangle her, but luckily, Poirot appeared in time to prevent him. Lynn and Rowland were eventually married. *Taken at the Flood.*

CLODE, CHRISTOBEL Simon Clode's deceased grand-daughter who had lived with him since her father was killed during World War I. She had participated in séances with Eurydice Spragg in an attempt to establish contact with her dead mother. "Motive v Opportunity" from *The Thirteen Problems.*

CLODE, GEORGE Simon Clode's nephew who possessed "an honest but not brilliant countenance," he asked Mr. Petherick to look into the Mrs. Spragg affair. "Motive v Opportunity" from *The Thirteen Problems.*

CLODE, MARY Simon Clode's niece, she was "a quiet, self-contained girl" who stood to lose her inheritance to Eurydice Spragg. "Motive v Opportunity" from *The Thirteen Problems.*

CLODE, SIMON The uncle of George and Mary Clode and the grandfather of the deceased Christobel Clode, Simon Clode was considered "a man of considerable wealth." Although "shrewd in practical matters," he was completely under the power of Mrs. Spragg—so much so that he tried to disinherit his niece and nephew and leave his fortune to Mrs. Spragg instead. "Motive v Opportunity" from *The Thirteen Problems.*

COBB, MR. A dignitary of the Harchester Galleries, he said to Mr. Satterthwaite: "Your name stands for a good deal in the artistic world." "The Dead Harlequin" from *The Mysterious Mr. Quin.*

COCKER, MRS. The "calm and unperturbable" cook and housekeeper to Gwenda and Giles Reed at Hillside, she accidentally discovered Helen Halliday's skeleton. She was "taken queer" but given some brandy to help her overcome the shock. The brandy was poisoned, but Mrs. Cocker recovered. *Sleeping Murder.*

COCKER, DORIS She was a housemaid who waited on the table at which Sir Bartholomew Strange died. Except for her absence during the previous murder of the Reverend Stephen Babbington, Sir Charles Cartwright—a self-appointed investigator—would have believed her guilty. *Three-Act Tragedy.*

CODDERS *See* LOMAX, THE HONOURABLE GEORGE.

CODSON, ANTHONY The former lover of the Mistress of La Paz and the father of her illegitimate son John, he had been told that he had only six months to live. He attempted suicide for the second time, but was interrupted by Mr. Satterthwaite, who said Codson led "the kind of life that practically inhibits thought of any description and substitutes sensation. To speak frankly, an animal's life." "The Man from the Sea" from *The Mysterious Mr. Quin.*

COGGINS Brutal assistant of the man presenting himself as Inspector Dymchurch, he used various instruments of torture and coercion to force the crucial Russian letter from Tommy Beresford. "The Adventure of the Sinister Stranger" from *Partners in Crime.*

COGHAN, MR. He revealed the secret of the hiding place in Andrew Marsh's fireplace to Poirot. "The Case of the Missing Will" from *Poirot Investigates.*

COHEN, SIR HERMAN *See* SALMON, SIR JOSEPH.

COLE, MR. (DETECTIVE INSPECTOR) Masquerading as a rather lunatic fringe member of the Flock of the Great Shepherd, Mr. Cole was really an undercover policeman observing the group at close range. Wearing "grass-green shorts," he recounted visions of ritual marriages of Sumerian deities, or the sacrifice of hundreds of virgins, and was quite convincing to Miss Carnaby. "The Flock of Geryon" from *The Labours of Hercules.*

COLE, ELIZABETH AKA Elizabeth Litchfield, she was the daughter of the tyrannical Mathew Litchfield and the sister of Margaret Litchfield. Hastings remarked that she was "a woman who had suffered and who was, in consequence, deeply distrustful of life." She suffered from horror and guilt after the murder of her father by her sister. In his last message to Hastings, Poirot suggested that his friend rescue her from the belief that life had passed her by, reminding Hastings that he was still attractive to women. *Curtain.*

COLEMAN, BILL An archaeologist with the American expedition at Tell Yarimjah, he described himself as "All British. See the trademark. Guaranteed guarantee," but others thought he more closely resembled "a large stupid dog dragging its tail and trying to please." *Murder in Mesopotamia.*

COLEMAN, MONKEY *See* DRAKE, VICTOR.

COLES, DR. Miss Marple's doctor at the Keston Spa Hydro was a "simple unsuspicious fellow who believed what he wanted to believe." "A Christmas Tragedy" from *The Thirteen Problems.*

COLES, DORIS Mr. Satterthwaite thought Doris had "no artistic justification for existence," but she helped to determine that Mabelle Annesley had been murdered by her inability to tune her ukulele. "The Bird with the Broken Wing" from *The Mysterious Mr. Quin.*

COLGATE, INSPECTOR He investigated the death of Arlena Marshall at the Jolly Roger Hotel. "Poirot liked Inspector Colgate. He liked his rugged face, his shrewd

eyes, and his slow unhurried manner."
Evil Under the Sun.

COLLINS, MISS She was Mrs. Waverly's companion when Johnnie Waverly was kidnapped. The only suspicions Poirot had about Miss Collins were that "we know very little about her, that she is obviously an intelligent young woman, and that she had only been here a year." Mrs. Waverly found Miss Collins an invaluable secretary-companion, as well as a very efficient housekeeper. "The Adventure of Johnnie Waverly" from *Three Blind Mice and Other Stories.*

COLLINS, BERYL Secretary and receptionist of Dr. John Christow, "she never made a mistake, she was never flurried or worried or hurried." Her answers to Inspector Grange were models of clarity, and she thought it was impossible that Gerda Christow could have shot Dr. Christow. *The Hollow.*

COLLODON, MISS Tommy Beresford's researcher "had grey hair which was slowly passing through the stage of recovering from a peroxide rinse designated to make her look younger (which it had not done). She was now trying various shades of artistic grey, cloudy smoke, steel blue and other interesting shades suitable for a lady between sixty and sixty-five, devoted to the pursuit of research." *Postern of Fate.*

"COLONEL" See **PEDLER, SIR EUSTACE.**

COMBEAU, PIERRE He was an old friend of Poirot's who knew the detective's methods well and aided him once in a deception. *The Big Four.*

CONRAD, MRS. According to Hastings, "Mrs. Conrad was a beautiful woman of thirty-five, with golden hair and a slight tendency to *embonpoint.*" A well-known lady in London society, she was connected with the enemy agents who were blackmailing Lord Alloway. "The Submarine Plans" from *The Under Dog.*

CONNEAU, GEORGES See **RENAULD, PAUL T.**

CONSTANTINE, DR. A Greek, he was "a small dark man" who boarded the *Orient Express* in Athens. He examined Samuel Edward Ratchett's body and was of the opinion that at least two persons were responsible for the dagger wounds on the corpse. *Murder on the Orient Express.*

CONSTANTINE, DR. CLAUDIUS See **ANTROBUS, DR.**

CONSTANTINE, DMITRI When Mr. Constantine screamed that his architect, Rudolf Santonix, was spending too much money designing his new house, he was told: "Don't give me any of your pettifogging middle-class economics. You want a house of quality and you're going to *get* it, and you'll boast about it to your friends and they'll envy you." *Endless Night.*

CONWAY, BRIDGET A cousin of Jimmy Lorrimer's, she lived with her aunt Mrs. Anstruther and "was like a delicate etching," according to Luke Fitzwilliam, who fell in love with her almost at once. Hardened from a recent unhappy love affair, she was considering marriage to Lord Easterfield purely for financial gain. In spite of the continual playful bickering with Fitzwilliam, Bridget was of great help in his investigation, and was the first to uncover the identity of the murderer. *Murder is Easy.*

CONWAY, SIR GEORGE Poirot felt "a sympathy for Sir George Conway. The man obviously wanted to tell him something—and as obviously had lost the art of simple narration. Words had become to him a means of obscuring facts—not revealing them. He was adept in the art of the useful phrase—that is to say the phrase that falls soothingly on the ears and is quite empty of meaning." "The

Augean Stables" from *The Labours of Hercules.*

COOKE, MISS AKA Miss Bartlett. With her companion Miss Barrow, she was Miss Marple's secret bodyguard on the Famous Houses and Gardens of Great Britain tour and successfully apprehended the killer. *Nemesis.*

COOMBE, ALICIA Her dress shop was haunted by the mysterious life-sized puppet doll: "She lay long and limp and sprawled in her green-velvet clothes and her velvet cap and the painted mask of her face. She was . . . the whim of Rich Women, the doll who lolls beside the telephone, or among the cushions of the divan. She sprawled there, eternally limp and yet strangely alive. She looked a decadent product of the twentieth century." The doll kept appearing in new positions and places when no one was watching. When Alicia threw the doll out of the window onto the pavement, a street urchin adopted it, saying that the doll needed love. "The Dressmaker's Doll" from *Double Sin.*

COOTE, LADY MARIA With her husband, Sir Oswald Coote, she rented Chimneys for a season and filled it with young people to ease her loneliness. She never could accustom herself to her husband's transformation from "that cheery young man in the bicycle shop" to a successful businessman. Her major indulgence was chatting with her servants, and she cheated at bridge. *The Seven Dials Mystery.*

COOTE, SIR OSWALD The husband of the long-suffering, timorous Lady Maria Coote, he had been the enterprising owner of a bicycle shop who, in rapid succession, bought a factory, became a steel magnate, was granted a peerage and eventually became one of the wealthiest men in England: "The kind of man you'd get if a steam-roller were turned into a human being." *The Seven Dials Mystery.*

COPE, JEFFERSON He had been in love with Nadine Boynton since her days as a penniless nursing candidate. Dr. Gerard said he possessed "a nice, upright, sentimental, normal American mind. He believes in good rather than evil." However, he credited Mrs. Boynton with maternal devotion rather than active malice. *Appointment with Death.*

COPES, MRS. The housekeeper to Colonel Pikeaway, she resembled a witch, "with a sharp nose and a sharp chin which almost met each other." *Postern of Fate.*

COPLEIGH, GEORGE AND LIZ They ran the guest house in Sutton Chancellor, and were questioned by Tuppence Beresford about the village. Content to let Mrs. Copleigh talk, Mr. Copleigh "barely opened his mouth. His conversation was mostly made up of amiable grunts, usually signifying an affirmative. Sometimes, in more muted tones, a disagreement." The information Liz gave was mostly hearsay, malice and imagination. *By the Pricking of My Thumbs.*

COPLING, NURSE AKA Zarida. While she was nursing Mrs. Pritchard, Miss Copling fell in love with George Pritchard, her patient's husband. After having left the Pritchard household, she returned as Zarida, a "Psychic Reader of the Future," and warned Mrs. Pritchard to beware of blue flowers. "The Blue Geranium" from *The Thirteen Problems.*

CORNELLY, LORD A modern-day Diogenes, this rich and eccentric peer with the "shrewd monkey-like face" hired Andrew MacWhirter as his personal representative in South America: "I thought to myself—that's the kind of chap *I* want. Man who can't be bribed to tell lies. You won't have to tell lies for me. I go about the world looking for honest men—and there are damned few of them." *Towards Zero.*

CORNER, SIR MONTAGU He gave the dinner party at which twelve people were fooled by Carlotta Adams' impersonation of Jane Wilkinson. Hastings remarked "His manner was affected to the last degree. . . . In the dim light he looked like some genie of mediaeval days." Sir Montagu, a connoisseur and collector of artifacts, was favourably impressed with the remarks on Greek art made by the young woman he thought was Jane Wilkinson. *Lord Edgware Dies.*

CORRIGAN, EILEEN AKA Rosaleen Cloade. David Hunter forced Eileen to take his dead sister's place and masquerade as Rosaleen Cloade, inherit Gordon Cloade's money and divide it with him. Poirot began to unravel the mystery when he saw her enter a Roman Catholic church in search of solace after the inquest. *Taken at the Flood.*

CORRIGAN, DR. JIM The police surgeon in the N.W. London division, he carried out the preliminary medical examination and found a list of names on the body of Father Gorman. He had a theory that a deficiency in the secretions of the Mandarian glands might make human beings criminals. *The Pale Horse.*

CORRIGAN, KATHERINE (GINGER) AKA Doreen Easterbrook. She was a friend of Rhoda Despard's, and collaborated with Mark Easterbrook by posing as his wife, Doreen, to help solve the mystery. *The Pale Horse.*

CORTMAN, MILDRED JEAN AKA Juanita; Miss Ellis. She was the wife of Sam Cortland and was described by Lady Matilda Checkheaton as "a pocket Venus." Sir Stafford Nye was quite taken by her beauty and likened her to a Persian cat. As Juanita, she was a member of Charlotte von Waldsausen's Youth Movement; as Miss Ellis, she was nurse to Robert Shoreham. *Passenger to Frankfurt.*

CORTMAN, SAM The husband of Mildred Jean Cortman and the American ambassador to the Court of St. James, he was gunned down on the steps of the American Embassy by a group of masked young men. *Passenger to Frankfurt.*

COURTENAY, COCO The night of the Victory Ball, at which this popular actress was dressed as Columbine, she had a heated disagreement with Lord Cronshaw when he took away her cocaine. The day after the ball she was found dead in her bed from an overdose. "The Affair at the Victory Ball" from *The Under Dog.*

COWLEY, PRUDENCE *See* BERESFORD, PRUDENCE.

CRABTREE, MRS. Patient of Dr. John Christow's at St. Christopher's Hospital, she suffered from Ridgway's disease. Christow was trying to cure her with hormone injections. "She was a fighter, not like that limp slug of a woman in the next bed. She was on his side, she wanted to live." After Christow was killed, Henrietta Savernake convinced Mrs. Crabtree to continue in the battle to survive. *The Hollow.*

CRABTREE, EMILY The wife of William Crabtree. Emily and Lily Crabtree often fought with one another, and lunch on the day that Lily died was no exception. "Sing a Song of Sixpence" from *The Listerdale Mystery.*

CRABTREE, LILY The aunt of Edward Crabtree and the great-aunt of Magdalen and Matthew Vaughan, Lily Crabtree was a "pernickity but kind-hearted" spinster. She died after suffering a severe bash on the back of the head, and left an estate totalling eighty thousand pounds. "Sing a Song of Sixpence" from *The Listerdale Mystery.*

CRABTREE, WILLIAM The husband of Emily Crabtree and the nephew of Lily Crabtree, he claimed to have been fiddling with his stamp collection when his aunt died. "Sing a Song of Sixpence" from *The Listerdale Mystery.*

CRACKENTHORPE, ALFRED Son of Luther Crackenthorpe and the brother of Edmund, Cedric, Harold, Henry, Edith and Emma Crackenthorpe, "Flash Alf" was the black sheep of the family. Having "sheer animal magnetism," he was a small-time crook cagey enough not to get caught. He was poisoned with arsenic which was at first presumed to be from poisonous mushrooms. *4.50 from Paddington.*

CRACKENTHORPE, LADY ALICE Although she may have really loved her husband, Harold Crackenthorpe, she also considered her marriage as an escape from poverty. "Her eyes were like windows in an empty house." *4.50 from Paddington.*

CRACKENTHORPE, CEDRIC Son and heir of Luther Crackenthorpe, he was a painter who lived on Iviza, and returned to England when a dead body was discovered on the family property. Miss Marple found a parallel to him in Thomas Eade, a bank manager's son, who was "always out to shock people." *4.50 from Paddington.*

CRACKENTHORPE, EMMA One of Luther Crackenthorpe's daughters, she possessed "the instinct some women have to make their menfolk happy." Miss Marple found in her a parallel to Geraldine Webb, who "had her hair cut and permed, and went off on a cruise, and came back married to a very nice barrister." Dr. Quimper nurtured the hope of marrying Emma. *4.50 from Paddington.*

CRACKENTHORPE, HAROLD A son of Luther Crackenthorpe's, he was married to Lady Alice and was "the perfect picture of a city gentleman and a director of important companies." In spite of his business acumen, he was having financial difficulties and considered himself "close to Queer Street." He was also dissatisfied by his childless marriage. According to Miss Marple, he "would go a long way to avoid scandal." He was murdered by aconite poisoning. *4.50 from Paddington.*

CRACKENTHORPE, LUTHER Son of Josiah Crackenthorpe, the founder of Rutherford Hall, and father of Edmund, Cedric, Harold, Henry, Alfred, Edith and Emma Crackenthorpe, this thorough curmudgeon was "a big gaunt man, his flesh hanging in loose folds. He had a face rather like a bulldog, with a pugnacious chin." Josiah had been disappointed that Luther refused to take an interest in the family business, and for this Luther hated his father. Luther transferred this animosity to his offspring and said: "None of my sons are any good." He was a stingy, bitter old man who indulged in being an invalid. He propositioned Lucy Eyelesbarrow. *4.50 from Paddington.*

CRACKENTHORPE, MARTINE The name signed to a letter sent to Emma Crackenthorpe, purportedly from the woman who married Edmund Crackenthorpe just before he was reported missing at Dunkirk, which claimed that a son had been born to Edmund. *See* **DUBOIS, MARTINE.** *4.50 from Paddington.*

CRADDOCK, MRS. The wife of Charles Craddock, she was described by Elsie Batt as "rather one for the gents." Her husband believed that her relationship with Dr. Roberts went beyond the normal one between doctor and patient. Mrs. Craddock died of an infection in Egypt. *Cards on the Table.*

CRADDOCK, CHARLES The husband of Mrs. Craddock, he was going to report Dr. Roberts to the General Medical Council for unprofessional conduct, but he died of anthrax before he could carry out his plan. *Cards on the Table.*

CRADDOCK, CHIEF INSPECTOR DERMOT ERIC Sir Henry Clithering's nephew and godson, Dermot Craddock had brains, imagination and the "self-discipline to go slow, to check and examine each fact and to keep an open mind until the very end of the case." A Detective Inspector with the Middleshire police, Craddock went on to become a top man at the New

Scotland Yard. "Nobody could make a better show of presenting a very small portion of the truth and implying it was the whole truth than Inspector Craddock." *A Murder is Announced;* "Sanctuary" from *Double Sin; 4.50 from Paddington; The Mirror Crack'd from Side to Side.*

CRAIG, DR. DONALD The fiancé of Hester Argyle, Craig thought that Hester had slain her mother Rachel with a poker. His only concern was: "It's *got* to be certain. . . . If Hester tells me, if she tells me herself, then—then it will be all right. We'll get married as soon as possible. I'll look after her." *Ordeal by Innocence.*

CRALE, AMYAS Husband of Caroline Crale, father of Carla Lemarchant and lover of, among many others, Elsa Greer, he was a famous painter who had been murdered sixteen years ago. "Great beer drinker. Went in for the lusts of the flesh and enjoyed them." His wife was convicted of poisoning his beer with hemlock. *Five Little Pigs.*

CRALE, CARLA *See* LEMARCHANT, CARLA.

CRALE, CAROLINE *Née* Spalding, she was wife of Amyas Crale, mother of Carla Lemarchant and half-sister of Angela Warren. Carla approached Poirot to reopen the investigation of the murder, so that she could vindicate the memory of her mother before marrying John Rattery. *Five Little Pigs.*

CRAM, GLADYS As the secretary to Dr. Stone, she was "noisy in manner, with a high colour, fine animal spirits and a mouth that always seems to have more than its full share of teeth." *Murder at the Vicarage.*

CRAWFORD, JOANNA Travelling with her aunt Geraldine Riseley-Porter, she met Emlyn Price, with whom she saw the figure in the rocks who had pushed the boulder onto Elizabeth Temple. *Nemesis.*

CRAWLEY, CHARLES Crawley's ex-fiancée, Sylvia Carslake, married the narrator instead, who had a vision of a man with a scar down the left side of his face strangling Sylvia. Crawley was "a tall, dark man" who also had a scar down the left side of his face. "In a Glass Darkly" from *The Regatta Mystery.*

CRAVEN, HILARY Suffering from a divorce and the recent death of her daughter, she was on the verge of committing suicide when approached by Mr. Jessop. He suggested that she choose a means of death almost as certain as sleeping tablets but which carried the possibility of resulting in great good. Hilary undertook the commission of impersonating Olive Betterton to penetrate the Brain Trust in the Atlas Mountains, and used marked cultured pearls from her broken necklace to guide Jessop to the site. *Destination Unknown.*

CRAVEN, NURSE Hired to care for Barbara Franklin, she realized that there was nothing at all wrong with her patient's health. Nurse Craven was involved with Major Allerton, but she hoped to start a more serious affair with Sir William Boyd Carrington, and laughed a good deal at his poor jokes. *Curtain.*

CRAY, VERONICA A glamorous movie actress, she had been engaged to John Christow fifteen years ago, but he broke off their engagement when she demanded that he give up his profession and accompany her to Hollywood. A confirmed egoist, she waited fifteen years after Christow rejected her before her campaign to recapture him. After the second meeting, she told Poirot that it was she who refused Christow. *The Hollow.*

CRESSWELL, MRS. The assumed name of Miss Greenshaw's housekeeper at the Folly, she was the second wife of Miss Greenshaw's brother-in-law and mother of Miss Greenshaw's nephew by marriage, Nat Fletcher. "Mrs. Cresswell had a marvellously dressed head of well-blued hair towering upwards in meticulously arranged curls and rolls. It was as though she had dressed her head to go as a French marquise to a fancy dress party. The rest of her middle-aged person was dressed in what ought to have been rustling black silk but was actually one of the shinier varieties of black rayon." She was fooled into working without wages by Miss Greenshaw, who told her the estate would be left to her, and claimed to have been locked in her room at the time of her employer's death. "Greenshaw's Folly" from *The Adventure of the Christmas Pudding.*

CRISPIN, ANGUS AKA Horsham, he was a member of British Intelligence sent to Tuppence and Tommy Beresford under the guise of a gardener. He was instrumental in rescuing Tuppence from the third attempt on her life. *Postern of Fate.*

CROFT, BERT Husband to Milly Croft, he resided at the lodge at End House. Poirot was suspicious of Bert and Milly, who exaggerated their Australian heritage. Bert suggested to Nick Buckley, his landlady, that she make up a will before a minor operation. The will was discovered after Nick's supposed death. *Peril at End House.*

CROFT, MILLY Bert Croft's wife was confined to a wheelchair. Her real identity was Milly Merton, a forger well acquainted with Inspector Japp. *Peril at End House.*

CROFTON LEE, SIR RUPERT Victoria Jones "disliked theatrical men who posed," and disapproved of Sir Rupert's "calculated sensationalism." During his travels, while he was prospecting for uranium in China, he happened upon the site where an illicit secret weapon was being constructed. His knowledge of this site, which he passed on to Henry Carmichael, led to his murder. *They Came to Baghdad.*

CROKER See LAVINGTON, MR.

CROME, INSPECTOR A young police inspector from Scotland Yard who was officially in charge of the A.B.C. murders case, he was scrutinized by Hastings: "for my taste, several shades too pleased with himself." Poirot, however, thought he was a "very able police officer." *The A.B.C. Murders.*

CRONSHAW, LORD CRONCH He was found stabbed to death in his harlequin costume at the Victory Ball after having argued with his supposed fiancée, Coco Courtenay. "The Affair at the Victory Ball" from *The Under Dog.*

CROSBIE, CAPTAIN An agent under the supervision of Mr. Dakin, he "strutted a little when he walked." Victoria Jones observed that "by the way his slightly protruberant eyes goggled at her ... he was susceptible to feminine charm." Captain Crosbie assisted in the arrest of Edward Goring and his group of subversives. *They Came to Baghdad.*

CROSSFIELD, SUPERINTENDENT In charge of investigating the death of Sir Bartholomew Strange, he was not above stretching the truth to save face when mere gentlemen uncovered clues he and his subordinates had missed. *Three-Act Tragedy.*

CROSSFIELD, GEORGE The son of Laura Abernethie Crossfield and nephew to Richard Abernethie, he lost money by faulty speculation and by gambling, but his inheritance covered his losses. His many other vices left him little time for women. *After the Funeral.*

CROTCHET, MR. See SIMPSON, MR.

CROWTHER, SYDNEY His Majesty's Secretary of State for Home Affairs, the Right Honourable Sydney Crowther had a delightful bonhomie to Poirot, who made him the executor of his estate in the event of his death. *The Big Four.*

CRUMP, MR. Alcoholic butler at Yew-tree Lodge and husband of the irascible cook Mrs. Crump, he was retained solely because of his wife's culinary talents. *A Pocket Full of Rye.*

CUNNINGHAM, DR. ALICE Hoydenish psychologist, she was engaged to Niki Rossakoff, son of Countess Vera Rossakoff. Poirot was alarmed that she considered everyone she met to be a potential case study for her book and she frequented the lounge, Hell, to observe Paul Veresco. Poirot chided her: "You wear the heavy coat and skirt with the big pockets as though you were going to play the game of golf. But it is not here the golf links, it is the underground cellar with the temperature of 71 Fahrenheit, and your nose is hot and shines, but you do not powder it, and the lipstick you put it on your lips without interest, without emphasizing the curve of the lips!" "The Capture of Cerberus" from *The Labours of Hercules.*

CURRY, INSPECTOR The policeman in charge of the investigation into the death of Christian Gulbrandsen at Stoneygates, he was "competent in his way . . . but he preferred not to make a parade of the fact." *They Do It with Mirrors.*

CURRY, R.H. *See* **DUGUESCLIN, QUENTIN.** R.H. Curry was the name found on a card in the pocket of the first murder victim. *The Clocks.*

CURTIS, MR. A former gardener at Sittaford House, he was married to Amelia Curtis and considered himself a philosopher: " 'Women . . . talk a lot.' He paused and thoughtfully removed an aged pipe from the right side of his mouth to the left side. 'And half the time they don't know the truth of what they are talking about.' " *The Sittaford Mystery.*

CURTIS, AMELIA Mr. Curtis' wife, she did for Major Burnaby. Charles Enderby and Emily Trefusis, posing as cousins, rented rooms from her in the course of their investigation. Always on the look-out for new gossip, she said: "Ah . . . now, what do you think? Are they sweethearts, or are they not? A lot of harm comes of cousins marrying, so they say. Deaf and dumbs and half-wits and a lot of other evils." *The Sittaford Mystery.*

CURTIS, SIR RALPH *See* **ALLOWAY, LORD.**

CURTISS After returning from Egypt, Poirot hired Curtiss as his manservant because George had left to tend his ailing father. Curtiss was charged with carrying Poirot down the stairs to the garden every day. George criticized his successor as being not a "particularly bright specimen": "He was strong physically, of course, but I should hardly have thought he was quite the class M. Poirot would have liked. He'd been assistant in a mental home at one time, I believe." *Curtain.*

CURTISS, MAJOR Underneath his soldierly exterior was a temperament more passionate than was suspected. He was present at the card party at Major Jack Rich's the night of Arnold Clayton's murder. "The Mystery of the Baghdad Chest" from *The Regatta Mystery.*

CUST, ALEXANDER BONAPARTE Cust's mother was responsible for giving him his "ridiculous names," intending that he should make something of himself, but instead, he felt stupid and insignificant. Mary Stroud saw him washing blood stains off his sleeve in his room at the Black Swan. *The A.B.C. Murders.*

CZARNOVA, COUNTESS *See* **VAUCHER, JEANNE.**

DACRE, DENIS *See* **DAVIS, DENIS.**

DACRE, JOAN Denis Dacre's second bigamous wife. Like Dacre's previous wife, Margery Dacre, she was "young, rather dowdy and very inconspicuous." "The Bloodstained Pavement" from *The Thirteen Problems.*

DACRE, MARGERY Denis Dacre's first bigamous wife met an untimely death by drowning. "The Bloodstained Pavement" from *The Thirteen Problems.*

DACRES, MR. Emily Trefusis' solicitor and James Pearson's defence lawyer, he informed Emily that James had "occasionally borrowed money—to use a euphemism—from his firm," and that James had requested help from his uncle, Captain Trevelyan, but was refused. However, Mr. Dacres did not believe that Pearson had killed Captain Trevelyan. *The Sittaford Mystery.*

DACRES, CYNTHIA Elegant wife of Captain Freddie Dacres, she was the proprietress of Ambrosine, Ltd., a dressmaking establishment, which was not without financial problems despite Mrs. Dacres' business acumen. She witnessed the deaths of Reverend Stephen Babbington and Sir Bartholomew Strange. She had "greenish-bronze hair" and a violent temper. The other characters hoped she was the murderess. *Three-Act Tragedy.*

DAKIN, MR. As an Intelligence supervisor, Mr. Dakin was the superior of the agents Henry Carmichael and Captain Crosbie. Although he was a sharp and perceptive man, he presented a lethargic face to the world. Mrs. Cardew Trench said: "He's a wet fish. Potters and dilly-dallies about—no stamina—no grip on life. Just one more Englishman who's come out East and gone to seed." *They Came to Baghdad.*

DALE, SYLVIA Martin Wylde was in love with Sylvia, who worked long and loyally to get him acquitted of the charge of murdering Lady Vivien Barnaby. "The Sign in the Sky" from *The Mysterious Mr. Quin.*

DALEHOUSE, HARRY The nephew of Hubert Lytcham Roche, he was surprised that the rigorous dinner schedule at Lytcham Close was altered due to Poirot's delayed train. "The Second Gong" from *Witness for the Prosecution.*

DANE CALTHORP, REVEREND CALEB The husband of Mrs. Dane Calthorp, he was the local vicar in Much Deeping, "a charming elderly scholar whose principal pleasure was finding some apposite comment from the classics. . . . The vicar never required acknowledgement of his sonorous Latin: his pleasure in having found an apt quotation was its own reward." *The Pale Horse; The Moving Finger.*

DANE CALTHORP, MAUD The wife of the Reverend Caleb Dane Calthorp, she was "a grey-haired weather-beaten woman with fine eyes," whose job, she felt, was to arrange and classify sin for her husband. She convinced Mark Easterbrook to investigate at Thyrza Grey's house, The Pale Horse, in Much Deeping. *The Pale Horse; The Moving Finger.*

DANIELS, CAPTAIN While employed as the secretary to Prime Minister David MacAdam, Daniels doubled as a German spy. He was an extremely fine linguist and spoke seven languages, but Poirot said that Daniels knew "too many languages for a good Englishman." "The Kidnapped Prime Minister" from *Poirot Investigates.*

DARNLEY, ROSAMUND A fashionable dressmaker whose enterprise was called Rose Mond Ltd., she was a life-long friend to Kenneth Marshall. Poirot "admired Rosamund Darnley as much as any woman he had ever met," and remarked to Colonel Weston: "She has brains and charm and chic. She is very pleasing to look at." She counselled Kenneth Marshall to divorce Arlena if not for his own peace of mind then at least for the benefit of his daughter Linda. After Arlena Marshall's death, Rosamund departed with Kenneth and his daughter to live in the country. *Evil Under the Sun.*

DARRELL, CLAUD AKA James; Dr. Quentin; Dr. Savaronoff; Micky Templeton. "Number Four" or "The Destroyer" in the crime organization the Big Four,

he appeared in a number of ingenious and convincing disguises including James, the second footman at Abe Ryland's country place; Dr. Quentin, who gave Mr. Paynter an injection on the night of Paynter's death; Dr. Savaronoff, a Russian chess champion; and Micky Templeton, Mr. Templeton's supposed son. Although he could change his looks, he couldn't change his habits. At the table, according to Flossie Monro, he would unconsciously fiddle with his bread: "He'd get a little piece between his fingers and then dab it 'round to pick up crumbs." He was probably killed in the explosion at Felsenlabyrynth. *The Big Four.*

DARRELL, RICHARD The husband of Theodora Darrell, Richard Darrell was the head of Hobson, Jekyll and Lucas, a firm that went under as a direct result of Darrell's shady dealings. "Magnolia Blossom" from *The Golden Ball.*

DARRELL, THEODORA She left both her husband, Richard Darrell, and her lover, Vincent Easton, and said: "For my sin I must pay in loneliness." "Magnolia Blossom" from *The Golden Ball.*

DASHWOOD, EVERETT Cheery young reporter on the staff of *The Branch*, he was described by his friend Poirot as having a reckless disposition: "You are the good sport, you like something that is out of the usual." He elicited Poirot's assistance in a scheme to discredit the *X-Ray News.* "The Augean Stables" from *The Labours of Hercules.*

DA SILVA, MRS. *See* **HOBHOUSE, VALERIE.**

DAUBREUIL, MADAME AKA Jeanne Beroldy. The mother of Marthe Daubreuil and the mistress of the Villa Marguerite near Merinville on the south coast of France, she was suspected of having been the mistress of the murdered Paul Renauld. As Jeanne Beroldy, the wife of Arnold Beroldy, she had encouraged the affections of Georges Conneau and, with him, contrived the murder of her husband. Conneau disappeared, and she was arrested, prosecuted and acquitted of the crime. Hastings remarked that "there was something almost exaggeratedly feminine about her, at once yielding and seductive. Though very well preserved, she was certainly no longer young, but her charm was of the quality which was independent of age." Poirot recognized her at once, having seen her photograph long ago in Belgium, and maintained that she was morally and virtually the murderer of her husband Arnold Beroldy. *Murder on the Links.*

DAUBREUIL, MARTHE She was the twenty-two-year-old daughter of Madame Daubreuil and the deceased Arnold Beroldy. Hastings, as usual, was besotted by her beauty, but Poirot thought she was "the girl with the anxious eyes." *Murder on the Links.*

DAUBREUIL, RAOUL The fiancé of Madame Simone, he forbade her to hold another séance for fear that her health would not be equal to the task. "The Last Séance" from *Double Sin.*

DAVENHEIM, MR. AKA Billy Kellet. The husband of Mrs. Davenheim, he was a senior partner in Davenheim and Salmon, well-known bankers and financiers. He once masqueraded as Billy Kellet, a petty thief, and in this disguise served three months in prison for pickpocketing. To conceal this incident he told his partners that he had gone to South America on business. "The Disappearance of Mr. Davenheim" from *Poirot Investigates.*

DAVENTRY, MR. A "grave young man of thirty-five," he worked for the Administrator of St. Honore, and Dr. Graham consulted him about Major Palgrave's death. *A Caribbean Mystery.*

DAVENTRY, VERA (SOCKS) A young society woman invited for weekends at Chimneys by Sir Oswald and Lady Coote, she was known most often as "Socks."

She was in on the alarm-clock joke perpetrated upon Gerald Wade. *The Seven Dials Mystery.*

DAVID, LUCY "A fresh buxom young woman of thirty," the cook at Simon Clode's house, she was one of the witnesses to Clode's new will. "Motive *v* Opportunity" from *The Thirteen Problems.*

DAVIDSON, MRS. The wife of Chris Davidson, Mrs. Davidson was dressed as Pierette to his Pierot at the Victory Ball. Along with Captain Digby and Mrs. Mallaby, she discovered the body of Lord Cronshaw. "The Affair at the Victory Ball" from *The Under Dog.*

DAVIDSON, CHRIS The husband of Mrs. Davidson, he was described by Hastings as "handsome enough in a rather obvious style, tall and dark, with the easy grace of the actor." He was also a dope pedlar and had hooked Coco Courtenay on cocaine. "The Affair at the Victory Ball" from *The Under Dog.*

DAVIS, MR. *See* **BLORE, WILLIAM HENRY.**

DAVIS, CAROL AKA Carol Harding. Denis Davis' legitimate wife, she used the name Carol Harding as his partner in an insurance swindle operation. "The Bloodstained Pavement" from *The Thirteen Problems.*

DAVIS, DENIS AKA Denis Dacre. Of his three marriages, only one—to Carol Davis, his partner in crime—was legitimate. Under the name of Denis Dacre, he had bigamously married two other women who became Joan Dacre and Margery Dacre. "The Bloodstained Pavement" from *The Thirteen Problems.*

DAVIS, GILES A former naval Commander, he was the loyal and admiring, but gloomy and sloppy, husband of Molly Davis and with her ran the Monkswell Manor boarding house in Berkshire. Giles thought Christopher Wren was by far the most likely suspect in the strangling of Mrs. Boyle, but this might have been attributed to his fear that Molly and Wren were having an affair. "Three Blind Mice" from *Three Blind Mice and Other Stories.*

DAVIS, JESSE AKA Mrs. Archer. As Mrs. Archer, she was the wife of a small-time crook. After his death she reverted to her maiden name. Eileen Brandon knew her as Jesse Davis when they had both worked for Zachariah Osborne's Customer's Reactions Classified. Just before she died, she gave Father Gorman the following list of names: "Omerod, Sandford, Parkinson, Hesketh-Dubois, Shaw, Harmondsworth, Tuckerton, Corrigan, Delafontaine." *The Pale Horse.*

DAVIS, MOLLY *Née* Molly Wainwright, she was the twenty-two-year-old bride of Giles Davis with whom she ran a boarding house, Monkswell Manor, which had been bequeathed to her by her aunt Katherine Emory. "Three Blind Mice" from *Three Blind Mice and Other Stories.*

DAVY, CHIEF INSPECTOR FRED A "large, heavy, bovine, placid and patient" man with a "deep countryman's voice," Fred Davy was known affectionately as "Father" by his men in Scotland Yard's Criminal Investigation Department. He was working on the disappearance of Canon Pennyfather with his assistant Inspector Campbell, and was suspicious of Bertram's Hotel. Davy had the temerity to consult the mysterious Mr. Robinson in his quest for information on the case, and also enlisted Miss Marple's aid. *At Bertram's Hotel.*

DAWES, RHODA *See* **DESPARD, RHODA.**

DAWLISH, LORD Mr. Ferguson's real identity was Lord Dawlish, an incredibly wealthy peer who converted to communism during his days at Oxford. *Death on the Nile.*

DEANE, MOLLY The fiancée of John Harrison, Molly was in love with her former fiancé, Claude Langton. Poirot had met her before, and described her as "a very charming, very beautiful girl." "Wasps' Nest" from *Double Sin.*

DEANE, MONICA The financially impoverished daughter of a clergyman, she and her invalid mother planned to transform Red House into a guest house, but it was plagued by a poltergeist which drove the guests away. Monica consulted Tuppence and Tommy Beresford about ridding Red House of its haunting spirit. "The Clergyman's Daughter" and "The Red House" from *Partners in Crime.*

DEBANHAM, MARY HERMIONE She was governess to Helena Goldenberg and also Sonia Armstrong's private secretary. She and Colonel Arbuthnot were having an affair. Dr. Constantine said of her: "She is cold. She has no emotions. She would not stab a man—she would sue him in the law courts." *Murder on the Orient Express.*

DE BATHE, COLONEL *See* **EUSTACE, MAJOR.**

DE BELLEFORT, JACQUELINE (JACKIE) Oldest and dearest friend to Linnet Doyle and fiancée to Simon Doyle before his marriage to Linnet, she was a "small slender creature with a mop of dark hair." Jackie followed Linnet and Simon to Egypt on their honeymoon and created as much embarrassment as her fertile mine could possibly imagine. Poirot hoped that the "star" she claimed to be following was not a "false" one. Except for the fact that she was with Nurse Bowers at the time Linnet was shot, she would have been the prime suspect of the murder. *Death on the Nile.*

DE CASTINA, MRS. *See* **GRÜNBERG, ANITA.**

DE HAVILAND, EDITH ELFRIDA The sister of Aristide Leonides' deceased first

72

wife Marcia, Edith de Haviland was the aunt of Roger and Philip Leonides and great-aunt of Sophia, Eustace and Josephine Leonides. Although Edith despised her brother-in-law, she agreed to move into his house and oversee the upbringing of his children: "*He* asked me to. Seven children—and the youngest only a year old. . . . Couldn't leave 'em to be brought up by a dago, could I?" *Crooked House.*

DELAFONTAINE, MARY The domineering wife of Henry Delafontaine and niece to the deceased Amelia Jane Barrowby, she was a tall woman with "authority in her voice, and contempt and a shade of well-bred irony." She inherited her aunt's estate, and her two passions in life were her husband and her garden. "How Does Your Garden Grow?" from *The Regatta Mystery.*

DELANGUA, PAUL He was a houseguest at Alderway until Sir James Dwighton discovered him making love to Lady Laura Dwighton. "There was something un-English about him—the easy grace of his movements, the dark, handsome face, the eyes set a little too near together. There hung about him the air of the Renaissance," according to Colonel Melrose. Paul confessed to the murder of Sir James Dwighton, but the others thought that this was merely to protect Lady Laura. "The Love Detectives" from *Three Blind Mice and Other Stories.*

DE LA ROCHE, COMTE ARMAUD The Count was an occasional lover of Ruth Kettering, having had an affair with her several years prior. "So very aristocratic-looking was the Count, that it would have seemed sheer heresy even to whisper that his father had been an obscure corn-chandler in Nantes—which, as a matter of fact, was the case." De la Roche used his fraudulent social position, his charm and his looks to entice women and then bilked them of whatever money or goods he could while keeping their letters as tools for blackmail. He convinced Ruth to bring the famous Heart of Fire rubies to him, but his plan to substitute a paste replica of the jewels was obstructed by Poirot. *The Mystery of the Blue Train.*

DEMETRIUS THE BLACK BROWED AKA "Mr. Parker Pyne," he was the head of a gang of Greek jewel thieves who assumed the identity of the investigator to deceive Mrs. Peters. "The Oracle at Delphi" from *Parker Pyne Investigates.*

DEMIROFF, OLGA AKA Olga Vassilovna, she was a Russian prostitute living in one of the less reputable quarters of Paris. She hid the famous Heart of Fire rubies under the ashes in her grating. *The Mystery of the Blue Train.*

DENBY, MR. The finance agent who looked after the Styles Court accounts, he provided Alfred Inglethorp with an alibi for the night of Emily Inglethorp's death. *The Mysterious Affair at Styles.*

DENMAN, MR. Geoffrey Denman's father, he was "rather a handsome old man . . . in his way. . . . Quite peaceful and well-behaved, but distinctly odd at times." He was quite upset that his son wanted to put him into a nursing home. "The Thumb Mark of St. Peter" from *The Thirteen Problems.*

DENMAN, ANNA AKA Anna Kharsanova; Anna Miklanova. "The immortal, the only Kharsanova!" gave up her passion for dance, a career and Prince Sergius Oranoff's devotion to marry John Denman and live the English countrywoman's life. She was known as "Anna Miklanova" to Prince Sergius. "Harlequin's Lane" from *The Mysterious Mr. Quin.*

DENMAN, GEOFFREY The son of old Mr. Denman and the husband of Mabel Denman, Geoffrey was a violent man who did not make his wife very happy. He also irritated his father by suggesting that the aged man move to a nursing home. "The Thumb Mark of St. Peter" from *The Thirteen Problems.*

DENMAN, JOHN "Tall, aloof and English," he was the husband of Anna Denman and the lover of Molly Stanwell. He was "devoid of imagination" and did not understand the whims of his Russian-born wife. "Harlequin's Lane" from *The Mysterious Mr. Quin.*

DENMAN, MABEL Miss Marple's niece and Geoffrey Denman's widow, she became suspect when her husband died suddenly, and sent for Miss Marple's help. According to Miss Marple, Mabel was "a nice girl, really a very nice girl, but just a trifle what one might call *silly.* Rather fond of being melodramatic and of saying a great deal more than she meant whenever she was upset." "The Thumb Mark of St. Peter" from *The Thirteen Problems.*

DEPLEACH, SIR MONTAGUE Lawyer for Caroline Crale's defence in the trial for the murder of her husband, "Depleach had force, magnetism, an overbearing and slightly bullying personality. He got his effects by a rapid and dramatic change of manner. Handsome, urbane, charming one minute—then an almost magical transformation, lips back, snarling smile—out for your blood." He told Poirot of his vain attempt to prove Amyas Crale's death as suicide, and expressed frustration in attempting to defend a woman who never tried to prove her innocence. He gave Poirot the opinion that his client had been guilty. *Five Little Pigs.*

DERING, MARTIN A moderately successful author, he claimed not to have been in attendance at the literary dinner the night Captain Trevelyan was murdered. Emily Trefusis said that he was "good-looking in a bold sort of way. Women talk about sex with him in corners. Real men hate him." *The Sittaford Mystery.*

DERING, SYLVIA *Née* Pearson, she was the wife of Martin Dering and the niece of Captain Trevelyan. "Her voice had that faintly complaining note in it which is about the most annoying sound a human voice can contain." She claimed to have seen her uncle only twice since her marriage. *The Sittaford Mystery.*

DEROULARD, MADAME The feeble mother of Paul Deroulard, she knew the true cause of her daughter-in-law's death, and took steps to rectify the matter. "The Chocolate Box" from *Poirot's Early Cases.*

DEROULARD, MONSIEUR LE BARON PAUL Son of Madame Deroulard, he was a notable French Deputy who would have become the Minister had he not died. His friendship with Monsieur de Saint Alard was strained by religious differences; Alard was as fanatically Catholic as Deroulard was anti-Catholic. He was unscrupulous in his behaviour with Virginie Mesnard. His death was reported to have been caused by apoplexy, but Poirot discovered that he had consumed John Wilson's heart medicine. "The Chocolate Box" from *Poirot's Early Cases.*

DE RUSHBRIDGER, MARGARET Mysterious and recent arrival from the West Indies, she was a patient at Sir Bartholomew Strange's sanitorium. A telegram to Poirot said she had valuable information about Sir Bartholomew's death, but she died from eating poisoned chocolates before he arrived. Poirot felt that she was murdered not to prevent her telling what she knew, but what she did not know. *Three-Act Tragedy.*

DERWENT, LADY FRANCES (FRANKIE) One of the "Bright Young People," she was a dark, plucky girl unmarred by the class-consciousness of her position as the wealthy daughter of Lord Marchington. She was searching for a purpose to her life: "Father gives me an allowance, and I've got lots of houses to live in and clothes and maids and some hideous family jewels and a good deal of credit at shops—but that's all the family, really. It's not *me.*" Among her many brilliant suggestions in her investigation with Bobby Jones, she convinced Dr.

George Arbuthnot to help her gain entrance into the Bassington-ffrench household. *Why Didn't They Ask Evans?*

DES ANGES, SISTER MARIE *See* **JONES, VICTORIA.**

DE SARA, MADELEINE As Maggie Sayers, which was her real name, she came from "an honest, hard-working family from Streatham," but under the name of Madeleine de Sara she worked for Parker Pyne. She assumed a number of disguises, including Dalores Ramona, Sanchia and the Grand Duchess Olga. Madeleine was "extremely attractive. . . . Almost dangerously so. . . . The sort of girl who cares only for men." Parker Pyne referred to her as the "Queen of the Vamps," and many young men suffered from "Madeleinitis" when they came under her spell. *Parker Pyne Investigates;* "Problem at Pollensa Bay" from *The Regatta Mystery.*

DESJARDEAUX, MONSIEUR The French Premier, he was "a tall thin man with a pointed black beard and a sensitive face" who at first refused to credit Poirot's contention that Madame Olivier was "Number Three" of the gang. *The Big Four.*

DESPARD, COLONEL JOHN HUGH The husband of Rhoda Dawes Despard, he had been a suspect in the Shaitana murder case when he was Major John Despard. By the time of the Pale Horse mystery he had been elevated in rank to Colonel and had become known as Hugh. He was one of Christie's retired military officers who had turned sportsman. Mark Easterbrook said: "He was a shrewd man, with an adventurous life behind him. One of those men who have a kind of sixth sense where danger is concerned." *Cards on the Table; The Pale Horse.*

DESPARD, RHODA DAWES The wife of Colonel John Hugh Despard and the cousin of Mark Easterbrook, she was in the business of "doctoring dogs" at Much Deeping, but she was not a veterinarian.

Each year she and her husband would host a fête. As Rhoda Dawes, she was Anne Meredith's roommate at Wendon Cottage and was involved in the Shaitana murder investigation. Perhaps Christie's most poignantly romantic scene was when Major John Despard and Rhoda paused, hand in hand, on the bank of the river from which he had just saved her. Her friendship with Ariadne Oliver dates from this early case. *Cards on the Table; The Pale Horse.*

DE TOREDO, SENORA ANGELICA *See* **SHAPLAND, ANN.**

DEVEREAUX, RONNY AKA Number Two, Two o'clock. He was "employed in a purely ornamental capacity at the Foreign Office." Bundle Brent thought she had run him over in her Hispano Suza but, from Dr. Cassell she learned that he had been fatally shot. His last words to her were: "Seven Dials. . . . Tell Jimmy Thesiger." *The Seven Dials Mystery.*

DEVERILL, CHRISTINE *See* **REDFERN, CHRISTINE.**

DIGBY, CAPTAIN A fellow officer of Lord Cronshaw, together with Mrs. Mallaby and Mrs. Davidson, he discovered Cronshaw's body "stretched on the ground with a table-knife in his heart." "The Affair at the Victory Ball" from *The Under Dog.*

DIGBY, MR. The butler at Lytcham Close was responsible for sounding the two dinner gongs. He also confirmed that Diana Cleves had picked the daisies for the dinner table. "The Second Gong" from *Witness for the Prosecution.*

DIGBY, SIR STANLEY The Air Minister, he attended the house party at Wyvern Abbey to negotiate with Herr Everhard for the scientist's secret metal formula. Bill Eversleigh noted him to be "a good-natured, tubby little chap." *The Seven Dials Mystery.*

DINSMEAD, MR. The husband of Maggie Dinsmead with whom he produced Magdalen and Johnnie, he was also the adoptive father of Charlotte Dinsmead. When he met Mortimer Cleveland, "Mr. Dinsmead talked and talked. He was expansive, genial, loquacious. He told the stranger all about himself." "S.O.S." from *Witness for the Prosecution.*

DINSMEAD, CHARLOTTE The adoptive daughter of Mr. and Mrs. Dinsmead and the adoptive sister of Magdalen and Johnnie Dinsmead, she was a foundling whose real father had just learned of her existence shortly before his death, just in time to leave her a fortune of sixty thousand pounds. Mortimer Cleveland, a psychic investigator and mental specialist, suspected her of inscribing an S.O.S. in the dust on his dressing table. "S.O.S." from *Witness for the Prosecution.*

DINSMEAD, JOHNNIE The young son of Mr. Dinsmead and his wife Maggie, he was the only member of the Dinsmead family not disturbed by Mortimer Cleveland's arrival. In explanation of his stained hands, he told Cleveland, "I'm always messing about with chemicals." He inadvertently provided the clue required to solve the mystery at the Dinsmead house. "S.O.S." from *Witness for the Prosecution.*

DINSMEAD, MAGDALEN She was the natural daughter of Mr. and Mrs. Dinsmead, but Mr. Dinsmead told Mortimer Cleveland that she was a foundling. Magdalen claimed to have written an S.O.S. on Cleveland's dressing table. "S.O.S." from *Witness for the Prosecution.*

DINSMEAD, MAGGIE The wife of Mr. Dinsmead, she was a nervous, shrieking, crockery-smashing woman. She often had hysterics, pressed her hand to her heart and cackled. "S.O.S." from *Witness for the Prosecution.*

DIRECTOR, HERR The almost mythical figurehead leader of Aristides' Brain Trust complex in the Atlas Mountains, he inspired a "Heil Hitler attitude" in his listeners. Mr. Aristides said: "He is very good . . . I pay him a very high salary. He used to run Revivalist Meetings." *Destination Unknown.*

DITTISHAM, LADY *See* **GREER, ELSA.**

DITTISHAM, LORD Third husband of Elsa Greer, Lady Dittisham, he was "not only a peer of the realm: he was a poet. Two of his fantastical poetic dramas had been staged at vast expense and had a *succès d'estime.* His forehead was rather prominent, his chin was eager and his eyes and his mouth unexpectedly beautiful." *Five Little Pigs.*

DIXON, GLADYS On the day of the St. John's Ambulance Association fête at Gossington Hall, she witnessed Heather Badcock spill a cocktail down the front of her gown. Gladys was in love with Giuseppe, the butler at Gossington Hall. After Giuseppe's murder, Miss Marple became concerned for Gladys' safety and sent her into seclusion at Bournemouth. *The Mirror Crack'd from Side to Side.*

DOBBS, MR. A gardener by profession, Mr. Dobbs was a local man who had never been outside of King's Gnaton and was one of the four suspects. "The Four Suspects" from *The Thirteen Problems.*

DODGE, BERNARD Mr. Dodge was a member of the War Cabinet and a close personal friend to David MacAdam, the British Prime Minister. Together with Lord Estair, he sought Poirot's help in the MacAdam kidnapping case. "The Kidnapped Prime Minister" from *Poirot Investigates.*

DODO *See* **MULLINS, IRIS.**

DONALDSON, DR. The physician to Lady Matilda Checkheaton, he at first did not understand when she suggested that perhaps she should take the cure: "He looked faintly puzzled for a moment, losing his air of medical omniscience, which, of course, so Lady Matilda reflected, was one of the slight disadvantages attached to having a younger doctor attending one rather than the older specimen to whom one has been accustomed for several years." *Passenger to Frankfurt.*

DONALDSON, DR. REX Fiancé to Theresa Arundell, he was a doctor of no small promise and of no financial means, but with complete confidence in his own abilities and future success. Others found him "namby-pamby" and Poirot thought he was "a little inhuman." He became Dr. Grainger's partner in Market Basing, married Theresa Arundell and ultimately made "a big name for himself" as an authority on the functions of ductless glands. *Dumb Witness.*

DONOVAN, SHEILA *See* **HOBHOUSE, VALERIE.**

DORTHEIMER, LADY NAOMI The wife of Sir Reuben Dortheimer, she was told by Jules: "You are not English—you cannot be English—to dance as you do. . . . You are the sprite, the spirit of the wind. Droushcka petrovka navarouchi." "The Case of the Distressed Lady" from *Parker Pyne Investigates.*

DORTHEIMER, SIR REUBEN The frightfully rich husband of Lady Naomi Dortheimer, he was much taken with the seductive Sanchia, female partner in the dance team of Jules and Sanchia. "The Case of the Distressed Lady" from *Parker Pyne Investigates.*

DOVE, MARY The housekeeper and manageress of Fortescue's Yewtree Lodge, she was responsible for hiring servants and was always in control, both of herself and of others. Inspector Neele thought she looked like a woman playing a part. *A Pocket Full of Rye.*

DOWNES, ROGER EMMANUEL A master at the Highfield School for Boys, Downes was described by Hastings as

"a middle-aged gentleman strongly resembling the frog footman in *Alice in Wonderland.* He was highly excited, and his voice was shrill with emotion." He had been sitting next to George Earlsfield, the fourth victim of the A.B.C. murderer, in the Regal Cinema in Doncaster. Colonel Anderson was convinced that Downes had been the intended victim because his name began with "D," and the A.B.C. murderer seemed to be following an alphabetical list. "E" for Earlsfield was out of order. *The A.B.C. Murders.*

DOYLE, LINNET *Née* Ridgeway, the first murder victim, she was shot in the head on board the S.S. *Karnak* while honeymooning with her husband Simon Doyle in Egypt. "She was the girl who had everything: an immense fortune inherited from an American grandfather, beauty and the man she loved." As a favour to her lifelong friend Jackie de Belleforte, she gave Jackie's fiancé Simon Doyle a job as estate manager and surprised herself and almost everyone else by marrying him as well. Linnet Doyle was a classic "poor little rich girl": she was betrayed by those to whom she felt closest. "She was used to being looked at, to being admired, to being the centre of the stage wherever she went." *Death on the Nile.*

DOYLE, SIMON Ex-fiancé of Jackie de Belleforte and husband of Linnet Doyle, he was a "tall, broad-shouldered young man, with very dark blue eyes, crisply curling brown hair, a square chin and a boyish, appealing, simple smile." Simon was shot in the leg the night his bride was murdered. Jackie described Simon as being "so childishly simple . . . he's got no imagination. . . . He always thought things would go right." He was later fatally injured. *Death on the Nile.*

DRAGE, LADY CYNTHIA "A middle-aged woman with a hard face and a liberal allowance of make-up," Cynthia Drage was a friend of Mr. Satterthwaite's who coached aspiring socialites for a living.

"The Shadow on the Glass" from *The Mysterious Mr. Quin.*

DRAGOMIROFF, PRINCESS NATALIA Great friend of Linda Arden and the godmother of Sonia Armstrong, she was one of the ugliest old women Poirot had ever seen. "It was an ugliness of distinction— it fascinated rather than repelled. She sat very upright. Round her neck was a collar of very large pearls which, improbable though it seemed, were real. Her hands were covered with rings. Her sable coat was pushed back on her shoulders. A very small and expensive black toque was hideously unbecoming to the yellow toad-like face beneath it." Her handkerchief, monogrammed "H," was discovered at the scene of the murder. *Murder on the Orient Express.*

DRAKE, ALLEN A cheerful, curious and talkative man, he generously referred to his partner Thomas Royde as "phlegmatic," because Royde's usual response in dialogue was along the line of "Ah-hum." *Towards Zero.*

DRAKE, LUCILLA The sister of Hector Marle, mother of Victor Drake and aunt to Rosemary Barton and Iris Marle, she had been married for only two years when she became the Reverend Caleb Drake's widow. She had been wearing black crêpe for twenty years since his death. "Motherhood, coming late and unexpectedly, had been the supreme experience of Lucilla Drake's life," but her son was a source of grief to her. *Sparkling Cyanide.*

DRAKE, ROWENA ARABELLA She had been a widow for two years. On reading the inscription on her husband's tombstone, " 'He giveth his beloved sleep'. . . . It occurred to Poirot, fresh from the impact of the dynamic Rowena Drake, that perhaps sleep might have come in welcome guise to the late Mr. Drake." Mrs. Drake had organized the Hallowe'en party at which the foolish and boastful Joyce Reynolds was murdered. *Hallowe'en Party.*

DRAKE, UNA The twin sister of Vera, Una Drake was a sporting Australian girl who bet Montgomery Jones that she could contrive an unbreakable alibi which would prove her to be in two places at once. She was seen in London at dinner and the theatre and at a hotel in Torquay on the same night. Jones, who had since fallen in love with her, consulted Tuppence and Tommy Beresford to win his bet. "The Unbreakable Alibi" from *Partners in Crime.*

DRAKE, VICTOR AKA Monkey Coleman and Pedro Morales, he was "the black sheep of the Marle family," the son of Lucilla Drake, and the cousin of Rosemary Barton and Iris Marle. He possessed a "practised ease with which he could play on the emotions." Ruth Lessing found that "the strength of Victor Drake was the strength of the devil. He could make evil seem amusing." After forging a cheque at Oxford, he was sent down and shipped off to a career that included being an actor, storekeeper, waiter, odd-job man, luggage porter, property man in a circus, candidate for President of a South American republic and prisoner. In prison, under the name of Monkey Coleman, he knew Tony Morelli, AKA Anthony Browne. As Pedro Morales, "a nasty bit of goods from Mexico—even the whites of his eyes are yellow," he was present at the Luxembourg with Christine Shannon the night George Barton was killed. *Sparkling Cyanide.*

DRAPER, MARY *Née* Riley, she was sister to Mary Gerrard's mother, Eliza Riley. A trained nurse who once lived in New Zealand, she had an unusually suspicious history. One of her patients, an old lady whose death was "somewhat of a puzzle to the doctor attending her," left Mary a legacy. After marrying a Mr. Draper, Mary Riley was to be left a considerable sum after his death which, when it came, was "sudden and unaccountable." Mary Draper returned to England under the name of Hopkins, the identity of a former colleague who had died abroad. She knew of Mary Gerrard's relation to the wealthy Laura Welman and proceeded to set her sights on Hunterbury Hall. Poirot said: "Other deaths may lie at her door. It is certain that she is a remorseless and unscrupulous woman." *Sad Cypress.*

DRIVER, INSPECTOR An Inspector from Scotland Yard who came to interview Anthony Eastwood after his valuable collection of old enamels was stolen, he was compared by Eastwood to the spurious Detective Inspector Joe Verall: "An unsympathetic man, Inspector Driver. . . . Distinctly stagy, in fact. Another striking example of the superiority of Art over Nature." "Mr. Eastwood's Adventure" from *The Listerdale Mystery.*

DRIVER, JENNY A great friend of Carlotta Adams', she had a hat shop in Moffat Street called Geneviève. She was "a small vivacious creature with flaming red hair" and reminded Hastings of a fox terrier. *Lord Edgware Dies.*

DROUET, INSPECTOR Disguised as the waiter Robert, he was at Rochers Neige in Switzerland and attempted to capture the killer Marrascaud, but was murdered, his face horribly mutilated, by the villain. "The Erymanthian Boar" from *The Labours of Hercules.*

DROWER, MARY The niece of Alice Ascher, she became a member of Poirot's "Special Legion" formed to track down the A.B.C. murderer. *The A.B.C. Murders.*

DUBOIS, MARTINE A young Frenchwoman, she was to marry Edmund Crackenthorpe, but he was killed at Dunkirk. She later married Lord Robert Stoddard-West. A letter signed with her name was sent to Emma Crackenthorpe, and the body in the sarcophagus was for a time identified as hers. *4.50 from Paddington.*

DUBOIS, VIVIAN Inspector Neele thought he was "the type that specialized in the young wives of rich and elderly men. . . . The type of man who 'understands' women." Adele Fortescue was his mistress and beneficiary to his will. A con artist obviously reluctant to confront police, he had had some previous difficulty from incriminating letters in the Edith Thompson case: "Women were all the same. They promised to burn things and then didn't." *A Pocket Full of Rye.*

DUBOSC, COLONEL He was of the opinion that "They have too much money, these Americans" and that honesty was "a nuance, a convention. In different countries it means different things. An Arab is not ashamed of stealing. He is not ashamed of lying. With him it is from *whom* he steals or to *whom* he lies that matters." "The Pearl of Price" from *Parker Pyne Investigates.*

DUBOSC, LIEUTENANT "A young French lieutenant, resplendent in uniform," who saw Poirot off at the station in Aleppo, Syria following a case involving the French military. He overheard his General thanking Poirot for saving the honour of the French Army. *Murder on the Orient Express.*

DUGUESCLIN, QUENTIN Quentin Duguesclin was the real name of the murdered "Mr. R.H. Curry" or "Harry Castleton." He was a distant Canadian cousin of Valerie Bland and had always been very fond of her. His dead body was discovered in Miss Pebmarsh's house on Wilbraham Crescent by Sheila Webb. *The Clocks.*

DUKE, MR. The secretive ex-Chief Inspector of Scotland Yard, he took his excursions into the supernatural world very seriously, but "the spirits, alas, paid very little attention to him." He was present at the séance the night of Captain Trevelyan's murder. *The Sittaford Mystery.*

DUNDAS, GEORGE The nephew of Ephraim Leadbetter, George Dundas was a beautifully dressed and well-turned-out young man who, with the adroit and calculated use of a banana peel, went down on one knee and proposed to Mary Montresor. "The Golden Ball" from *The Golden Ball*.

DUNN, ELIZA Mrs. Todd's cook, she disappeared from her employ without giving notice. When Poirot found her through an advertisement, she explained that a solicitor had come to her with an inheritance, a house and a yearly income which she was required to claim immediately. Poirot cautioned her against forgetting how to cook. "The Adventure of the Clapham Cook" from *The Under Dog*.

DUPONT, ARMAND A distinguished French archaeologist whose specialty was pottery, he was on board the *Prometheus* with his son Jean at the time of Madame Giselle Morisot's death. Although the presence of Kurdish pipes in their luggage indicated that they may have had some connection to the blow-gun murder weapon, Poirot felt the Duponts were innocent of the crime: "Their concentration would be such that they would be quite blind and deaf to the outside world. They would be existing, you see, in 5000 or so BC. Nineteen hundred and thirty-four AD would have been nonexistent for them." *Death in the Clouds*.

DUPONT, JEAN The son of Armand Dupont, he killed the wasp which was at first thought responsible for Giselle Morisot's death. He firmly stated that he could not have killed Madame Giselle: "She was far too ugly! . . . If a woman is good-looking, you are fond of her; she treats you badly; she makes you jealous, mad with jealousy. . . . But an ugly old woman like Giselle—who would want to kill her?" He and Jane Grey were attracted to each other. *Death in the Clouds*.

DURAND, SIR GEORGE He was travelling in the train compartment shared by Canon Parfitt, Dr. Clark and Raoul Letardeau. "His profession was so clearly the law that no one could have mistaken him for anything else for a moment." "The Fourth Man" from *Witness for the Prosecution*.

DURRANCE, MR. A former photographer, he sold films, postcards and greeting cards in Hollowquay. Tuppence Beresford consulted him about the old photograph album she had found in her new house. *Postern of Fate*.

DURRANT, AMY Mary Barton's cousin, she drowned while they were holidaying at the Metropole Hotel in Teneriffe on Grand Canary Island. "The Companion" from *The Thirteen Problems*.

DURRANT, MARY The wife of Philip Durrant and the first adoptive child of Leo and Rachel Argyle, she was a tidy imperturbable woman who seemed quite passionless except for her overriding love for her husband. Philip guessed that she "had not the imagination to understand that her pleasure in his dependence upon her sometimes irked him." *Ordeal by Innocence*.

DURRANT, MARY The niece of Elizabeth Penn, she was an auburn-haired beauty. When Hastings was immediately attracted to her, Poirot remarked: "Auburn hair—always the auburn hair." She was carrying a case of Cosway miniatures to J. Baker Wood in Charlock Bay, but *en route*, the case was stolen. She suspected Norton Kane of the theft. "Double Sin" from *Double Sin*.

DURRANT, PHILIP The husband of Mary Durrant, he had been a dashing young pilot when afflicted with polio, which left him paralyzed and confined to a wheelchair. Since he had been disabled, he became "keenly observant of the differences and realities of human personality. . . . People—really that was all that life held for him now. People to study, to find out about, to sum up." He undertook an independent investigation of his mother-in-law's death. *Ordeal by Innocence*.

DUTCH PEDRO A Herzoslavakian, he stole the secret code letters signed "Virginia Revel," thinking he could blackmail the adulterous author. After Jimmy McGrath saved his life, he left the letters for his friend as a way to gain some cash, but instead, Jimmy commissioned Anthony Cade to return the letters. *The Secret of Chimneys.*

DUVAL, ARISTIDE *See* **CARTWRIGHT, SIR CHARLES.**

DUVEEN, BELLA With her twin sister Dulcie, she performed in the vaudeville duo, The Dulcibella Kids. She was suspected of being the Englishwoman with whom Paul Renauld was involved. However, she had been jilted by Jack Renauld, Paul's son, in favour of Marthe Daubreuil. Bella falsely confessed to the killing of Paul Renauld in order to save Jack, who had been arrested for the crime, from the guillotine. She and Jack eventually married and left for South America to assume the duties of his late father's business interests. *Murder on the Links.*

DUVEEN, DULCIE *See* **HASTINGS, DULCIE.**

DWIGHTON, SIR JAMES The owner of Alderway and the husband of Lady Laura Dwighton, he was found in his library with his skull bashed in by a bronze statuette of Venus. He was reputed to be "tightfisted in the extreme." Paul Delangua threatened to kill Sir James after discovering that Lady Laura Dwighton had been mistreated by Sir James, who subsequently expelled him from Alderway. Sir James had also dismissed his valet Jennings without a character reference. "The Love Detectives" from *Three Blind Mice and Other Stories.*

DWIGHTON, LADY LAURA The wife of Sir James Dwighton, she was apparently in love with Paul Delangua. When Colonel Melrose and Mr. Satterthwaite interviewed her, she "looked like a visitor from another world. She was dressed in

a clinging medieval tea gown of dull-blue brocade." She confessed to the murder of her husband, but it was thought that she had done so to protect her beloved, Paul Delangua, from suspicion. "The Love Detectives" from *Three Blind Mice and Other Stories.*

DYMCHURCH, DETECTIVE INSPECTOR He consulted the International Detective Agency in an attempt to warn "Mr. Blunt" (Tommy Beresford) about Dr. Charles Bower's account of secret papers. "The Adventure of the Sinister Stranger" from *Partners in Crime.*

DYSON, GREG With his wife Lucky, he was an American botanist who visited St. Honore every year with the Hillingdons. Even though he was genuinely fond of his wife, calling her his "lucky" piece, he was also an incurable flirt: Edward Hillingdon reported that "Gregory Dyson finds it difficult to keep his hands off any good-looking woman." Suffering from heart trouble, his medication was discovered in Major Palgrave's room and caused the Major's death to appear accidental. Miss Marple found in him a parallel to the St. Mary Mead butcher, Mr. Murdoch: "Mr. Murdoch had had rather a bad reputation, but some people said it was just gossip, and that Mr. Murdoch himself liked to encourage the rumours!" *A Caribbean Mystery.*

DYSON, LUCKY *Née* Greatorex, she was the second wife of Gregory Dyson, a botanist, and travelled with him and their friends and colleagues the Hillingdons each year to St. Honore. Her golden blond hair was not natural. Before her marriage to Gregory she had had an affair with Edward Hillingdon, and pressed him to aid her in her scheme to become the second Mrs. Dyson. She was drowned in an accident of mistaken identity. *A Caribbean Mystery.*

EARDSLEY, JOHN *See* **RAYBURN, HARRY.**

EARL, WILLIAM The young undergardener at Styles Court, he witnessed Emily Inglethorp's new will the day before her death. *The Mysterious Affair at Styles.*

EARLSFIELD, GEORGE A barber and the fourth victim of the A.B.C. murderer, he was stabbed in the Regal Cinema in Doncaster while watching *Not a Sparrow. The A.B.C. Murders.*

EASTERBROOK, DOREEN *See* **CORRIGAN, KATHERINE.**

EASTERBROOK, MARK The cousin of Rhoda Despard and the godson of Lady Hesketh-Dubois, whom he referred to as "Aunt Min," Mark Easterbrook was preparing a book on "certain aspects of Mogul architecture." Easterbrook and his friend Ariadne Oliver attended a church fête in Much Deeping at the home of Rhoda Despard. While he was in Much Deeping, he met Thyrza Grey and began to decipher the Pale Horse mystery. *The Pale Horse.*

EASTERFIELD, LORD The pompous and boorish lord of Ashe Manor, Easterfield was Gordon Ragg before his elevation to the peerage. He ran a group of "nasty little weekly newspapers," and was ready to talk endlessly on the subject of himself. He was one of Luke Fitzwilliam's suspects in the death of Lavinia Fullerton. *Murder is Easy.*

EASTLEY, ALEXANDER Son of the deceased Edith Crackenthorpe and her husband Bryan, he was an enterprising young man, and proposed to Lucy Eyelesbarrow on behalf of his father, who needed "a proper home life." Alexander was to inherit Edith Crackenthorpe's share of the estate. *4.50 from Paddington.*

EASTLEY, BRYAN Widower of Edith Crackenthorpe and father of Alexander, he was "an amiable-looking young man of thirty-odd with brown hair, rather plaintive blue eyes and an enormous fair moustache." A Squadron Leader and fighter pilot in World War II who received the D.F.C., he really had not managed to keep up with the rest of the world after the war, and his son treated him with a protective, almost fatherly attitude. *4.50 from Paddington.*

EASTNEY, PHIL Charlie Burns' rival for the love of Gillian West, Phil Eastney worked in a glass-blowing factory, but was a musical genius. While dining with him, Mr. Satterthwaite "realized that he was talking to an exceptional brain," and could not understand why Gillian did not prefer him to Charlie Burns. "The Face of Helen" from *The Mysterious Mr. Quin.*

EASTWOOD, ANTHONY A romantic young mystery writer of liberal persuasions, he fancied that he had "a very pretty collector's taste in small things," and was quite proud of his set of old enamels which were subsequently conned from him by the Patterson gang. He was writing a story called "The Mystery of the Second Cucumber." "Mr. Eastwood's Adventure" from *The Listerdale Mystery.*

EBENTHAL, BERTHA AKA Mrs. Everard. "A tall handsome woman of middle age," she was a German spy posing as Mrs. Everard, the aunt of Captain Daniels. It was at her house in Hampstead that Prime Minister David MacAdam and his chauffeur O'Murphy were detained. "The Kidnapped Prime Minister" from *Poirot Investigates.*

EBERHARD, HERR The creator of a formula which would simultaneously strengthen and lighten steel for use in the aircraft industry, he was invited to the house party at Wyvern Abbey to negotiate with government officials. Bill Eversleigh said: "This man sucks in soup and eats peas with a knife. Not only that, but the brute is always biting his fingernails—positively gnaws at them." *The Seven Dials Mystery.*

ECCLES, MR. A poker-faced lawyer for the ostensibly reputable, respectable and old-fashioned solicitors' firm of Partingdale, Harris, Lockeridge and Partingdale, he was considered by Ivor Smith as having one of the best criminal brains in the country, but was far too cautious and slick to involve himself in any culpable fashion. His firm handled Mrs. Lancaster's interests. *By the Pricking of My Thumbs.*

ECCLES, MR. Pam Eccles' husband and William Sandbourne's brother-in-law, he arrived in Chipping Cleghorn with his wife to collect the personal effects of the man Bunch Harmon found dying in her husband's church. "Sanctuary" from *Double Sin.*

ECCLES, PAM The wife of Mr. Eccles and the sister of William Sandbourne, she accompanied her husband to Chipping Cleghorn to visit Bunch Harmon. "Sanctuary" from *Double Sin.*

ECKSTEIN, PROFESSOR Considered by many to be Britain's top scientist and weapons expert, Eckstein "seemed supremely unimportant. ... He had the manner of one anxious to apologize for his existence." He was consulted by Cedric Lazenby's cabinet regarding England's potential in chemical warfare. *Passenger to Frankfurt.*

EDGE, BELLA The wife of Mr. Edge the chemist and daughter of the village tobacconist, she had been an old flame of Harry Laxton's and the village opinion was that Harry should purchase his toothbrushes at the Boots in Much Benham instead of at Mr. Edge's store. "The Case of the Caretaker" from *Three Blind Mice and Other Stories.*

EDGERTON, SIR JAMES PEEL "The most celebrated KC in England" whose special hobby was criminology, "just a shade over average height, he nevertheless conveyed the impression of a big man." He was rumoured to be the future Prime Minister of England. Tommy Beresford felt he had "read him through and through like an open book. ... Sir James took in everything, but gave out only what he chose." *The Secret Adversary.*

EDGWARE, THE FIFTH BARON, LORD *See* MARSH, RONALD.

EDGWARE, LORD *See* MARSH, GEORGE.

EDMUNDS, ALFRED Managing clerk of Mahew's law firm at the time of the Crale murder case, he was visited by Poirot. *Five Little Pigs.*

EDMUNDSON, JOHN Third secretary to the British Embassy at Ramat at the time of the revolution, he was a friend of Bob Rawlinson's. They had a code: if Rawlinson mentioned a girl who was "out of this world," it meant he had an urgent message for Edmundson. *Cat Among the Pigeons.*

EDNA The cousin of Gladys Holmes, she was Miss Marple's maid and was uneasy over Gladdie's situation—or loss thereof—at the Skinners'. Edna consulted Miss Marple in the hope that she could put things straight. "The Case of the Perfect Maid" from *Three Blind Mice and Other Stories.*

EDNA Vacant, idiotic, half-witted adolescent girl who frequented Mrs. Sweetiman's confectionary shop, she had enough sex appeal to attract two men simultaneously. One of her suitors was married. *Mrs. McGinty's Dead.*

EGERTON, RICHARD Partner in the law firm of Egerton, Forbes and Wilborough, he was "a handsome man, tall, dark with a touch of grey at the temples and very shrewd grey eyes. His advice was always good advice, but he seldom minced his words." Elivra Blake consulted him on the particulars of the seven hundred pounds his firm held and managed in trust for her. *At Bertram's Hotel.*

ELLEN Amelia Viner's maid and cook, she was originally named Helen, but "Helen is not a suitable name for a servant," so Miss Viner called her Ellen. "Ellen does a steak with grilled tomatoes pretty fairly," said Miss Viner, "she doesn't do it well, but she does it better than anything else." *The Mystery of the Blue Train.*

ELLEN Maidservant to Emily Arundell at Littlegreen House, she discovered and mailed her dead mistress' letter to Poirot two months after it was written. *Dumb Witness.*

ELLESWORTHY, MR. The creepy and effete bachelor who ran the antique shop in Wychwood, Ellesworthy dabbled in the mysteries of Satanic witchcraft. Luke Fitzwilliam thought that he was a "nasty bit of goods," and suspected him in the deaths of Lydia Horton, Amy Gibbs, Tommy Pierce, Lillian Fullerton and Dr. Humbleby. *Murder is Easy.*

ELLIOT, MRS. With the baker, she discovered the dead body of her neighbour, Mrs. McGinty. *Mrs. McGinty's Dead.*

ELLIOT, JAMES A smuggler who was conveying the stolen painting by Rubens to France, he engineered the kidnapping of Winnie King with the help of the "flashy bit of goods" who posed as his wife. "He's got a bad reputation, suspected by the police of being mixed up in some questionable transactions." "The Girdle of Hippolyta" from *The Labours of Hercules.*

ELLIOT, LADY NOREEN Leader of a set called the "Bright Young People," Lady Noreen Elliot had recently become engaged to Captain James Folliot, V.C., of the Household Cavalry. She had a habit of stealing jewellery, wearing it for a while and then returning the goods. "The Manhood of Edward Robinson" from *The Golden Ball.*

ELLIS Jane Wilkinson's maid, Ellis was reputedly loyal to her employer, and was sent to Paris to fetch a gold box encrusted with rubies forming the initials "C.A." *Lord Edgware Dies.*

ELLIS, MISS *See* **CORTMAN, MIL-DRED JEAN.**

ELLIS, JOE Ellis was in love with Rose Emmott, the murdered girl, and had been determined to marry her despite her pregnant condition. However, his landlady, Mrs. Bartlett, was in love with him and had different ideas about the matter. A carpenter by trade, Ellis was from "good old village stock," which is to say that he was "not overly intelligent." "Death by Drowning" from *The Thirteen Problems.*

ELLIS, JOHN A persona of Sir Charles Cartwright's, Ellis was the butler at the home of Sir Bartholomew Strange for about two weeks who mysteriously disappeared the night Sir Bartholomew was poisoned. Drafts of blackmail notes stating that he had information about the death of Sir Bartholomew were found under the grating in his gas heater. *See* **CARTWRIGHT, SIR CHARLES.** *Three-Act Tragedy.*

ELLIS, LOU Lou Ellis was the "ash blond, dank hair, medium height rather bosomy" young woman whom Mark Easterbrook witnessed in a fight with Thomasina Tuckerton at a Chelsea espresso bar. About a week after the fight, during which Lou yanked out some of her opponent's hair by the handful, Thomasina suddenly died. *The Pale Horse.*

ELSA First and only legitimate wife of James Folliat, she met her husband in Italy after his desertion during the war. She was an Italian criminal from Trieste with a sunburned complexion and bronze-red curls. She aided him in his complicated plot to secure his ancestral home, Nasse House. As husband and wife, they were devoted to each other. *Dead Man's Folly.*

ELSIE Madam Simone's housemaid, Elsie was a good Catholic who disapproved of her mistress's séances. She thought that Madame Simone was "trafficking with the devil." After Madame Exe's rapid departure, she discovered Madame Simone's body but could not understand why it was only half its natural size. "The Last Séance" from *Double Sin.*

ELSPETH The supervisor of the dressmakers employed by Alicia Coombe, she was "a stern woman who looked as though her mouth should always be full of pins." "The Dressmaker's Doll" from *Double Sin.*

EMLYN, MISS The grey-haired Headmistress of The Elms, the site of the Hallowe'en party and of the murder of Joyce Reynolds, knew about all the intricate goings-on at the school. *Hallowe'en Party.*

EMMOTT, DAVID American assistant archaeologist with the expedition at Tell Yarimjah, "he seemed to be the best and most dispassionate judge of Mrs. Leidner's personality." He ultimately married the strong-willed Sheila Reilly, but it was claimed, he's "no doormat—he'll keep her in her place." *Murder in Mesopotamia.*

EMMOTT, ROSE The murdered girl, Miss Emmott had been pregnant by Rex Sandford and loved by Joe Ellis. Sandford remarked that "she was pretty . . . very pretty and very alluring. And—and she made a dead set at me. . . . She wouldn't let me alone." "Death by Drowning" from *The Thirteen Problems.*

EMMOTT, TOM Rose Emmott's father and the owner of the Blue Boar, he firmly believed that the unsavoury Rex Sandford had corrupted his daughter and that, when she became pregnant, rather than do the right thing by her, Sandford had killed her. "Death by Drowning" from *The Thirteen Problems.*

ENDERBY, CHARLES A reporter with the *Daily Wire,* he journeyed to Sittaford to scoop an inside story on the death of Major Burnaby's close friend, Captain Trevelyan. Emily Trefusis contrived to win his allegiance to help her in the investigation she had undertaken to clear her fiancé, James Pearson, of suspicion. *The Sittaford Mystery.*

ENDICOTT, MR. Elderly lawyer from a respectable firm, he was Sir Arthur Stanley's solicitor. His "impregnable legal calm" was shattered by Poirot's amazing and accurate surmises about Sir Arthur: "Really, Poirot! In the Middle Ages you would certainly have been burnt at the stake." *Hickory Dickory Dock.*

ENGLEMOUNT, LORD *See* **CARTWRIGHT, SIR CHARLES.**

ENRICO Cuban cook in the Golden Palm Hotel kitchens, he saw Molly Kendal pass through the kitchen with a knife in her hand just before Victoria Johnson was stabbed. *A Caribbean Mystery.*

ENTWHISTLE, MISS Irritable but well-meaning sister of Mr. Entwhistle, to whom she used "the indignant and bullying tones adopted by devoted sisters towards brothers for whom they keep house," she strongly disapproved of her brother's part in the Abernethie family affairs. She told him that funerals were fatal for a man of his age. *After the Funeral.*

ENTWHISTLE, MR. Shrewd and elderly solicitor two years retired, he still managed the Abernethie estate as the family lawyer because he was an old friend of Richard Abernethie. His suspicions were aroused concerning the death of Richard Abernethie after Cora Lansquenet suggested murder. He investigated to some extent himself and then consulted Poirot. *After the Funeral.*

ERICSSON, TORQUIL A brilliant young physicist, this solemn-looking Norwegian had read papers before the Royal Society before defecting to Mr. Aristides' Brain Trust complex in the Atlas Mountains. He told Hilary Craven: "The scientists must be masters. They must control and rule. They and they alone are the Supermen. It is only the Supermen who matter. The slaves must be well treated, but they *are* slaves." *Destination Unknown.*

ERSKINE, MAJOR RICHARD SETOUN The husband of Janet Erskine, he had met and fallen in love with Helen Halliday. He remained with Janet for the sake of the two children. *Sleeping Murder.*

ESA The mother of Imhotep and the grandmother of Yahmose, Sobek, Renisenb and Ipy, Esa was the reigning matriarch of this distinguished Egyptian family. After Imhotep brought home Nofret, his beautiful young concubine, Esa said to him: "Men are made fools by the gleaming limbs of women, and lo, in a minute they are become discoloured carnelians. . . . A trifle, a little, the likeness of a dream, and death comes as the end. . . . All life is a jest, Imhotep—and it is death who laughs last." *Death Comes as the End.*

ESTAIR, LORD The leader of the House of Commons during the years of World War I, he, along with Bernard Dodge, appealed to Poirot for help in the MacAdam case. "The Kidnapped Prime Minister" from *Poirot Investigates.*

ESTCOURT, MERVYN (BUGLER) Effusive long-time friend of Tommy Beresford, Bugler was with the beautiful and popular actress Gilda Glen when they met Tuppence and Tommy at the Adlington Hotel. Bugler informed the Beresfords about Gilda Glen's character. "The Man in the Mist" from *Partners in Crime.*

ESTRAVADOS, PILAR *See* **LOPEZ, CONCHITA.**

EUSTACE, MAJOR A military-looking man of about forty-five with a bowler hat and a toothbrush moustache, he knew Barbara Allen when she lived in India. He was described as a "bit hairy at the heel. Definitely not out of the top drawer" and good-looking in a coarse, crafty way. Colonel de Bathe was among his assumed identities. "Murder in the Mews" from *Murder in the Mews.*

EVANS A Secret Service man assisting Mr. Carter, he helped Tommy Beresford break into Mrs. Van Snyder's suite. "The Man Who Was No. 16" from *Partners in Crime.*

EVANS, INSPECTOR The retired C.I.D. inspector's philosophy included: "Acting on information received." He also believed in accumulating his own information. It was this professional instinct which prompted him to follow up the Anthony poisoning case when he recognized Mrs. Merrowdene at the fête. He knew her as the notorious Mrs. Anthony, who was acquitted of murdering her husband. "Accident" from *Witness for the Prosecution.*

EVANS, ALBERT AKA Lance Fortescue. As Bert Evans, he wooed Gladys Martin and convinced her that he had to mix "truth serum" in Rex Fortescue's morning marmalade. Before Gladys died, she sent Miss Marple a letter detailing her relationship with Bert and enclosed a picture of the two lovers. *A Pocket Full of Rye.*

EVANS, CHARLES (CHUBBY) The fourth husband of Lady Rosalie Tamplin, he was described by his step-daughter Lenox Tamplin: "An expensive luxury" who knew "a jolly sight too well which way his bread is buttered" to make a play for Katherine Grey. Evans was one of those "staunch patriot Britons who, having made a portion of a foreign country their own, strongly resent the original inhabitants of it." *The Mystery of the Blue Train.*

EVANS, DORIS The small and fair typist who met Anthony Sessle at a cinema, she was thereafter invited to dinner at his home. Later, they took a walk, during the course of which Sessle became violent and threatened to enforce a suicide pact between them. Doris escaped, but was later arrested for stabbing Sessle through the heart with a hatpin. "The Sunningdale Mystery" from *Partners in Crime.*

EVANS, GLADYS *See* **ROBERTS, GLADYS.**

EVANS, REBECCA The recent wife of Robert Evans, Captain Trevelyan's man, she was the daughter of Mrs. Belling and an excellent cook. Captain Trevelyan, a misogynist, refused to have her or any other woman servant in his house. *The Sittaford Mystery.*

EVANS, ROBERT HENRY Newlywed husband of Rebecca Evans, this retired sailor was the daily manservant of Captain Trevelyan, and was upset that the "Capting" did not take to the idea of having a woman cook about his house. *The Sittaford Mystery.*

EVERARD, MRS. *See* **EBENTHAL, BERTHA.**

EVERETT, MR. A theatrical friend of Poirot's, he had come to Marsdon Manor to play the part of the deceased Mr. Maltravers. "The Tragedy at Marsdon Manor" from *Poirot Investigates.*

EVERSLEIGH, BILL AKA Number Three, Three o'clock. A member of the Seven Dials group, he became the fiancé of Bundle Brent. He had "a pleasantly ugly face, a splendid set of white teeth and a pair of honest brown eyes." He was "employed in a purely ornamental capacity at the Foreign office" where he was George Lomax's dog's-body. *The Secret of Chimneys; The Seven Dials Mystery.*

EVESHAM, LADY LAURA KEENE Tom Evesham's superstitious wife, she hoped that it would be "a dark man who first steps over the door step on New Year's

Day," and was appeased by the appearance of Harley Quin. "The Coming of Mr. Quin" from *The Mysterious Mr. Quin.*

EVESHAM, TOM The husband of Lady Laura Evesham and MP for West Kidleby, he related the story of Derek Capel, the former owner of Royston, who shot himself in the house while both Evesham and Sir Richard Conway were present. He participated in Harley Quin's belated "court of inquiry" into the death of Capel. "The Coming of Mr. Quin" from *The Mysterious Mr. Quin.*

EXE, MADAME The pseudonym of the woman who had lost her only child, Amelie, for whom Madame Simone performed the last séance. To Madame Simone she represented the elementary primitive power of motherhood, a force to be feared: "A mother's love for her child is like nothing else in the world. It knows no law, no pity, it dares all things and crushes down remorselessly all that stands in its path." "The Last Séance" from *Double Sin.*

EYELESBARROW, LUCY Thirty-two-year-old friend of Miss Marple, she took a First in Mathematics at Oxford and was "acknowledged to have a brilliant mind." Much to her friends' and fellow scholars' surprise, she entered the field of domestic service: "Her success was immediate and assured. By now, after a lapse of some years, she was known all over the British Isles." She was hired by Miss Marple to find the body of the woman Mrs. McGillicuddy saw being murdered from the train, and discovered the body in a sarcophagus on the grounds of Rutherford Hall. *4.50 from Paddington.*

FANE, ELEANOR The widow of the solicitor Mr. Fane, she was the meddling mother of Robert, Gerald and Walter Fane. She disapproved of Robert's wife on the grounds that she was Roman Catholic. She attempted to ruin her son Walter's chance at happiness with Helen Spenlove Kennedy, but circumstances managed that without her capable hand. Henry was her "asthmatic spaniel whose liquid eyes burned with greed." *Sleeping Murder.*

FANE, WALTER The son of Mr. and Mrs. Fane and youngest brother of Gerald and Robert Fane, he left to manage a tea plantation in Ceylon after Helen Spenlove Kennedy refused to marry him. Gwenda Reed said: "What a *quiet* face Walter Fane had. You might see a house like that—a house with all the blinds pulled down." Miss Marple said he was "The devoted type of young man whom women ignore and marry only because the man they love does not return their affection." He lived with his elderly mother. *Sleeping Murder.*

FANSHAW, ADA Eighty-three-year-old aunt to Tommy Beresford, she resided at the Sunny Ridge Nursing Home. Opinions on this lady by those who knew her varied as widely as did her own moods: to Tommy, she was a vitriolic tartar; to Dr. Murray, her physician, she had been "a woman of considerable mental capacity, though she often pretended otherwise"; to Nurse O'Keefe she was "a good spirit . . . sharp as a needle"; to Tuppence she was a crotchety old lady triumphant at outliving her friends. Tuppence and Tommy visited Aunt Ada during the last three weeks of her life; she sent Tuppence from the room but to Tommy she said, "Come back. I'll talk to you. I don't want the woman. No good her pretending she's your wife, I know better. Shouldn't bring that type of woman in here." Upon her death, Aunt Ada left Tommy and Tuppence all her possessions, among them a painting by William Boscowan, "House by a Canal." In her old-fashioned desk, Albert Batt discovered a secret drawer containing a letter marked "Confidential" which detailed some suspicious circumstances at Sunny Ridge Nursing Home. *By the Pricking of My Thumbs.*

FANTHORPE, JAMES LECHDALE He was William Carmichael's nephew and worked as a lawyer in Carmichael's firm. Poirot found him "intelligent—yes. He does not talk, but he listens very attentively, and he also watches. Yes, he makes good use of his eyes. Not quite the type you would expect to find travelling for pleasure in this part of the world. I wonder what he is doing here." Dispatched by his uncle, Fanthorp was in Egypt to prevent an American business manager, Andrew Pennington, from swindling his client, Linnet Doyle. He conveyed Jackie de Belleforte to her cabin after Simon Doyle was shot in the leg, and made sure she was under constant surveillance. *Death on the Nile.*

FARLEY, BENEDICT Eccentric millionaire husband of Louise Farley and father of Joanna Farley, he was "a well-known figure of legend. There were his strange meannesses, his incredible generosities, as well as more personal details—his famous patchwork dressing-gown, now reputed to be twenty-eight years old, his invariable diet of cabbage soup and caviar, his hatred of cats." His death occurred in such a manner that it could almost only have been suicide. "The Dream" from *The Adventure of the Christmas Pudding.*

FARLEY, JOANNA Daughter of Benedict Farley and step-daughter of Louise Farley, she was the inheritress of the residue of her father's estate. Joanna's ex-fiancé had lost his job as a result of her father's wrath at the match. She was very candid in her answers to Poirot. "The Dream" from *The Adventure of the Christmas Pudding.*

FARLEY, LOUISE Second wife of Benedict Farley and stepmother of Joanna Farley, she "gave absolutely no clue to her emotions. She appeared perfectly self-possessed." She substantiated Hugo Cornworth's tale of the hauntingly self-destructive dream which plagued her husband. "The Dream" from *The Adventure of the Christmas Pudding.*

FARQUHAR, ESMÉE She hired Poirot to discover what really happened to the sto-

len Liberty Bonds that her fiancé, Philip Ridgeway, was escorting to New York aboard the *Olympia.* Esmée was about twenty-five, with big brown eyes and a perfect figure. Predictably, Hastings was charmed. "The Million Dollar Bond Robbery" from *Poirot Investigates.*

FARR, STEPHEN *See* **GRANT, STEPHEN.**

FARRADAY, LADY ALEXANDRA CATHERINE (SANDRA) The daughter of Lord William and Lady Victoria Kidderminster, she possessed a keen intelligence and an iron will and was completely devoted to her husband Stephen Farraday, an obscure but brilliant Tory MP. Rosemary Barton, who stole Stephen's affections for a time, "used to say that if you pricked Sandra, sawdust would ooze out." To her husband, she was "rather like a racehorse—so well-groomed, so instinct with breeding, so proud. He found her an ideal companion; their minds raced alike to the same quick conclusions." Sandra hated the vapid Rosemary Barton with a passionate intensity which, in her mother's opinion, rendered her capable of murder. *Sparkling Cyanide.*

FARRADAY, STEPHEN The husband of Lady Alexandra Farraday, he was "Leopard" to Rosemary Barton's "Black Beauty" in their love letters. Eventually, he saw the folly of his affair with Rosemary, but she intended to expose their passion after her birthday party and run away with him. Since she could easily damage his career, he was a prime suspect in her murder. *Sparkling Cyanide.*

FARRELL, DETECTIVE INSPECTOR He was on the trail of a group headed by an "American girl bandit" when the robbery at Lady Anchester's Orion House occurred. He knew that the real Grand Duchess Pauline had eloped with a chauffeur in Paris on the morning that she was apparently attending the bazaar at Orion House. "Jane in Search of a Job" from *The Golden Ball.*

FAT IKEY *See* **ISAACSTEIN, HERMAN.**

FAULKENER, JIMMY A friend of Donovan Bailey's and Mildred Hope's, he loved Patricia Garnett, as did Donovan. With Donovan, Jimmy found the body of a woman in the flat below Patricia's. "The Third-Floor Flat" from *Three Blind Mice and Other Stories.*

FAULKNER, LESLIE The name given to a young playwright whom Jane Helier was going to use as a dupe in her scheme to expose "Mary Kerr," the wife of her ex-husband Claud Averbury. "The Affair at the Bungalow" from *The Thirteen Problems.*

FELICE A domestic at the Deroulard residence, she "responded eagerly" to Poirot's questions, wishing to free herself from the accusation that she had stolen a bottle of John Wilson's heart medicine. "The Chocolate Box" from *Poirot's Early Cases.*

FELLOWS-BROWN, MRS. One of Alicia Coombe's preferred customers, she possessed a rather unfortunately large derrière that seemed to be smaller in Alicia Coombe's dresses: "There's something about the way you cut, it really does minimize my behind. I almost look as though I hadn't got one—I mean only the usual kind that most people have. . . . It's always been a bit of a trial to me. Of course, for years I could pull it in, you know, by sticking out my front. Well, I can't do that anymore because I've got a stomach now as well as a behind. And I mean—well, you can't pull it in both ways, can you?" "The Dressmaker's Doll" from *Double Sin.*

FENN, ARDWYCK Described as "a very big shot in the Television and Moving Picture world," Ardwyck Fenn had known Marina Gregg for a number of years. In response to Craddock's questions as to who might want to kill Miss Gregg, Fenn replied: "I have nothing to say on the subject. And that, Chief Inspector Craddock, is all you'll get out of me." *The Mirror Crack'd from Side to Side.*

FENN, KATHLEEN The deceased mistress of Cecil Aldbury, Mrs. Burton-Cox's late first husband, she was the natural mother of Desmond Burton-Cox. When offering Desmond to Mrs. Burton-Cox for adoption, Kathleen claimed that he was the son of Cecil Aldbury, but Mr. Goby doubted this as Miss Fenn had a number of admirers at the time. She subsequently became a highly successful pop star and vainly attempted to regain her son. When she died, she left her son a sizeable legacy. *Elephants Can Remember.*

FEODOR, COUNT *See* **PAUL, PRINCE OF MAURANIA.**

FERGUSON, DR. He certified Mrs. Llewellyn-Smythe's death as due to natural causes and "looked Poirot up and down, with shrewd eyes under bristling eyebrows." *Hallowe'en Party.*

FERGUSON, MR. The assumed name of the immensely wealthy Communist peer Lord Dawlish. Mr. Ferguson criticized Linnet Doyle, saying there were "hundreds and thousands of wretched workers slaving for a mere pittance to keep her in silk stockings and useless luxuries." He attacked Poirot as an "established institution," and called him "one of your dressed-up, foppish good-for-nothings." *Death on the Nile.*

FERRAREZ, CARMEN The assumed identity of a member of the Patterson gang who participated in the plot to fleece Anthony Eastwood of his collection of old enamels, she was born in Hampstead, but purported to be Spanish. "Mr. Eastwood's Adventure" from *The Listerdale Mystery.*

FERRARS, MRS. The widow of Ashley Ferrars, she was unofficially engaged to marry Roger Ackroyd when she took her own life with an overdose of veronal. *The Murder of Roger Ackroyd.*

FERRIER, DAGMAR Wife of the present Prime Minister, Edward Ferrier, and daughter of John Hammett, Lord Conworthy, the previous Prime Minister, she was reputed to be a model respectable British wife. Scandalous photographs of her look-alike and an Argentine gigolo were circulated in the *X-Ray News.* "The Augean Stables" from *The Labours of Hercules.*

FERRIER, EDWARD Lean, dark, tired-looking Prime Minister, he was the husband of Dagmar Ferrier and the son-in-law of the previous Prime Minister, John Hammet, Lord Conworthy. "Edward Ferrier was considered sound—just that—not brilliant, not great, not a particularly eloquent orator, not a man of deep learning." He and Sir George Conway consulted Poirot about the scandal-mongering *X-Ray News*, which was in the process of exposing graft in the former government, which he feared would cause a decline in national morale. "The Augean Stables" from *The Labours of Hercules.*

FERRIER, LESLEY A clerk in the solicitors' firm of Fullerton, Harrison and Leadbetter, he was a suspected forger. He was a friend to Olga Seminoff, who inherited all of Mrs. Llewellyn-Smythe's money in a codicil to the will. Ferrier was knifed to death following an affair with the wife of a short-tempered village publican. *Hallowe'en Party.*

FINCH, SALLY American Fulbright scholar, she lived in Mrs. Nicoletis' youth hostel and proposed marriage to Len Bateson, who gratefully accepted. *Hickory Dickory Dock.*

FINN, JANE AKA Janet Vandemeyer, she was the cousin of Julius Hersheimmer and was sailing on the *Lusitania.* She survived the sinking of the ship, and secured a packet of papers containing a secret Draft Treaty from a British Intelligence agent. Tuppence Beresford assumed the identity of Jane Finn in a search for the documents, which were feared to have been confiscated by Bolshevist revolutionaries. The real Jane Finn was admitted to Dr. Roylance's care under the name of Janet Vandemeyer, and was, according to Tuppence, "the loveliest thing" she had ever seen. *The Secret Adversary.*

FINNEY, MAJOR The Chief Constable, he agreed with Inspector Huish that Jacko Argyle was guilty of the Rachel Argyle murder. When he consulted Dr. Calgary concerning some aspects of the case, "the Chief Constable's eyebrows climbed slowly up his forehead in a vain attempt to reach the receding line of his grey hair. He cast his eyes up to the ceiling, and then down again to the papers on his desk. 'It beggars description!' he said." *Ordeal by Innocence.*

FISH, HIRAM An American interested in rare books, roses and paintings, he had been invited down for the weekend at Chimneys to make the party seem an entirely normal one instead of a high-level political conference. He roused suspicion in his host, Lord Caterham, for never offering his own opinions on the books he had allegedly come to discuss. *The Secret of Chimneys.*

FITZROY, MR. Lord Alloway's secretary, he was described by Hastings as "a pale, thin young man with pince-nez and a frigid expression." "The Submarine Plans" from *The Under Dog.*

FITZWILLIAM, LUKE Known as Fitz, was Jimmy Lorrimer's best friend. A retired policeman who had just returned to England after many years' duty in the Mayang Straits, he met Miss Lavinia Fullerton on the train to London. She told him of her intention to consult Scotland Yard about suspicious deaths in her town of Wychwood, and several coincidental occurrences prompted him to undertake an investigation at once. He disguised himself as Bridget Conway's cousin, a writer working on a book about superstitions, to gain entrance into the closed village society. He fell in love with Bridget during his adventure. *Murder is Easy.*

FLAVELLE, HIPPOLYTE AND MARIE The Comte de la Roche's manservant and cook at the Villa Marina, they were instructed to lie about the day of the Count's return to his villa. Poirot extracted the truth when he informed them that the reason for the Count's delay was not a woman, as they had supposed, but a murder. *The Mystery of the Blue Train.*

FLEETWOOD, MR. A big, truculent engineer on board the S.S. *Karnak,* he bore a grudge against Linnet Doyle for exposing him as a married man with three children. He had been courting Marie, her former maid. *Death on the Nile.*

FLEMMING, MR. He was Professor Beddingfeld's London solicitor, an ardent anthropologist and a great admirer of his client's work. He invited Anne Beddingfeld to stay with him and Mrs. Flemming after the professor's death. *The Man in the Brown Suit.*

FLEMMING, MRS. The wife of Mr. Flemming, she was "a stout, placid woman of the 'good wife and mother' type," but not very pleased when her husband brought Anne Beddingfeld to stay with them in Kensington Square. Out of "sheer Christian charity," she offered Anne a permanent position as governess, but instead, Anne sailed to South Africa. *The Man in the Brown Suit.*

FLETCHER, AGNES Parlourmaid for the Morleys and present the day of the murder, she was a garrulous Cockney who waited a rather long time before saying that she saw Frank Carter enter the den-

tist's surgery at a time he claimed to be absent from the premises. She had a fear of police matters. *One, Two, Buckle My Shoe.*

FLETCHER, NAT Although Miss Greenshaw referred to him as her "nephew," Nat Fletcher was the son of Miss Greenshaw's brother-in-law by his second wife, Mrs. Cresswell. He appeared shortly after Miss Greenshaw was murdered by an arrow through the neck. "Greenshaw's Folly" from *The Adventure of the Christmas Pudding.*

FLORENCE Former parlourmaid to Emily Barton, she operated a boarding house in Lymstock. "A tall, raw-boned, fierce-looking woman . . . clearly a dragon," she blamed the Bartons for her current situation and complained of living in rooms rather than in her own home. However, she had strong maternal feelings about Emily Barton. *The Moving Finger.*

FOGG, QUENTIN, KC Bespectacled junior partner of the Crown Attorney in the Crale murder case, "Quentin Fogg was thin, pale, singularly lacking in what is called personality. His questions were quiet and unemotional, but they were steadily persistent." *Five Little Pigs.*

FOLLIAT, AMY Wife of the Major and mother of James and Henry Folliat, she was "a very small and compact little person, dressed in shabby tweed. The most noticeable feature about her was her clear china-blue eyes. Her grey hair was closely confined by a hair-net." Enthusiastic about gardening and attached to Nasse House, her old home, she continued to live on Sir George Stubb's estate, inhabiting the gardener's cottage. Poirot recognized the ruthless side to her nature. *Dead Man's Folly.*

FOLLIAT, JAMES The wild, ruthless son of Mrs. Amy Folliat, he was reported dead when he deserted during the war in Italy. He allowed his mother to engineer a match between himself and her half-witted but rich ward, Hattie, in an effort to maintain the Folliat ancestral home, Nasse House. However, he neglected to tell his mother that he was already married to an Italian woman, Elsa. Hattie was easily bilked of her entire fortune according to plan, but Folliat then substituted his first wife in Hattie's place, who did not figure in his mother's scheme. *Dead Man's Folly.*

FOLLIOTT, MRS. RICHARD The wife of Captain Richard Folliott, Mrs. Folliott was not anxious for anyone to know that Ursala Bourne was her sister. She did not approve of Ursala's secret marriage to Ralph Paton (Roger Ackroyd's step-son) nor her position, below her proper station in life, as a parlourmaid at Roger Ackroyd's Fernly Park. *The Murder of Roger Ackroyd.*

FORBES, GENERAL A crotchety old army man, he was highly indignant that John Clapperton, whom he considered to be a mere music-hall entertainer, should be sporting the title "Colonel." During his many bouts of consternation, he tugged at his military moustache and his face became bright red. He circled the deck exactly forty-eight times a day. "Problem at Sea" from *The Regatta Mystery.*

FORBES, OLGILVIE The discreet, shrewd lawyer for the Chevenix-Gores and an old friend of the family, he was their guest when Sir Gervase was slain. Along with Colonel Bury, he shared a passion for Vanda Chevenix-Gore when she was young, and remained attached to her for years. "Dead Man's Mirror" from *Murder in the Mews.*

FORD, MONICA *See* **GLEN, ASPASIA.**

FORRESTER, MRS. "A sickly, neurotic woman" from Park Lane Court, she was one of Dr. John Christow's hypochondriac patients: "Once again it was easy money. Once again he listened, asked questions, reassured, sympathized, infused something of his own healing energy. Once again he wrote out a prescription for an expensive proprietary," and she left his office "with a firmer step, with colour in her cheeks, with a feeling that life might possibly after all be worth while." *The Hollow.*

FORTESCUE, ADELE Young second wife of Rex Fortescue, married two years, she "*was* a sexy piece . . . glamour all through. Her appeal was obvious, not subtle. It said simply to every man 'Here I am. I'm a woman.' . . . She liked men—but she would always like money even better." Poisoned with cyanide at tea-time, she left her estate to her lover, Vivian Dubois. She would have been beneficiary to her husband's will had she survived him a month. *A Pocket Full of Rye.*

FORTESCUE, ELAINE Daughter of Rex Fortescue by his first wife Elvira, and sister of Lancelot and Percival Fortescue, she was, according to Mary Dove, "one of those great schoolgirls who never grow up. She plays games quite well and runs Guides and Brownies and all that sort of thing." She was involved with Gerald Wright until her father discovered her young man's "Communistic ideas" and attacked them "like a ton of bricks." Miss Marple found a parallel to Elaine in Marion Bates of St. Mary Mead, whose husband was only interested in her financial expectations. *A Pocket Full of Rye.*

FORTESCUE, JENNIFER AKA Ruby MacKenzie. As Ruby MacKenzie, she nursed Percival Fortescue back to health after a bout of pneumonia and then married him. There was a mutual dislike between her and her father-in-law Rex Fortescue, who thought his son "Val" could have made a better marriage. Miss Marple discovered a similarity between Jennifer and Mrs. Emmett, a lady who was eager to talk because she did not feel comfortable in her environment. *A Pocket Full of Rye.*

FORTESCUE, LANCELOT AKA Albert Ellis, he was the son of Rex and Elvira Fortescue and brother of Percival and

Elaine. He met his wife Patricia in East Africa where he had hurriedly retired after a cheque forgery. He sincerely loved his new wife, but adopted the persona of Albert Ellis to romance Gladys Martin, housemaid to the Fortescues at Yewtree Lodge. A photograph of him in company with Gladys was sent to her old mistress, Miss Marple. *A Pocket Full of Rye.*

FORTESCUE, PATRICIA Widow of Lord Frederick Antice and also of the fighter pilot Don, she met and married Lancelot Fortescue in Kenya. The daughter of an Irish peer, she spent a happy childhood in Ireland but was distressed during her adult life, thinking that she brought bad luck to those around her. Miss Marple found her gravity and simplicity quite attractive. *A Pocket Full of Rye.*

FORTESCUE, PERCIVAL (VAL) Son of Rex and Elvira Fortescue, he had been married to Jennifer Fortescue for three years. He was also "mean about money." "A neat fair man of thirty-odd, with pale hair and eyelashes and a slightly pedantic way of speech," he was nicknamed "Percy Prim." He had quarrelled with his father over the investments of the family company. *A Pocket Full of Rye.*

FORTESCUE, REX Husband of the deceased Elvira Fortescue, with whom he produced Lancelot, Percival and Elaine, he was later married to the young Adele. A moody and extravagant man, he was not amicable with any of his children. He had cheated his partner MacKenzie out of the Blackbird mine in Africa, and probably left him to die there. He died from taxine poisoning, an alkaloid found in the berries of the yew tree, and was found wearing a jacket with a pocket full of rye. *A Pocket Full of Rye.*

FOSCARELLI, ANTONIO At one time, he was chauffeur to the Armstrong family, but had since become a naturalized American citizen. He had a "swift, cat-like tread," and "a typical Italian face, sunny-looking and swarthy." Poirot and his assistants made the mistake of asking him whether he was an agent for Ford automobiles: "A voluble explosion followed. At the end of it anything that the three men did not know about Foscarelli's business methods, his journey, his income and his opinion of the United States and most European countries seemed a negligible factor. This was not a man who had to have information dragged out of him. It gushed out." He and Edward Masterman shared the same berth and provided each other with alibis for the time of the murder. *Murder on the Orient Express.*

FOSCATINI, COUNT Count Foscatini was not genuine; Poirot noted that his name was not included in the *Almanack de Gotha.* He had been a successful blackmailer until he was murdered. "The Adventure of the Italian Nobleman" from *Poirot Investigates.*

FOTHERGILL, SIR HUGO One of Ariadne Oliver's "elephants," he was: "Quite an old pet—but useless as a source of information. Obsessed by some people called Barnet who did have a child killed in an accident in Malaya. But nothing to do with the Ravenscrofts." *Elephants Can Remember.*

FOURNIER, MONSIEUR The French Inspector from the Sûreté who collaborated with Inspector Japp and Poirot in the investigation of Madame Giselle Morisot's murder, he was pleasantly surprised by the restaurant where they dined: "After all, it is possible to eat well in England." *Death in the Clouds.*

FOWLER, MRS. She was convinced that Franz Ascher murdered his wife, despite the fact that Ascher had an unshakable alibi. Poirot offered her five pounds for an interview, claiming to be from the *Evening Flicker* newspaper. She told him "all that she knew not once but many times over." *The A.B.C. Murders.*

FOX, SYBIL The fabric cutter at Alicia Coombe's dress shop, Sybil became more and more distressed by the perversity of the puppet doll and said: "I've got a nasty frightened feeling—a horrid feeling that she's too strong for us." "The Dressmaker's Doll" from *Double Sin*.

FRANCOIS Anti-clerical butler at the Deroulard residence, he informed Poirot about Paul Deroulard's passion for chocolates. "The Chocolate Box" from *Poirot's Early Cases*.

FRANKLIN, BARBARA (BABS) Unhappily wed to Dr. John Franklin and an old friend of Sir William Boyd Carrington's, she was, said Hastings, of "the madonna type," a "sickly creature, though pretty in a frail, chocolate-box way." Others, among them Nurse Craven and Judith Hastings, saw through her feigned illnesses. Judith Hastings commented: "She's a very stupid woman. . . . She never reads anything but the cheapest kind of novel." Poirot replied to Judith, "she uses her little grey cells in ways that you, my child, know nothing about." She died from consuming alkaloids from the Calabar bean in her coffee. *Curtain*.

FRANKLIN, DR. JOHN Husband of the invalid Babs Franklin, he was a brilliant doctor dedicated to the research of tropical diseases. Although he was a cheerful man, he once said: "Lots of people I'd like to kill. . . . Don't believe my conscience would keep me awake at night afterward. It's an idea of mine, you know, that about eighty percent of the human race *ought* to be eliminated. We'd get on much better without them." After his wife's death, he promptly married his assistant, Judith Hastings, and they journeyed to Africa to continue investigations into the mysterious properties of the Calabar bean. *Curtain*.

FRASER, DONALD The fiancé of the murdered Elizabeth Barnard, he was ex-

tremely jealous and once threatened to murder Elizabeth if he caught her dating other men. *The A.B.C. Murders*.

FREEBODY, MISS *See* DEBANHAM, MARY, HERMIONE.

FRENCH, EMILY The elderly murder victim, she was a friend and benefactor of Leonard Vole's and the employer of Janet Mackenzie, the maid. Despite her reputation as "a good woman of business," she asked Vole to manage her finances, and left him most of her money when she died. "Witness for the Prosecution" from *Witness for the Prosecution*.

FRENCH, IRENE *See* HOBHOUSE, VALERIE.

FROBISHER, COLONEL GEORGE He was very fond of his friend Admiral Charles Chandler's son, Hugh Chandler, and was concerned about the Chandler family's legacy of insanity, but refused to interfere in the Admiral's personal affairs. "The Cretan Bull" from *The Labours of Hercules*.

FULLERTON, JEREMY The senior partner of the old-fashioned, respectable firm of Fullerton, Harrison and Leadbetter, he was Mrs. Llewellyn-Smythe's solicitor. When visited by Poirot concerning the Joyce Reynolds murder case, Mr. Fullerton feared that the detective was senile. *Hallowe'en Party*.

FULLERTON, LAVINIA A victim of the Wychwood murderer, she was on the way to Scotland Yard with a story of many suspicious deaths in her village when she met Luke Fitzwilliam. Miss Fullerton had provided the retired inspector with one clue before she died: she said the killer was someone whom no one would ever suspect. *Murder is Easy*.

GAIGH, LADY ELIZABETH The daughter of the Marquis of Axminster and the sister of Lord Rowland Gaigh, Lady Elizabeth impersonated the Grand Duchess Anastasia so that her brother and the real Grand Duchess could be married in anonymity. George Rowland wanted to marry her, not only because she was a beauty but because his uncle, William Rowland, was a snob, and would appreciate her social standing to the extent that he might offer George a partnership. Elizabeth agreed not only because she thought him gallant, but also because he was wealthy; she adored spending money and her father was "yearning for a rich son-in-law." It was a marriage "made in heaven and approved on earth." "The Girl in the Train" from *The Golden Ball*.

GAITSKILL, MR. A small, elderly man, he was a partner in the very respectable firm of Gaitskill, Callum and Gaitskill and Aristide Leonides' cautious solicitor. He had a precise way of speaking and an incredibly accurate memory, but was duped by his shrewd client into overseeing a secret will. Mr. Gaitskill's sensitive professional pride and his faith in the friendship he had with Aristide were hurt by this incident. *Crooked House*.

GALBRAITH, MR. The father of Gladys Galbraith and the retired senior partner of the realty firm Messrs. Gailbraith and Penderly, he was over eighty years old and had recently suffered a stroke. The "old gentleman with a white walrus moustache" had served in India. Gwenda Reed compared him to "a very old gramophone, repeating a worn record." *Sleeping Murder*.

GALE, MARGERY The daughter of Lady Stranleigh by Charles Gale, Margery "might have inherited . . . some mental kink from her mother's side of the family" according to Mr. Satterthwaite. She was in love with Noel Barton, but was pursued by Roley Vavasour who, after her, was next in line to the Stranleigh title. "The Voice in the Dark" from *The Mysterious Mr. Quin*.

GALE, NORMAN AKA James Richards, he was flying home on the *Prometheus* when Madame Giselle Morisot collapsed, and offered his aid as a dentist. His profession was disparaged by Jane Grey's co-workers: "Why, if he was going to kiss you, you'd feel he was going to say, 'Open a little wider, please'." He fell in love with Jane and with her aided Poirot in the investigation of the murder. Poirot sent him as "John Robinson" to blackmail Lady Cicely Horbury, and said of Gale's disguise: "Name of a name of a name. . . . What do you think you are? A Santa Claus dressed up to amuse the children? . . . But what a beard. . . . Then there are your eyebrows—but is it that you have a mania for false hair? The spirit gum, one smells it several yards away. . . . You are a blackmailer, not a comedian. I want her ladyship to fear you, not to die of laughing when she sees you." His real name was James Richards and he had spent some time on a farm in South America. *Death in the Clouds.*

GAPP, FLORENCE (FLOSSIE) *See* **RIVAL, MERLINA.**

GARCIA, DR. ALAN He was the distinguished and twinkling-eyed Home Office analyst full of learned terms who "spoke with gusto of the stomach contents of the murdered Mary Gerrard" at the trial of Elinor Carlisle, and who discovered traces of arsenic in the exhumed body of Mrs. Charles Oldfield. *Sad Cypress*; "The Lernean Hydra" from *The Labours of Hercules.*

GARDENER, CARRIE The wife of Odell C. Gardener, Carrie Gardener was "a garrulous American tourist" who spent all her waking hours boring everyone within earshot with her non-stop chatter which was punctuated only, it seemed, by the confirmations elicited from her pliant husband. *Evil Under the Sun.*

GARDINER, JOHN The secretary of Hugo Lemesurier, he was Sadie Lemesurier's lover and with her produced a son, Ronald Lemesurier. After Hugo's death, he married Sadie. "The Lemesurier Inheritance" from *The Under Dog.*

GARDNER, MRS. A Cornish farmwoman, she was indebted to Mr. Parker Pyne for having saved her only son from penal servitude. She initially broke the news to Amelia Rymer that Amelia was

really Hannah Moorehouse. "The Case of the Rich Woman" from *Parker Pyne Investigates.*

GARDNER, JENNIFER After marrying Robert Gardner, she was estranged from her brother, Captain Trevelyan. Emily Trefusis thought Jennifer "had enough character for two and three-quarter people instead of one," and found her beautiful and terrible, "like something out of a Greek play." Jennifer adored her husband, and cultivated open antipathy for her husband's Nurse Evans; when Emily commented upon that woman's beauty, Jennifer shot back, "Nonsense. With her ugly, beefy hands?" *The Sittaford Mystery.*

GARDNER, CAPTAIN ROBERT The husband of Jennifer Gardner and lover of Nurse Evans, he was an invalid with no visible disability but had lost the use of his limbs from psychological disorder. He seemed to enjoy being a petulant invalid, but Emily Trefusis wondered if he enjoyed being adored as much as his wife delighted in adoring him. *The Sittaford Mystery.*

GARFIELD, MICHAEL Mystical, narcissistic and talented architect, he had been commissioned by Mrs. Llewellyn-Smythe to transform her Quarry Wood into an enchanted garden, and was bequeathed the property when she died. Poirot was slightly unnerved by him: "It is always difficult to know if you like anyone beautiful. . . . Hercule Poirot was not at all sure that he liked beauty in men." Garfield called Poirot "Senor Mustachios" and thought the detective sartorially ambitious because he preferred the painful elegance of his patent-leather shoes to footwear more appropriate for tramping about country lanes. He died at Kilterbury Ring. *Hallowe'en Party.*

GARFIELD, RONALD Pitifully weak nephew of Caroline Percehouse, he was Mrs. Gardner's godchild and was present at the séance the night of Captain Trevelyan's murder. His aunt treated him as a half-wit, but regretted his spinelessness: "Look at what he stands from me. And he hasn't got the brains to see that I would like him just ten times better if he stood up to me now and again and told me to go to the devil." *The Sittaford Mystery.*

GARNETT, PATRICIA (PAT) The beloved of Jimmy Faulkener and of Donovan Bailey, she was also a friend of Mildred Hope's, who "was not nearly so attractive as the impulsive and troublesome Pat." Pat lived in a third-floor flat in Friar's Mansions. When she locked herself out one night, Jimmy and Donovan broke in, but found themselves instead in the second-floor flat with the dead body of a woman. "Third-Floor Flat" from *Three Blind Mice and Other Stories.*

GARROD, GRACE Philip Garrod's wife and the niece of Simon Clode, she stood to be disinherited by Simon Clode if he decided to favour Eurydice Spragg instead. "Motive *v* Opportunity" from *The Thirteen Problems.*

GARROD, PHILIP The husband of Grace Garrod, Philip was a clever young research chemist who saved the family from Eurydice Spragg's manoeuvers to inherit all of Simon Clode's money. He filled Simon Clode's pen with evanescent ink so that when Clode made his new will two months before his death, it faded away shortly afterward and only a blank sheet of paper remained. "Motive *v* Opportunity" from *The Thirteen Problems.*

GARROWAY, CHIEF SUPERINTENDENT The head of the investigation at the time of the Ravenscroft tragedy at Overcliffe and a friend of Superintendent Spence's, Garroway had "grey hair which left a small round spot like a tonsure, so that he had a faint resemblance to an ecclesiastic." He did not agree that the deaths of General and Lady Ravenscroft were suicides. *Elephants Can Remember.*

GASCOIGNE, HENRY "Old Father Time," as the waitresses called him, was a regular at the Gallant Endeavour every Tuesday and Thursday night for the past ten years, during which time he was never known to eat thick soup, suet pudding or blackberries. An artist, he was Anthony Gascoigne's twin brother and George Lorrimer's uncle, but he had not associated with his brother since Anthony married and gave up art. He died by falling headlong down a flight of stairs, ostensibly owing to the loose cord on his ragged dressing gown. Henry shocked the staff of the Gallant Endeavour by appearing on the Monday night before his death and ordering thick soup, suet pudding and blackberries. "Four and Twenty Blackbirds" from *The Adventure of the Christmas Pudding.*

GASKELL, MARK Previously married to Rosamund Jefferson, who had died, he was disliked by almost everyone. Miss Marple agreed with Sir Henry Clithering, who said: "the man had charm but he was unreliable—talked too much, was occasionally boastful—not quite to be trusted." Colonel Melchett noted that Gaskell was "one of those men who usually get their own way and whom women frequently admire." He kept his second marriage to Josephine Turner a secret in order to inherit half of Conway Jefferson's money. *The Body in the Library.*

GAUNT, EMMA The housemaid at Simon Clode's home, she had been in service there for many years and nursed Clode devotedly. She was called in to witness Clode's new will favouring Eurydice Spragg. "Motive *v* Opportunity" from *The Thirteen Problems.*

GEORGE A gentleman's gentleman, George was Hercule Poirot's impeccable and imperturbable valet. He was "an intensely English, rather wooden-faced individual" who was in the tradition of Lord Peter Wimsey's Bunter and Albert Campion's Magersfontein Lugg. Before coming to Poirot, some time after the departure of Arthur Hastings for the Argentine at the conclusion of the Renauld Case *(Murder on the Links)*, George had been in the employ of Lord Edward Frampton. Only after Poirot had been received at Buckingham Palace did George decide that the great detective would make a suitable employer. His amazing knowledge of the English aristocracy was often tapped by Poirot, but when he tried to extract an opinion from the valet, Poirot often said: "You press admirably the trousers, George . . . but the imagination you possess it not." Hastings, who found George "clearly not good at thinking" informed George of his master's death in *Curtain:* "George reacted as George would react. He was distressed and grieved and managed very nearly to conceal the fact." *The Mystery of the Blue Train;* "Murder in the Mews" from *Murder in the Mews; Dumb Witness; One, Two, Buckle My Shoe;* "The Nemean Lion," "The Lernean Hydra" and "The Apples of the Hesperides" from *The Labours of Hercules; Taken at the Flood;* "Four and Twenty Blackbirds" from *The Adventure of the Christmas Pudding;* "The Under Dog" from *The Under Dog; Mrs. McGinty's Dead; After the Funeral; Hickory, Dickory, Dock; Cat Among the Pigeons; The Clocks; Third Girl; Hallowe'en Party; Elephants Can Remember; Curtain.*

GEORGE, UNCLE The uncle of Jack Hartington, he owned the blue jar that Jack brought to Heather Cottage in the hope of contacting Mrs. Turner's ghost. "A white-haired old gentleman wheezing with mirth," he came home from a trip on the Continent unexpectedly early. "The Blue Jar" from *Witness for the Prosecution.*

GERARD, DR. THEODORE An eminent psychologist on vacation in Jerusalem at the time of the Boynton murder case, he had immediate access to the personalities of the Boynton family members. He outlined his professional philosophy to Jefferson Cope: "My dear sir, I have made a life's study of the strange things that go on in the human mind. It is no good turning one's face only to the fairer side of life; there lies a vast reservoir of strange things—as, for instance, delight in cruelty for its own sake. But when you have found that, there is something deeper still—the desire, profound and pitiful, to be appreciated. If that is thwarted, if through an unpleasing personality a human being is unable to get the response it needs, it turns to other methods—it must be *felt*—it must *count*—and so to innumerable strange perversions." A hypodermic needle with some digitoxin was discovered to be missing from his doctor's bag. *Appointment with Death.*

GERRARD, BOB *See* **GERRARD, EPHRAIM.**

GERRARD, EPHRAIM Alleged father of Mary Gerrard, he resented having to raise someone else's daughter as his own and jeered "at her schooling and her fine ways." *Sad Cypress.*

GERRARD, MARY The bastard child of Laura Welman and Sir Lewis Rycroft, she was brought up by Mr. and Mrs. Gerrard, who worked at the lodge at Hunterbury Hall. Sir Lewis later paid for her education—French, piano lessons, and "things"—and Laura Welman quite naturally wished that Mary be provided for after her death. Roderick Welman, already engaged to Elinor Carlisle, fell in love with this "lovely creature with a kind of wild-rose unreality about her." Mary Gerrard was poisoned by morphine in the fish paste sandwiches which were served to her by Elinor Carlisle. *Sad Cypress.*

GERTIE An "old friend" of Inspector Japp's, this member of the jewel thief gang was apprehended at Poirot's residence.

(*See* **VAUGHN, LADY MILLICENT CASTLE.**) "The Veiled Lady" from *Poirot's Early Cases.*

GIBBS, AMY Lord Easterfield's maid, according to Miss Waynflete, was "always wanting to go out. . . . She was fond of admiration and was inclined to think a lot of herself." She was engaged to Jim Harvey. Easterfield had fired the sluttish and impertinent girl over her noticeable lack of moral sense. She swallowed red hat paint, thinking it was cough syrup, and succumbed to oxalic acid poisoning. The death was attributed to suicide because her door had been locked from the inside. *Murder is Easy.*

GIBSON, OLD MOTHER A very aged lady who owned and operated an antique glassware shop, she had "a budding moustache that many an undergraduate might have envied, and a truculent manner." Her upstairs room was used by the Patterson gang in their plot to fleece Eastwood of his collection of old enamels. "Mr. Eastwood's Adventure" from *The Listerdale Mystery.*

GILCHRIST, MISS "Lady-like" and "old-maidish" housekeeper-companion to Cora Lansquenet, she found herself cooking, fetching and carrying for the hypochondriac Leo Abernethie after Cora Lansquenet was murdered. She told Poirot that she eavesdropped on Cora's conversation with Richard Abernethie: "It's not so bad telling you because you're not English." She almost died of an overdose of arsenic in a piece of wedding cake which mysteriously arrived in the mail, but the Victorian habit of placing the cake under her pillow to encourage dreams of a future husband saved her life. *After the Funeral.*

GILCHRIST, DR. MAURICE Marina Gregg's resident physician at Gossington Hall, he had a sympathetic attitude to his patient's needs. "When you're shooting a picture everything's taken out of sequence. It's a monotonous grinding business. It's exhausting. You live in luxury, of course, you have soothing drugs, you have baths and creams and powders and medical attention, you have relaxations and parties and people, but you're always in the public eye. You can't enjoy yourself quietly. You can't really—ever relax." *The Mirror Crack'd from Side to Side.*

GILES, DR. The doctor called in to examine the body of Walter Prothero, he was "a tall man dressed in sporting tweeds, with a clever, capable face, and who was clearly in command of the situation." "The Market Basing Mystery" from *The Under Dog.*

GILLIAT, BERYL Simon Gilliat's second wife, she was the step-mother of Timothy Gilliat (Simon's son by his first wife) and the mother of Rolland Gilliat (by her deceased first husband Christopher Eden). Beryl lived at Thomas Addison's Doverton Kingsbourne, where she plotted to ensure that her son Roland, and not Addison's blood grandson, Timothy, would inherit the Addison fortune. "The Harlequin Tea Set" from *Winter's Crimes 3.*

GILLIAT, LILY Daughter of Thomas and Pilar Addison, the first wife of Simon Gilliat and the mother of Timothy Gilliat, she had died in an automobile accident in Kenya. Mr. Satterthwaite was apparently thanked by her spirit for saving the life of her son Timothy. "The Harlequin Tea Set" from *Winter's Crimes 3.*

GILLIAT, ROLAND (ROLY) The son of Beryl Gilliat and her first husband Christopher Eden, Roland was step-son of Simon Gilliat and the step-brother of Timothy Gilliat. Roland looked very much like Timothy, and most people mistook him for Lily Gilliat's son, an error which Beryl Gilliat greatly encouraged. However, Mr. Satterthwaite "could see no resemblance in Roland to his grandfather. Nor apart from his red hair did he look like his father." In addition, Roland did not suffer from Dalton's disease. "The Harlequin Tea Set" from *Winter's Crimes 3.*

GILLIAT, SIMON A Squadron Leader in the Royal Air Force, during World War II, Simon Gilliat was the father of Timothy Gilliat by his deceased first wife Lily Addison Gilliat, and the step-father of Roland Gilliat, the son of his second wife Beryl Gilliat by her deceased first husband Christopher Eden. "The Harlequin Tea Set" from *Winter's Crime 3.*

GILLIAT, TIMOTHY The son of Simon Gilliat and his deceased first wife Lily Addison Gilliat, he was the step-son of Beryl Gilliat, half-brother of Roland Gilliat, grandson of Thomas Addison and the cousin of Inez Horton. For many years Beryl had been passing off Roland as the son of Lily Addison Gilliat, and thus the heir to the Addison fortune. Timothy also inherited Dalton's disease or colour-blindness from his grandfather Thomas Addison. "The Harlequin Tea Set" from *Winter's Crimes 3.*

GINCH, MISS A clerk with Richard Symmington's law firm, she was "forty at least, with pince-nez and teeth like a rabbit . . . frizzy hair and simpered." After Symmington received a poison pen letter accusing them of illicit relations, she quit the law firm "to avoid even the appearance of evil." *The Moving Finger.*

GIRAUD, MONSIEUR The famous detective with the Paris Sûreté, he was in charge of the investigation into the death of Paul Renauld. Giraud and Poirot took an instant dislike to one another. Poirot called him "the human foxhound" because he was always on all fours sniffing out clues. In turn, Giraud regarded Poirot as senile. The tension between them was

the clash of the old and the new methods of the science of detection and the gap between age and youth. For a while, Hastings sided with Giraud, seeing him as a man of action concerned with hard evidence, and his old friend, Poirot, as a passive person given to concentrating on unimportant details. In the end Giraud's methods proved inconclusive. *Murder on the Links.*

GISELLE, MADAME AKA Marie Angelique Morisot, she was a "frightfully ugly . . . stoutish middle-aged woman dressed in heavy black," murdered with a blowgun dart dipped in the venom of the South American boomslang snake while en route from Paris to England. She was the most famous money-lender in Paris, and maintained a file of unpleasant information on each of her clients which she kept as security for their loans; if they reneged, she simply ruined them. Her estate, valued at over one hundred thousand pounds, was left to her daughter Anne Morisot Leman Richards. *Death in the Clouds.*

GIUSEPPE The butler employed by Marina Gregg at Gossington Hall, he was admired by Gladys Dixon. "He's awfully handsome. Flashing eyes. He's got a terrible temper. When we go and help there, he chivvies us girls something terrible. . . . But none of us really mind. He can be awfully nice sometimes." Cherry Baker warned her ". . . you'd better be careful, my girl. You know what these wops are like! Affiliation orders all over the place. Hot-blooded and passionate, that's what these Italians are." Gladys "sighed ecstatically" in response. The charming Giuseppe was shot dead at Gossington Hall after he had returned from a trip to London. *The Mirror Crack'd from Side to Side.*

GLADYS The third housemaid at the Astwell household, Gladys told Poirot that Victor Astwell was in love with Lily Margrave. She brought him the dress that her mistress wore on the night of the murder of Sir Reuben Astwell, saying "we all know that French gentlemen are interested in ladies' dresses." "The Under Dog" from *The Under Dog.*

GLADYS (GLADDIE) The kitchenmaid at Colonel Lucius Protheroe's Old Hall, she looked "more like a shivering rabbit than anything human." *Murder at the Vicarage.*

GLEN, ASPASIA AKA "The Weeping Lady with the Silver Ewer"; "The Woman with the Scarf"; Monica Ford. A brilliant impersonator, she was considered a ruthless egoist by Mr. Satterthwaite. As Monica Ford, she had been the nursery governess who wrote to Lord Reginald that she was pregnant by him. "The Dead Harlequin" from *The Mysterious Mr. Quin.*

GLEN, GILDA The famous English actress' provocative beauty was in inverse proportion to her intelligence. Bugler Estcourt maintained that she had "the brains of a rabbit." Tuppence and Tommy Beresford had seen her in *The Secret of the Heart, Pillars of Fire* and in countless other productions. "Her smile said many things. It asserted, for instance, that she knew perfectly well that she herself was the thing best worth looking at certainly in England and possibly in the whole world." It was a closely-guarded secret that she was sister to Mrs. Honeycott, and that she was married to a policeman, from whom she sought a divorce. She was murdered by a blow to her skull. "The Man in the Mist" from *Partners in Crime.*

GLYDR, MAJOR BORIS ANDREI PAVLOV AKA Andrew Peters; Glider; Glyn; Sidi. He was the nephew of Professor Mannheim and the cousin of Mannheim's daughter Elsa, both brilliant scientists. Major Glydr, the slightly sinister Pole, consulted with Jessop concerning the disappearances of several major scientific minds across the world. As An-

drew Peters, Glydr was an agent of the F.B.I. masquerading as a research chemist at Mr. Aristides' Brain Trust in the Atlas Mountains. Andrew Peters had come to the complex not out of love of money, freedom or fascism, as had the others, but because he felt "it's the only way. We're leaving the Past and stepping out towards the Future. . . . the world of science, clean away from the scum and the driftwood." As Sidi, he was a Moroccan servant at the Brain Trust. He fell in love with Hilary Craven on his mission. *Destination Unknown.*

GLYNNE, LAVINIA BRADBURY-SCOTT Niece of Colonel Bradbury-Scott and sister of Clotilde and Anthea Bradbury-Scott, she was an "entirely normal and pleasant woman but not very happy" according to Miss Marple. *Nemesis.*

GOBY, MR. An old friend of Hercule Poirot's, Mr. Goby was a celebrated private investigator whose specialty was acquiring information quickly: "Give him twenty-four hours and he would lay half the private life of the Archbishop of Canterbury before you." Goby was "so nondescript as to be practically nonexistent," and "had never been known to address the human being he was working for directly. He selected always the cornice, a radiator, a television set, a clock, sometimes a carpet or a mat." He was hired by Rufus Van Aldin in *The Mystery of the Blue Train,* and came out of retirement to assist Poirot in *After the Funeral, Third Girl* and *Elephants Can Remember.*

GOEDLER, BELLE The invalid widow of Randall Goedler, she lived in Scotland and would have been dead years ago if she did not have an "intense enjoyment and love of being alive." Belle had inherited her husband's immense fortune, and on her death the estate was to pass on to Letitia Blacklock, his former secretary. *A Murder is Announced.*

GOLD, DOUGLAS CAMERON Husband of Marjorie Gold, with whom he was vacationing in Rhodes, he was bowled over by the attention he received from Valentine Chantry, and would have hanged for her murder had Poirot not solved the case. "Triangle at Rhodes" from *Murder in the Mews.*

GOLD, MARJORIE EMMA Wife of Douglas Gold for five years, she was in love with Tony Chantry. Although she had a meek and mild appearance, Poirot correctly labelled her "a cold-blooded devil." "Triangle at Rhodes" from *Murder in the Mews.*

GOODBODY, MRS. She was the local witch and cleaning lady at Woodleigh Common. She provided Poirot with incisive and perfectly accurate portraits of the members of the Reynolds family, disburdened him of the misapprehension that her blue witch-ball was used for fortune-telling and disposed of so-called "black magic" Satanism as being "for people who like to dress up and do a lot of tomfoolery. Sex and all that." Her pronouncement on Olga Seminoff, a cryptic "Ding dong bell, pussy's in the well," was one small example of her tremendous psychic sensitivity. *Hallowe'en Party.*

GOODMAN, ADAM Cover name of the Special Branch agent Ronnie, who posed as a gardener at Meadowbank. The part of a gardener came easily to him, for he once had the "Your Garden" column in the *Sunday Mail. Cat Among the Pigeons.*

GORDON LEIGH, THE HONOURABLE HERMIONE *Née* Crane, she was the widow of Maurice Gordon Leigh, the second daughter of Lord Lanchester and fiancée of the explorer Gabriel Stavansson, who consulted Tuppence and Tommy Beresford's International Detective Agency when she disappeared. "The Case of the Missing Lady" from *Partners in Crime.*

GORING, EDWARD A criminal mastermind, he posed as Dr. Rathbone's "yesman and dog's-body." During World War

II, he had been a fighter pilot with the R.A.F. and had received the D.F.C. Goring ran his operation from the Olive Branch, a coffee shop and meeting place in Baghdad. Victoria Jones felt that she was madly in love with him at first sight, but Goring returned her affections by using her in one of his schemes because she bore a striking resemblance to Anna Scheele. Dr. Rathbone said: "He knows just when to charm and when to bully." *They Came to Baghdad.*

GORMAN, FATHER Father Gorman was "a tall elderly priest" at St. Dominic's Presbyterian church and lived with his housekeeper Mrs. Gerahty. He was called to Jesse Davis' deathbed at Mrs. Coppin's boarding house and there received a list of names from the dying woman. While he was returning to the presbytery, he was knocked on the head and killed in West Street, Paddington. Because there was a hole in his pocket, he put the list in his shoe. The list was found when the police searched his body and it provided the first clue to the Pale Horse mystery. *The Pale Horse.*

GORMAN, MICHAEL (MICKEY) Commissionaire doorman at Bertram's Hotel, he was the first and only legitimate husband of Lady Bess Sedgwick, who eloped with him when she was only sixteen. Although she was brought back home, the marriage was never legally dissolved, and it rendered all her other marriages void. Gorman saw Bess accidentally at the hotel and when he jokingly threatened to expose the internationally renowned adventuress' first marriage, she threatened to shoot him. Later, he was shot to death and Bess confessed to his murder before she drove her car into a rail. *At Bertram's Hotel.*

GORRINGE, MISS Well-respected and well-liked receptionist of Bertram's Hotel for fourteen years, she had the capacity for remembering an amazing number of the guests and their needs. Even with her unusually keen appraisal of human nature, she missed the shrewd side of Chief Inspector Davy's character and thought he was a "yokel." She coached Ruth Sheldon on the story to be related to officials concerning Canon Pennyfather's disappearance. *At Bertram's Hotel.*

GOTTLIEB, PROFESSOR JOHN In discussion, he "scratched his ear with a rather monkey-like gesture which was characteristic of him. He looked rather like a monkey anyway. A prognathous jaw, a high mathematical head which make a slight contrast in terms and small wizened frame." He was introduced to Mary Ann, also known as Countess Renata Zerkowski, by a letter from the President of the United States. He informed her about Project Benvo. *Passenger to Frankfurt.*

GRACE Although she had been courting James Bond for three years, she had attracted the attention of Claud Sopworth, a man whom James loathed. Grace thought that James dressed poorly and laughed at him when he said that he too might one day be a peer. She persuaded James to holiday with her at the fashionable resort town of Kimpton-on-Sea. He could ill-afford the luxury, and while she stayed in a posh hotel, James lodged at a boarding house. "The Rajah's Emerald" from *The Golden Ball.*

GRACE, INSPECTOR A police inspector from Scotland Yard, he worked on the case of the Ambassador's boots with Tuppence and Tommy Beresford. Unfortunately Albert, the Beresfords' office boy, had been reading too many American westerns and related: "lassoed him in the nick of time, I did. . . . It's wonderful what those chaps can do on the prairies, sir." "The Ambassador's Boots" from *Partners in Crime.*

GRACE, PATIENCE Neither graceful nor patient, she snorted cocaine, promulgated its use and shot at her drug-dealing boyfriend, Anthony Hawker, in a narcotic-induced hysteria. "The Horses of Diomedes" from *The Labours of Hercules.*

GRAHAM, DR. Exceedingly kind physician residing in the Golden Palm Hotel, he chatted with Miss Marple after discussing her game knee, which was not bothering her at the time, because he felt she might be lonely. He instituted the investigation of Major Palgrove's death. *A Caribbean Mystery.*

GRAHAM, ROGER The son of Mrs. Graham, he was engaged to Madge Keeley, but had fallen under the spell of Mabelle Annesley. He had decided to tell Mabelle that he intended to return to the more human if commonplace charms of Madge Keeley when Mabelle Annesley was murdered. "The Bird with the Broken Wing" from *The Mysterious Mr. Quin.*

GRAINGER, DR. Physician to Emily Arundell and partner of Dr. Rex Donaldson, he was described as the type of doctor who "fair bullies you into living whether you want to or not." The combination of the curry that the Arundells had for supper the night Emily died, and his own loss of smell following a bout of influenza prevented him from detecting the garlic-like odour of phosphorus on Miss Arundell's breath. *Dumb Witness.*

GRANBY, MRS. A guest at the Crown Hotel in Barnchester, she was suspected by Miss Marple as having disguised herself as a man and of taking part in the murder of Mrs. Rhodes. "Miss Marple Tells a Story" from *The Regatta Mystery.*

GRANDIER MADAME A guest at Rochers Neige, she returned to the hotel every year in remembrance of her husband who was killed while climbing near there. Poirot was taken with her beauty: "I think that anyone might well mount ten thousand feet for her sake." The wrecking of the funicular, which cut the hotel off from the rest of the world, was a matter of indifference to Madame Grandier. "The Erymanthian Boar" from *The Labours of Hercules.*

GRANDIER, ELISE The personal maid to the murdered Madame Giselle, she had been deceived by a man, left with a child and robbed of her life savings. Madame Giselle had made all the arrangements for the child to be cared for in the country. After Madame Giselle's death, Elise burnt all the documents relating to Madame's clients except one small notebook which she turned over to Poirot. *Death in the Clouds.*

GRANGE, INSPECTOR Chief Inspector for the area around The Hollow, he was convinced that Gerda Christow was motivated by jealousy and had murdered her husband. *The Hollow.*

GRANT, GENERAL Father of "four blinking girls," among them Sheila and Pam Grant, he was described as "a retired General—blood and thunder, shoot 'em down—pukka Sahib—all that sort of thing." His foot was bandaged for the gout he claimed to have, and he did not notice when Poirot once clutched his foot when he stumbled. "The Horses of Diomedes" from *The Labours of Hercules.*

GRANT, MR. A friend of Mr. Carter's in British Intelligence, he was "an attractive person with an easy manner." Although Grant wished to employ only Tommy Beresford in the case, he was thwarted by Tuppence's natural curiosity, ingenuous duplicity and thirst for adventure. Grant sent Tommy, under the guise of Mr. Meadows, to Leahampton, where Tuppence portrayed a Mrs. Blenkensop. Grant

assumed the disguise of a fisherman so that he could remain near the village for Tommy's consultation and, with Albert Batt, he rescued both Tuppence and Tommy from their respective kidnappers. *N or M?*

GRANT, ERNESTINE The wife of eight years to Donovan Bailey, she lived in the second-floor flat below Patricia Garnett's and had written a note to Patricia the morning she was shot requesting to see her. Poirot thought it ironic that Mrs. Grant had come to live in Friar's Mansions. "Third-Floor Flat" from *Three Blind Mice and Other Stories.*

GRANT, GERDA AKA Sylvia Chapman and Helen Montressor. Gerda Grant was Alistair Blunt's first wife. In the guise of Helen Montressor, she played the part of her husband's cousin, who had died in Canada seven years ago. As a young woman, she was an actress and knew Mabelle Sainsbury Seale. She enjoyed portraying a large repertoire of characters while married to Blunt. *One, Two Buckle My Shoe.*

GRANT, PAM Alleged sister of Sheila Grant and daughter of General Grant, "the girl was small and fair—her face was pink and white and suspiciously angelic. Her eyes, Poirot noticed at once, were alert and suspicious." "The Horses of Diomedes" from *The Labours of Hercules.*

GRANT, ROBERT AKA Abraham Biggs. According to Hastings, Grant was "a man of medium height, with a somewhat unpleasing cast of features." An ex-convict, he was Jonathan Whalley's manservant. *The Big Four.*

GRANT, SHEILA AKA Sheila Kelly. The alleged daughter of General Grant and sister of Pam Grant, she was treated for cocaine poisoning by Dr. Michael Stoddart, who fell in love with her and said: "I mean, she'd *describe* herself as hardboiled. But she's really just very young—a bit wild and all that—but it's just kid foolishness. She gets mixed up in a racket like this because she thinks it's smart or modern or something like that." Poirot discovered that her true identity was Sheila Kelly, a convicted shoplifter, and convinced her to reject the cocaine business. "The Horses of Diomedes" from *The Labours of Hercules.*

GRANT, STEPHEN The beloved of Mary Jones, Stephen Grant had looked after Captain Richard Harwell's horses at Ashley Grange until Harwell disappeared. Grant was suspected of foul play, but no evidence could be produced and he was set free. "At the Bells and Motley" from *The Mysterious Mr. Quin.*

GRANT, STEPHEN AKA Stephen Farr. Born and raised in South Africa, Stephen Grant was the bastard son of Simeon Lee. He posed as Stephen Farr, the son of Ebenezer Farr (an old business partner of Simeon Lee's) to gain entrance at Gorston Hall and to learn about his natural father. He was often mistaken for Harry Lee and Superintendent Sugden; they were all brothers by different mothers. He returned to South Africa engaged to Conchita Lopez (AKA Pilar Estravados). *Hercule Poirot's Christmas.*

GRAVES, CONSTABLE A police constable for the area of Sittaford, he knew Major Burnaby well, and with the Major and Dr. Warren broke into Captain Trevelyan's bungalow to discover the Captain's body the night of the séance. Major Burnaby was impatient at the constable's lack of perspicacity. *The Sittaford Mystery.*

GRAVES, INSPECTOR Inspector from London who arrived to aid in the investigation, he was "a tall lantern-jawed man in plain clothes" whose specialty was anonymous letter cases. His professional admiration for the poison-pen letters in Lymstock seemed strange to the locals. He had a "deep lugubrious voice like a depressed bloodhound." *The Moving Finger.*

GRAVES, MR. He was Count Foscatini's valet and butler at the Count's flat in Regent's Court, St. John's Wood. "The Adventure of the Italian Nobleman" from *Poirot Investigates.*

GRAVES, SERGEANT A "tactful young man," Graves was a member of the Warmsley Vale constabulary helping Superintendent Spence in his investigation of the death of "Enoch Arden." He had quite a good French accent, but wisely chose not to use it in front of Spence. *Taken at the Flood.*

GRAVES, SIR RONALD Assistant Commissioner of Scotland Yard, he presided over the conference on robberies and "according to his custom he did more listening than talking." He had a habit of doodling cat figures on his desk blotter when deep in thought. Although he had the highest respect and affection for Chief Inspector Fred "Father" Davy, he was apprehensive about obtaining the clearance necessary for Davy to consult Mr. Robinson, whom he called "the top brains behind the international financiers of Europe." *At Bertram's Hotel.*

GRAYLE, LADY ARIADNE The wife of Sir George Grayle and aunt of Pamela Grayle, "she had suffered since she was sixteen from the complaint of having too much money." Grayle consulted Mr. Parker Pyne, a fellow traveller on board the S.S. *Fayoum,* about her suspicions that she was being poisoned by her husband. She was full of complaints and incapable of enjoying anything, except the company of her darling Basil West. "Death on the Nile" from *Parker Pyne Investigates.*

GRAYLE, SIR GEORGE The long-suffering and docile husband of Lady Ariadne Grayle and the uncle of Pamela Grayle, he was not very clever but was civil to everyone. He particularly doted on the capable nurse, Miss MacNaughton; in turn she found him pathetic and childlike. Because all her attacks of illness took place when he was present, and never while he was absent, Lady Grayle suspected Sir George of poisoning her. Mr. Parker Pyne hoped that Sir George would derive some enjoyment in future: "He's been treated like a worm for ten years." "Death on the Nile" from *Parker Pyne Investigates.*

GRAYLE, PAMELA The niece of Sir George and Lady Ariadne Grayle, she called her uncle, Sir George Grayle, "Nunks," and thought little of her aunt, Lady Ariadne, although the older lady paid for all the younger lady's pleasures. Her lover was Basil West. "Death on the Nile" from *Parker Pyne Investigates.*

GREEN, CYRIL He informed the police about a car he had noticed near Sunny Point the night of Rachel Argyle's murder. "Breathing hard in the effort of remembrance," Cyril recalled that it was a bubble car, a new model at the time. The young man's original theory was that "it's them Russians . . . they come down in that sputnik of theirs and they must have got in and killed her." *Ordeal by Innocence.*

GREENHOLTZ, MR. Victoria Jones' employer at Greenholtz, Simons and Lederbetter, he fired her for doing a quite wicked but funny impersonation of his wife, and wrote on the reference letter: "Miss Jones has been with me for two months as a shorthand typist. Her shorthand is inaccurate and she cannot spell. She is leaving owing to wasting time in office hours." *They Came to Baghdad.*

GREENSHAW, KATHERINE DOR-OTHY Daughter of Nathaniel Greenshaw and mistress of Greenshaw's Folly, she had not paid her companion-housekeeper Mrs. Cresswell for several years, telling her instead that she would leave the Folly to her. She hid her will in the book, *Lady Audley's Secret.* Miss Marple understood this lady's Victorian sensibilities and referred to the case of Mr. Naysmith, who kept bees and also had

a strange sense of humour. Miss Greenshaw was slain with an arrow through her neck, but in the end she outwitted both Mrs. Cresswell and her avaricious nephew by leaving the Folly to the grandson of one of her grandfather's numerous bastards, Alfred Pollock. "Greenshaw's Folly" from *The Adventure of the Christmas Pudding.*

GREER, ELSA One-time mistress of the painter Amyas Crale, and current wife of Lord Dittisham, she was previously married to a famous aviator and also to Arnold Stevenson. Crale was just finishing a portrait of her, his "best," when he died from hemlock (coniine) poisoning. Although the Crales' marriage had survived a multitude of mistresses, it was alleged that Caroline Crale murdered him out of jealousy when Elsa Greer told her that Amyas would soon leave her. Poirot likened her grey eyes to "dead lakes." Since the death of her lover, and his wife, she had lost all interest in life and maintained that it was not they but she who had died. *Five Little Pigs.*

GREGG, BETTY Fiancée to Basil Chester, whom she met at the Hotel Pino d'Oro, in Adela Chester's eyes, "The girl was dreadful. She drank, swore—she wore no clothes to speak of." Parker Pyne "noticed her—her grey flannel trousers—the scarlet handkerchief tied loosely around her breast—the vermilion mouth and the fact that she had chosen a cocktail in preference to tea." Eventually the breach between Adela and Betty was healed. "Problem at Pollensa Bay" from *The Regatta Mystery.*

GREGG, ERNIE One of the delinquent boys who lived at Stoneygates, he was "a perishing liar" who was killed because he boasted that he had seen the murderer of Christian Gulbrandsen. He had given Gina Hudd "valuable lessons in the manipulation of locks." *They Do It with Mirrors.*

GREGG, MARINA The wife of Jason Rudd and a famous film actress, Marina Gregg had been married many times according to Dolly Bantry: "An early one that didn't count, and then a foreign Prince or Count, and then another film star, Robert Truscott. . . . And then Isidore Wright, the playwright. That was rather serious and quiet, and she had a baby. . . . Very much built up. Motherhood with a capital M. And then, I believe, it was an imbecile, queer or something—and it was after that that she had this breakdown and started to take drugs and all that. . . . She married the present man about two years ago, and they say she's quite all right again now." The first husband was Alfred Beadle, AKA Arthur Badcock, and the third, Robert Truscott, was stolen away by Lola Brewster. Marina was about fifty years old at the time of the fête, and did not notice Margot Bence, whom she had adopted and forsaken long ago. In the end, life proved to be unbearable for Marina Gregg, and she committed suicide. *The Mirror Crack'd from Side to Side.*

GREGG, MAUREEN *See* **LYON, MRS.**

GREGSON, GARRY An author for whom Miss Martindale had once been a typist, he sold a manuscript copy of one of his unpublished books to Poirot who was researching detective fiction. The manuscript provided Poirot with a valuable clue to the solution of the murders. *The Clocks.*

GRETA "Haughty blond" secretary to Sir Joseph Hoggin, she gave Poirot a "disdainful glance in passing" when he came to interview Sir Joseph about the dognapping. On entering Sir Joseph's office, just vacated by Greta, Poirot noticed lipstick all over Sir Joseph's chin. Greta was disappointed in her plans to become the second Lady Hoggin. "The Nemean Lion" from *The Labours of Hercules.*

GREY, DETECTIVE SERGEANT A detective with the Berkshire police, he assisted Poirot in the denouement of Mrs.

Charles Oldfield's murderer. He brought in the compact case found in Jean Moncrieffe's bureau and tasted the contents, commenting that it certainly wasn't face powder. Poirot informed him that "white arsenic does not taste." "The Lernean Hydra" from *The Labours of Hercules.*

GREY, MRS. *See* **GRÜNBERG, ANITA.**

GREY, JANE Quick-witted hairdresser at Monsieur Antoine's in London, she was returning from a holiday made possible by Irish Sweepstakes winnings and was on board the *Prometheus* when Madame Giselle was killed. She fell in love with Norman Gale in a casino on vacation, but received the attentions of Jean Dupont on the flight. She aided Poirot in his investigation by assuming the guise of a secretary to the Duponts. *Death in the Clouds.*

GREY, KATHERINE The cousin of Lady Rosalie Tamplin, she took the post of companion to Miss Amelia Viner, an old lady dying of cancer. "Katherine Grey was born with the power of managing old ladies, dogs and small boys, and she did it without any apparent sense of strain. At twenty-three she had been a quiet girl with beautiful eyes. At thirty-three she was a quiet woman with those same grey eyes, shining steadily out on the world with a kind of happy serenity that nothing could shake." *The Mystery of the Blue Train.*

GREY, THORA For over two years Miss Grey had been Sir Carmichael Clarke's secretary. Although Sir Clarke admitted only to feeling fatherly toward her, he was planning to ask her to marry him on the death of his ailing wife. She was dismissed by Lady Charlotte Clarke after Sir Clarke was murdered. Her beauty intoxicated Hastings: "She had the almost colourless ash hair—light grey eyes—and transparent glowing pallor that one finds amongst Norwegians and Swedes. She looked to be about twenty-seven and seemed to be as efficient as she was decorative." Poirot responded by humming: "Some of the time I love a brunette, some of the time I love a blond (who comes from Eden by way of Sweden)." *The A.B.C. Murders.*

GREY, THYRZA Residing at the Pale Horse, in the village of Much Deeping, she was "very occult. . . . Goes in for spiritualism and trances, and magic. Not quite black masses, but that sort of thing." When Rhoda Despard remarked that there was "something really awe-inspiring about Thyrza. . . . You feel she knows just what you're thinking. She doesn't talk about having second sight—but everyone says that she has got it." Mark Easterbrook's meeting with Thyrza Grey led him to investigate The Pale Horse mystery. *The Pale Horse.*

GRIFFITH, MISS The efficient head typist with Consolidated Investments Trust for sixteen years, she sailed "through the typist's room without deigning to give anyone a word or glance. The typists might have been so many blackbeetles." She called in Sir Edwin Sandeman of Harley Street when Rex Fortescue was taken with his fatal fit. A snob and a romantic, she was quite besotted with Lancelot Fortescue. *A Pocket Full of Rye.*

GRIFFITH, AIMÉE Sister of Owen Griffith, the village doctor, she had "all the positive assurance her brother lacked." She had wanted to be a doctor but her parents refused to pay the fees. "A handsome woman in a masculine weatherbeaten way with a deep voice . . . cheery, mannish and successful," she possessed a very aggressive personality, a hearty and overwhelming manner, a jolly laugh and an ability to put people's backs up. She was in love with and neurotically jealous of Richard Symmington. *The Moving Finger.*

GRIFFITH, DR. OWEN Brother of Aimée, this melancholy doctor at Lymstock, "was dark, ungainly, with awkward ways of moving and deft, very gentle hands. He

had a jerky way of talking and was rather shy." He fell in love with Joanna Burton and ultimately married her. *The Moving Finger.*

GROSJEAN, MONSIEUR LE PRESIDENT The president of France, he called an historic meeting of powerful personages to discuss the worldwide student problem. "He was a worried man doing his best to slide over things with facility and a charm of manner that had often helped him in the past." *Passenger to Frankfurt.*

GROSVENOR, IRENE Personal secretary to Rex Fortescue, she was "just a necessary part of the office decor—which was all very luxurious and very expensive . . . an incredibly glamorous blond. She wore an expensively cut little black suit and her shapely legs were encased in the very best and most expensive black market nylons." When she discovered Mr. Fortescue in the midst of his fatal fit, she went all to pieces and lost her Mayfair accent. *A Pocket Full of Rye.*

GRÜNBERG, ANITA AKA Nadina; Mrs. Grey, Mrs. de Castina. The wife of L.B. Carton and a confederate of the man called the "Colonel," Anita Grünberg was described by Harry Rayburn as "an actress. Quite young and beautiful. She was South African born, but her mother was a Hungarian, I believe. There was some sort of mystery about her . . . Delilah—that's what she should have been called." Anita first appeared under the name Nadina, "the Russian dancer who had taken Paris by storm." She booked cabin 71 on the *Kilmorden Castle* under the name of Mrs. Grey. Under the name of Mrs. de Castina she viewed the Mill House in Marlow, a house owned by Sir Eustace Pedler, where she was later found dead. *The Man in the Brown Suit.*

GUDGEON, MR. The grey-headed butler at The Hollow, he was fiercely loyal to Lady Angkatell and had a keen sense of etiquette between servant and master.

He habitually cleaned up after Lady Angkatell, replacing the kettles she burned out and removing a live lobster she left in the card-tray in the hall. *The Hollow.*

GULBRANDSEN, CHRISTIAN The son of Eric Gulbrandsen, half-brother of Mildred Strete and the step-son of Carrie Louise Serrocold, he was one of the trustees of the Gulbrandsen Institute. He was killed at Stoneygates. *They Do It with Mirrors.*

GUSTAVE Name given to the "skillful and adroit" waiter at the Rochers Neige hotel in Switzerland. "He darted here and there, advising on the menu, whipping out his wine list." He deplored the fact that the high altitude and low boiling point of water made it impossible to produce a good cup of coffee. He claimed to be Inspector Drouet at the trial of the killer Marrascaud. "The Erymanthian Boar" from *The Labours of Hercules.*

GUTEMAN, ELLIE *See* **ROGERS, ELLIE.**

GUTHRIE, ALEXANDER Elderly art critic and friend of Cora Abernethie Lansquenet's, he usually visited her once a year to evaluate her acquisitions. He had a very low opinion of most of the "daubs" she purchased. Even though he attended her funeral and the inquest, melancholia did not come naturally to him, "his own inclination being to beam." *After the Funeral.*

HALE, CAPTAIN BINGO He lived with Sir Arthur and Lady Vere Merivale and ultimately became Lady Vere's lover. As "the gentleman dressed in newspaper" from *Alice in Wonderland* at the Three Arts Ball, he had a midnight tryst with Lady Vere at the Ace of Spades but was given a note purportedly from Lady Vere warning him away from the meeting. She was murdered that night and her last words were "Bingo did it." "Finessing the King" and "The Gentleman Dressed in Newspaper" from *Partners in Crime.*

HALL, DR. Operator of a private nursing home in Bournemouth, he treated Jane Finn, who had been brought in as "Janet Vandemeyer," shortly after the sinking of the *Lusitania.* She suffered loss of memory and was unable to speak in her own language. *The Secret Adversary.*

HALLIDAY, MR. The husband of Mrs. Halliday, he was a British scientist experimenting with the concentration of wireless energy. While travelling to Paris to meet with Madame Olivier, he vanished, but was eventually found by Poirot. *The Big Four.*

HALLIDAY, MR. An American millionaire, Halliday was the father of Flossie Carrington and was described by Hastings as "a large, stout man, with piercing eyes and an aggressive chin." "The Plymouth Express" from *The Under Dog.*

HALLIDAY, MRS. The wife of Mr. Halliday, she was "a tall, fair woman, nervous and eager in manner" who resided at Chetwynd Lodge near the village of Cobham in Surrey. *The Big Four.*

HALLIDAY, ARTHUR He had been after Joyce Lambert to marry him for a long time, and even though she hated him, he enjoyed the chase. She finally did agree to marry him, but after the death of her dog, she broke the engagement. "Next to a Dog" from *The Golden Ball.*

HALLIDAY, HELEN SPENLOVE KENNEDY The half-sister of Dr. James Kennedy, the second wife of Major Kelvin Halliday, and the step-mother of Gwenda Reed, she was a woman whom every man found captivating and few women could abide. When she disappeared, her husband committed suicide in an insane asylum, convinced that he had murdered her for her infidelities. Gwenda Reed bought St. Catherine's, the house where she had lived as a small child with her father and step-mother, and to Miss Marple, she recounted a flashback concerning vivid psychic impressions of having seen Helen. *Sleeping Murder.*

HALLIDAY, MAJOR KELVIN JAMES The widower of Megan Danby Halliday, father of Gwenda Halliday and the husband of Helen Spenlove Kennedy Halliday, he was utterly convinced that he had murdered his second wife. He sent his young daughter Gwenda off to live with Megan's family in New Zealand, committed himself into Saltmarsh House insane asylum and died by his own hand two years later. His psychiatrist, Dr. Penrose, remembered him as "a gentle, kindly and well-controlled individual." *Sleeping Murder.*

HAMER, SILAS He was a "complacent man whose millions were a matter of public knowledge." One evening, while returning from a dinner with Dick Borrow, he was attracted by the sound of a flute, which had a hypnotic effect: it made him feel free, unshackled by the chains of materialism. Eventually Hamer gave all of his money to Dick Borrow's East End Mission so that he could pursue life as a free spirit. On the very first day of his new life, he was killed while saving a boy who had fallen on the subway tracks. "The Call of Wings" from *The Golden Ball.*

HAMILTON CLIPP, MRS. The apparent wife of George Hamilton Clipp, Mrs. Hamilton Clipp was "a short bird-like sharp-eyed little woman" who worked as an operative for Edward Goring. Under the pretense of having a broken arm, she hired Victoria Jones as a companion-escort to accompany her on her trip to Baghdad. Mrs. Hamilton Clipp "had spent a large portion of her life jumping from boats into aeroplanes and from aeroplanes into trains with brief intervals at expensive hotels in between." *They Came to Baghdad.*

HAMILTON CLIPP, GEORGE "An immensely tall and very thin grey-haired American of kindly aspect and slow deliberate speech," he worked for Edward Goring's subversive network. Posing as the husband of Mrs. Clipp, he was approached by Victoria Jones who applied for the position of companion-escort to Mrs. Clipp on their trip to Baghdad. *They Came to Baghdad.*

HAMMOND, MR. Roger Ackroyd's solicitor, he was, according to James Sheppard, "a small dried-up little man, with an aggressive chin and sharp grey eyes, and 'lawyer' written all over him." *The Murder of Roger Ackroyd.*

HARDCASTLE, DETECTIVE INSPECTOR Official in charge of the murder case, he was "a tall, poker-faced man with expressive eyebrows, godlike" who always saw "that what he had put into motion was being done, and done properly." He was an old friend of Colin Lamb's, and had an amazing memory for faces. *The Clocks.*

HARDCASTLE, MRS. Replacing Miss Grosvenor, she was "a hard-faced woman of middle age" with a forbidding manner. Lance Fortescue found her a "Gorgon," and referred to her as "Horseface Hetty." *A Pocket Full of Rye.*

HARDCASTLE, CLAUDIA The half-sister of Rudolf Santonix, the ex-wife of Stanford Lloyd and a friend to Major Phillpot and Ellie Rogers, she lived near Gipsy's Acre. This fine horsewoman was allergic to animals, which somewhat hampered her riding activities, but she disclosed that "Camels do it to me worse than horses." Major Phillpot said she was "anti-man." Her death occurred shortly after Ellie Rogers'. *Endless Night.*

HARDCASTLE, MIDGE Young first cousin of Lady Lucy Angkatell, she was a poor relation of the family and was forced to take a job at Madame Alfredge's dreadful dress shop. She was hopelessly in love with Edward Angkatell, and stopped him from committing suicide after she broke off their engagement. They were eventually reconciled. *The Hollow.*

HARDEN, GRETE One of Mr. Dakin's operatives, Grete Harden was sent by Dakin to infiltrate Edward Goring's group of subversives. She was supposed to impersonate Anna Scheele, but the Goring group captured her and replaced her with Victoria Jones. *They Came to Baghdad.*

HARDING, CAROL *See* DAVIS, CAROL.

HARDMAN, CYRUS BETHMAN An American, he was an agent for the McNeil Detective Agency of New York who disguised himself as a travelling typewriter ribbon salesman. To Poirot, he was "a common-looking man with terrible clothes. He chews the gum, which I believe is not done in good circles." He was in love with Susanne Michel. He told Poirot that Samuel Edward Ratchett hired him as a bodyguard. Poirot thought he epitomized "the true Western spirit of hustle." *Murder on the Orient Express.*

HARDMAN, MARCUS "A small man, delicately plump, with exquisitely manicured hands and a plaintive tenor voice," he had a hobby of collecting people and things. This "elderly social butterfly" hired Poirot to locate a priceless emerald necklace, which was thought to have once belonged to Catherine de Medici. It was stolen the night he hosted a soirée and Hardman wished to avoid publicity in the matter. "The Double Clue" from *Double Sin.*

HARDT, ELSA A German spy who once posed as a concert singer while on assignment in Washington, D.C., Miss Hardt received some stolen naval plans and, after keeping a low profile for a while, planned to sell them to the highest bidder. She had been implicated in a murder

with her friend Luigi Valdarno. "The Adventure of the Cheap Flat" from *Poirot Investigates.*

HARFIELD, MARY ANNE The wife of Samuel Harfield and a distant cousin of Jane Harfield through marriage, she was described by Dr. Arthur Harrison as "a perfectly poisonous person." Although she had nothing to do with Jane Harfield, she became venomously upset when she discovered that Katherine Grey had inherited Jane's fortune, and attempted to have Katherine disqualified as heiress. *The Mystery of the Blue Train.*

HARGRAVES, LAURA *See* UPWARD, LAURA.

HARGREAVES, MRS. The wife of Mr. Hargreaves the church organist, she proffered a large green plastic pail for the apple-dunking at the Hallowe'en party. "In the end it was decided that a galvanized bucket was preferable to the more meretricious charms of a plastic pail which overturned rather too readily." If Mrs. Hargreaves had had her way, the likelihood that the plastic pail could have withstood Joyce Reynold's death throes without tipping over was remote, and the girl may not have drowned. *Hallowe'en Party.*

HARGREAVES, LOIS The good friend of Mary Chilcott and niece of the late Lady Radclyffe, she lived at Thurnley Grange after her aunt disinherited Dennis Radclyffe, Lois' cousin and Lady Radclyffe's son. Lois sought Tuppence and Tommy Beresford's aid after she was almost killed by eating poisoned chocolates. She was eventually murdered by Ricin poisoning in fig paste sandwiches. "The House of Lurking Death" from *Partners in Crime.*

HARKER, CAPTAIN Friend of the Duke of Blairgowrie's, Harker was to have captured Tuppence Beresford after the Duke had taken Tommy, but these plans were foiled by Albert's vigilance. "Blindman's Buff" from *Partners in Crime*.

HARMON, DIANA (BUNCH) The wife of the Reverend Julian Harmon and Jane Marple's favourite godchild who was "christened by her optimistic parents Diana, Mrs. Harmon had become Bunch at an early age for somewhat obvious reasons and the name had stuck to her ever since." Miss Marple was staying with her in Chipping Cleghorn when Rudy Scherz was murdered at Little Paddocks, and together with her godmother she later unravelled the mystery surrounding Walter St. John, who had died in her husband's church. *A Murder is Announced;* "Sanctuary" from *Double Sin.*

HARMON, REVEREND JULIAN The husband of Bunch Harmon, he was described by Mr. Butt, the village atheist: "Our vicar's a highly educated gentleman—Oxford, not Milchester, and he gives us the full benefit of his education. All about the Romans and the Greeks he knows, and the Babylonians and the Assyrians, too. And even the vicarage cat Tiglath Pileser is called after an Assyrian king!" *A Murder is Announced;* "Sanctuary" from *Double Sin.*

HARPER, MR. The senior Mr. Bleibner's American secretary and a member of the Men-her-Ra expedition, Mr. Harper was "a pleasant lean young man wearing the national insignia of horn-rimmed spectacles." "The Adventure of the Egyptian Tomb" from *Poirot Investigates.*

HARPER, SUPERINTENDENT A member of the Glenshire Police, he worked with Colonel Melchett and Inspector Slack on the Ruby Keene case. "Never do too much at once was Superintendent Harper's rule. Bare routine inquiry for the first time. That left the persons you were interviewing relieved, and predisposed them to be more unguarded in the next interview you had with them." *The Body in the Library.*

HARRIS, MYRNA "A pretty girl with a glorious head of red hair and a pert nose," Miss Harris was a waitress at The Grill in the Royal Spa Hotel. She had dated the victim, Rudi Scherz, and gave Inspector Craddock information that suggested Scherz's death was not suicide but murder. *A Murder is Announced.*

HARRISON, MRS. "Voluble" proprietress of Glengowrie Court where Mabelle Sainsbury Seale lodged, she was a pleasant woman who was sincerely concerned about her boarder. She helped Poirot and Inspector Japp examine Mabelle's rooms. *One, Two, Buckle My Shoe.*

HARRISON, NURSE A nurse in the employ of Dr. Oldfield at the time of Mrs. Oldfield's death, she had fallen in love with her employer and thought that he would ask her to marry him after his wife died. Disappointed that he didn't, she began to spread rumours of foul play which implicated Dr. Oldfield and Jean Moncrieff in Mrs. Oldfield's death. "The Lernean Hydra" from *The Labours of Hercules.*

HARRISON, DR. ARTHUR The husband of Polly Harrison, father of Johnnie Harrison, he was Jane Harfield's doctor in St. Mary Mead. Harrison assured Katherine Grey of Jane Harfield's soundness of mind, and cautioned her against taking Mary Anne Harfield's attempts to disqualify her inheritance seriously. *The Mystery of the Blue Train.*

HARRISON, JOHN Poirot met Harrison along with Claude Langton at a dinner party. Engaged to Molly Deane, Harrison recently learned that he had only a few months to live and that Molly was falling in love with her former fiancé, Claude Langton. "Wasps' Nest" from *Double Sin.*

HARRY The fiancé of Lily Price, he failed to help Lily when she almost tumbled from a first floor window. The incident was witnessed by Miss Marple. *The Mirror Crack'd from Side to Side.*

HARTE, MISS Rustling and gracious manageress of the Balaclava Private Hotel, she exuded "a strong smell of Devonshire violets." Only with difficulty did Poirot escape from being rented a room. "The Nemean Lion" from *The Labours of Hercules.*

HARTER, MARY Patrick Harter's elderly widow for twenty-five years, she was the aunt of Miriam Harter and Charles Ridgeway. She did not care for the intrusion of modernity into her life, nor did she like to have strange men in her house: "She suspected them one and all of having designs on her old silver." However, she thought her nephew was a charming acquisition, and changed her will in his favour after he proved more gracious than her niece, Miriam Harter. Three months after obtaining a new radio, Mrs. Harter began to hear the voice of her dead husband over the set which she took to be a premonition of her own death. "Where There's a Will" from *Witness for the Prosecution.*

HARTER, PATRICK *See* **RIDGEWAY, CHARLES.**

HARTIGAN, TOM Lily Marbury's young man, he examined the fact that Alexander Bonaparte Cust was always at the same place whenever the murders occurred. He went to see Inspector Crome, whom he thought to be a bit "la-di-da" and set the police on Cust's trail. *The A.B.C. Murders.*

HARTINGTON, JACK Uncle George's nephew, he was a golf fanatic who began to hear a faint but distinct voice crying "Murder—help! Murder" at 7:25 A.M. each morning at the Stourton Heath links. Jack traced the sound to Heather Cottage, where the inhabitant, Mademoiselle Marchaud, had heard a voice in a dream in which a blue jar also figured. "The Blue Jar" from *Witness for the Prosecution.*

HARTNELL, AMANDA Miss Marple's next-door neighbour in St. Mary Mead, Miss Hartnell was an old village pussy who was "weather-beaten and jolly and much dreaded by the poor." She often embellished her stories, and it was difficult for her listeners to know "where narrative ends and interpretation begins." *Murder at the Vicarage; The Body in the Library;* "Tape Measure Murder" and "The Case of the Perfect Maid" from *Three Blind Mice and Other Stories.*

HARVEY, JIM A mechanic at Pipewell's Garage in Wychwood, he had been engaged to Amy Gibbs. They had argued before her alleged suicide. *Murder is Easy.*

HARWELL, ELEANOR *See* **LE COUTEAU, ELEANOR.**

HARWELL, CAPTAIN RICHARD *See* **MATHIAS, JOHN.**

HASSAN Sir John Willard's devoted native servant, he assisted Poirot in trapping the murderer of his employer. "The Adventure of the Egyptian Tomb" from *Poirot Investigates.*

HASTINGS, CAPTAIN ARTHUR O.B.E. The husband of Dulcie Duveen Hastings and the father of Grace, Judith and two sons, and the brother of at least two unnamed sisters, Captain Arthur Hastings was Poirot's Watson—his long and trusted friend, his confederate, his confidant and the avid chronicler of a number of the little Belgian's greatest cases. By July of 1916, he had recently been sent home from the Front in World War I and, after spending some months in convalescence; he ran into his childhood friend John Cavendish, who invited him to Styles Court. There he encountered Hercule Poirot, whom he had met before the war while working for Lloyd's of London, when Poirot was a private inquiry agent in Europe. By September, 1916, Hastings had been posted to a "half-hearted Army job" recruiting at the War Office in London and later became private secretary to a Member of Parliament, after helping to rescue Prime Minister David Mac-Adam (in "The Kidnapped Prime Minister" from *Poirot Investigates*). In London, Hastings and Poirot took rooms together at 14 Farraway Street where Poirot resumed his career as a private inquiry agent and together they worked on many cases. During *Murder on the Links,* Hastings met his Cinderella—Dulcie Duveen (a slight inconsistency occurs in *Peril at End House,* where Hastings refers to Dulcie by her sister's name, Bella). Hastings married Dulcie and together they went to the Argentine to manage a ranch for Jack Renauld. Hastings returned many times to aid his old friend, and during Poirot's last case in *Curtain,* they resided at Styles Court, now a guest house, where the Poirot saga began.

Poirot said that Hastings was "occasionally of an imbecility to make one afraid," and that he had "a lamentable absence of order and method." Nevertheless, Poirot respected Hastings, who, he maintained, "has a knack of stumbling over the truth unawares—without noticing it himself." Poirot once said to him: "As in a mirror I see reflected in your mind exactly what the criminal wishes me to believe. That is terrifically helpful and suggestive." Hastings was quite easily led astray by women, and imagined himself to be in love with almost every auburn-haired lady he saw. Poirot said that he had the blood of a Turk, and ought to establish a harem.

Hastings appeared in eight novels and twenty-one short stories in the Christie canon. (*See* Bibliography.)

HASTINGS, DULCIE DUVEEN AKA Cinderella; Cinders. The wife of Captain Arthur Hastings and the mother of four children, she was the twin sister of Bella Duveen and the other half of the vaudeville act, The Dulcibella Kids. She was

American-born, but had spent most of her life in England. Hastings met her in 1921, when both were involved in the Renauld murder case; she introduced herself to the stuffy Hastings as Cinderella. At the conclusion of the case, Hastings and Dulcie married and moved to the Argentine, marking the virtual disappearance of Hastings, with a few notable exceptions, from the Poirot saga. *Murder on the Links.*

HASTINGS, JUDITH Daughter of Cinders (*See* **DUVEEN, DULCIE**) and Arthur Hastings, she was the child whom Hastings "had always loved best," although he "never for one moment understood her." She earned her B.Sc. and worked as research assistant for Dr. Franklin, and married him after his wife died. They moved to Africa to continue their research on obscure tropical diseases. *Curtain.*

HAUTET, MONSIEUR The Examining Magistrate in the Renauld case, he was described by Poirot: "A famous old imbecile, that one! Of a stupidity to make pity." *Murder on the Links.*

HAVERING, ROGER The second son of the Fifth Baron Windsor and the husband of Zoe Havering, he received a sizeable inheritance from his uncle, Harrington Pace. Shortly afterward, he and his wife were killed in an aeroplane crash. "The Mystery of Hunter's Lodge" from *Poirot Investigates.*

HAVERING, ZOE AKA Zoe, Carrisbrook. The wife of Roger Havering and the fourth daughter of William Crabb, she was once an actress at the Frivolity where her stage name had been Zoe Carrisbrook. "A very handsome young woman," she died with her husband in the crash of the *Air Mail* flight to Paris. "The Mystery of Hunter's Lodge" from *Poirot Investigates.*

HAWKER, DR. Dr. Hawker was a bachelor who "lived in a gloomy old house a few streets away" from the residence that Poirot and Hastings occupied temporarily. It was "the genial doctor's habit to drop in sometimes of an evening and have a chat with Poirot, of whose genius he was an ardent admirer." "The Adventure of the Italian Nobleman" from *Poirot Investigates.*

HAWKER, ANTHONY The unpleasant boyfriend of Patience Grace, shot by her when she was in a drug-induced frenzy, he was a "nasty-looking fellow with his eyes too close together." "The Horses of Diomedes" from *The Labours of Hercules.*

HAWES, MR. The new curate in St. Mary Mead, he held High Church views and fasted on Fridays. Leonard Clement, the vicar in St. Mary Mead, was not very fond of him, and it was eventually discovered that Mr. Hawes embezzled church funds. He suffered from narcolepsy or "sleeping sickness." *Murder at the Vicarage.*

HAWKINS, EDWARD *See* **JONES, ROBERT.**

HAWORTH, ALISTAIR The maternal wife of Maurice Haworth, she was the daughter of a celebrated psychic medium. Mr. Macfarlane said: "Perfect unquestionable beauty is rare, and perfect unquestionable beauty was what Alistair Haworth possessed." She had second sight, which she had inherited from her mother, and had warned Dickie Carpenter about returning to the house of Arthur Lawes too soon. When Macfarlane asked if he might visit her again, she replied: "I don't know. I—I fancied that we shouldn't meet again—that's all. . . . Goodbye." The next day she was dead. "The Gipsy" from *The Golden Ball.*

HAY, SERGEANT Assistant to Inspector Neele, he was industrious and thorough,

but not very imaginative. Present at Rex Fortescue's death, he discovered the "cereal" in the jacket of the corpse. On the telephone, heavy breathing was "an inevitable prelude to Sergeant Hay's conversation." *A Pocket Full of Rye.*

HAYDOCK, CAPTAIN An old crony of Inspector Evans', he tried to disuade his friend from investigating the Anthony murder case. He spoke to the woman at the village fête whom Inspector Evans recognized as Mrs. Anthony. "Accident" from *Witness for the Prosecution.*

HAYDOCK, COMMANDER AKA "N" and Dr. Binion, Haydock was a "stout fellow." As Haydock, he was a well-known patriotic inhabitant of Smugglers Rest, which was situated on a clifftop and had previously been the residence of a spy. As "N," Haydock was identified by British Intelligence as one of the two leaders of the Fifth Column; as Dr. Binion, he borrowed his dentist's name and surgery to interrogate Mrs. Blenkensop (alias Tuppence Beresford). *N or M?*

HAYDOCK, DR. The Police Surgeon in St. Mary Mead, Dr. Haydock was Miss Marple's physician and next-door neighbour. Haydock felt that crime might be a result of physical malfunction: "One should no more hang murderers than people suffering from tuberculosis." He took on the young Dr. Sandford as a partner when he went into semi-retirement. *Murder at the Vicarage;* "Death by Drowning" from *The Thirteen Problems; The Body in the Library;* "The Case of the Caretaker" from *Three Blind Mice and Other Stories; The Mirror Crack'd from Side to Side; Sleeping Murder.*

HAYDON, ELLIOT The cousin of Sir Richard Haydon, Elliot Haydon was dressed as a brigand chief the night of the fancy dress party when he was found stabbed in the shoulder near the altar of Astarte. Haydon later died in an expedition to the South Pole. "The Idol House of Astarte" from *The Thirteen Problems.*

HAYDON, SIR RICHARD The cousin of Elliott Haydon, he was in love with Diana Ashley and was an old college friend of Dr. Pendar's. He tripped and fell during Diana Ashley's frightening performance as Astarte and was stabbed through the heart with a long thin knife. "The Idol House of Astarte" from *The Thirteen Problems*.

HAYES, SERGEANT He investigated the death of Walter St. John, the man Bunch Harmon found dying in her husband's church and accepted Pam Eccles' statement that the dead man was her brother, William Sandbourne. "Sanctuary" from *Double Sin*.

HAYMES, PHILLIPA (PIP) The widow of Captain Haymes, she was the daughter of Sonia Stamfordis, sister of Emma Stamfordis and a niece to Randall Goedler. "The sort of girl . . . who would keep a secret well," Pip worked for Mrs. Lucas as an assistant gardener at Dayas Hall in Chipping Cleghorn, and boarded at Letitia Blacklock's Little Paddocks. With her sister Emma Stamfordis, she stood to inherit Goedler's fortune if Letitia Blacklock died before Belle Goedler (*see* **GOEDLER, RANDALL**). *A Murder is Announced*.

HAYWARD, SIR ARTHUR The father of Charles Hayward, who called him "The Old Man," he was an Assistant Commissioner of Scotland Yard. When he allowed his cigar to go out, it was a sign to his son just how upset the "Old Man" was over the Leonides case. Charles Hayward and his father had a special relationship: "Our meeting after five years of war would have disappointed a Frenchman. Actually all the emotion of reunion was there all right." Like his fiancée Sophia Leonides, Charles was confident that Sir Arthur knew exactly what went on in his son's mind. *Crooked House*.

HAYWARD, CHARLES He was the son of Sir Arthur Hayward, and had worked for the Special Branch. Charles met Sophia Leonides while they were both employed in the Diplomatic Service and he was determined to marry her when the war was over. Sophia Leonides liked his "funny way of doing things" while Sir Arthur stated that Charles didn't lose his head easily. *Crooked House*.

HAZY, LADY SELINA A guest at Bertram's Hotel, she had come from Leichestershire to consult doctors about her arthritis and teeth. The Harley Street specialists, she thought, had done her some good: "Took me by the neck when I wasn't looking and wrung it like a chicken." Lady Selina "regarded writers, artists and musicians as species of clever performing animals." A combination of short-sightedness and optimism caused her to continually mistake strangers for friends. *At Bertram's Hotel*.

HEARN, DETECTIVE INSPECTOR The English Inspector who co-operated with what Japp called the "Frenchies" in the disappearance of Winnie King, he was consulted by Poirot. "The Girdle of Hippolyta" from *The Labours of Hercules*.

HEATH, DR. The doctor summoned by Alice Bennet to examine the body of Carlotta Adams, he was "a fussy elderly man somewhat vague in manner" according to Hastings. "He knew Poirot by repute and expressed a lively pleasure at meeting him in the flesh." *Lord Edgware Dies*.

HEAVYWEATHER, SIR ERNEST The renowned K.C. engaged to defend John Cavendish on the charge of wilful murder of his step-mother Emily Agnes Inglethorp, he was particularly pompous and self-satisfied. Heavyweather, remarked Hastings, was "famous all over England for the unscrupulous manner in which he bullied witnesses." *The Mysterious Affair at Styles*.

HEILGER, ROMAINE See **VOLE, ROMAINE**.

HELIER, JANE AKA Jane Helman. A "beautiful and popular actress," Jane Helier was "a little bit dense—constantly making all sorts of inane comments." "The Affair at the Bungalow" from *The Thirteen Problems;* "Strange Jest" from *Three Blind Mice and Other Stories.*

HELLIN, MARIE Foul-tempered lady's maid to Katrina Samoushenka, she was dismissed from her mistress's employ under mysterious circumstances. A resident at the boarding house where Marie once lived recalled: "wicked temper she had—real Eyetalian—her black eyes snapping and looking as if she'd like to put a knife in you." Poirot tracked her down and realized that she was definitely not the missing maid that Ted Williamson loved. "The Arcadian Deer" from *The Labours of Hercules.*

HELMAN, JANE *See* **HELIER, JANE.**

HEMMING, MRS. Neighbouring the house where the first murder was discovered, Mrs. Hemming kept twelve cats and claimed that they understood every word she said to them. "Facing them was a lady in a pale moss-green, rather rubbed, velvet tea gown. Her hair, in flaxen grey wisps, was twirled elaborately in a kind of coiffure of some thirty years back. Round her neck she was wearing a necklet of orange fur" which turned out to be Sunbeam the cat. *The Clocks.*

HEMMINGWAY, GERALD AKA Stephens, Hemmingway was described by Poirot as "a very promising young actor." As Stephens the window cleaner, he claimed to have seen Dr. Roberts administering some medicine to Mrs. Lorrimer. *Cards on the Table.*

HENDEN Butler to the Stubbs family at Nasse House, he "looked as though blackmailing letters would be well within his scope." He was a virtuoso of the dinner gong: "The butler, having finished a most artistic performance, crescendo, forte, diminuendo, rallentando, was just re-placing the gong stick on its hook. His dark melancholy face showed pleasure." *Dead Man's Folly.*

HENDERSON, DR. First witness for the prosecution in the libel case against the *X-Ray News,* Dr. Henderson, the Bishop of Northumbria, testified that during the time Dagmar Ferrier was supposed to be with the Argentine gigolo Ramon, she was staying with him and his wife. "The Augean Stables" from *The Labours of Hercules.*

HENDERSON, DIEDRE Daughter of Mrs. Weatherby and step-daughter of Mr. Weatherby, she inherited a great deal of money from an aunt and consequently controlled the purse-strings in the household. Poirot reflected that "Diedre Henderson seemed a rather simple young woman—simple to the point of gaucheness." He decided to match her up with James Bentley. *Mrs. McGinty's Dead.*

HENDERSON, ELLIE A spinster, she fell in love with Colonel Clapperton on a voyage to Egypt. She was "a woman of forty-five who was content to look her age." Poirot thought her adept at handling the crusty General Forbes, whom she had pumped for information about the Colonel. She also had a love of scandal—"the more ill-natured, the better!" "Problem at Sea" from *The Regatta Mystery.*

HENET Imhotep's housekeeper, Henet "was one of those people whose fate it is to be devoted to others and have no one devoted to them." Imhotep was the only one who was fond of her, and she obeyed his word completely. She hated Esa and Renisenb. Henet worshipped the god Amun, a local deity whom she thought would one day be the greatest god in Egypt. Her end came when she was mummified alive. *Death Comes as the End.*

HENGRAVE, MRS. The widow of Major Hengrave and owner of Hillside House, formerly St. Catherine's, "Mrs. Hengrave was an interloper—a woman who did up rooms in mustard-cum-biscuit colour and liked a frieze of wisteria in her drawing room." *Sleeping Murder.*

HENRY The maitre d'hotel at Bertram's, Henry was "a large and magnificent figure, a ripe fifty, avuncular, sympathetic and with the courtly manners of that long vanished species, the perfect butler." He had the ability to appear magically when a client was in need, "like some travesty of Ariel who could materialize and vanish at will." *At Bertram's Hotel.*

HENSLEY, MR. One of the twelve travellers journeying from Damascus to Baghdad, he was the best friend of Captain Smethurst but nonetheless a suspect in murder because he sat behind Smethurst during the trip. "A quiet man . . . he belonged to the public works department of Baghdad." He was further incriminated by the presence of sand in his pocket, when it appeared as though Smethurst had been bludgeoned with a sandbag. "The Gate of Baghdad" from *Parker Pyne Investigates.*

HERMANSTEIN, IKEY See **ISAAC-STEIN, HERMAN.**

HERSHEIMMER, JULIUS P. The wealthy American cousin of Jane Finn offered one million pounds to Sir James Peel Edgerton to locate Miss Finn, who had disappeared along with her side of the family years before. He was very attached to his gun, "Little Willie," which he felt could always be trusted to save the day. Julius' favourite expression was "Put me wise." He asked Tuppence to marry him at one point, but she realized his lack of sincerity. *The Secret Adversary.*

HETHERINGTON, JANET One of Jessop's agents, she worked the circuit between Spain and Morocco and was assigned to tail Hilary Craven. She "could not have been mistaken for anything but travelling English . . . knitting one of those melancholy shapeless-looking garments that English ladies of middle age always seem to be knitting." At the Hotel St. Louis in Fez, Morocco, she "talked only to the English and Americans of what she considered a certain social standing," and reacted to the arrival of a Swedish magnate and a blond film star: " 'Not married, I understand,' she breathed, disguising her pleasure with a correct disapproval. 'One sees so much of that sort of thing abroad'." *Destination Unknown.*

HIGGINS, BILL John Newman's diver engaged in the search for the gold cargo of the sunken Spanish galleon *Juan Fernandez,* he was "a wooden-faced individual, extremely taciturn, and his contributions to . . . conversation were mostly monosyllabic." "Ingots of Gold" from *The Thirteen Problems.*

HIGGINS, MARY See **SKINNER, EMILY.**

HIGGS, WILLIAM The small, rat-like Cockney dog-trainer who worked with the police, he induced the guard dog Cerberus of the lounge Hell to follow him to police headquarters where he could be examined. When Cerberus' owner, the Countess Vera Rossakoff, wanted to know how he did it, he replied: " 'Ardly like to say afore a lady. But there's things no dogs won't resist. Follow me anywhere a dog will if I want 'im to. Of course you understand it won't work the same with bitches—no, that's different, that is.' " "The Capture of Cerberus" from *The Labours of Hercules.*

HIGLEY, MILLY A waitress at the Ginger Cat who worked with Elizabeth Barnard, she was a buxom and rather foolish girl, and considered to be quite vulgar by Elizabeth. Poirot, however, complimented her ankles, and ogled her in such a way that Hastings was "startled and almost shocked." *The A.B.C. Murders.*

HILL, FLORENCE The faithful Florence, once maidservant to Miss Marple, resided in Brackhampton where she took in respectable lodgers. She looked after Miss Marple while Lucy Eyelesbarrow worked at Rutherford Hall. "A tall, grim-looking woman, dressed in black with a large knob of iron-grey hair," she had a nice smile and was very protective of her old mistress. *4.50 from Paddington.*

HILL, MARY A chambermaid at the Crown Hotel, she was on duty when Mrs. Rhodes was murdered. She was the only person Mr. Rhodes saw before he discovered his wife's corpse that night, but he did not believe she had committed the crime. "Miss Marple Tells a Story" from *The Regatta Mystery.*

HILLINGDON, COLONEL EDWARD Husband to Evelyn Hillingdon, Hillingdon was a botanist, and a colleague and friend of the Dysons', with whom he and his wife travelled to the West Indies annually. Although his marriage seemed happy, he and Evelyn had actually barely spoken to one another for three years. He had recently broken off an affair with Lucky Dyson. Since then, she had tormented him with his part in her plot to become the second Mrs. Dyson. This demanded that the first Mrs. Dyson, Gail, be somehow removed. *A Caribbean Mystery.*

HILLINGDON, EVELYN Wife of Colonel Edward Hillingdon and mother of their two school-age boys, with her husband she was a botanist and journeyed each year with their colleagues the Dysons to St. Honore. Even though her husband's affair with Lucky Dyson had embittered her, when Edward showed a sincere wish to be rid of Lucky and old associations she was eager to make a clean start. *A Caribbean Mystery.*

HINCHCLIFFE, MISS Made of stern and "single-minded stuff," Miss Hinchcliffe

lived with Amy Murgatroyd on a small piece of land where they kept pigs and poultry. Amy talked her into going to Little Paddocks to witness the murder that had been advertised in the *Chipping Cleghorn Gazette. A Murder is Announced.*

HOBHOUSE, VALERIE Elegant, "clever dark girl" whose "sarcastic way of talking" earned few friends, she worked at Mrs. Lucas' "Sabrina Fair" beauty parlour and lived at the youth hostel run by her mother, Mrs. Nicoletis. Besides operating the beauty business, she ran a lucrative smuggling operation. She assumed numerous false identities: Mrs. da Silva, Miss Irene French, Mrs. Olga Kohn, Miss Nina Le Mesurier, Mrs. Gladys Thomas, Miss Moira O'Neele, Madame Mahmoudi and Sheila Donovan. She also convinced Celia Austin to feign kleptomania so that the disappearance of certain articles from the hostel would not be incriminating to herself. *Hickory Dickory Dock.*

HOD An orderly at Dr. Graham's clinic appointed by Poirot to confine Nick Buckley for his own protection, he was "a stupid but honest-looking young fellow of about twenty-two." He delivered the box of poisoned chocolates to Nick. *Peril at End House.*

HODGSON, MR. He was employed by McNeil and Hodgson, Poirot's solicitors. Flossie Monro went to Mr. Hodgson's office in response to Poirot's advertisement seeking information on Claud Darrell. *The Big Four.*

HOFFMAN, ROBERT He and his brother Wilhelm were respectable Dutch diamond merchants although Assistant Commissioner Graves called them "those scoundrels." Robert Hoffman "gave the appearance of being carved out of wood—preferably teak." Chief Inspector Fred Davy went to great lengths to ascertain that the Hoffman brothers owned Bertram's Hotel. Mr. Robinson supplied Davy with this information and also told him that, although Robert Hoffman was not involved in illegal schemes in England, his brother in Europe had handled some highly questionable operations, and that they grew richer every year. *At Bertram's Hotel.*

HOGBEN, SUPERINTENDENT *See* **JIM.**

HOGG, DORIS Member of the live-in domestic staff at Meadowbank, she gave "a negative spate of information" when questioned about the murder of Miss Springer: "She couldn't say, she was sure. She didn't know nothing." *Cat Among the Pigeons.*

HOGG, FREDERICK A son of Mr. and Mrs. James Hogg and brother to Eddie, he was a witness to Major Eustace's departure from Barbara Allen's flat the night she died. He was "an impish-faced bright-eyed lad, considerably swollen with self-importance." "Murder in the Mews" from *Murder in the Mews.*

HOGGIN, SIR JOSEPH Wealthy businessman and husband of Lady Milly Hoggin, he described himself as "a plain man.... No frills about me." He hired Poirot to investigate the dognapping of his wife's Pekinese Shan Tung. Sir Joseph, however, received more detection than he had expected: Poirot recounted to him the case of a wealthy soap manufacturer in Belgium who resembled Sir Joseph in appearance. This soap manufacturer had poisoned his wife in order to marry his blond secretary. "A faint sound came from Sir Joseph's lips—they had gone a queer blue colour. All the ruddy hue had faded from his cheeks." "The Nemean Lion" from *The Labours of Hercules.*

HOGGIN, LADY MILLY Wife to Sir Joseph Hoggin, Lady Milly was "a stout, petulant-looking woman with dyed henna red hair." Her precious Pekinese Shan Tung was dognapped while being walked in Kensington Park by her companion, Miss Amy Carnaby. Because of her terror at the dognapper's threat to cut off Shan Tung's ears and tail if she went to the police, her husband hired Poirot to investigate. She was equally devoted to her dog as she was callous to her servants. "The Nemean Lion" from *The Labours of Hercules.*

HOLLABY, MR. Father of Mr. Hollaby, Jr. and friend of Anthony Sessle's as well as partner in Sessle's Porcupine Assurance Company, Mr. Hollaby was playing golf with Sessle the afternoon his friend was murdered. He was one of the last persons to see Sessle alive: Hollaby related that Sessle was approached by a tall woman in brown on the sixth green. When Sessle returned, near dusk, he played like an entirely different man. The next day Sessle's body was discovered on the links. "The Sunningdale Mystery" from *Partners in Crime.*

HOLLAND, DESMOND A friend of Nicholas Ransome's, this seventeen-year-old became a suspect in the murder of Joyce Reynolds because he was once remanded owing to a psychiatric report. Desmond enthusiastically offered Poirot original, if fanciful, speculations of the identity of the murderer: "Whittaker for my money.... Yes. Real old spinster, you know. Sex starved. And all that teaching, bottled up among a lot of women.... What about the curate? ... He might be a bit off his nut. You know, original sin perhaps, and all that, and the water and the apples and the things...." He and Nicky saved Miranda Butler's life. *Hallowe'en Party.*

HOLLAND, ELSIE Extremely beautiful nursery governess in the Symmington household, she had "the perfect features, the crisply curling golden hair, the tall exquisitely shaped body ... she walked like a goddess—a glorious, an incredible, a breath-taking girl" until she opened her mouth. Her "flat, competent voice" utterly destroyed her image. She received one of the poison-pen letters. *The Moving Finger.*

HOLMES, MR. Employed by the Farleys, he was "a perfect specimen of the genus butler." He acquiesced with distaste to many of the eccentric whims of his master. "The Dream" from *The Adventure of the Christmas Pudding.*

HOLMES, MR. *See* **OBOLOVITCH, PRINCE MICHAEL.**

HOLMES, GLADYS (GLADDIE) The cousin of Emily, Miss Marple's little maid, Gladdie Holmes was formerly the maid to the Misses Skinner. Gladdie was a stout, giggling girl of unshakably equable temperament, bouncing and self-opinionated, adenoidal, but intrinsically honest, which caused Miss Marple to doubt that Gladdie had stolen Emily Skinner's brooch—ostensibly the reason for her dismissal. "The Case of the Perfect Maid" from *Three Blind Mice and Other Stories.*

HONEYCOTT, MRS. She was mistress of White House, where her sister Gilda Glen was murdered. Mrs. Honeycott was a violent anti-papist who referred to the Roman Catholic Church as "The Scarlet Woman" and feared that Gilda had converted: "And to think of those convents—quantities of beautiful young girls shut up there, and no one knowing what becomes of them—well, it won't bear thinking about." "The Man in the Mist" from *Partners in Crime.*

HOPE, EVELYN The identity assumed by Eva Kane on leaving England after the Craig murder case, it was also the name she gave to her son. On leaving Australia he was adopted by his patron, Mrs. Upward, and took her name by deed-pole. *Mrs. McGinty's Dead.*

HOPE, MRS. GERALD Mother of Henrietta, she brought her daughter to Meadowbank school. Miss Bulstrode managed to avoid Mrs. Hope's anger at not being allowed to take her daughter on holiday in mid-term by complimenting her on the "very charming Balenciaga model" she wore. *Cat Among the Pigeons.*

HOPKINS, JESSIE The District Nurse who came every morning to assist Laura Welman with the bedmaking and toilet, she partook of the fish-paste sandwiches which proved fatal to Mary Gerrard. She had convinced Mary to leave her money to her "aunt from New Zealand," Mary Riley. She penned an anonymous letter to Elinor Carlisle, which she signed "Well-Wisher," warning that "Girls Are very Artful and Old Ladies is soft when Young Ones suck up to Them and Flatter them." She was referring to Mary Gerrard and Laura Welman. *Sad Cypress.*

HOPKINSON, MR. Mary Harter's legal adviser, he was a precise old gentleman who was in charge of her various wills. Mr. Hopkinson informed Charles Ridgeway that his office had sent back the will the Tuesday before Mrs. Harter's death. "Where There's a Will" from *Witness for the Prosecution.*

HORBURY, LADY CICELY AKA Martha Jebb, she was a "clever, calculating cat of a chorus girl" who managed to marry Lord Stephen Horbury. She was seated with Venetia Kerr during the flight of the *Prometheus* when Madame Giselle was murdered. She was a cocaine addict and an inveterate gambler. Poirot referred to her as "a nasty piece." Estranged from her husband, who had fallen for her "delicately made-up, Dresden-china face," she refused him a divorce until Poirot convinced her otherwise. *Death in the Clouds.*

HORBURY, LORD STEPHEN Husband of Lady Cicely Horbury, he was the typical English country aristocrat who, although once besotted with Cicely's lovely face, soon came to the grim realization that he and she lived in two drastically different worlds. They agreed to separate, and he had since fallen in love with Venetia Kerr, but for the sake of the family name, he refused to give his wife grounds for divorce. Lady Cicely quickly returned to Horbury after the possibility of scandal after Madame Giselle's death. *Death in the Clouds.*

HORBURY, SYDNEY He was employed as a male nurse attendant to the invalid Simeon Lee. He was not well-liked by the members of the family because of his habit of creeping around like a cat and appearing from behind. "His manner was unctuous." *Hercule Poirot's Christmas.*

HORI Imhotep's "man of business and affairs," Hori was described by his employer: "In every way my right hand— and a man of good sense and discrimination." To Renisenb, Hori "was like the cliffs themselves—steadfast, immovable, unchanging." Hori's speculations about the murders in Imhotep's house were correct. He saved Renisenb's life, and although she was deeply affected by the attentions of Kameni, Renisenb eventually decided to spend her life with Hori. *Death Comes as the End.*

HORLICK The nervous undergardener at Hunterbury Hall, he discussed with Elinor Carlisle the possibility of securing a post as main gardener to Major Somervell after the sale of the Hall. He was planning to be married in the fall, and would have liked to have been sure of his future. His Adam's apple jerked "up and down in a spasmodic fashion" during this conversation. *Sad Cypress.*

HORRISTON, DR. He operated The Grange in Sussex, a clinic for desperate and overweight women, and used secret injections for weight reduction. Tommy Beresford found Dr. Horriston an "unpleasant-looking brute . . . shifty-looking beggar." "The Case of the Missing Lady" from *Partners in Crime.*

HORSEFALL, PAMELA A reporter, she wrote an article titled, "Where Are These Women Now?" concerning women in-

volved in murder cases, which Mrs. McGinty had carefully saved. She was "tall, manly-looking, a hard drinker and smoker, and it would seem, looking at her, highly improbable that it was her pen which had dropped so treacly a sentiment in the *Sunday Comet.*" When Poirot questioned her on the veracity of her reporting, she replied: "My dear man. No point in accuracy. Whole thing was a romantic farrago from beginning to end. I just mugged up the facts a bit and then let fly with a lot of hou ha." She neighed like a horse. *Mrs. McGinty's Dead.*

HORSEFIELD, SIR RODERICK Uncle of Andrew Restarick with poor eyesight, he spurned with horror Poirot's offer of a *sirop de cassis* in favour of a whisky, against his doctor's orders: "Doctors are all fools, as we know. All they care for is stopping you having anything you've a fancy for." In the process of writing his memoirs, he discovered some of his papers to be missing and consulted Poirot about their return. *Third Girl.*

HORSHAM *See* **CRISPIN, ANGUS.**

HORSHAM, HENRY A Security man, he was well-known as a discreet and unobtrusive carrier of messages which called for a high degree of secrecy. "Mr. Horsham had a moustache. He found it useful to have a moustache. It concealed moments when he found it difficult to avoid smiling." His security clearance was such that he was present at the confidential meetings about Project Benvo with high government officials. Henry Horsham had access to classified information, and he had known Lisa Neumann when she had been with Shoreham at the Leveson Foundation years before. *Passenger to Frankfurt.*

HORTON, DR. The husband of Maria Horton (*née* Addison) and the father of Inez Horton, he was a "good general practitioner, unambitious but reliable and devoted . . . to his daughter." "The Harlequin Tea Set" from *Winter's Crimes 3.*

HORTON, MAJOR A retired military man who served in India, and the formerly hen-pecked widower of Lydia Horton, he was "a small man with a stiff moustache and protuberant eyes." The Major appeared to have doted on his late wife, though Luke Fitzwilliam thought his married life must have been "like a military campaign." The Major said: "Fellow needs a wife to keep him up to scratch. . . . Otherwise he gets slack—yes, slack." *Murder is Easy*.

HORTON, INEZ The nineteen- or twenty-year-old daughter of Maria Horton and Dr. Horton and the grand-daughter of Thomas Addison, she was a beautiful, dark girl who took after her grandmother, Pilar Addison. Inez lived with her parents in a house next to Thomas Addison's Dovercourt Kingsbourne. Both Timothy and Roland Gilliat were in love with her. "The Harlequin Tea Set" from *Winter's Crimes 3*.

HORTON, LYDIA The domineering, nagging wife of Major Horton, she was the first victim of the Wychwood murderer. Bridget Conway referred to her as "the most disagreeable woman . . . that I've ever known." When she died, "the bulldogs brightened at once." Fitzwilliam learned from the Major that his wife held rather stringent domestic values and went through fifteen cooks and parlourmaids in one year. Easterfield had sent her some of his hothouse grapes shortly before her death from gastroenteritis. *Murder is Easy*.

HORTON, MARIA The wife of Dr. Horton and the mother of Inez Horton, Maria Horton was the daughter of Thomas Addison and his deceased wife Pilar and the sister of the deceased Lily Gilliat. She had died in childbirth. "The Harlequin Tea Set" from *Winter's Crimes 3*.

HOSKINS, ROBERT (BOB) Local Police Constable, he had a "rural wisdom" and, according to Mrs. Tucker, spent "his time looking into parked cars on the Com-mon." He had an "ingrained prejudice against foreigners," and was an "absolute specialist on the subject of sexual 'goings on'." *Dead Man's Folly*.

HOWARD, EVELYN (EVIE) John Cavendish enthusiastically remarked that she was Emily Inglethorp's "factotum, companion, Jack of all trades! A great sport— old Evie! Not precisely young and beautiful, but as game as they make them." "Her conversation, I soon found, was couched in the telegraphic style." Poirot ventured: "She is an excellent specimen of well-balanced English beef and brawn. She is sanity itself." *The Mysterious Affair at Styles*.

HOWELL, MRS. The housekeeper at Chimneys, she was "that dignified, creaking lady who had struck such terror to the heart of Lady Coote." Bundle Brent affectionately called her "Howelly" and learned from her the changes in Chimneys' staff around the time of Gerald Wade's death. When she expressed displeasure, Mrs. Howell "shivered all down her reactionary aristocratic spine." *The Seven Dials Mystery*.

HUBBARD, MRS. Sister of Felicity Lemon, Poirot's secretary, she was a widow for four years and the matron of Mrs. Nicoletis' student hostel. The disappearance of numerous articles from the hostel led her to consult Poirot, who saw in her "a definite resemblance to her sister. She was a good deal yellower of skin, she was plumper, her hair was more frivolously done and she was less brisk in manner than her sister, but the eyes that looked out of a round and amiable countenance were the same shrewd eyes that gleamed through Miss Lemon's pince-nez." He thought her to be a Miss Lemon softened by marriage and by the years she spent in Singapore. *Hickory Dickory Dock*.

HUBBARD, CAROLINE MARTHA Her real identity was the celebrated tragic actress, Linda Arden, who retired from the stage after calamities struck her family. Mother of Sonia Armstrong and Helena Goldenberg and grandmother of Daisy Armstrong, she pretended to be an American visiting a fictitious daughter and son-in-law on the staff of an American college in Smyrna. The source of many false clues surrounding the murder, Poirot felt she played the part of "the perfectly natural, slightly ridiculous American fond mother" to perfection. *Murder on the Orient Express.*

HUDD, GINA The wife of Walter Hudd, the daughter of Pippa and Guido San Severiano and the grand-daughter of Carrie Louise Serrocold, Gina was "a very beautiful young woman . . . not only beautiful but expensive." Knowing that her youth and beauty could not last, she enjoyed them to the fullest while she could. Most of the men at Stoneygates were in love with her. *They Do It with Mirrors.*

HUDD, WALTER (WALLY) Gina Hudd's American husband, "Wally was a big young man with brushed-up hair on his head and a sulky expression." He was the only outsider at Stoneygates and thought that all of Gina's relatives were batty. Walter longed to return to America with his wife. *They Do It with Mirrors.*

HUISH, SUPERINTENDENT The police Superintendent assigned to the Argyle murder case, he "was a tall, sad-looking man. His air of melancholy was so profound that no one would have believed that he could be the life and soul of a children's party, cracking jokes and bunging pennies out of little boys' ears, much to their delight." *Ordeal by Innocence.*

HUMFRIES, MR. Manager of Bertram's Hotel, running it from his "inner sanctum," Mr. Humfries was "often taken by the uninitiated as Mr. Bertram in person," a misapprehension he never bothered to rectify. "He could, at any moment, be all things to all people. He could talk racing shop, cricket, foreign politics, tell anecdotes of royalty, give motor show

information, knew the most interesting plays at present." However, he did not convince the shrewd Chief Inspector Davy: "You know the sort of feeling one gets. Smarmy sort of chap." *At Bertram's Hotel.*

HUMBLEBY, JESSIE ROSE The widow of the murdered Dr. Humbleby, and the mother of Rose Humbleby, she was extremely grieved by her husband's death. Luke Fitzwilliam visited her home where he found her sitting in "a curiously huddled-up position. . . . Her voice was rather monotonous, but its very lack of feeling seemed to emphasize the fact that actually feeling was in her, strenuously held back." She told Luke there was evil going on in Wychwood, and he got the impression that she knew more about her husband's death than she admitted. *Murder is Easy.*

HUMBLEBY, DR. JOHN WARD Yet another victim of the Wychwood murderer, he was survived by his grief-stricken wife Jessie Rose and his daughter Rose Humbleby, and was succeeded in his practice by his partner, Dr. Thomas, who was in love with Rose. He was of the old school of physicians. Easterfield called Humbleby an "opinionated, muddle-headed old fool." Humbleby contracted an accute septicaemia from an infected cut. Miss Fullerton had told Luke Fitzwilliam on their way to London that she feared Dr. Humbleby would be the next victim. *Murder is Easy.*

HUMBLEBY, ROSE The daughter of Dr. and Mrs. Humbleby, she and Dr. Thomas were in love and wished to marry but her father opposed the match. She and Dr. Thomas delayed their marriage in deference to her bereaved mother's feelings after her father was murdered, but planned to wed as soon as feasible. *Murder is Easy.*

HUNT, VERITY After her parents' fatal plane crash in Spain, she became a ward of their good friend, Clotilde Bradbury-Scott. Verity had been a student of Elizabeth Temple's at the Fallowfield School. Verity had been engaged to the ne'er-do-well Michael Rafiel, who was convicted of her murder after the disfigured body of Nora Broad had been identified as hers. *Nemesis.*

HUNTER, DAVID The brother of Rosaleen Cloade, he survived the air raid that killed his sister and her husband. He then convinced Eileen to take his sister's place and claim the Cloade inheritance. Much to Rowley Cloade's distress, Hunter fell in love with Lynn Marchmont and she with him. When "Enoch Arden" wrote him a letter about Robert Underhay, his sister's first husband, Hunter went to the Stag to pay Arden off. When he arrived with the money, "Enoch Arden" was dead. *Taken at the Flood.*

HUNTER, MEGAN Twenty-year-old daughter of Captain and Mona Hunter and half-sister to Colin and Brian Symmington, Megan was "a tall awkward girl." Jerry Burton, distressed by her drab, unconcerned dress, took her to Joanna's dressmaker and hair dresser in London, which did wonders for Megan's self-esteem. She found Agnes Woddell's body and aided police in dangerous and unusual ways to apprehend the killer. Jerry Burton fell in love with her and they married. *The Moving Finger.*

HURST, JIM The secretary to Mr. Blundell, he had once been caught stealing from his employer, but Carol Blundell convinced her father to give the young man another chance. Jim and Carol wished to wed, against her father's own wishes that she marry Sir Donald Marvel. "The Pearl of Price" from *Parker Pyne Investigates.*

IMHOTEP The husband of the deceased Ashayet, the father of Yahmose, Sobek, Renisenb and Ipy (the latter by Imhotep's mistress, Ipi) and the son of Esa, Imhotep was the ka-priest or mortuary priest responsible for maintaining the Tomb of Meripath. When Imhotep brought Nofret, a nineteen-year-old concubine, into his house, tension mounted. Already his sons were against him because he would not make them partners in his business and treated them like slaves. To make matters worse, he had disinherited his family in favour of Nofret. Shortly afterward members of his household started to die one by one. *Death Comes as the End.*

INCH Inch's Taxi Service was the official name of old Mr. Inch's company, even though ownership had passed to a Mr. Roberts. "The older ladies of the community continued to refer to their journeys as going somewhere 'in Inch,' as though they were Jonah and Inch was a whale." *The Mirror Crack'd from Side to Side; Nemesis.*

INGLES, JOHN Ingles was an expert on internal Chinese affairs and political personalities. Poirot consulted Ingles about the possible connection between the Big Four gang and the Chinese opium underworld. Ingles mysteriously disappeared from the S.S. *Shanghai* shortly after the ship left Marseilles. His Chinese servant was murdered trying to get a message to Hastings. *The Big Four.*

INGLETHORP, ALFRED The husband of Emily Inglethorp, Alfred Inglethorp first came to Styles Court on the pretext of being the cousin of Evelyn Howard, Emily's "factotum." Emily hired him as her secretary, and not long after that they announced their plans to marry. John Cavendish, Emily's step-son, was shocked by the engagement and let it be known that he, for one, considered Alfred Inglethorp nothing more than "a bare-faced fortune hunter." Poirot described Alfred as a "man of method," a comment which approached the highest praise that Poirot could bestow on any individual. *The Mysterious Affair at Styles.*

INGLETHORP, EMILY AGNES The wife of Alfred Inglethorp and the step-mother of John and Lawrence Cavendish, she was "not a day less than seventy" and was "an energetic, autocratic personality, somewhat inclined to charitable and social notoriety, with a fondness for opening bazaars and playing the Lady Bountiful." One of her more interesting projects was to provide housing for a number of Belgian refugees in Leastways Cottage, a small lodge that she owned next to the gates of Styles Court. One of her boarders was Hercule Poirot. Emily Inglethorp's death was very painful; poisoned by strychnine, she suffered from tetanic convulsions. Hercule Poirot decided to repay her hospitality by discovering her murderer and thus the saga of Hercule Poirot in England began. *The Mysterious Affair at Styles.*

INGLEWOOD, SIR MORTIMER "Dignified and full of righteous indignation," Sir Mortimer Inglewood, K.C., opened the case for the prosecution in the libel suit against the *X-Ray News.* He spoke "with bitter disparagement of Fascists and Communists both of whom sought to undermine Democracy by every unfair machination known." "The Augean Stables" from *The Labours of Hercules.*

INGRID Credulous maid to the Brown household, she was "a big blond Nordic girl with a flushed face and wearing gay-coloured clothing." In the process of being taught English by Geraldine Brown, she learned that the English equivalent for *auf wiedersehen* was "get the hell out of here!" but this phrase did not quite produce the desired results when she used it on Miss Bulstrode the next day. *The Clocks.*

INSTOW, JEAN She thought that Mary Pritchard ought to die since she was a miserable woman who made everyone else miserable. She was in love with George Pritchard, Mary Pritchard's husband. "The Blue Geranium" from *The Thirteen Problems.*

IPY Ipy was Imhotep's third and youngest son and was the product of an alliance between Imhotep and his one-time mistress, Ipi. Imhotep defended and indulged his son: "Ipy is high-spirited. He does not like taking orders." Ipy considered himself the "superior intelligence of the family." He was found dead, face down, in the stream that ran near the family home. *Death Comes as the End.*

ISAACSTEIN, HERMAN AKA Ikey Hermanstein; Nosystein; Fat Ikey. This member of the "strong, silent yellow men of finance" represented the all-British syndicate that wished to lend Prince Michael Obolovitch money in return for oil concessions in Herzoslavakia. He was present at the conference at Chimneys when Prince Michael was murdered. "His voice was deep and rich, and had a certain compelling quality about it. It had stood him in good stead at board meetings in his younger days." The gun used to murder Prince Michael was found in his suitcase. *The Secret of Chimneys.*

IVANOVITCH, BORIS AKA Count Stepanov; Monsieur Krassine. One of the few characters to appear in the adventures of different sleuths, Ivanovitch first appeared in a Tuppence and Tommy book where as Count Stepanov he was a member of a revolutionary Bolshevist gang. Later, in a Poirot novel, he posed as Monsieur Krassine, a member of the Russian Embassy in Paris, where he worked with Olga Demeroff in the Heart of Fire ruby theft. Ivanovitch was "a little man with a face like a rat. . . . In an Empire where rats ruled he was king of the rats." *The Secret Adversary; The Mystery of the Blue Train.*

IVANOVITCH, SERGIUS *See* **ORANOFF, PRINCE SERGIUS.**

J

JACKSON, ARTHUR Nurse valet, attendant and masseur to Mr. Rafiel, he had been with Rafiel for nine months, a record for manservants to the irascible millionaire. Because he was once employed in the pharmaceutical field, he recognized the various drugs including datura (Jimson weed) in Molly Kendall's cosmetics. *A Caribbean Mystery.*

JACOBS, MISS Frances Cary ran to this elderly lady when she found Norma Restarick holding a bloody knife over the body of David Baker. Miss Jacobs was "not the kind of woman who screams," and promptly called the police emergency phone number. She made an excellent witness. *Third Girl.*

JAMES *See* **DARRELL, CLAUD.**

JAMES, CAROLINE The wife of John James was described by Sir Eustace Pedler: "Caroline is the lady who cooks for me. Incidentally she is the wife of my gardener. What kind of wife she makes I do not know, but she is an excellent cook. James, on the other hand, is not a good gardener—but I support him in idleness and give him the lodge to live in solely on account of Caroline's cooking." *The Man in the Brown Suit.*

JAMESON, COMMISSIONAIRE He discovered the murdered George Earlsfield in the Regal Cinema at Doncaster. He also found an A.B.C. railway guide under Earlsfield's seat. *The A.B.C. Murders.*

JAMESON, MRS. Mrs. Jameson's business sign read: "DIANE. Hair Stylist." "The bulk of Mrs. Jameson's clientele was a bunch of solid, stick-in-the-mud middle-aged ladies who found it extremely hard to get their hair done the way they wanted it anywhere else." Mrs. Jameson gave Miss Marple copies of *Movie News* and *Amongst the Stars* so that she could read about Marina Gregg. *The Mirror Crack'd from Side to Side.*

JAMESON, RICHARD A fellow tourist of Miss Marple's on the Famous Houses and Gardens of Great Britain excursion, he was "a tall thin man of about thirty with a highly technical vocabulary, clearly an architect." Jameson was "the kind of young man who is fond of hearing his own voice," and lectured the group monotonously during one point on the tour. *Nemesis.*

JANE A friend of Tuppence Beresford's, this girl "of an accommodating disposition" supplied four photographs for breaking one of Una Drake's alibis. Unfortunately, this tactic failed. "The Unbreakable Alibi" from *Partners in Crime.*

JANET She was an elderly housemaid at Enderby Hall "who, although enjoying frequent acid disputes with Landscombe, was nevertheless usually in alliance with him against the younger generation" of servants. During her interview with the impertinent foreigner Monsieur Pontarlier (alias Poirot), she was "grim-faced and resentful," her lips fixed in a sour line. *After the Funeral.*

JANET Eleven-year-old daughter of Deborah Beresford, and grand-daughter of Tuppence and Tommy Beresford, she was the sister of Andrew and Rosalie, and was referred to as "the Rosa Dartle of the family." *Postern of Fate.*

JAPP, CHIEF INSPECTOR JAMES James Japp's long association with Hercule Poirot began in 1904, when Poirot was with the Belgium Police and Japp was a detective with Scotland Yard. They worked on the unrecorded Abercrombie forgery case and subsequently on the Baron Altara case. Hastings described Japp as "a little, sharp, dark, ferret-faced man," and Japp and Poirot remained good friends despite what Poirot considered Japp's unfortunate lack of method in his investigations: "Japp is the 'younger generation knocking at the door.' And *ma foi!* They are so busy knocking that they do not notice that the door is open!" Among Japp's more memorable characteristics was his ability to constantly mispronounce "Moosier Poirot's" name; he was also a zealous amateur botanist. He once said to Poirot: "I shouldn't wonder if you ended by detecting your own death. . . . That's an idea, that is. Ought to be put in a book." *The Mysterious Affair at Styles; Poirot Investigates; The Big Four; Peril at End House; Lord Edgware Dies; The A.B.C. Murders; Death in the Clouds;* "Murder in the Mews" from *Murder in the Mews; One, Two, Buckle My Shoe;* "The Girdle of Hippolyta," "The Flock of Geryon" and "The Capture of Cerberus" from *The Labours of Hercules;* "The Plymouth Express," "The Affair at the Victory Ball" and "The Market Basing Mystery" from *The Under Dog.*

JARROLD, DETECTIVE INSPECTOR Detective Inspector Jarrold of Scotland Yard was "a small man with ginger hair and moustache and a suggestion of horsiness in his apparel." He had been on the trail of Mardenberg, a known spy, when he noticed that George Rowland was also watching Mardenberg rather intently. They eventually crossed paths at a second-class hotel in Portsmouth, where all three had taken rooms. "The Girl in the Train" from *The Golden Ball.*

JARROW, DOROTHEA (DOLLY) *Née* Preston-Grey, Dolly Jarrow was Molly Ravenscroft's twin sister and the aunt of Celia and Edward Ravenscroft. She came under the care of Dr. Willoughby's father, who had met her when he was doing a study of twins. General Alistair Ravenscroft had at first been in love with her, but her emotional instability caused him to transfer his affections to her twin, Molly. After Molly Ravenscroft's death, she disguised herself as her dead sister with the help of four wigs. *Elephants Can Remember.*

JEFFERSON, ADELAIDE The widow of Frank Jefferson (her second husband) and the mother of Peter Carmody, she was in a difficult financial position owing to her deceased husband's unwise speculations in the stock market. She was a devoted mother who resented Conway Jefferson's proposed adoption of Ruby Keene because it would have deprived her son of his inheritance. Both Raymond Starr and Hugo McLean were in love with her. She agreed to marry McLean. *The Body in the Library.*

JEFFERSON, CONWAY His wife, son and daughter—Margaret Jefferson, Frank Jefferson and Rosamund Gaskell—were all killed in the plane crash that left him crippled and permanently confined to a wheelchair. He had adapted to his new life admirably: "It was as though the injuries which had left him a cripple had resulted in concentrating the vitality of his shattered body into a narrower and more intense focus." Much to the surprise and dismay of a number of people, Jefferson intended to adopt Ruby Keene and bequeath to her fifty thousand pounds. *The Body in the Library.*

JEFFRIES, EDWARD An American, he had been married to Elsie Jeffries only one and a half years when a spectre from his past, Mrs. Rossiter, emerged. The gallant Edward had once allowed Mrs. Rossiter to stay the night with him to avoid the threats of her violent husband, who wished to shoot her. He believed in rigorous, sober, strait-laced puritanism. He did not feel his wife, whom he had put on a pedestal of the purest and most virginal sort, could have borne hearing about this seeming indiscretion. Mr. Pyne said to the young man: "You, my dear sir, fall naturally into the category of victims." "Have You Got Everything You Want?" from *Parker Pyne Investigates.*

JEFFRIES, ELSIE The young American wife of Edward Jeffries, she discovered some clues that her husband had had a past, and discussed this with Mr. Parker Pyne on the train. She was robbed of her jewels en route. Mr. Parker Pyne told Edward "Your wife . . . is a charming, innocent, high-minded girl, and the only way she is going to get any kick out of her life with you is to believe that she had reformed you." "Have You Got Everything You Want?" from *Parker Pyne Investigates.*

JENKINS, MISS Secretary in the realty firm Messrs. Gable and Stretcher, she was "a young woman with adenoids and a lack-lustre eye." Intelligence was not one of her gifts: she found it impossible to relate a four-digit number accurately to Mr. Gable. *Dumb Witness.*

JENNINGS The valet to the murdered Sir James Dwighton and the beloved of Janet, Lady Laura Dwighton's maid, he had been sent into the library to help his master at 6:10 P.M. "A man, thought Mr. Satterthwaite, who would easily murder his master if he could be sure of not being found out." Although the loyal Janet did her best to keep the police from suspecting him, Lady Laura reported that Jennings was dismissed for pilfering. "The Love Detectives" from *Three Blind Mice and Other Stories.*

JENNSON, MISS Mademoiselle La Roche, Miss Jennson's colleague at Mr. Aristides' Brain Trust complex, exclaimed about this thin, dark, spectacled girl: "Ah! That one, what man will look at her twice?" The man proved to be Andrew Peters, who noted a certain "Heil Hitler" attitude in Jennson's approach to the Herr Director; he wooed her to find out more: "These plain, angular, short-sighted girls respond immediately when given the treatment. . . . That girl . . . can be very useful. She's in the know about all the arrangements here." *Destination Unknown.*

JESMOND, MR. The Foreign Office man, he asked Poirot to take on the commission of finding the royal ruby for Prince Ali. "Everything about Mr. Jesmond was discreet . . . his agreeable, well-bred voice which rarely soared out of an agreeable monotone, his light-brown hair just thinning a little at the temples, his pale, serious face." Through Lady Edwina Morcombe, Poirot was invited to Kings Lacey for the Christmas vacation. Mr. Jesmond managed to attract Poirot by mentioning the variety of modern conveniences available at Kings Lacey.

"The Theft of the Royal Ruby" from *Double Sin.*

JESSOP, MR. A member of a special Intelligence unit, he worked with Janet Hetherington in the Mediterranean, Monsieur Leblanc on the Continent and Andrew Peters in the United States. "This man, you felt, was an indoor man. A man of desks and files. The fact that to reach his office you had to walk through long twisting underground corridors was somehow strangely appropriate." He prevented Hilary Craven from suicide, and suggested that if she was serious about taking her life, perhaps she could better choose a means which would also benefit the British government, and worked with her on the Aristides case. *Destination Unknown.*

JETHROE, JOHNNY "A young man with exuberant hair and a pink and white face," he worked with Margot Bence in her photography studio just off the Tottenham Court Road. He drew a very good comparison when he suggested to Dermot Craddock that a murder case "develops . . . like a photograph." *The Mirror Crack'd from Side to Side.*

JIM AKA Superintendent Hogben; Sergeant Trotter. One of the "Three Blind Mice," he had been raised by John and Maureen Gregg. Jim vowed to revenge the death of his brother Georgie, who had been neglected by the Greggs. As Superintendent Hogben, he informed Molly Davis that Sergeant Trotter would be coming to question her. As Sergeant Trotter, he was the energetic, well-bronzed and cheerful police officer and an excellent skier. As the man witnessed by Bill and Joe who ran like a "scurrying rabbit," he dropped the notebook which was turned over to Inspector Parminter. "Three Blind Mice" from *Three Blind Mice and Other Stories.*

JOBSON, MR. The taxi driver who disproved the alibi of Geraldine and Ronald Marsh at the opera, the old man had a ragged moustache and spectacles, and "a hoarse, self-pitying voice." *Lord Edgware Dies.*

JOHN With his friends Evelyn and Sara, he was another aspiring young medium who was contacted by the Ouijah spirit Ada Spiers. He was told he would "marry someone named Gladys Bun almost immediately." John's Ouijah board was taken over by Harley Quin to send Mr. Satterthwaite the message that he was to take Madge Keeley up on her invitation to Laidell. "The Bird with the Broken Wing" from *The Mysterious Mr. Quin.*

JOHN A young squadron leader in Baghdad and a friend of Mrs. Kelsey's, he provided Nurse Leatheran with background information on the members of the American expedition at Tell Yarimjah. He described Mrs. Leidner as "a bit long in the tooth," but had once been "completely bowled over" by her. *Murder in Mesopotamia.*

JOHNSON The "impenetrable butler" to Sir Alington West, he overheard the argument between his master and Dermot West. A short while later, just as he was going to bed, Johnson heard a shot and discovered Sir Alington's body with a bullet wound through the heart. "The Red Signal" from *Witness for the Prosecution.*

JOHNSON, COLONEL The Chief Constable for Middleshire, he was visited by Hercule Poirot on Christmas Eve when the death of Simeon Lee was reported. A pecadillo that particularly irritated Poirot was the Colonel's preference for a wood fire instead of central heating; Poirot loved to be warm. *Hercule Poirot's Christmas.*

JOHNSON, COLONEL Chief Constable in Yorkshire and a friend of Mr. Satterthwaite's, he said: "I know criminals. Chicken-livered, most of them." He introduced Superintendent Crossfield to Mr. Satterthwaite and Sir Charles Cartwright and also investigated the background of John Ellis, the butler. *Three-Act Tragedy.*

JOHNSON, CONSTABLE An assistant to Inspector Badgworthy in Market Basing, he was "very new to the Force, with a downy unfledged look about him, like a human chicken." He and his superior were quite excited about the murder, quite a rarity in their vicinity although he said " 'I'm sorry it were a foreigner' . . . with some regret. It made the murder seem less real. Foreigners, Johnson felt, were liable to be shot." He had been looking forward to a hanging. *The Secret of Chimneys.*

JOHNSON, MISS Daughter of "Old" Johnson, she was the "plump fair-haired girl" working the bar at the Crown and Feathers in Croydon who was being courted by Albert Davis, second steward on board the *Prometheus. Death in the Clouds.*

JOHNSON, MISS *See* **WILLETT, VIOLET.**

JOHNSON, MR. A servant at the Leonides' residence Three Gables, he was paid a substantially increasing bonus each year in lieu of any bequest in Aristide Leonides' will, so it was to Mr. Johnson's advantage that the old man live as long as possible. Johnson was one of the witnesses to the secret will with which Aristide tricked his family and his solicitor, Mr. Gaitskill. *Crooked House.*

JOHNSON, MRS. *See* **BLIGH, GERTRUDE.**

JOHNSON, MRS. *See* **WILLETT, MRS.**

JOHNSON, ANNE As the general bottlewasher with the American expedition at Tell Yarimjah, Miss Johnson described herself as "faithful but jealous" and a "cross-grained, complaining old dog. Conservative—liking things always the same." She worshipped her employer, Dr. Leidner. She was murdered with a glass of hydrochloric acid exchanged for the customary glass of water she always drank in the middle of the night, but her observation of the architecture of the house provided Poirot with his most important clue in solving the murders. *Murder in Mesopotamia.*

JOHNSON, ELIZABETH Nicknamed "Black Bess" by the other students who lived with her at Mrs. Nicoletis' youth hostel, she was intelligent, slightly anti-social and a member of the Communist party. "Behind her modest, pleasant manner, here was a young woman who was positively arrogant in her appraisement of her own qualities." She had "the ego of a Napoleon." *Hickory Dickory Dock.*

JOHNSON, VICTORIA Enterprising black maid at the Golden Palm Hotel, she was the common-law wife of Big Jim Ellis, the father of two of her children. She was "a magnificent creature with a torso of black marble such as a sculptor would have enjoyed." She discovered that the bottle of pills found in Major Palgrave's room did not belong to him, but when she attempted to blackmail the person she thought was responsible, she was stabbed to death. *A Caribbean Mystery.*

JOLIET, MADAME Stout manageress of the Ballet Maritski in Paris and former employee of Anna Stravinska, she was consulted by Detective Inspector Craddock and Armand Dessin, Prefect of the Paris Police. She was "a brisk business-like Frenchwoman with a shrewd eye, a small moustache and a good deal of adi-

pose tissue." She disliked the police and invariably thought that men were the only reason her girls left the Ballet. *4.50 from Paddington.*

JONATHAN, CALEB Head of the firm of solicitors, Jonathan and Jonathan, which represented the Crales, he was approached by Poirot. "After a courteous exchange of letters, Hercule Poirot received an invitation, almost royal in its character, to dine and sleep. The old gentleman was decidedly a character. After the insipidity of young George Mahew, Mr. Jonathan was like a glass of his own vintage port." *Five Little Pigs.*

JONES AKA Detective Inspector Merrilees. Jones, who "was about forty, his face keen and hawklike," was Lord Edward Campion's valet and was with Lord Campion at Kimpton-on-Sea when the Rajah of Maraputna's emerald was stolen. Disguised as Detective Inspector Merrilees, Jones accosted James Bond for questioning regarding the emerald, but Bond saw that Merrilees' badge was a medallion from the Merton Park Super Cycling Club. "The Rajah's Emerald" from *The Golden Ball.*

JONES, DETECTIVE SERGEANT A police officer aiding the investigation into the murder of Lady Tressilian, he carefully lifted a full set of fingerprints from the heavy niblick used to bash her skull: "Lovely set of prints on that club," he said. The prints were identified as those of Nevile Strange. *Towards Zero.*

JONES, MR. The husband of Mrs. Jones and father of Hetty Jones, he was Wychwood's bank manager. Luke Fitzwilliam questioned him about the numerous deaths in the village. Apart from the theory that the murderer was the least likely person, Mr. Jones aroused no suspicion in his interrogator. He told Fitzwilliam, however, that both Major Horton and Mr. Abbot had been absent from Wychwood on Derby Day, the day Miss Fullerton was killed in London. *Murder is Easy.*

JONES, MRS. The wife of Albert Jones, she was "a rather commonplace woman of about forty-five." Her death was at first attributed to botulism poisoning from eating a bad lot of tinned lobster. "The Tuesday Night Club" from *The Thirteen Problems.*

JONES, ALBERT According to Sir Henry Clithering, Albert Jones was "a traveller for a firm of manufacturing chemists." He inherited eight thousand pounds from his wife after her death. Gladys Linch was pregnant by him and died in childbirth after he had abandoned her. "The Tuesday Night Club" from *The Thirteen Problems.*

JONES, POLICEWOMAN ALICE A strong swimmer, she faked drowning while a tourist boat went by, thus proving Inspector Bland's theory that Lady Hattie Stubbs could have been drowned without anyone on a passing tourist boat noticing. *Dead Man's Folly.*

JONES, MARY The daughter of William Jones, Mary Jones was in love with Stephen Grant and worked in her father's inn the Bells and Motley in Kirtlington Mallet. "At the Bells and Motley" from *The Mysterious Mr. Quin.*

JONES, MONTGOMERY The rich son of Lady Aileen Montgomery, he consulted Tuppence and Tommy Beresford in an attempt to win a bet he had made with Una Drake and thereby gain her admiration. From the letter he wrote, the sleuths deduced that Jones was "not one of the world's best spellers, thereby proving that he has been expensively educated." "The Unbreakable Alibi" from *Partners in Crime.*

JONES, ROBERT (BOBBY) AKA Edward Hawkins, Frederick Spragge and George Parker, he was the fourth son of Reverend Thomas Jones, the vicar of Marchbolt. He had been the childhood friend of Lady Frances Derwent, whom he dearly loved. Badger Beadon was his best friend and business associate. With his friend Dr. Thomas, he discovered the rapidly expiring body of a man later identified as Alex Pritchard at the bottom of a cliff. Aided by Lady Frankie, he began a private investigation of the death. As Edward Hawkins, he masqueraded as her chauffeur; assuming the identity of the venerable solicitor Frederick Spragge, he interviewed various parties; and as George Parker he registered at the hotel in Ambledever. After solving the mystery, he obtained both the hand of Lady Frankie and the job of managing a coffee plantation in Kenya for Lord Marchington, Frankie's father. *Why Didn't They Ask Evans?*

JONES, REVEREND THOMAS "A man of extremely nervous temperament," he was the vicar of Marchbolt and father of many sons—Bobby Jones was the fourth and most problematic of his offspring. "He was *par excellence* a fusser and when he fussed, his digestive apparatus collapsed and he suffered agonizing pain." Bobby thought the war had caused the gap between himself and the older generation: "It upset them and they never got straight again." He disliked Bobby's friend Badger Beadon intensely, "spoke very little and was obviously bearing his fourth son's presence as a Christian should. Once or twice he quoted Shakespeare on how sharper than a serpent's tooth, etc." *Why Didn't They Ask Evans?*

JONES, VICTORIA AKA Sister Marie des Anges, she was an adventurous, comical and lovable heroine. "Her principal defect was a tendency to tell lies at both opportune and inopportune moments. The superior fascination of fiction to fact was always irresistible to Victoria. She lied with fluency, ease and artistic fervour." She was especially talented at mimicry, and was once fired for doing rather outrageous imitations of her boss' wife. She fell in love with Edward Goring, and followed him to Baghdad where she worked for him because of her startling resemblance to Anna Scheele. She also assumed the alias of Sister Marie des Anges, and was hired by Mr. Dakin to spy on Goring. She subsequently fell in love with Richard Baker. Rosa Clayton described Victoria best: "an amiable nitwit with a lot of common sense." *They Came to Baghdad.*

JONES, WILLIAM The father of Mary Jones and the proprietor of the Bells and Motley in Kirtlington Mallet, William Jones was "a big burly man of fifty" who related the story of the disappearance of Captain Richard Harwell to Harley Quin and Mr. Satterthwaite. "At the Bells and Motley" from *The Mysterious Mr. Quin.*

JORDAN, MARY A member of British Intelligence during World War I in Hollowquay, she posed as a nursery governess to Alexander Parkinson while investigating a suspicious political movement in that village. She was poisoned with foxglove (digitalis). Alexander suspected foul play and entered a coded message in R.L. Stevenson's *The Black Arrow,* which over half a century later was discovered and decoded by Tuppence Beresford who set out to untangle the mystery. *Postern of Fate.*

JOSEPH, FRANZ *See* **ARGUILEROS, KARL.**

JUANITA *See* **CORTMAN, MILDRED JEAN.**

JUDD, HENRY Henry Judd was Rosina Nunn's latest in a long line of husbands. According to Mr. Vyse, Judd treated his wife "just as though she were a dog. . . . Cuts up her food for her." He was a part of the group that included Rosina Nunn, Mr. Vyne, Mr. Satterthwaite, the Duchess of Leith, Harley Quin, Mr. Tomlinson and Naomi Carlton-Smith who met when they rushed for cover from the sudden snow squall at Coti Chiaveeri. "The World's End" from *The Mysterious Mr. Quin.*

JULES Knowledgeable maitre d'hotel at the exclusive Chez Ma Tante, he "composed" a "little meal" for Poirot which was, in the words of the restaurant's proprietor Monsieur Blondin, "a poem—positively a poem!" *Death on the Nile.*

JULES *See* **LUTTRELL, CLAUDE.**

JUVET *See* **ANDRÉ.**

KAIT The wife of Sobek, "was devoted to her children and seldom thought or spoke about anything else." Satipy said to her: "You are as stupid as your children, Kait, and that is saying a good deal!" After Nofret's death, however, Kait became more assertive, and realized that the future of her children was threatened by Imhotep's hasty and ill-considered disinheritance of the family. She was not sorrowed by her husband's death: "A handsome braggart—a man who was always going to other women. . . . And what are men anyway? They are necessary to breed children, that is all. But the strength of the race is in the women. . . . As for men, let them breed and die early." Kait, Renisenb and Imhotep were the only ones of the family to survive. *Death Comes as the End.*

KAMENI When Renisenb first saw Kameni she thought that he was her deceased husband Khay "returned from the Underworld." Kameni slowly wooed Renisenb with love songs. In a spirit of urgency and daring, he proposed to Renisenb. She accepted unenthusiastically because, although he made her heart beat a little faster, she did not love him. After the murders were solved and the need to escape the household of Imhotep had evaporated, Renisenb reconsidered and decided to marry Hori instead. *Death Comes as the End.*

KANE, NORTON This young man was taking the Charlock Bay motor-coach only as far as Mockhampton. He interested Poirot because he was "trying to grow a moustache and as yet the result is poor." Blustering, denying and contradicting, he was suspected of stealing Mary Durrant's case of miniatures from the motor-coach. "Double Sin" from *Double Sin.*

KARL, PRINCE The cousin of the Grand Duchess Anastasia, Prince Karl, in the words of Elizabeth Gaigh, was "a horrid pimply person." Prince Osric, who was the Grand Duchess Anastasia's uncle, was under pressure from Sturm, the chancellor of Catonia, to force a marriage between Prince Karl and the Grand Duchess. After George Rowland refused Prince Karl the pleasure of a duel, Karl attempted to pull George's nose (this seemed to be accepted procedure in Catonia), and George promptly set about dispatching the Prince in a good English fashion that did not involve the pulling of noses. "The Girl in the Train" from *The Golden Ball.*

KATE, KILLER *See* LANCASTER, JULIA.

KEANE, MARCIA A "tall, dark girl" who was very keen on horses, she was Margery Gale's closest friend. She was skeptical about the ghosts that Margery thought were in Abbot's Mead, but agreed to participate in Mrs. Lloyd's séance. "The Voice in the Dark" from *The Mysterious Mr. Quin.*

KEBLE, ELLEN Blushing, stammering and murmuring companion to Mrs. Samuelson, she had been walking her mistress' Pekinese Nanki Poo when he was dognapped. "Thin and scraggy," as well as "voluble and slightly breathless," she had the standard spinster's love for infants, and was admiring a baby outside of Harrod's when Nanki Poo disappeared. "The Nemean Lion" from *The Labours of Hercules.*

KEELEY, DAVID The father of Madge Keeley and the owner of Laidell, he was "a most brilliant mathematician and had written a book totally incomprehensible to ninety-nine hundredths of humanity. But like so many men of brilliant intellect, he radiated no bodily vigour or magnetism." David Keeley thought that Mabelle Annesley had committed suicide because she had sung "Swan Song" the night before she died. He agreed to show Mr. Satterthwaite Mabelle's body, saying, "I'd forgotten you have a penchant for human tragedies." "The Bird with the Broken Wing" from *The Mysterious Mr. Quin.*

KEELEY, MADGE The daughter of David Keeley, fiancée of Roger Graham, and a friend of Mr. Satterthwaite's, whom she thought was "rather a duck," Madge was as energetic as her father was unobtrusive: "Mr. Satterthwaite received a message from the Ouijah board and decided to visit her. Her fiancé was enthralled by the fey charms of Mabelle Annesley. "The Bird with the Broken Wing" from *The Mysterious Mr. Quin.*

KEENE, SERGEANT The Sergeant in Charge at Kingston Bishop, he was "a square sensible man" whom Michael Rogers consulted about the sinister warnings of the gipsy curse on Gipsy's Acre. Keene, more sympathetic to the gipsies than he might have been, knowledgeably discussed them with Michael Rogers. He showed Rogers a gold cigarette case, inscribed with the monogram C, which his men had found in the Folly at Gipsy's Acre after Ellie Rogers' death. *Endless Night.*

KEENE, GEOFFREY The secretary to Hubert Lytcham Roche, he was the object of Diana Cleves' flirtatious attention in an effort to disguise her infatuation with Captain John Marshall and deceive her father. He blushed often, and she gave him an embroidered rose the evening before Hubert's murder. "The Second Gong" from *Witness for the Prosecution.*

KEENE, RUBY AKA Rosy Legge (her real name), she was Josephine Turner's cousin. Assessments of Ruby Keene's character were numerous and varied. When she was first missing from the Majestic Hotel in Danemouth, the following description was telephoned to Colonel Melchett at Much Benham police headquarters: "Ruby Keene, eighteen, occupation, professional dancer, five-feet-four inches, slender, platinum blond hair, blue eyes, retroussé nose, believed to be wearing white diamanté evening dress, silver sandal shoes." Adelaide Jefferson said: "Poor little rat, she had to fight for what she wanted. She wasn't bad. . . . It was just that she was quick to take advantage of a possibility and she knew just how to appeal to an elderly man who was lonely." Conway Jefferson, Adelaide's father-in-law, decided to adopt Ruby Keene to fill his empty life after his family died in a plane crash which left him alone and crippled. He also planned to bequeath her fifty thousand pounds, but before he could, she was murdered. Her body was mistaken with Pamela Reeves' body found in Arthur Bantry's library, but was later discovered burnt almost beyond recognition in George Bartlett's stolen Minoan 14 automobile. *The Body in the Library.*

KEENE, SYLVIA The niece of Sir Ambrose Bercy and the fiancée of Jerry Lorimer, she died from eating a salad laced with foxglove, the active ingredient of which is digitalis. "The Herb of Death" from *The Thirteen Problems.*

KELLETT, BILLY *See* **DAVENHEIM, MR.**

KELLY, SHEILA *See* **GRANT, SHEILA.**

KELSEY, DETECTIVE INSPECTOR Gentle, kind and efficient officer in charge of the Meadowbank murder case, "Inspector Kelsey was a perceptive man. He was always willing to deviate from the course of routine if a remark struck him as unusual or worth following up." He once worked with Poirot in a case years before under the direction of Inspector Warrender. *Cat Among the Pigeons.*

KELSEY, INSPECTOR An inspector working with Inspector Crome on the A.B.C. murders case, he was given to mimicking Miss Merrion's "mincing tone." *The A.B.C. Murders.*

KELSEY, MAJOR With his wife, he lived in Baghdad and hired Nurse Leatheran to join them there to care for their child. He was surprised to learn of the "queer tension" within the expedition at Tell Yarimjah—"They seemed like a happy family—which is really surprising when one considers what human nature is!" *Murder in Mesopotamia.*

KELSEY, MARY Delicate, nervous wife of Major Kelsey, she invited the midwife Nurse Leatheran to join her and her baby in Iraq, but she lost her to the employ of Mrs. Louise Leidner. Mrs. Kelsey was "quite nice, though rather the fretting kind." *Murder in Mesopotamia.*

KELVIN, MR. The landlord of the Three Anchors in the Cornish village of Polperran, according to Raymond West, Kelvin "was a remarkable-looking man, dark and swarthy, with curiously broad shoulders. His eyes were bloodshot, and he had a curiously furtive way of avoiding one's glance." "Ingots of Gold" from *The Thirteen Problems.*

KEMP, CHIEF INSPECTOR A Scotland Yard detective, Kemp had worked under Superintendent Battle for many years, and "he bore about him the same suggestion of being carved all in one piece—but whereas Battle had suggested some wood such as teak or oak, Chief Inspector Kemp suggested a somewhat more showy wood—mahogany, say, or good old-fashioned rosewood." He worked with Colonel Race on the Barton murders. *Sparkling Cyanide.*

KENDALL, MOLLY Wife of Tim Kendall, she and her husband ran the Golden Palm Hotel in St. Honore, West Indies. "An ingenuous blond of twenty-odd . . . she had a wide generous mouth that laughed easily." She had been suffering from nightmares, hallucinations and blackouts for a period of time, which was discovered by Arthur Jackson to be the result of drugs, including datura, in her cosmetics. The drugs induced the impression that she was mad, and the effects were strong enough to drive her to suicide. *A Caribbean Mystery.*

KENDALL, TIM Husband of Molly, with his wife he ran the Golden Palm Hotel in St. Honore. A "lean dark man in his thirties," he was told by his wife to care for the female guests: "You charm the old pussies and manage to look as though you'd like to make love to the desperate forties and fifties, and I ogle the old gentlemen and make them feel sexy dogs—

or play the sweet little daughter the sentimental ones would love to have had." He was very solicitous of Miss Marple, offering her bread-and-butter pudding—which she refused—instead of the more exotic island fare. *A Caribbean Mystery.*

KENNEDY, DR. JAMES The half-brother of the missing Helen Spenlove Kennedy Halliday, he was the local physician to Dillmouth and was rumoured to be a wonder with rheumatic knees. He explained that he had been apologetic about his half-sister, whose twenty-years' absence he regarded as typical, and he told Gwenda Reed: "I was always a straight-laced sort of fellow—a believer in marital fidelity." *Sleeping Murder.*

KENT, CAPTAIN A member of the United States Secret Service, Kent, according to Hastings, had "a singularly impassive face which looked as though it had been carved out of wood." Kent was investigating the Halliday disappearance case and was introduced to Poirot by Inspector Japp. *The Big Four.*

KENT, CHARLES The illegitimate son of Mrs. Russell, Roger Ackroyd's housekeeper at Fernly Park, Kent had visited his mother the night Roger Ackroyd was killed. He was a drug addict. *The Murder of Roger Ackroyd.*

KENT, DR. MARCUS Jerry Burton's doctor, he advised his patient after the aeroplane crash: "Go to some part of the world where you haven't any friends. Get away from things. Take an interest in local politics, get excited about village gossip, absorb all the local scandal. Small beer—that's the prescription for you. Absolute rest and quiet." Lymstock, however, was plagued by anonymous poison pen letters and later, murder. *The Moving Finger.*

KERR, DR. The police surgeon at Andover who first examined Alice Ascher's body, he was "a competent-looking middle-aged man" who spoke "briskly and with decision." From a psychological standpoint, he did not feel that Alice's murder was a woman's crime. *The A.B.C. Murders.*

KERR, MARY The name given by Jane Helier to the woman who was married to Claud Leason but having an affair with Sir Herman Cohen. Mary Kerr was also the name that Miss Helier gave to the actress who had stolen her husband, Claud Averbury, and then had married him. Both Miss Kerrs were having affairs with men who had supplied the ladies with little cottages and lavished jewels upon them. "The Affair at the Bungalow" from *The Thirteen Problems.*

KERR, THE HONOURABLE VENETIA ANNE She was travelling on board the *Prometheus* with Lady Cicely Horbury, whom she thought was "a little tart." She was in love with Cicely's husband, Lord Stephen Horbury, who would marry her if Cicely would give him a divorce. Although it was against her code to show surprise, she was openly amazed at Cicely's arrival at Horbury after Madame Giselle's death, since Lord and Lady Horbury had been since separated. Poirot managed to convince Lady Cicely to grant the divorce so that the lovers could wed. *Death in the Clouds.*

KETTERING, DEREK The husband of Ruth Kettering, who was hoping to divorce him, he was the son of Lord Leaconbury, whose title he was due to inherit. Destitute and in debt, Derek was accused of marrying Ruth for her money, and it was speculated that she married him for his future title. Kettering was a man of numerous infidelities; he was having an affair with Mirelle the dancer and was in love with Katherine Grey. *The Mystery of the Blue Train.*

KETTERING, RUTH The daughter of Rufus Van Aldin and the wife of Derek Kettering, she was an auburn beauty, the kind of woman who would have appealed to Arthur Hastings if he had met her. Her father convinced her to divorce her husband on the basis of infidelity, but Ruth was not without her own "special friends," among them the Comte de la Roche. She was given the famous Heart of Fire rubies and was murdered on the *Blue Train* on the way to a tryst with her lover on the Isle D'Or. *The Mystery of the Blue Train.*

KHARSANOVA, ANNA *See* **DENMAN, ANNA.**

KIDD, GRACIE *See* **MASON, JANE.**

KIDD, KITTY *See* **MASON, ADA BEATRICE.**

KIDDER, MRS. The slatternly, suspicious woman who cleaned at Rutherford Hall, she was a good source of gossip about the Crackenthorpes. After the poisonings, Lucy Eyelesbarrow often heard her mumble: "Nasty things, mushrooms." *4.50 from Paddington.*

KIDDERMINSTER, LADY VICTORIA (VICKY) The wife of Lord William, Earl of Kidderminster, and the mother of Lady Alexandra Farraday, her "large rocking-horse face was familiar on public platforms and on committees all over England." This tough, unsentimental woman thought Stephen Farraday, her prospective son-in-law, was "a useful man to know." She also thought her daughter Alexandra was passionately capable of murder. *Sparkling Cyanide.*

KIDDERMINSTER, LORD WILLIAM EARL OF The husband of Lady Victoria Kidderminster, he was, "with his little imperial, his tall distinguished figure ... known by sight everywhere," and exerted a powerful influence on Conservative politics. He generally approved of the match between his daughter, Lady Alexandra, and Stephen Farraday. *Sparkling Cyanide.*

KIDDLE, MRS. With her husband, Bert the plasterer, and son Ernie, she moved into Mrs. McGinty's house after the murder. She was somewhat proud of the notoriety that went with living at the murder location, and happily showed Poirot where Mrs. McGinty was slain. "Poirot looked round him. Hard to visualize that this rampant stronghold of haphazard fecundity was once the well-scrubbed domain of an elderly woman who was house-proud." *Mrs. McGinty's Dead.*

KIMBLE, LADY ABBOT The wife of Jim Kimble, she was the high-spirited parlourmaid at Hillside in Dillmouth when Helen Kennedy Halliday was murdered. She read one of Gwenda Reed's advertisements in a local newspaper and, disregarding her husband's advice not to get involved, decided to meet with Dr. James Kennedy, Helen's brother, and discover what it was that Gwenda Reed wanted to know about her former mistress. On the day of her appointment with Dr. Kennedy, she was murdered only minutes after she stepped off the train. *Sleeping Murder.*

KING, ALIX *See* **MARTIN, ALIX.**

KING, BEATRICE The housekeeper to the Oldfields, she was dismissed almost immediately upon Mrs. Oldfield's death, and denied overhearing the conversation between Dr. Oldfield and Jean Moncrieffe alluded to by Nurse Harrison. "The Lernean Hydra" from *The Labours of Hercules.*

KING, MURIEL AKA Lady Esther Carr. Formerly the maid to Esther Carr, she was loved by Herr Schlagal. As Muriel King, she was a "frightened girl, ignorant and untravelled" when her mistress took her to Persia. There she assumed the identity of Lady Esther Carr, and to protect herself, feigned an extreme interest in native ways, and would not have "anything to do with anything or anyone British." Parker Pyne said: "There was something decidedly offensive in her voice." "The House at Shiraz" from *Parker Pyne Investigates.*

KING, SARAH On holiday in Jerusalem in an attempt to forget an unhappy love affair, she had just received her MB. She was interested in Raymond Boynton but was annoyed that he would allow his step-mother to turn him into another shy, boorish, rude American who would not even look at her. She likened their relationship to "St. George and the Dragon reversed" with her playing the canonical role, he that of the young maiden and Mrs. Boynton, the serpent. Sarah determined the time of Mrs. Boynton's death. *Appointment with Death.*

KING, WINNIE Daughter of Canon and Mrs. King of Cranchester, she was kidnapped by James Elliot on her way to Miss Pope's establishment for girls in Neuilly, France. She was to facilitate smuggling his stolen Rubens painting into France. "The Girdle of Hippolyta" from *The Labours of Hercules.*

KINGSTON BRUCE, BEATRICE Ill-natured daughter of Colonel and Mrs. Kingston Bruce, she had been forced to consult the International Detective Agency concerning the theft of a pink pearl stolen from Mrs. Betts-Hamilton, her parents' houseguest. Beatrice was romantically involved with the unpopular Mr. Rennie, a Socialist. "The Affair of the Pink Pearl" from *Partners in Crime.*

KINGSTON BRUCE, COLONEL CHARLES AND MRS. The parents of Beatrice Kingston Bruce, they owned The Laurels, site of the theft of Mrs. Betts-Hamilton's pink pearl while she was a houseguest. They personally suspected Mr. Rennie, a Socialist, of the theft. "The Affair of the Pink Pearl" in *Partners in Crime.*

KIRKWOOD, FREDERICK The lawyer of Captain Trevelyan, he was a partner in the firm of Walters and Kirkwood. Although clearly agog with curiosity when Major Burnaby, executor of Trevelyan's will, visited him, "he rose, put on his mourning face, and shook hands with the Major." *The Sittaford Mystery.*

KLEEK, SIR JAMES (JAMIE) The son of one of Lord Edward Altamount's oldest friends and Lord Edward's right-hand man, he was Brutus to Lord Edward's Julius Caesar. Sir Stafford Nye thought this spokesman for the committee of inquiry into the Youth Movement "a restless, fidgety type. Sharp, suspicious glances that never rested anywhere for long. He had the contained eagerness of a sporting dog awaiting the word of command. Ready to start off at a glance from his master's eye." *Passenger to Frankfurt.*

KNIGHT, MISS Miss Marple's paid nurse-companion was hired by Raymond West, her nephew, to tend to her daily needs. "Devoted maidservants," lamented Miss Marple, "had gone out of fashion. In real illness you could have a proper hospital nurse, at vast expense and procured with difficulty, or you could go to hospital. But after the critical phase of illness had passed, you were down to the Miss Knights." She thought the Miss Knights of the world treated their charges as "slightly mentally afflicted children." Miss Marple later referred to her in *Nemesis*, calling her "Miss Castle," "Miss Rook" and "Miss Bishop." *The Mirror Crack'd from Side to Side.*

KNIGHTON, MAJOR AKA Monsieur le Marquis. As Major Knighton, he procured the position of Rufus Van Aldin's resourceful and charming secretary. In reality he was Monsieur le Marquis, the famous international jewel thief with a passion for historical gems. Working in collaboration with Ada Beatrice Mason (AKA Kitty Kidd) he had staged various jewel thefts in Switzerland, France, the United Kingdom and the United States. He was currently working with Demetrius Papopolous to acquire Van Aldin's

Heart of Fire rubies. *The Mystery of the Blue Train.*

KOHN, OLGA *See* **HOBHOUSE, VALERIE.**

KRAMENIN Also known as "Number One," he was the "man behind bolshevism, the real author of the Russian Revolution, and had come to London to foment rebellion in England, He was "a small man, very pale, with a gentle, almost womanish air," and "strange light eyes that had a burning presence." He gave the impression of possessing some unusually potent force. Julius Hersheimmer kidnapped Kramenin, and as they were leaving to rescue his cousin Jane

Finn, he ventured a comment regarding his prisoner's coat: "Fur-lined? And you a Socialist?" *The Secret Adversary.*

KRANIN, COLONEL He had "a thick, rather foreign-looking moustache," and interviewed Jane Cleveland at Messrs. Cuthbertons' for the position of impersonating the Grand Duchess Pauline. He then sent Jane to see Count Streptitch at Harridge's Hotel. "Jane in Search of a Job" from *The Golden Ball.*

KRAPP, CHARLOTTE *See* **VON WALDSAUSEN, THE GRÄFIN CHARLOTTE.**

KRASSINE, MONSIEUR *See* **IVANOVITCH, BORIS.**

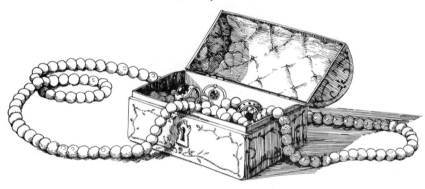

LACEY, COLIN The fifteen-year-old grandson of Em Lacey and Colonel Horace Lacey and the cousin Sarah Lacey, he was heir to Kings Lacey on the death of his grandfather. Colin and Michael, a school friend, and Sarah Lacey planned Poirot's Boxing Day surprise. "The Theft of the Royal Ruby" from *Double Sin.*

LACEY, EM The wife of Colonel Horace Lacey and the grandmother of Colin and Sarah Lacey, she was Poirot's very genial hostess at Kings Lacey during the Christmas vacation. She insinuated Poirot into her household to extricate her granddaughter Sarah from the clutches of Desmond Lee-Wortley. "The Theft of the Royal Ruby" from *Double Sin.*

LACEY, COLONEL HORACE The husband of Em Lacey, grandfather of Colin and Sarah Lacey and Poirot's host at Kings Lacey, "he might have been taken for a farmer rather than lord of the manor." A member of "the old school," he disapproved of both Poirot (though only at first) and Desmond Lee-Wortley (whom he would have liked to horse-whip). "The Theft of the Royal Ruby" from *Double Sin.*

LACEY, SARAH The cousin of Colin Lacey, she was the grand-daughter of Colonel Horace Lacey and Em Lacey, who said: "Sarah has got in with what they call the coffee-bar set. She won't go to dances or come out properly or be a deb or anything of that kind. Instead she has two rather unpleasant rooms in Chelsea down by the river and wears these funny clothes that they like to wear, and black stockings or bright green ones." Sarah thought she was in love with Desmond Lee-Wortley and made tentative plans to elope with him to the Continent. Unknown to her, Lee-Wortley's motive was the pursuit of the fortune that Sarah had inherited from her mother. "The Theft of the Royal Ruby" from *Double Sin.*

LAIDLAW, MAJOR Husband to Marguerite Laidlaw and an avid follower of the race track, the Major was suspected by Scotland Yard of counterfeiting. He requested the aid of Tuppence and Tommy Beresford for his defence. "The Crackler" from *Partners in Crime.*

LAIDLAW, MARGUERITE The attractive French wife of Major Laidlaw, she had produced evidence of possessing counterfeit notes three times, which put her high on Tommy Beresford's suspect list. She purportedly found five hundred pounds while on a treasure hunt with her friend Hank Ryder in Whitechapel. 'The Man in the Mist" from *Partners in Crime*.

LAKE, CAPTAIN JOHN Tall and fair-haired husband of Ruth Chevenix-Gore, he was Sir Gervaise Chevenix-Gore's estate agent. Frank and intelligent, he was good at his job and everyone liked him. In comparison with his wife, to whose wishes he deferred, he was quite mild-mannered. "Dead Man's Mirror" from *Murder in the Mews*.

LAL, CHANDRA An Indian student of medicine who lived at Mrs. Nicoletis' youth hostel, he was obsessed by the oppression of native races: "His mind is entirely occupied with politics and persecution mania." A few subversive pamphlets were discovered among his belongings. *Hickory Dickory Dock*.

LAL, RAM After the young Hindu student assaulted the Prime Minister, Alistair Blunt tried to protect Ram Lal: "He's a nice kid. A bit excitable but he feels the wrongs of India very keenly." *One, Two, Buckle My Shoe*.

LAMB, DETECTIVE SERGEANT A pencil-licking police sergeant, he did not think that Laurence Brown had committed the crime, but later, he and Inspector Tavener arrested Brenda Leonides and Laurence Brown for the murder of Aristide Leonides. *Crooked House*.

LAMB, COLIN Assumed name of the agent working for the Special Branch and to that end posing as a police constable, he discussed the international repercussions of the murder of "Mr. R.H. Curry" with Poirot. He fell in love with Sheila Marsh, a suspect in the case, and later married her, moved to Australia and took a post as a marine biologist at a university there. *The Clocks*.

LAMBERT, JOYCE The widow of Michael Lambert, she was a young woman of twenty-nine who felt sixty-nine. All of her attentions were riveted in an abnormally intense way on her little dog, Terry. Her poverty induced her to accept a proposal of marriage from Arthur Halliday, although she despised him. When Terry died, Joyce was free to accept a job overseas as the governess of Mr. Allaby's young son. "Next to a Dog" from *The Golden Ball*.

LANCASTER, MRS. The mother of Geoffrey Lancaster and the daughter of Mr. Winburn, she purchased a house that was haunted by the ghost of a young boy who had starved to death after his father had committed suicide. "The Lamp" from *The Golden Ball*.

LANCASTER, GEOFFREY The small son of Mrs. Lancaster and the grandson of Mr. Winburn, he came with his mother and grandfather to live in Weyminster, where he claimed to have seen a small boy crying in the attic, and later in the doorway of the nursery. When Geoffrey became ill and died, his spirit apparently left the sickroom to join the apparition in the attic. "The Lamp" from *The Golden Ball*.

LANCASTER, JULIA AKA Julia or Lilian Charrington, Killer Kate, Lady Julia Starke and Mrs. Yorke, Julia Lancaster the assumed name of an elderly, vague resident of the Sunny Ridge Nursing Home. As either Julia or Lilian Charrington she was the daughter of a dancer, a ruined and abandoned woman who committed suicide. As Killer Kate, she followed her mother's wild proclivities until the gang cashiered her for mental unbalance. As Lady Julia Starke, she was married to Sir Philip Starke who secreted her away in different rest homes and hired Nellie Bligh to watch her. As Mrs. Yorke, she received mail at the Rosetrellis Court for Elderly Ladies in Cornwall. Tuppence Beresford traced Mrs. Lancaster to Watermead, the house in William Boscowan's painting, where she was cared for by Alice and

Amos Perry. She died after drinking a glass of poisoned milk. *By the Pricking of My Thumbs.*

LANE, PATRICIA Student of archaeology living in Mrs. Nicoletis' youth hostel, she was robbed of a diamond solitaire ring. Poirot said she had no allure: "And her clothes! What is it they say? Dragged through a hedge backwards? *Ma foi*, that expresses it exactly!" She was slugged on the back of the head with a paperweight-stuffed sock. *Hickory Dickory Dock.*

LANE, REVEREND STEPHEN "His Reverence's trouble was an obsession about the Devil—especially the Devil in guise of a woman—scarlet woman—whore of Babylon." Arlena Marshall represented all the "evil under the sun" to Lane. Two women were strangled within twelve miles of the vicar's living in Whiteridge before Arlena Marshall's death. *Evil Under the Sun.*

LANGTON, CLAUDE Poirot met Claude Langton and John Harrison at a party. Langton was Mary Deane's ex-fiancé and was working toward a reconciliation with her. He told Poirot that he was going to Harrison's house to destroy a wasps' nest with petrol. "Wasps' Nest" from *Double Sin.*

LANSCOMBE The ancient butler of Enderby Hall, he sorely missed the old days and waged a losing battle against modernity, which was represented in part by the younger generation of servants at the Hall. About ninety years old, he moved "totteringly from room to room" and, when called on for speed, broke "into a shuffling trot." Loyally devoted to the Abernethies, he was also intensely patriotic. To him, polishing a Georgian silver teapot in the Abernethie household was an act of love. *After the Funeral.*

LANSQUENET, CORA ABERNETHIE Youngest sibling of Richard Abernethie, and widow of Pierre Lansquenet, she was "decidedly an afterthought" whose birth terminated her mother's life at age fifty. "Rather cushion-like in shape," she had "no judgement, no balance and a crude childish point of view, but she had also the child's uncanny knack of sometimes hitting the nail on the head." She remarked that her father had been murdered, which initiated an investigation and resulted in her death the day after his funeral. *After the Funeral.*

LA PAZ, THE MISTRESS OF As a young orphan girl, the anonymous owner La Paz, had married a young English swimmer. When he tragically drowned, she was relieved because he had been a cruel sadist and caused the stillbirth of their child. Because more than anything else she wanted a baby, she had a brief affair with Anthony Codson and bore him a son. She had a rejuvenating effect on men: "When she was in the room the sun seemed to be shining twice as brightly as when she was out of it, and presently a curious feeling of warmth and aliveness began to steal over Mr. Satterthwaite. It was as though he stretched out thin, shrivelled hands to a reassuring flame." "The Man from the Sea" from *The Mysterious Mr. Quin.*

LARKIN, MRS. Sister of Millicent Pebmarsh, aunt and stepmother of Sheila Webb, she had a rather "gipsyish" appearance. *The Clocks.*

LARKIN, BERYL Lady Carmichael suspected her vague neighbour, Mrs. Larkin, of drug addiction or perhaps the murder of her husband. She hosted cocaine parties, supplied by her pusher Anthony Hawker. "The Horses of Diomedes" from *The Labours of Hercules.*

LA ROCHE, MADEMOISELLE A former vendeuse in one of the Parisian *haut-couture* houses, she was employed by Mr. Aristides in the dress department of his Brain Trust complex. Possessed of a thrillingly feminine manner and a cheering laugh, she admitted to Hilary Craven, "*Entre nous*, my work is sometimes disappointing. These scientific ladies often take very little interest in *la toilette*." *Destination Unknown*.

LARRABY, DR. When asked by Mr. Entwistle about the possibility of foul play in the death of Richard Abernethie, the usually good-humoured Dr. Larraby "looked as though he had grave suspicions of Mr. Entwistle's own stability of mind." *After the Funeral*.

LATIMER, EDWARD (TED) A childhood friend of the unpopular Kay Strange, he had "lithe South American charm," and remarked that Latimer always turned up near his wife like "the faithful dog— or faithful lizard might be more apt." Superintendent Battle said: "He's the type that would smash in his own grandmother's head if he thought he could get away with it and knew he'd make something of it." Battle pursued a direct but novel means of discovering whether or not Latimer could swim. *Towards Zero*.

LAURIER, HENRI "A small Frenchman who looked like a commercial traveller," he acted as a contact agent between the Brain Trust complex and prospective members. Hilary Craven, disguised as Olive Betterton, was approached by Monsieur Laurier in Fez, Morocco; she gave the correct passwords, and was then given instructions for continuing her journey to meet Thomas Betterton. *Destination Unknown*.

LAVERTON-WEST, CHARLES An MP for Hampshire, he had two ambitions: to be a good public speaker and to get on in the world. He was engaged to Barbara Allen, who adored him, but Inspector Japp thought he was a "bit of a stuffed fish . . . *and* a boiled owl." "Murder in the Mews" from *Murder in the Mews*.

LAVIGNY, FATHER Working as an epigraphist with the American expedition at Tell Yarimjah, he informed Poirot that he was a member of the Pères Blancs at Carthage. After the murder of Anne Johnson, Father Lavigny disappeared. *See*

MENIER, RAOUL. *Murder in Mesopotamia*.

LAVINGTON, MR. AKA Croker or Reed, he was a member of the jewel thief gang headed by Gertie. He pretended to be blackmailing Lady Millicent Castle Vaughn, who subsequently consulted Poirot. He double-crossed Gertie and the rest of the gang. Hastings "felt a positive tingling" in the end of his boot, so keen was his desire to "kick him down the stairs." "The Veiled Lady" from *Poirot's Early Cases*.

LAVINGTON, DR. AMBROSE One of Jack Hartington's fellow guests at the small hotel near Stourton Heath links, he described himself as a doctor of the soul. He did not hear the mysterious voice that Jack claimed to hear every morning at 7:25, and recommended that they hold a séance. They hoped to contact the ghost of Mrs. Turner, who had been murdered at Heather Cottage. "The Blue Jar" from *Witness for the Prosecution*.

LAWES, ESTHER The sister of Rachel Lawes and the deceased Arthur Lawes, she was "six-foot-one of Jewish perfection." After her brother died, she wrote to Dickie Carpenter at sea, and when Dickie returned, they decided to marry. Esther soon broke their engagement. "The Gipsy" from *The Golden Ball*.

LAWES, RACHEL The younger sister of Esther Lawes and the deceased Arthur Lawes, Rachel Lawes was engaged to Mr. Macfarlane. She possessed a "childlike face and honest brown eyes. . . . Not a beauty like Esther. . . . But unutterably truer and sweeter." "The Gipsy" from *The Golden Ball*.

LAWSON, EDGAR The illegitimate son of Lewis Serrocold, Lawson was "a pathetic undersized young man in a neat dark suit, a young man that few people would look at twice, or remember if they did look." Lawson was brought to Stoneygates by his father, where he pretended to be a schizophrenic paranoid. Had he been less an actor and more a swimmer he might not have drowned. *They Do It with Mirrors.*

LAWSON, WILHELMINA Also called "Mina" and "Minnie," the "slave" and companion of Emily Arundell was favoured over the Arundell family as the beneficiary of her employer's will. In her last illness Miss Arundell asked Lawson for the new will and, fearing a change of heart in her employer, Wilhelmina lied and told her it had been sent to the solicitor. An ardent spiritualist, she and the weird Tripp sisters induced Miss Arundell to join in a séance. The "luminous ribbon issuing from Miss Arundell's mouth" at the séance was symptomatic of phosphorus poisoning. After Poirot solved the case, "Miss Lawson, in an acute attack of conscience, had to be restrained forcibly from denuding herself of every penny," and finally shared her fortune with Charles and Theresa Arundell and the Tanios children. *Dumb Witness.*

LAXTON, HARRY The son of Major Laxton and owner of Kingsdean House, he was once a wicked young scapegrace who had grown up, worked hard, become wealthy and married Louise, a lovely young girl. The village had always had a soft spot for Harry: "He had broken windows, robbed orchards, poached rabbits and later had run into debt, got entangled with the local tobacconist's daughter—had been disentangled and sent off to Africa—the village as represented by various aging spinsters had murmured indulgently, 'Ah, well! Wild oats! He'll settle down!' " The only blight upon Harry and Louise Laxton's bliss was the muttering imprecations of old Mrs. Murgatroyd who, with her husband, had taken care of old Kingsdean House for thirty years. He settled with her, but his happiness was short-lived. Louise died soon after. Dr. Haydock presented the case of Harry Laxton as a literary puzzle to spark Miss Marple's failing interest in life. "The

Case of the Caretaker" from *Three Blind Mice and Other Stories.*

LAXTON, LOUISE The bride of Harry Laxton, she was an object of envy in the village because of her looks, youth, money and breeding. The village spinsters hoped that Harry's mis-spent youth would catch up with the happy couple. She died following a fall from her sensitive chestnut stallion, Prince Hal. "The Case of the Caretaker" from *Three Blind Mice and Other Stories.*

LAZARUS, JIM Wealthy friend of Nick Buckley, he was interested in Frederica Rice and with his father owned a Bond Street art gallery. *Peril at End House.*

LAZENBY, DR. Police surgeon in the district surrounding Gull's Point, he suggested that a bloodied golf club may have been the weapon used to murder Lady Tressilian, and that the blow seemed to have been struck by a left-handed person. *Towards Zero.*

LAZENBY, CEDRIC The Prime Minister of England, during the Youth Movement and student unrest, he "was beginning to think that it was only in the privacy of his Cabinet Meetings that he could relax his face into an unhappy expression, and could abandon that look which he presented usually to the world . . . Mr. Lazenby had an incurable fund of optimism seldom justified by results." *Passenger to Frankfurt.*

LEACH, INSPECTOR JAMES (JIM) The nephew of Superintendent Battle, he was under the misapprehension that a fine sportsman such as Nevile Strange could not possibly be a murder suspect. *Towards Zero.*

LEADBETTER, MR. He was sitting behind George Earlsfield, the fourth victim of the A.B.C. murderer, at the Regal Cinema and was so intensely involved in the film that he could only be irritated at the distraction of a murder in front of him. Inspector Crome found him "about as bad a witness" as one could imagine. *The A.B.C. Murders.*

LEADBETTER, MRS. The widow of Canon Leadbetter, she came to the Stag for a month every year on the anniversary of her husband's death. She told Poirot that she had seen a woman in the room of "Enoch Arden" the night of the murder. *Taken at the Flood.*

LEADBETTER, EPHRAIM A partner in Leadbetter and Gilling, he had fired his nephew George Dundas from the firm because of "the criminal folly and wickedness of a young man, who has his way to make, taking a day off in the middle of the week without even asking leave." He gave George a lecture on "opportunities and taking them." George took these words to heart when he met Mary Montresor, a wealthy society girl. "The Golden Ball" from *The Golden Ball.*

LEAMAN, HARRIET A cleaning-lady to Mrs. Llewellyn-Smythe and other residents of Woodleigh Common, she consulted Ariadne Oliver, whom she knew as a famous detective fiction writer, about a codicil ("some word like codi. Like the fish I mean") to her mistress' will. After witnessing the codicil, Harriet hid the will in the Victorian volume, *Enquire Within Upon Everything. Hallowe'en Party.*

LEASON, CLAUD *See* **AVERBURY, CLAUD.**

LEATHERAN, MISS "The worst cat of the lot," according to Jean Moncrieffe, she was a villager in Market Loughborough. Poirot amused himself by counting the number of times she used the phrase "of course" in their conversation. Pretending to be from the Home Office, he counted on her lack of discretion and eagerness to spread gossip when he casually mentioned the possibility of an exhumation. "The Lernean Hydra" from *The Labours of Hercules.*

LEATHERAN, AMY The companion to Lady Matilda Cleckheaton, "Amy, Lady Matilda thought suddenly, would look exactly like a sheep when she was ten years older. A nice, faithful, kindly sheep. At the moment, Lady Matilda was glad to think she looked still like a very agreeable plump lamb with nice curls of hair, thoughtful and kindly eyes, and able to give kindly baa's rather than to bleat." *Passenger to Frankfurt.*

LEATHERAN, NURSE AMY A "generous-natured woman with a romantic disposition," she journeyed to Iraq to help Mrs. Kelsey care for her baby; later, she was hired by Dr. Leidner to care for his wife Louise, who suffered from "fancies." She found Hercule Poirot like "a hairdresser in a comic play," did not expect him to be "quite as foreign as he was" and thought him so comic that she could not imagine him with a wife or a mistress. Nevertheless, they became a team to discover who murdered Mrs. Leidner and Anne Johnson. *Murder in Mesopotamia.*

LEATHERN, EVE AKA Maria Amalfi, she was the young daughter of Samuel Leathern and one of Isaac Pointz' guests at the Regatta in Dartmouth Harbour. She bet Mr. Pointz that she could successfully steal his Morning Star diamond from under his nose; if she could, he was to pay her half a dozen pairs of nylon stockings; if she was caught, she would owe him a tobacco pouch. The light-hearted stunt became grave when the diamond disappeared from Eve's hiding place. As Maria Amalfi, she was the wife of Pietro Amalfi, son of the famous jewel thief, Amalfi. Parker Pyne reported her to be an "amazing creature, twenty-seven at least, and nearly always played a part of sixteen." "The Regatta Mystery" from *The Regatta Mystery.*

LEATHERN, SAMUEL AKA Amalfi, he was an American businessman, the father of Eve Leathern and irritated his host, Isaac Pointz, with his "disconcerting habit of requiring precise information." As Amalfi, he was the father of Pietro Amalfi and the head of an international gang of jewel thieves. "The Regatta Mystery" from *The Regatta Mystery.*

LEBLANC, MONSIEUR A stocky Frenchman, he worked with Jessop in locating and exposing Mr. Aristides' Brain Trust complex in the Atlas Mountains. In Monsieur Leblanc's opinion, "it is easier to control temperamental opera singers than it is to control a scientist." *Destination Unknown.*

LECKIE, MARTHA Sir Bartholomew Strange's cook, she was horrified that the police had to have their noses in the dustbins during their investigation. *Three-Act Tragedy.*

LECKY, MR. Major Barnard's golfing partner, he reported seeing Anthony Sessle speak with a woman during his game. When Sessle returned from the conversation, Lecky noticed that he played much worse than before. "The Sunningdale Mystery" from *Partners in Crime.*

LE CONTEAU, ELEANOR AKA Eleanor Harwell. The young owner of Ashley Grange was married to Captain Richard Harwell, who had disappeared the day they returned from their honeymoon. She was "a very beautiful young lady, and well thought of, for all she was a Canadian and a stranger." As Eleanor Harwell, she posed as the wife of Richard Harwell, and belonged to an acrobatic troupe, the Clondinis, which was a front for a theft organization. "At the Bells and Motley" from *The Mysterious Mr. Quin.*

LEE, ALFRED The eldest son of Simeon Lee, husband of Lydia Lee and the brother of George, Harry and David Lee and the deceased Jennifer Estravados (*née* Lee), Alfred Lee "gave a curious impression of inertia." He was the only son still living at the Lee home and for most of his adult life he had waited on his father hand and foot, but Simeon Lee detested him be-

cause he was so dull. There was also a long-standing animosity between Alfred and his brother Harry. *Hercule Poirot's Christmas.*

LEE, DAVID The youngest son of Simeon Lee, he was married to Hilda Lee. He was overly devoted to the memory of his mother, Adelaide Lee (*See* **LEE, SIMEON**), whom he believed had died from a "broken heart." David left home at a young age to pursue the life of an artist in London. He was living on a small allowance from his father and had not been home in twenty years. *Hercule Poirot's Christmas.*

LEE, DINAH The legal wife of Basil Blake, Dinah pretended to be his mistress with "scarlet lips, blackened eyelashes and a platinum-blond head" solely to aggravate village gossip in St. Mary Mead. *The Body in the Library.*

LEE, ESTHER (OLD MOTHER LEE) A sinister old creature, she lived in a cottage on Major Phillpot's land near Gispy's Acre. She was the local witch and fortune-teller in Kingston Bishop, and had been warning the inhabitants of Gipsy's Acre, among them Michael and Ellie Rogers and Greta Anderson, of impending doom. Sergeant Keene thought that she had sent the many anonymous notes, some tied to rocks thrown through windows, in the area. Old Mother Lee disappeared shortly before Ellie Rogers' death, and was discovered several days later dead from a fall into a disused quarry. She was an old hag, frightening and menacing but she did have, as she pointed out, the gift of prophecy. *Endless Night.*

LEE, GEORGE The second eldest son of Simeon Lee, he was married to Magdalene Lee. He was MP for Westeringham, and only pretended affection toward his father. His father disliked him because he was a boring, slow, penny-pinching and stupid person. *Hercule Poirot's Christmas.*

LEE, HENRY (HARRY) The third son of Simeon Lee, he was also the prodigal son: he left home to roam around the world after having forged his father's name on a cheque. Simeon Lee would nevertheless wire Harry funds when he was broke and summoned him home for Christmas. After their reconciliation, Simeon found his son Harry to be the most spirited of all his legitimate children and eventually, Simeon offered to change his will in Harry's favour. *Hercule Poirot's Christmas.*

LEE, HILDA The wife of David Lee, she was constantly trying to subdue her husband's obsession with his dead mother. She was: "An over-stout dumpy middle-aged woman—not clever—not brilliant—but with something about her that you couldn't pass over. Force! Hilda Lee had force!" *Hercule Poirot's Christmas.*

LEE, LYDIA The wife of Alfred Lee, she was "an energetic, lean greyhound of a woman." Simeon Lee liked her because she had "spirit," but she detested him because he manipulated people and harrassed her husband. *Hercule Poirot's Christmas.*

LEE, MAGDALENE The wife of George Lee, she was twenty years younger than her husband, "a slender creature, a platinum blond with plucked eyebrows and a smooth egg-like face. It could, on occasions, look quite blank, devoid of any expression whatever." Known to see other men, she had once lived with Commander Jones although they pretended that the relationship was one between father and daughter. *Hercule Poirot's Christmas.*

LEE, SIMEON The patriarch of the Lee family, his legitimate children were Alfred, George, Harry and David Lee and the deceased Jennifer Estravados (*née* Lee). His bastard sons were Stephen Grant (AKA Stephen Farr) and Superintendent Sugden. He had made life miserable for his wife Adelaide, since deceased, and his children. Lee called his far-flung family together at Christmas for the express purpose of tormenting them and amusing himself. On Christmas Eve he was found brutally murdered. *Hercule Poirot's Christmas.*

LEECH, ANDREW AKA Monsieur Antoine, he was "Iky Andrew ... the old devil" to his employees. Andrew Leech was the real name of Monsieur Antoine of Antoine's beauty salon, where Jane Grey worked. It was "second nature for him to speak in broken English once within the portals of Bruton Street." He lost Jane, his drawing-card, when one of his clients began to resemble her pet Pekinese too closely. *Death in the Clouds.*

LEE-WORTLEY, DESMOND A young man who had a reputation for preying on young heiresses, he arrived at Kings Lacey at the invitation of Em Lacey with a woman playing the role of his sister. His current victim was Sarah Lacey. "The Theft of the Royal Ruby" from *Double Sin.*

LEGGE, ALEC Mean-tempered husband to Sally Legge, he was considered "more unfortunate than reprehensible" by Poirot. He was an atom scientist horrified at the mess of the modern world; this and his sense of injustice caused him to become involved with "a certain political party" as a sort of espionage agent. *Dead Man's Folly.*

LEGGE, ROSY *See* **KEENE, RUBY.**

LEGGE, SALLY Wife of the unfortunate Alec, she was a friendly, attractive redhead who told fortunes at the fête under the name of Madame Zuleika. An intelligent university graduate, she once had an art studio in Chelsea. Sir George Stubbs made a pass at her. After three years of marriage, Alec's moodiness and obsessions distressed her so much that she left him for her old friend Michael Weyman. *Dead Man's Folly.*

LEGGE, SIR THOMAS An Assistant Commissioner of Scotland Yard, he discussed the Indian Island case with his assistant, Inspector Maine: "The whole thing's fantastic—impossible. Ten people killed on a bare rock of island—and we don't know who did it, or why, or how." *And Then There Were None.*

LEICESTER, MARJORY The friend and flat-mate to Una Drake, she testified that Una had slept at home the night of the bet. "The Unbreakable Alibi" from *Partners in Crime.*

LEIDNER, DR. ERIC The distinguished archaeologist in charge of the expedition at Tell Yarimjah, he was the husband of Louise Leidner. His love for her was "the ruling passion of his life," and he hired Nurse Leatheran to care for her because she suffered from "fancies." (*See* **BOSNER, FREDERICK.**) *Murder in Mesopotamia.*

LEIDNER, LOUISE One-time wife of Frederick Bosner and later of Dr. Eric Leidner, she was a woman possessed of remarkably contradictory characteristics. She was called "a mass of affectation" and a "champion liar," and was "the sort of woman who could easily make enemies." Poirot said she was "one of those women who do inspire devouring devotions in men, the type of devotion which can become an obsession." Her husband and her lover, Richard Carey, were both affected by her "calamitous magic." Following several weeks of terror caused by the anonymous, threatening letters she received, she was murdered by a blow to the head from a heavy quern. *Murder in Mesopotamia.*

LEITH, DUCHESS OF Distantly related to Naomi Carlton-Smith, the Duchess of Leith appealed to the snobbish side of Mr. Satterthwaite's nature because she was both the daughter of a duke and the wife of one. "She had quantities of diamonds in old-fashioned settings, and she wore them as her mother before her had worn them: pinned all over her indiscriminately. Someone had suggested once that the Duchess stood in the middle of the room while her maid flung brooches at her haphazard." Bored of the high prices in Cannes, the Duchess dragged Mr. Satterthwaite off to Corsica, saying, "we needn't be afraid of scandal at our time of life." "The World's End" from *The Mysterious Mr. Quin.*

LEJEUNE, INSPECTOR Mark Easterbrooke remarked: "He had an air of quiet ability. I thought, too, that he was an imaginative man—the kind of man who would be willing to consider possibilities that were not orthodox." *The Pale Horse.*

LeMAITRE, CHARLES *See* **MARTIN, GERALD.**

LEMAN, ANNE MORISOT *See* **MORISOT, ANNE.**

LEMARCHANT, CARLA Daughter of Caroline and Amyas Crale, Carla wished to commission Poirot to reopen the case of her father's murder to clear the memory of her mother so that she could marry her fiancé, John Rattery, with a clear past. *Five Little Pigs.*

LE MARCHANT, JIMMY Jimmy verified Una Drake's story of having had dinner with him at the Savoy the night of the bet, and quite proudly showed the Beresfords the notation of their date in his appointment book. He also mentioned that a friend, Dicky Rice, had seen Una in Torquay on the day in question. "The Unbreakable Alibi" from *Partners in Crime.*

LE MARQUIS, MONSIEUR *See* **KNIGHTON, MAJOR.**

LEMENTEUIL, COMMISSIONAIRE Swiss Commissionaire of Police and an old friend and colleague of Poirot's, he slipped Poirot a note which began: "Impossible to mistake those moustaches!" He told Poirot of the "race-course" killer Marrascaud whom he had traced to the resort Rochers Neige high in the Swiss Alps. Poirot helped in the search and Lementeuil arrived by helicopter to arrest Marrascaud. "The Erymanthian Boar" from *The Labours of Hercules.*

LEMESURIER, HUGO The husband of Sadie Lemesurier, he was the father of Gerald Lemesurier, the nominal father of Ronald Lemesurier and the uncle of Captain Vincent Lemesurier. The family curse—that the first-born Lemesurier should never inherit—became an obsession with him. "The Lemesurier Inheritance" from *The Under Dog.*

LE MESURIER, NINA *See* **HOBHOUSE, VALERIE.**

LEMESURIER, MAJOR ROGER A cousin from a distant branch of the Lemesurier family, he recounted the legend of the family curse to Poirot. In mediaeval times, Baron Hugo Lemesurier suspected his wife of infidelity and killed her. She protested her innocence, and to gain vengeance, cursed the first-born son of the Lemesurier family forever. Since then, none of the first-born sons had inherited. "The Lemesurier Inheritance" from *The Under Dog.*

LEMESURIER, RONALD He was the son of Hugo's wife, Sadie, and his secretary, John Gardiner. Several suspicious accidents occurred to the eight-year-old heir to the Lemesurier estate: he scarcely escaped drowning, the ivy he climbed was mysteriously severed by a saw and he unfortunately contracted ptomaine poisoning. "The Lemesurier Inheritance" from *The Under Dog.*

LEMESURIER, SADIE The wife of Hugo Lemesurier and the mother of Ronald Lemesurier (by John Gardiner) and Gerald Lemesurier, she married John Gardiner after her husband's death. "The Lemesurier Inheritance" from *The Under Dog.*

LEMESURIER, CAPTAIN VINCENT The son of John Lemesurier and the nephew of Hugo Lemesurier, he lived in fear of the Lemesurier curse. (*See* **LEMESURIER, MAJOR ROGER.**) Ill from shellshock, he became even more disturbed at the news of his father's fall from a horse and impending death. "The Lemesurier Inheritance" from *The Under Dog.*

LEMOINE, MONSIEUR An inspector from the Sûreté in Paris, he was to have come to Chimneys to locate King Victor, but he was unavoidably detained. When he finally did arrive at Chimneys, he had "a foppish appearance slightly marred by a bandage around the head." (*See* **VICTOR, KING.**) *The Secret of Chimneys.*

LEMON, FELICITY The sister of Mrs. Hubbard, Felicity Lemon began as Mr. Parker Pyne's secretary, but quickly moved on to work for Hercule Poirot. Miss Lemon was "unbelievably ugly and incredibly efficient . . . composed entirely of angles—thus satisfying Poirot's demand for symmetry. . . . Her general effect was that of a lot of bones flung together at random. She had a passion for order almost equalling that of Poirot himself, and though capable of thinking, she never thought unless told to do so. . . . She was very nearly the perfect machine, completely and gloriously uninterested in all human affairs. Her real passion in life was the perfection of a filing system besides which all other filing systems should sink into oblivion." "The Case of the Middle-Aged Wife," "The Case of the Distressed Lady" from *Parker Pyne Investigates;* "How Does Your Garden Grow" from *The Regatta Mystery;* "The Nemean Lion" and "The Capture of Cerberus" from *The Labours of Hercules; Hickory, Dickory, Dock; Dead Man's Folly;* "The Mystery of the Spanish Chest" from *The Adventure of the Christmas Pudding; Third Girl; Elephants Can Remember.*

LEONIDES, ARISTIDE The wealthy Greek restaurateur and businessman, he was the widower of Marcia de Haviland, father of Roger and Philip Leonides, father-in-law of Clemency and Magda Leonides, the brother-in-law of Edith de Haviland and the grandfather of Sophia, Eustace and Josephine Leonides. At the age of seventy-four, he met Brenda, a twenty-four-year-old waitress at his restaurant, The Gay Shamrock, and married her, much to the shock and chagrin of the rest of his family. Far from causing widespread resentment, the benign old patriarch was generally beloved. Inspector Tavener admitted: "Funny thing was, he was attractive. He'd got personality, you know. You could feel it. Nothing much to look at. Just a gnome—ugly little fellow—but magnetic—women always fell for him." Aristide exercised his shrewd business acumen to the end of his life. In the secret will that Mr. Gaitskill unknowingly managed, he stated: "In a family . . . there is always one strong character and it usually falls to this person to care for, and bear the burden of, the rest of the family. In my family I was that person." Aristide Leonides died in his eighty-fourth year; he suffered from glaucoma and diabetes, and was killed when someone adulterated his daily insulin injection with er-serine. *Crooked House.*

LEONIDES, BRENDA She was a young, single and pregnant waitress before she married Aristide Leonides. Sophia Leonides, his elder grand-daughter, said, "Oh, Grandfather wasn't taken in. . . . Grandfather was never taken in by anybody. He wanted Brenda. He wanted to play Cophetua to her beggar-maid." Brenda reminded Inspector Tavener of "a cat, a big purring lazy cat"; Magda Leonides referred to her as "that woman upstairs. . . . Horrible creature!" The flat-voiced, large-eyed Brenda, whose wide mouth "curled up sideways in a queer, sleepy, smile," was arrested with her step-children's tutor, Laurence Brown, for the murder of her husband. *Crooked House.*

LEONIDES, CLEMENCY The wife of Roger Leonides and daughter-in-law of Aristide Leonides, she was a scientist working on the radiation effects of atomic disintegration. Charles Hayward said she was "one of those rare people to whom money does not appeal. They dislike luxury, prefer austerity and are suspicious of possessions." He also found her boudoir uncomfortably reminiscent of an operating-theatre. He commented: "Love for Roger, I saw, made up her whole existence. He was her child, as well as her husband and her lover." *Crooked House.*

LEONIDES, EUSTACE The sixteen-year-old son of Philip and Magda Leonides and grandson of Aristide Leonides, he contracted infantile paralysis which left him "not exactly lame, but his walk was a halting one." He resented having a private tutor and sharing his lessons with his sister Josephine. In the secret will, Aristides said that Eustace was "indolent and very easily influenced by the ideas of anyone whom he meets." Moody, arrogant and odd, he took himself very seriously. *Crooked House.*

LEONIDES, JOSEPHINE The daughter of Philip and Magda Leonides and grand-daughter of Aristide Leonides, she was "a fantastically ugly child with a very distinct likeness to her grandfather." Inspector Tavener suspected that the precocious eleven-year-old was "wise to everything that goes on in that house." Three attempts had been made on her life, which prompted investigators to surmise that the murderer was aware of Josephine's insight. Josephine admitted she had not liked her grandfather much, since he had kept her from studying ballet; she also resented Nannie for encouraging Magda to send her away to a Swiss school. The only person she loved, she confided to Charles Hayward, was her aunt Edith de Haviland. *Crooked House.*

LEONIDES, MAGDA AKA Magda West, her stage name, Magda Leonides was the wife of Philip Leonides, the mother of Sophia, Eustace and Josephine Leonides, and daughter-in-law of Aristide Leonides, whom she referred to as "Sweetie

Pie." She feared that what Charles Hayward found "a delightfully tip-tilted nose" would forever consign her to playing comedy roles. Eustace told Hayward that she was "always haring up and down to London and bullying tame dramatists to rewrite plays for her, and making frightful fusses about nothing at all." *Crooked House.*

LEONIDES, PHILIP The husband of Madga Leonides, brother of Roger and son of Aristide Leonides, he was the author of numerous books which no one read. His father had settled a hundred and fifty thousand pounds in various bonds and securities upon him, making him financially independent, but what Philip really wanted from his father was love and attention. In his secret will, Aristide stated: "My son Philip is too unsure of himself to do anything but retreat from life." Philip's daughter, Sophia, thought his "studied coldness" was "probably a kind of unconscious self-defence" against her mother's "absolute orgies of emotion." *Crooked House.*

LEONIDES, ROGER The eldest son of Aristide Leonides and the husband of Clemency Leonides, he was lovable, friendly and companionable, but an utter failure at business. His great admiration and devotion for his father was the only reason he kept on trying in business, knowing full well that he had no aptitude. Roger inspired a mixture of affection, pity and resentment among his family. Roger's inability to live up to his father's success was his one great sorrow. *Crooked House.*

LEONIDES, SOPHIA The daughter of Philip and Magda Leonides and granddaughter of Aristide Leonides resembled her grandfather in character more than any other member of the Leonides clan.

Her grandfather stated in his secret will: "Only my grand-daughter Sophia seems to me to have the positive qualities required. She has brains, judgement, courage, a fair and unbiased mind and, I think, generosity of spirit." He left her in control of his entire estate. Her fiancé, Charles Hayward, said to her: "Sophia, I fully believe that all that is bravest and best in the Leonides family has been handed down to you." *Crooked House.*

LEONIE Mrs. Vanderlyn's coquettish maid was "very good to look at" in Poirot's opinion. She admitted to Poirot that she had not really seen a ghost, but had been overwhelmingly surprised by Reggie Carrington's embrace and had merely invented the tale of a mysterious figure in white. After satisfactorily answering Poirot's questions, the French minx said to the detective, "Thank you, Monsieur. If I meet Monsieur on the stairs, be well assured that I shall not scream." "The Incredible Theft" from *Murder in the Mews.*

LESSING, RUTH George Barton's loyal, efficient secretary, "good-looking in a severe black and white kind of way, she was the essence of efficiency combined with fact." Colonel Race suspected her of being "one of those women who can be kindled to unlikely passion by one particular man." *Sparkling Cyanide.*

LESTER, CHARLES The young bank clerk on board the S.S. *Assunta* with Wu Ling, he was drugged by a Chinese posing as Wu Ling and then released, but shortly thereafter was charged with the murder of Wu Ling. Poirot cleared him of the crime. "The Lost Mine" from *Poirot's Early Cases.*

LESTRANGE, MRS. The first wife of Colonel Lucius Protheroe and the mother of Lettice Protheroe, she had an enigmatic presence, and Laurence Redding called her the "Mystery Lady of St. Mary Mead." The name Lestrange was an alias assumed to cover an unknown identity.

She had a secret meeting with Colonel Protheroe the night before his death. *Murder at the Vicarage.*

LETARDEAU, RAOUL The "fourth man," he shared a train compartment with Dr. Campbell Clark, Sir George Durand and Canon Parfitt, and listened to their discussion of body, soul, spirit, multiple personalities and the case of Felicie Bault. He provided them with clues to the source of the girl's four personalities. "The Fourth Man" from *Witness for the Prosecution.*

LEVERSON, CHARLES The nephew of Sir Reuben Astwell, he had quarrelled with Sir Astwell the night before his uncle's murder. "The Under Dog" from *The Under Dog.*

LI CHANG YEN Li Chang Yen was "Number One" in the Big Four gang. He was the most intelligent member of the group and controlled the East. Of the mandarin class, he was complimented by Poirot who called him "the finest criminal brain ever known." *The Big Four.*

LINCH, GLADYS A young maid, she was pregnant by Albert Jones and died in childbirth after he deserted her. "The Tuesday Night Club" from *The Thirteen Problems.*

LINDSTROM, KIRSTEN (KIRSTY) A Swedish nurse and masseuse at Rachel Argyle's wartime nursery, she stayed on with the Argyles as housekeeper after the war. Dr. Calgary thought that Kirsten's "should have been a nun's face! It demanded the crisp white coif . . . framed tightly round the face, and the black habit and veil. It was the face, not of a contemplative, but of the lay-sister who peers at you suspiciously through the little opening in the thick door, before grudgingly admitting you and takes you to the visiting parlour or to Reverend Mother." The family members agreed that Kirsten had been "really quite devoted" to Rachel. She was said to be "as plain as a current bun." *Ordeal by Innocence.*

LINGARD, MISS Once mistress to Anthony Chevenix-Gore and mother of his bastard child Ruth, she remained unrecognized by the family when she came ostensibly to aid Sir Gervase in writing a history of the Chevenix-Gores. Her real motive was to see her daughter again. "Dead Man's Mirror" from *Murder in the Mews.*

LIONEL, SIR An Assistant Commissioner of the C.I.D. at Scotland Yard, he was furious at the suggestion that the A.B.C. murderer would work through the alphabet to "z": "In my day if a man was mad he was mad and we didn't look for scientific terms to soften it down. I suppose a thoroughly up-to-date doctor would suggest putting a man like A.B.C. in a nursing home, telling him what a fine fellow he was for forty-five days on end and then letting him out as a responsible member of society." *The A.B.C. Murders.*

LIPPINCOTT, ANDREW P. A lawyer, he was "Uncle Andrew" to his ward Ellie Guteman, of whom he was very fond. Concerned with his young ward's safety, he hired two private detectives, Carson and his wife, and installed them as butler and cook in her household at Gipsy's Acre. *Endless Night.*

LIPPINCOTT, BEATRICE The publican of the Stag in Warmsley Vale, she thought that Rowley Cloade was "a fine figure of a man," and when she realized that her mysterious guest, "Enoch Arden," had dealings with David Hunter, she eavesdropped on their conversation. She then informed Rowley that Arden attempted to blackmail Hunter about Robert Underhay. *Taken at the Flood.*

LIPSCOMB "Abominably rude" and "immune from the general sweetness and light of Green Hills," he lived in the Lodge which gave admission to the Flock of the Shepherd at Green Hills in Devonshire. He was Dr. Andersen's "faithful watchdog. He is a crude—primitive soul—but faithful—utterly faithful." He followed

Miss Carnaby to the tea-shop where she met Poirot for a strategy conference. "The Flock of Geryon" from *The Labours of Hercules*.

LISKEARD, PROFESSOR Meek archaeologist and friend of the Countess Rossakoff's, he was the decorator of her lounge, Hell. The Countess took his "good steak" to demonstrate the manners of her well-trained dog, Cerberus. "The Capture of Cerberus" from *The Labours of Hercules*.

LISTERDALE, LORD AKA Quentin. The cousin of Colonel Maurice Carfax, he had "the meditative calm of an archbishop." In repentance for having led what he believed to be a totally selfish life, Lord Listerdale hit upon the idea of retiring his butler, Quentin, assuming Quentin's identity and serving as butler at his London house, which he had let to Mrs. St. Vincent. He announced that he had gone to East Africa, but young Rupert St. Vincent was suspicious: "Depend upon it, he was murdered in that house. You say there's a lot of panelling?" After he was unmasked, Listerdale asked Mrs. St. Vincent to marry him. "The Listerdale Mystery" from *The Golden Ball*.

LITCHFIELD, ELIZABETH See **COLE, ELIZABETH**.

LITTLEDALE, JAMES ARTHUR A chemist employed by the chemical wholesalers Jenkins and Hale, he confirmed the fact that the fragment of a label found near the scene of Mary Gerrard's murder was not from a container of morphine, as police originally thought, but from apomorphine, a powerful emetic that counteracts morphine poisoning. *Sad Cypress*.

LITTLEWORTH, MR. *See* **SANDERS, JACK**.

LIVINGSTONE, MISS Ariadne Oliver's new secretary who proved to be not as efficient as her old one, Miss Sedgwick, she was sent on an exhaustive search for Mrs. Oliver's old address books and her birthday book. *Elephants Can Remember*.

LLEWELLYN, EVAN One of Isaac Pointz' guests at the Regatta in Dartmouth Harbour, he "was a dark young man—there was a faintly hungry wolfish look about him which some women found attractive." He was a writer and had made a large sum of money at the racetrack at the same time that the Morning Star, Mr. Pointz' diamond mascot, had been stolen. Parker Pyne assured him that he was not a criminal type: "Not, that is, the particular type that steals jewellery. There are crimes, of course, you might commit—but we won't enter into that subject." "The Regatta Mystery" from *The Regatta Mystery*.

LLEWELLYN-SMYTHE, MRS. Extremely wealthy, short-tempered aunt to Hugo Drake, she had a fight with Hugo and his wife Rowena, disinherited them and added a codicil to her will which left all her money to her "opera" (*au pair*) girl Olga Seminoff. The codicil was found to be an obvious forgery, and Mrs. Llewellyn-Smythe and Hugo Drake died soon after each other. The final disposition left her land and house to Michael Garfield, her landscape designer, and her money to Rowena Drake. *Hallowe'en Party*.

LLOYD, MRS. Mrs. Casson heralded Mrs. Lloyd as "simply the most wonderful medium that every existed," and brought her to Abbot's Mead to conduct a séance for Margery Gale. She wore a chain of moonstones and several rings and would only eat fruit before conducting a séance. "The Voice in the Dark" from *The Mysterious Mr. Quin*

LLOYD, STANFORD A trustee of Ellie Guteman's he managed her investments and was at one time married to Claudia Hardcastle. When Michael Rogers met him, he thought that "there was something about Stanford Lloyd that was almost too good to be true. He was a banker, and he looked like a banker. He was a rather handsome man thought not young. He was very polite to me and thought dirt of me though he tried not to show it." Rogers fired Lloyd as investment manager to the Guteman estate after he began to suspect him of swindling. *Endless Night.*

LOFTUS, SQUADRON LEADER *See* **LONG, SAMUEL.**

LOGAN, MISS The companion of the late Lady Radclyffe, she was housekeeper for Lois Hargreaves at Thurnley Grange. She ate the Ricin-poisoned fig paste sandwiches which killed Lois Hargreaves, and died from the shock of Hannah's maniacal arson attempt. "The House of Lurking Death" from *Partners in Crime.*

LOLLIPOP, BARON *See* **LOLOPRETJZYL, BARON.**

LOLOPRETJZYL, BARON A Herzoslavakian baron in Prince Michael Obolovitch's entourage, he was called Baron Lollipop by Anthony Cade because his real name sounded like "a cross between gargling and barking like a dog." He attempted to obtain the late Count Stylptitch's memoirs from Anthony Cade, who was masquerading as Jimmy McGrath. *The Secret of Chimneys.*

LOMAX, THE HONOURABLE GEORGE Virginia Revel's cousin and the owner of Wyvern Abbey, he was nicknamed Codders because of his protruding fish-like eyes. He was Undersecretary of State for Foreign Affairs. Bill Eversleigh, who worked under Lomax, described him as "a disgusting wind-bag, an unscrupulous, hypocritical old hot-air merchant— a foul, poisonous self-advertiser." *The Secret of Chimneys; The Seven Dials Mystery.*

LOMBARD, CAPTAIN PHILIP A *soi-disant* soldier of fortune, he was invited to Indian Island and accused of the deaths of twenty-one members of an East African tribe. He said it was a "matter of self-preservation." He became the ninth victim, fatally shot with his own revolver by Vera Claythorne when they appeared to be the only ones left on the Island. *And Then There Were None.*

LONG, SAMUEL AKA Squadron Leader Loftus. Signor Poli related to Mr. Parker Pyne that Long was "a great criminal, that man. Even in Italy we have suffered. He inspired confidence all over the world. He is a man of breeding, too, they say." He claimed that his talents did not include murder. As Squadron Leader Loftus, he was among the twelve people travelling from Damascus to Baghdad. "The Gate of Baghdad" from *Parker Pyne Investigates.*

LONGMAN, PROFESSOR A scientist interested in spiritualism, he was recruited by Philip Garrod to test the authenticity of Eurydice Spragg. He came to the conclusion that Mrs. Spragg was a fraud, but he could not detect her method. "Motive *v* Opportunity" from *The Thirteen Problems.*

LOPEZ, CONCHITA AKA Pilar Estravados. Conchita Lopez assumed the identity of her dead friend Pilar Estravados, the daughter of Jennifer Estravados (*née* Lee), Simeon Lee's only grandchild. She had "the mouth of a child or a kitten— a mouth that knew only its own desires and that was as yet unaware of pity." Poirot recognized that she could not be the real Pilar Estravados because she had brown eyes while both parents were blue-eyed. Later, Conchita travelled to South Africa to marry her admirer, Stephen Grant. *Hercule Poirot's Christmas.*

LORD, DR. PETER He engaged the services of Poirot on behalf of the accused murderess Elinor Carlisle, with whom he had fallen in love. He said: "I like my job. I like *people* . . . and I like ordinary everyday diseases. . . . I've got absolutely no ambition." *Sad Cypress.*

LORIMER, JERRY He was the "really charming boy" who was engaged to Sylvia Keene. Sir Ambrose Bercy, Sylvia's uncle, had initially opposed the engagement but relented after a year. Maud Wye and Lorimer were seen kissing by Dolly Bantry. "The Herb of Death" from *The Thirteen Problems.*

LORRIMER, DR. GEORGE Nephew to Anthony and Henry Gascoigne, he neglected to notice his Uncle Henry's diet. "Four and Twenty Blackbirds" from *The Adventure of the Christmas Pudding.*

LORRIMER, MRS. One of the suspects in the death of Mr. Shaitana, she had been a guest at his last dinner and bridge party. She was killed by an overdose of Evipan. *Cards on the Table.*

LUCAS, HARRY He was John Eardsley's fellow diamond prospector and victim of the charms of Anita Grünberg. According to Harry Raymond (AKA John Eardsley), Anita's betrayal of him "tore up the very roots of his life. The blow stunned him and left him paralysed." Dispirited by the scandal caused by Anita in Kimberly (*see* Grünberg, Anita) both Eardsley and Lucas joined the Army and Lucas died trying to regain his honour. *The Man in the Brown Suit.*

LUSCOMBE, COLONEL DEREK Godfather, guardian and one of the managers of Elvira Blake's trust, he undertook to raise her after her father died. He was very fond of his charge but incapable of communicating with her, and was oblivious to her true nature. *At Bertram's Hotel.*

LUTTRELL, CLAUDE A "hardened gigolo" in the employ of Mr. Parker Pyne, "Claude Luttrell was one of the handsomest specimens of lounge lizard to be found in England." "The Case of the Middle-Aged Wife" and "The Case of the Distressed Lady" from *Parker Pyne Investigates.*

LUTTRELL, DAISY (MRS. COLONEL) Owner of the Styles Court guest house and wife to Colonel George Luttrell, she had a "vinegar tongue" and a sharp, curt, irritable manner. Poirot said that if he were her husband, he would take a hatchet to her. She was ruthless at bridge and ignored all the rules. She was accidentally shot by her husband, who mistook her for a rabbit. *Curtain.*

LUTTRELL, COLONEL GEORGE (TOBY) Husband of the vitriolic Daisy Luttrell and owner of the Styles Court guest house, he was often humiliated by his wife. After mistaking her for a rabbit and shooting her, she became a gentler person. *Curtain.*

LUXMORE, MRS. The wife of Professor Timothy Luxmore, she fabricated the story that her husband was shot by Major John Despard. She thought that Despard had "been trying to shoot the old boy in cold blood—for love of her." *Cards on the Table.*

LYALL CAPTAIN A Royal Flying Corps officer, he conveyed Prime Minister David MacAdam to the Court of Versailles after Poirot had secured the Prime Minister's release from the kidnappers. "The Kidnapped Prime Minister" from *Poirot Investigates.*

LYALL, PAMELA A guest at the hotel in Rhodes where she was vacationing with her friend Susan Blake, her "principal interests in life were the observation of people round her and the sound of her own voice." She had a very un-English ability to speak to strangers on sight. She and Susan enjoyed the mounting tension as Valentine Chantry and Douglas Gold spent increasing amounts of time together. "Triangle at Rhodes" from *Murder in the Mews.*

LYON, MAUREEN AKA Maureen Gregg and The Farmer's Wife. She was the widow of John Gregg, and with him, had lived at Longridge Farm, the site of an infamous case of criminal child neglect. Of three evacuee children billeted with them during the war, one named George had died from lack of care. She was "The Farmer's Wife" in the song the murderer used as a signature after strangling her. "Three Blind Mice" from *Three Blind Mice and Other Stories.*

LYTCHAM ROCHE, HUBERT The husband of Mrs. Lytcham Roche, the adoptive father of Diana Cleves, the uncle of Harry Dalehouse, the friend of Gregory Barling and the employer of both Geoffrey Keene and John Marshall, he owned Lytcham Close, one of the most famous houses in England. At Lytcham Close, absolute punctuality reigned: "Anyone who had the temerity to be late for the second gong was henceforth excommunicated—and Lytcham Close shut to the unlucky diner forever." Poirot thought he suffered from *manie de grandeur* and responded to his request: "Well, I agree. I come. Not quite so soon as Mr. Lytcham Roche wishes—for after all I have other affairs, and Mr. Lytcham Roche, he is not

quite the King of England, though he seems to think he is." Hubert Lytcham Roche was found shot through the head. A note reading "Sorry" was left beside him. "The Second Gong" from *Witness for the Prosecution.*

LYTTON GORE, HERMOINE (EGG) Impatient and determined daughter of Lady Mary Lytton Gore, she was present at both the party where the Reverend Stephen Babbington was murdered and the dinner where Sir Bartholomew Strange was killed. She had a "pash" on Sir Charles Cartwright which masked her real love for Oliver Manders. She was one of Sir Charles' few friends, and together with him and Mr. Satterthwaite, formed a committee to try and solve the murders. She was nicknamed "Egg" because of her roly-poly shape when she was a toddler. *Three-Act Tragedy.*

LYTTON GORE, LADY MARY Poor and unpretentious fifty-five-year-old mother of Egg Lytton Gore and widow of Ronald Lytton Gore, she served Mr. Satterthwaite tea and "microscopic sandwiches." Because her own marriage was so unhappy and because of her intense devotion to her daughter, she was very worried about Egg's former attachment to Oliver Manders and encouraged her daughter's infatuation with Sir Charles Cartwright. *Three-Act Tragedy.*

"M" *See* **Sprot, Millicent.**

Maberly, Diana Hugh Chandler broke his engagement to Diana for fear he would pass the Chandler family mental illness on to his offspring, and because of this she consulted Poirot. "The Cretan Bull" from *The Labours of Hercules.*

MacAdam, David The Prime Minister of England during World War I, Mac-Adam was kidnapped the day before he was to speak at the Allies Conference in Versailles. Nicknamed "Fighting Mac" by his own Party, "he was more than England's Prime Minister—he *was* England." "The Kidnapped Prime Minister" from *Poirot Investigates.*

MacAndrews, Dr. Physician attending upon the death of Henry Gascoigne, he provided Poirot with particulars of the Gascoigne brothers, especially in connection with the colour of Henry's teeth. "Four and Twenty Blackbirds" from *The Adventure of the Christmas Pudding.*

MacArthur, General John Gordon, C.M.G., D.S.O. Of all the guests on Indian Island, the General was the only one who welcomed death as a release from thirty years of torment. Death came swiftly and mercifully to him; his skull was crushed, answering the rhyme: "Eight little Indian boys travelling in Devon; One said he'd stay there and then there were seven." *And Then There Were None.*

Macatta, Mrs., MP Present at Lord Mayfield's house at the time of the bomber plans theft and possessed of an earnestness of purpose, she perverted Poirot's interrogation of her movements during that evening into a forum for her views on the rising importance of women in government and on the evils of gambling. "The Incredible Theft" from *Murder in the Mews.*

Mace, Albert A young assistant in the chemist's shop in Styles St. Mary, Mace testified at the inquest into the death of Emily Inglethorp that he had sold strychnine to Alfred Inglethorp on the Monday preceding Emily's death. *The Mysterious Affair at Styles.*

Macfarlane, Mr. The fiancé of Rachel Lawes, Macfarlane was "a dour Scot, with a Celtic imagination hidden away somewhere." Alistair Haworth credited him with having the "gift—curse—call it what you like" of second sight, though it seemed to be quite under-developed. "The Gipsy" from *The Golden Ball.*

MACKENZIE, HELEN Widow of Rex Fortescue's dead partner MacKenzie, she was a voluntary patient at the Pinewood Private Sanatorium. She was convinced that Rex Fortescue murdered her husband or left him to die in Africa, and raised her children to hate Fortescue and made them promise to kill him. *A Pocket Full of Rye.*

MACKENZIE, RUBY AKA Jennifer Fortescue. Her mother, Helen MacKenzie, made Ruby promise every night to kill Rex Fortescue, the alleged murderer of Ruby's father. When Ruby married Percival Fortescue, her mother struck her name from the family Bible. *A Pocket Full of Rye.*

MACMASTER, DR. A retired physician in Drymouth, Dr. MacMaster gave Dr. Calgary valuable information about the Argyle family and the Rachel Argyle murder. *Ordeal by Innocence.*

MACNAUGHTON, ELSIE The nurse to Lady Ariadne Grayle and travelling with her on board the S.S. *Fayoum*, Miss MacNaughton thought that if her patient had a few floors to scrub and several children to raise, she would be relieved of her largely non-existent illnesses. "Death on the Nile" from *Parker Pyne Investigates.*

MACQUEEN, HECTOR WILLARD The son of the District Attorney who handled the Daisy Armstrong case, MacQueen was Samuel Edward Ratchett's private secretary. Poirot was appalled when MacQueen thought he was "a woman's dressmaker." *Murder on the Orient Express.*

MACWHIRTER, ANDREW Called a "damned pig-headed Scot" by his former employer, Herbert Clay, MacWhirter was subsequently hired by the eccentric Lord Cornelly who was impressed by his innate honesty. MacWhirter discovered crucial evidence in the murder of Lady Tressilian which cleared Audrey Strange of suspicion. *Towards Zero.*

MADELEINE *See* **MORISOT, ANNE.**

MAHEW, GEORGE "A thin, dry, cautious gentleman," Mr. Mahew was a solicitor who met Poirot in *Five Little Pigs* and "The Under Dog" from *The Under Dog.*

MAHMOUDI, MADAME *See* **HOBHOUSE, VALERIE.**

MAINE, INSPECTOR An inspector at Scotland Yard, he investigated the backgrounds of the ten murder victims on Indian Island. *And Then There Were None.*

MAITLAND, CAPTAIN Moustachioed captain of police in the area of Tell Yarimjah, he was in charge of investigating the murder of Mrs. Leidner and later of Anne Johnson. *Murder in Mesopotamia.*

MALINOWSKI, LADISLAUS For two successive years a world champion racing driver, this half-French, half-Polish celebrity was the lover of both Elvira Blake and her mother, Lady Bess Sedgwick. His gun was used to kill Micky Gorman. *At Bertram's Hotel.*

MALLABY, MRS. An American widow, Mrs. Mallaby was dressed as Pulcinella at the Victory Ball, and together with Captain Digby and Mrs. Davidson she discovered the dead body of Lord Cronshaw. "The Affair at the Victory Ball" from *The Under Dog.*

MALTRAVERS, MRS. An extraordinarily beautiful woman, Mrs. Maltravers had been married only a year when her husband apparently died from an internal hemorrhage, leaving her a large insurance policy and the family home Marsdon Manor in Essex. "The Tragedy at Marsdon Manor" from *Poirot Investigates.*

MANDERS, OLIVER Languid, supercilious young man of about twenty-five, he was, in Poirot's estimation, the most obvious of the suspects in the deaths of the Reverend Stephen Babbington and Sir Bartholomew Strange. He was an illegitimate child, had a foreign heritage and an inferiority complex, and embraced the Communist doctrine. *Three-Act Tragedy.*

MANELLI, GIUSEPPE A member of the Comrades of the Red Hand, he was sent to steal the memoirs of Count Stylptitch. When he tried to blackmail Virginia Revel, he was murdered and his body was found in her home. *The Secret of Chimneys.*

MANNING The old head gardener at Styles Court, he witnessed Emily Inglethorp's new will. *The Mysterious Affair at Styles.*

MANNING Seventy-five years old, Miss Marple hired him to supplement the gardening activities of the even more ancient Mr. Foster at Hillside house, and to provide information about the Kennedy family. *Sleeping Murder.*

MARCH, CICELY AKA Eileen O'Hara, she was a "fair-haired and extremely pretty" girl who answered Tuppence and Tommy Beresford's advertisement requesting information on Eileen O'Hara. She ran a beauty parlour on Bond Street and had discovered a slip of paper in Ambassador Wilmott's boot which, when wetted, disclosed tracings of a harbour plan. *Partners in Crime.*

MARCHINGTON, LORD Lady Frances Derwent's extremely wealthy father, he suffered from gout which "some free imbibing of the family port had not improved." After his daughter and Bobby Jones solved the manifold mysteries involved in Alan Carstairs' death, he appointed Bobby as manager of a coffee plantation in Kenya and assured Badger Beadon's success by patronizing his new garage business. *Why Didn't They Ask Evans?*

MARCHMONT, ADELA Gordon Cloade's widowed sister and the mother of Lynn Marchmont, she found herself in financial difficulty after the war and borrowed five hundred pounds from Rosaleen Cloade (alias Eileen Corrigan). *Taken at the Flood.*

MARCHMONT, LYNN The daughter of Adela Marchmont, niece of Gordon Cloade and the fiancée of her cousin, Rowley Cloade, she found the sense of sameness, security and slowness in Warmsley Vale disturbing after her experience abroad. She fell in love with the excitement surrounding David Hunter. When she informed Rowley about her passion for Hunter and broke their engagement, Rowley tried to strangle her. Luckily, Poirot arrived on the scene in time to save her. Eventually, she married Rowley. *Taken at the Flood.*

MARDENBERG Pursued by Detective Inspector Jarrold of Scotland Yard, Mardenberg was a spy who planned to despatch the Portsmouth harbour defence plans to Germany disguised as a love letter. The code was ridiculously simple, and involved connecting the dotted i's. "The Girl in the Train" from *The Golden Ball.*

MARGRAVE, LILY AKA Lily Naylor, which was her real name, Lily Margrave was the sister of Captain Humphrey Naylor, and had been Lady Nancy Astwell's paid companion for about a year. Suspecting foul play involving her brother, she forged her references to obtain a post in the Astwell house so that she might discover some evidence against Sir Astwell. Lady Astwell sent Lily to consult Poirot after the death of Sir Astwell. "The Under Dog" from *The Under Dog*.

MARGUERITE *See* **VANDEMEYER, RITA.**

MARIE Linnet Doyle's former maid, she suffered mental anguish when her mistress revealed that her lover Fleetwood, an engineer on the S.S. *Karnak*, was already wed to a native woman and had three children. *Death on the Nile*.

MARLE, IRIS The sister of Rosemary Barton, she was the sister-in-law of George Barton, cousin of Victor Drake and niece of Lucilla Drake. The terms of Paul Bennet's will stipulated that his money, on Rosemary's death, would go to Iris. Iris became a prime suspect in the murder of her sister. *Sparkling Cyanide*.

MARPLE, JANE The elderly spinster with a swarm of relatives, including the celebrated novelist Raymond West, her nephew, this famous first lady of detection has been called everything from a "dithering old maid who is all caught up in her knitting," to a "nasty old cat." Far from Margaret Rutherford's film version, Agatha Christie's Jane Marple was tall and thin with great masses of snowy white hair piled high on her head, pale blue eyes, "a pink crinkled face" and seventy-four years old when she first appeared in *Murder at the Vicarage*. Miss Marple based her methods on the belief that "human nature is much the same everywhere, and, of course, one has opportunities of observing it at closer quarters in a village." She regarded St. Mary Mead as a microcosm of the world. Her favourite pastimes were birdwatching and gardening and "in the art of seeing without being seen," said Leonard Clement, the vicar, "Miss Marple had no rival." She often compared people to one another, finding parallels in character traits. She also maintained that no one was above suspicion, "and that you simply cannot afford to believe everything that people

tell you."

Among Miss Marple's acquaintances and friends were Leonard and Griselda Clement, Dr. Haydock, Amanda Hartnell and Caroline Weatherby, Colonel Arthur and Dolly Bantry and Sir Henry Clithering. Miss Marple was still active, although extremely aged, at the conclusion of *Nemesis*. Leonard Clement summarized the endearing old lady: Miss Marple "is not the type of elderly lady who makes mistakes. She has got an uncanny knack of being always right." *See* Bibliography and Appendix A.

MARRASCAUD A vicious killer, he was tracked by Commissionaire Lementeuil to the resort of Rochers Neige in Switzerland, where he was supposed to rendezvous with his gang. Psychologically, he was "a wild boar, ferocious, terrible, who charges in blind fury." Commissionaire Lementeuil interested Poirot in the case, and the killer was finally apprehended. "The Erymanthian Boar" from *The Labours of Hercules*.

MARSDEN, CHIEF INSPECTOR He assured Poirot of Elinor Carlisle's guilt in the Mary Gerrard murder, and stated with cheerful certainty: "This time I can go ahead with a clear conscience." *Sad Cypress*.

MARSDON, ANTHONY (TONY) A colleague of Deborah Beresford's in British Intelligence, he was considered "one of the most brilliant beginners in the coding department and was thought likely to go far." *N or M?*

MARSH, ANDREW The brother of Roger Marsh and the uncle of Violet Marsh, whom he had sheltered and treated as his own daughter, Marsh left his niece all of his vast estate, but only if she could find his hidden will. "The Case of the Missing Will" from *Poirot Investigates*.

MARSH, GERALDINE (DINA) The daughter of George Marsh, step-daughter of Jane Wilkinson and cousin of Ronald

Marsh, she was terrorized by her father who had hated his first wife, Geraldine's mother, for leaving him. She showed little remorse at her father's death, and confided to Poirot her hope that the murderer would escape. *Lord Edgware Dies.*

MARSH, GEORGE ALFRED ST. VINCENT, THE FOURTH BARON EDGWARE The estranged husband of Jane Wilkinson, uncle of Captain Ronald Marsh and father of Geraldine Marsh, he was "very near the border line of madness" and possessed "a deep-rooted instinct of cruelty." Volumes by the Marquis de Sade were displayed in his library in silent testimony to his perversity. His death did not come as a great shock to any of those who knew him. *Lord Edgware Dies.*

MARSH, CAPTAIN RONALD, THE FIFTH BARON EDGWARE The nephew of George Marsh and the cousin of Geraldine Marsh, he succeeded to the title of Lord Edgware on his uncle's death. He had a round, pleasant, vacuous face "and an absurdly small black moustache that gave one the impression of being marooned in the middle of a dent." *Lord Edgware Dies.*

MARSH, VIOLET The niece of Andrew Marsh, she was bequeathed his vast estate on the condition that she could find his hidden will. She hired Poirot to help her solve the puzzle. "The Case of the Missing Will" from *Poirot Investigates.*

MARSHALL, ANDREW The solicitor to the Argyle family, he was a partner in the firm Marshall and Marshall, which had acted for Rachel Argyle over a number of years. It was the solicitor's personal opinion that Sunny Point, the Argyle home, was much more accurately described by its original name, Viper's Point. *Ordeal by Innocence.*

MARSHALL, ARLENA AKA Helen Stuart, her maiden name; Arlena Stuart, her stage name. The wife of Captain Kenneth Marshall and the step-mother of Linda Marshall, Arlena Marshall attracted the obsessive attentions of a number of men with drastic results. At the Jolly Roger Hotel in Leathercombe Bay she was the "evil under the sun." Her tragic death in Pixy Cove did not elicit a great deal of sympathy from her fellow guests. *Evil Under the Sun.*

MARSHALL, EDWARD JOHN Former resident of New Zealand and witness at Elinor Carlisle's trial for the murder of Mary Gerrard, he identified Nurse Jessie Hopkins as Mary Draper, *née* Riley, sister of Mary Gerrard's mother. *Sad Cypress.*

MARSHALL, CAPTAIN KENNETH The husband of Arlena Marshall and the father of Linda Marshall, Kenneth Marshall's only fault, said his childhood friend Rosamund Darnley, was "a penchant for making unfortunate marriages." After Arlena's death he proposed to Rosamund Darnley. *Evil Under the Sun.*

MARSHALL, LINDA The daughter of Kenneth Marshall, she said of her stepmother, Arlena Marshall: "I'd like to kill her. Oh! I wish she'd die." She borrowed a book on sorcery and stuck pins through waxen images of Arlena that she crafted herself. When Arlena died, Linda tried to expiate her enormous guilt by an overdose of sleeping pills, but she survived to be graced with a new "sensible" stepmother, Rosamund Darnley. *Evil Under the Sun.*

MARSTON, ANTHONY JAMES (TONY) A supercilious young guest at the house party on Indian Island, he was accused of murdering John and Lucy Coombes, to which he replied: "Must have been a couple of kids I ran over near Cambridge. Beastly bad luck." His death coincided with the dictates of the first verse of the nursery rhyme: "Ten little Indian boys went out to dine; One choked his little self and then there were nine." *And Then There Were None.*

MARTHA The mother of that "bad lot," Ben, Martha was the maid, cook and housekeeper to Lily Crabtree for thirty years. She was the last person to see Lily Crabtree alive, and provided Palliser with some information regarding a sixpence coin, "one of the new ones with oak leaves on it," that enabled Palliser to solve the mystery of Miss Crabtree's death. "Sing a Song of Sixpence" from *The Listerdale Mystery.*

MARTIN, ALIX The wife of Gerald Martin, she was distressed on learning that her husband had said she would be away in London indefinitely, and that Mr. Ames had received only two thousand of the three thousand pounds she had given her husband to buy Philomel Cottage. "Philomel Cottage" from *Witness for the Prosecution.*

MARTIN, BRIAN An actor who had starred with Jane Wilkinson in several films, he was in love with her but she threw him over for the Duke of Merton. *Lord Edgware Dies.*

MARTIN, ELIZABETH An American from Sargon Springs, Elizabeth Martin "was 'doing Europe' in a stern conscientious spirit." She was Mr. Satterthwaite's guest at the 'Hedges and Highways' party that Harley Quin arranged in Monte Carlo. "The Soul of the Croupier" from *The Mysterious Mr. Quin.*

MARTIN, GERALD AKA Charles LeMaitre, he was the husband of Alix Martin with whom he lived at Philomel Cottage. As Charles LeMaitre, he was "a long-bearded, scholarly-looking gentleman" who, although acquitted of murdering some of his numerous bigamous wives, had served a prison sentence for other charges. "Philomel Cottage" from *Witness for the Prosecution.*

MARTIN, GLADYS Adenoidal, half-witted parlourmaid at the Fortescue's Yewtree Lodge, she was seduced by Lancelot Fortescue who, under the name Albert Evans, promised to marry her. He convinced her to put "truth serum" into Rex Fortescue's marmalade. She was strangled and found dead with a clothespin on her nose, but not before she had sent Miss Marple, her former employer, a letter and a photograph of herself and Bert Evans. A *Pocket Full of Rye.*

MARTINDALE, HILDA *See* **BLAND, VALERIE.**

MARTINDALE, KATHERINE "Sandy Cat" to her employees at the Cavendish Secretarial and Typing Bureau, she "was of the type that the French label so aptly a *femme formidable." The Clocks.*

MARTINELLI, CONTESSA "Old Macaroni" was plagued by her students who worked very hard to deceive her and giggled to recall their "successful wickedness." Any attempts to circumvent her watchful eye needed "a lot of planning." *At Bertram's Hotel.*

MARVEL, SIR DONALD, MP A member of the tourist party travelling from Amman to Petra, Sir Donald, "a tired-looking Englishman," wished to marry Carol Blundell, but she thought that he was a "stuffed fish." "The Pearl of Price" from *Parker Pyne Investigates.*

MARVELL, MARY The wife of Gregory Rolf, Mary Marvell was an American film actress who possessed the "Western Star," a great diamond which, as the "Star of the East," had once belonged to Lady Yardly. "The Adventure of 'The Western Star' " from *Poirot Investigates.*

MARY One of the housemaids at the Keston Spa Hydro, she died within twenty-four hours from a septic finger. Her body was initially mistaken for that of Gladys Sanders. "A Christmas Tragedy" from *The Thirteen Problems.*

MARY ANN *See* **ZERKOWSKI, COUNTESS RENATA.**

MASON, ADA BEATRICE AKA Kitty Kidd, the actress and male impersonator. She was a partner in crime with Major Knighton (AKA Monsieur le Marquis) and was involved in Knighton's bid to steal the Heart of Fire rubies belonging to Rufus Van Aldin. Her part was to play the role of Ruth Kettering's maid. *The Mystery of the Blue Train.*

MASON, JANE AKA Gracie Kidd, her real name, she travelled with her mistress The Honourable Mrs. Rupert Carrington on the *Plymouth Express,* but was also working for the jewel fence Red Narky. "The Plymouth Express" from *The Under Dog.*

MASSINGTON, MRS. This nosy and sympathetic friend to Iris Wade was a good companion because both women "were afflicted with athletic husbands who talked stocks and shares and golf alternately." "The Case of the Discontented Husband" from *Parker Pyne Investigates.*

MASTERMAN, EDWARD HENRY Formerly Colonel Armstrong's batman in World War I, he became Samuel Edward Ratchett's valet and travelled with him on the *Orient Express. Murder on the Orient Express.*

MASTERTON, CONNIE The wife of Wilfred Masterton the politician, she "was a somewhat monumental woman who reminded Poirot of a bloodhound. She had a full underhung jaw and large, mournful, slightly bloodshot eyes." She was the power behind her husband's success. *Dead Man's Folly.*

MATCHAM, MRS. Ariadne Oliver's old nanny, she was one of Mrs. Oliver's "elephants" and recalled quite a lot about the Ravenscrofts—especially the fact that Dolly Jarrow, Molly Ravenscroft's twin sister, had spent some time in Dr. Willoughby's father's mental clinic. Mrs. Matcham coined the phrase "Elephants don't forget." *Elephants Can Remember.*

MATHIAS, JOHN AKA Captain Richard Harwell. As John Mathias he was the gardener at Eleanor Le Couteau's Ashley Grange in Kirtlington Mallet and the last person to see Captain Richard Harwell. As Richard Harwell, he was "a dashing rider to the hounds, a handsome laughing daredevil of a fellow" who had come to stay at the Bells and Motley and had subsequently met and married young Eleanor Le Couteau of Ashley Grange. Mathias was also a member of the Clondinis, an acrobatic troupe that stole precious art treasures. "At the Bells and Motley" from *The Mysterious Mr. Quin.*

MAUD The fiancée of Edward Robinson, "Maud was very superior. She was good-looking and clever and very ladylike, and she was always right about everything. . . . Her qualities were all excellent qualities, but sometimes Edward wished that she had more faults and less virtues. It was her virtues that drove him to desperate deeds." "The Manhood of Edward Robinson" from *The Golden Ball.*

MAVERICK, DR. He was the chief psychiatrist at Stoneygates, a home for delinquent boys run by the Serrocolds and the Gulbrandsen Institute. Miss Marple decided that he was "distinctly abnormal" after he commented: "We're all mad, dear lady. . . . That's the secret of existence. We're all a little mad." *They Do It with Mirrors.*

MAYERLING, MR. A British Secret Service man who had disappeared in Russia and was missing for five years, he brought Poirot news regarding the Big Four gang and shortly thereafter died from inhaling strong prussic acid. *The Big Four.*

MAYFIELD, LORD, SIR CHARLES McLAUGHLIN The host of a weekend gathering at his country place in Sussex, he had intended to review the plans of a new bomber with Sir George Carrington, when the documents were suddenly stolen from his library. "The Incredible Theft" from *Murder in the Mews*.

MAYHERNE, MR. The solicitor in charge of Leonard Vole's case, he was convinced of Vole's innocence. He interviewed Mrs. Vole and discovered that she intended to turn King's evidence against her husband and attempted to find some way of undermining her testimony. "Witness for the Prosecution" from *Witness for the Prosecution*.

MCCRAE, DETECTIVE CONSTABLE Dour police officer aiding in the investigation of events at the Hickory Road Hostel, he thought that naming a beauty salon "Sabrina Fair" was blasphemous. *Hickory Dickory Dock*.

MCGILLICUDDY, ELSPETH She was returning from Christmas shopping and on the way to visit her friend, Miss Marple, when she observed a murder on her 4.50 from Paddington. *4.50 from Paddington*.

MCGINTY, MRS. Washerwoman and cleaning lady, she was hit on the back of the head with a sharp, heavy instrument and her life savings of thirty pounds were stolen. *Mrs. McGinty's Dead*.

MCGRATH, JIMMY While pursuing his favourite pastime, following up purported gold strikes, McGrath encountered his friend Anthony Cade in Bulaways, Africa. He asked Cade to convey a manuscript to a British publishing house and to return a packet of letters to its rightful owner, one Virginia Revel. *The Secret of Chimneys*.

MCKAY, ELSPETH Widowed sister to Superintendent Spence, she had lived in Woodleigh Common for two or three years and had been joined by her brother on his retirement. This perceptive woman seldom required being told anything. *Hallowe'en Party*.

MCLAREN, COMMANDER JOCK Best friend of Arnold Clayton, he was an old friend to the family. There was the distinct possibility that, following the death of her husband and the conviction of Major Rich for murder, Mrs. Margharita Clayton might have turned to Commander McLaren for comfort. "The Mystery of the Spanish Chest" from *The Adventure of the Christmas Pudding*.

MCLAUGHLIN, SIR CHARLES *See* **MAYFIELD, LORD**.

MCLEAN, HUGO "A tall middle-aged man with a thin brown face," Hugo McLean, in love with Adelaide Jefferson, was at her beck and call. Mark Gaskell referred to him as "William Dobbin," a character of blind, faithful love from William Makepeace Thackeray's *Vanity Fair*. *The Body in the Library*.

MCNABB, COLIN Post-graduate student taking a course in psychiatry, he lived in Mrs. Nicoletis' student hostel. McNabb ignored Celia Austin's adoration until she feigned kleptomania to attract his attention. He eventually asked her to marry him, but she was murdered that same night. *Hickory Dickory Dock*.

MCNAUGHTON, MRS. The wife of Angus McNaughton; on being shown a photograph of a murdered man, she thought she recognized him, but Hardcastle later said: "I doubt it. She just wants to think she's seen him. I know that type of witness only too well." *The Clocks*.

MCNAUGHTON, ANGUS Retired Scottish professor, he was husband of Mrs. McNaughton but his real love seemed to have been his garden. "In it all day long, and mad on compost. Really, he's quite a bore on the subject of compost." His home bordered the house where the first murder victim was found. *The Clocks*.

MCNEIL, MR. He was a member of McNeil and Hodgson, Hercule Poirot's solicitors, the firm Flossie Monro visited in response to Poirot's advertisement soliciting information about Claud Darrell. *The Big Four.*

MCNEIL, SIR ANDREW The governor of Manstone Prison and a close friend of Professor Wanstead's, he was convinced from the start that Michael Rafiel had not murdered his fiancée Verity Hunt. Of Miss Marple, he thought: "That old lady gives me the creeps." *Nemesis.*

MEADOWS, DETECTIVE INSPECTOR Anne Beddingfeld gave him information about the death of L.B. Carton and a description of the "Man in the Brown Suit." *The Man in the Brown Suit.*

MEAUHOURAT, MADEMOISELLE ZELIE The French governess who replaced Mademoiselle Rouselle at Overcliffe, she knew the secret of the deaths of General Alistair and Lady Molly Ravenscroft, and travelled with Poirot to Overcliffe to lay to rest the ghosts that remained there for Desmond Burton-Cox and Celia Ravenscroft. *Elephants Can Remember.*

MELCHETT, COLONEL The Chief Constable for Radfordshire and a resident of Much Benham, he was an "irascible-looking" but "dapper little man who had a habit of snorting suddenly and unexpectedly." His territory included St. Mary Mead, which brought the deaths of Lucius Protheroe, Rose Emmott, Pamela Reeves and Ruby Keene under his jurisdiction. *Murder at the Vicarage;* "Death by Drowning" from *The Thirteen Problems; The Body in the Library;* "Tape Measure Murder" from *Three Blind Mice and Other Stories.*

MELFORD, MILDRED Cousin of Colonel Derek Luscombe and with him guardian to Elvira Blake, Cousin Mildred was described by her charge as "fearfully easy to deceive." Chief Inspector Davy found her, during their "singularly unprofitable interview," a person who "knew nothing, had heard nothing, had seen nothing and

had apparently deduced very little." *At Bertram's Hotel.*

MELROSE, COLONEL The Chief Constable for the area which included Market Basing and King's Abbot (the site of Roger Ackroyd's Fernly Park) Colonel Melrose was an old friend of Lord Caterham's and had often been to Chimneys, where on two occasions he met Superintendent Battle. He also became acquainted with Mr. Satterthwaite. *The Secret of Chimneys; The Seven Dials Mystery;* "The Love Detectives" from *Three Blind Mice and Other Stories.*

MENIER, RAOUL "One of the cleverest thieves known to the French police," he specialized in stealing art objects from museums and exhibitions. As Father Lavigny, whom he was impersonating, he worked with Ali Yusef to replace artifacts found at Tell Yarimjah with clever electroplated copies. He disappeared after the murder of Anne Johnson, but both he and his colleague Ali Yusef were apprehended in Baghdad. *Murder in Mesopotamia.*

MERCADO, JOSEPH Husband of Marie Mercado and in his second year with the American expedition at Tell Yarimjah, he was a secret drug addict "in an advanced stage of the craving," whose habit was cleverly discovered by Poirot's judicious use of a sharp pin. *Murder in Mesopotamia.*

MERCADO, MARIE Wife of Joseph Mercado and in her second year with the American expedition at Tell Yarimjah, she was fiercely jealous and maternally protective of her husband, and helped him conceal his drug habit. She was "a thoroughly spiteful little cat," who hated Louise Leidner passionately, fearing her husband was attracted to that woman's "calamitous magic." *Murder in Mesopotamia.*

MERDELL Ninety-two years old, he continued to work at the ferry docks until he was pushed into a river. *Dead Man's Folly.*

MEREDITH, ANNE A suspect in the Shaitana murder case, Anne Meredith was one of the guests at Shaitana's dinner and bridge party. She drowned in the same river from which Major John Despard saved Rhoda Dawes. *Cards on the Table.*

MERIVALE, SIR ARTHUR Husband of the murdered Lady Vere Merivale, he had attended the Three Arts Ball dressed as a seventeenth-century executioner. "The Gentleman Dressed in Newspaper" from *Partners in Crime.*

MERIVALE, LADY VERE Wife to Sir Arthur Merivale and mistress of Captain Bingo Hale, Lady Merivale had arranged a midnight tryst with her lover at the Ace of Spades following the Three Arts Ball, where she was discovered stabbed through the heart with a jewelled dagger. Her last words, overheard by Tuppence Beresford, were: "Bingo did it." "Finessing the King" and "The Gentleman Dressed in Newspaper" from *Partners in Crime.*

MERRILEES, DETECTIVE INSPECTOR *See* **BOND, JAMES.**

MERRION, MISS The proprietress of the Ginger Cat, she employed Elizabeth Barnard and Milly Higley and was given to bleating in a "high, distressed gentlewoman voice." *The A.B.C. Murders.*

MERROWDENE, GEORGE The second husband of Margaret Merrowdene, he had just insured his life at his wife's request. Mrs. Merrowdene's former husband had similarly insured himself just before being poisoned with arsenic. "Accident" from *Witness for the Prosecution.*

MERROWDENE, MARGARET Acquitted earlier of poisoning her first husband Mr. Anthony, she had been happily married for six years to George Merrowdene, a former chemistry professor, when she asked him to take out life insurance.

"Accident" from *Witness for the Prosecution.*

MERRYPIT, MRS. Proprietress of the wool and woolens shop in Carristown, she helped Miss Marple match some wool, and gave her own opinion of the Verity Hunt case and the Bradbury-Scott family. *Nemesis.*

MERSU, DIVINE FATHER Mersu was "a skilled physician of great experience" who attended to Yahmose in his sickness. Despite his skill, he could not save the life of Sobek who, like his brother, had drunk poisoned wine. *Death Comes as the End.*

MERTON, DOWAGER DUCHESS OF The Duke of Merton's mother, she wished to terminate the relationship between her son and Jane Wilkinson, and attempted to convince Poirot to support her cause. Hastings thought her a tartar, but admired her; Poirot said she "wishes to arrange the universe to her manner of thinking." *Lord Edgware Dies.*

MERTON, DUKE OF The son of the Dowager Duchess of Merton and the fiancé of Jane Wilkinson, Merton "looked more like a weedy young haberdasher than like a duke." He was an Anglo-Catholic religious fanatic who refused to marry a divorcée, and "his infatuation for the extremely modern Jane Wilkinson was one of those anachronistic jokes that Nature so loves to play." *Lord Edgware Dies.*

MERTON, MRS. Closest friend of Sylvia Chapman, she was "a loquacious lady, with snapping black eyes, and an elaborate coiffure." Poirot and Inspector Japp learned from Mrs. Merton that Mr. Chapman may have worked in government intelligence. *One, Two, Buckle My Shoe.*

MERTON, MILLY *See* **CROFT, MILLY.**

MESNARD, VIRGINIE Impoverished young cousin of the late Madame Deroulard, she had lived at the Deroulard residence for three years. She consulted Poirot about the death of Paul Deroulard who, though he had made up to her, had no intention of marrying her. She ultimately took the veil. "The Chocolate Box" from *Poirot's Early Cases.*

METCALF, DR. He was Conway Jefferson's physician, and felt that it was probably better to burn oneself out living a full life than to be terrified of dying. *The Body in the Library.*

METCALF, MAJOR *See* **TANNER, INSPECTOR.**

MEYNELL, DR. The physician to Mrs. Harter, he performed an autopsy on her body and discovered that her heart condition was further advanced than he had thought. He gave the distressing news to her nephew Charles Ridgeway that old Mary Harter could not have lasted another two months. "Where There's a Will" from *Witness for the Prosecution.*

MICHAEL Actor with the Repertory in Cullenquay, he told Maude Williams of a playwright from Australia named Evelyn Hope who had changed his name to Robin Upward. *Mrs. McGinty's Dead.*

MICHEL, PIERRE The father of Susanne Michel, he was a conductor on the *Orient Express* and was on duty the night that Samuel Ratchett was murdered and discovered the body. More than likely, he was the same Pierre Michel who was a conductor on the *Blue Train* and discovered the body of Ruth Kettering. *The Mystery of the Blue Train; Murder on the Orient Express.*

MIKLANOVA, ANNA *See* **DENMAN, ANNA.**

MILLER, INSPECTOR Hastings called Inspector Miller, "conceited, ill-mannered and quite insufferable . . . both obstinate and an imbecile." Miller "was one to say that Hercule Poirot was much overrated." "The Disappearance of Mr. Dav-

enheim" from *Poirot Investigates;* "The Under Dog" from *the Under Dog;* "The Mystery of the Spanish Chest" from *The Adventure of the Christmas Pudding;* "The Lost Mine" from *Poirot's Early Cases.*

MILLY Ariadne Oliver's maid, Milly, said Mark Easterbrook, was "an efficient dragon who guarded her mistress from the onslaughts of the outside world." *The Pale Horse.*

MILRAY, MRS. A woman "almost ludicrously unlike her daughter" Violet Milray, she was "an immense dumpling of a woman, immovably fixed in an armchair conveniently placed, so that she could, from the window, observe all that went on in the world outside." Sir Charles Cartwright and Egg Lytton Gore interviewed her about the murder of the Reverend Babbington. *Three-Act Tragedy.*

MILRAY, VIOLET Daughter of the invalid Mrs. Milray, she was called "the perfect robot" by her employer of six years, Sir Charles Cartwright, who kept her as a glorified housekeeper. "Plain as sin," and possessed of a "rugged countenance," she was secretly in love with Sir Charles and would have done anything for his pleasure. *Three-Act Tragedy.*

MILSON *See* **WEST, DERMOT.**

MINKS, ARTHUR AKA Count Sergius Paulovitch; Reverend Edward Chichester; Miss Pettigrew. Arthur Minks' ingeniousness for disguise may have been a model for Claud Darrell in *The Big Four.* He was very closely involved with the "Colonel," and Sir Eustace Pedler called him "a clever actor—but a fool." As Count Sergius Paulovitch, he stopped by to see Nadina (AKA Anita Grünberg), the Russian dancer, and learned of her plans to deal from a marked deck to the "Colonel." As the Reverend Edward Chichester he made an extremely agitated attempt to gain occupancy of Cabin 17 aboard the *Kilmorden Castle,* but lost it to Anne Beddingfeld. As Miss Pettigrew he was Sir

Eustace Pedler's "slab-faced" secretary on a trip to Rhodesia. *The Man in the Brown Suit.*

MINTON, SOPHIA Considered by Mrs. Blenkensop to be "the *compleat* British spinster," she did not excel at bridge; "sometimes, Tuppence thought to herself, it would save time if Miss Minton just put her hand down on the table to show them all. She was quite incapable of not telling them exactly what was in it." *N or M?*

MIRABELLE The current favourite of the king of Bosnia, Mirabelle excited jealousy in the Countess Czarnova. "She was dressed in something that looked like a glorified bird of paradise, and she wore chains of jewels hanging down her bare back." "The Soul of the Croupier" from *The Mysterious Mr. Quin.*

MIRELLE A dancer in Paris, she was Derek Kettering's mistress. She abandoned Kettering when it appeared that he was about to lose his wife and only source of income. However, she tried to win him back when he inherited his wife's two million pounds. A passenger on the *Blue Train* when Ruth Kettering was murdered, she told Poirot that Derek killed his wife. *The Mystery of the Blue Train.*

MIROTIN *See* **GREY, MARY.**

MITCHELL, HENRY CHARLES Husband to Ruth Mitchell, he was the chief steward on board the *Prometheus* and the discoverer of Madame Giselle's body. He recognized Madame Giselle as the woman who usually took the earlier flight and remembered her as a good tipper. *Death in the Clouds.*

MITCHELL, RUTH The wife of Henry Mitchell, she was the product of many

generations of Dorset people. She thought the "Bolshies" were behind the murder of Madame Giselle, and that it was "a dirty trick to have done . . . in a British aeroplane." *Death in the Clouds.*

MITZI A European refugee, Mitzi was the somewhat hysterical maid at Letitia Blacklock's Little Paddocks. She had a reputation for lying and was given to fits of outrage, but was talked into helping Miss Marple set a trap for the murderer of Rudi Scherz. *A Murder is Announced.*

MOGSON, MRS. *See* **VOLE, ROMAINE.**

MOHAMMED The Arabian lift-operator at Mr. Aristide's Brain Trust, he promised to secure Andrew Peters a native costume and other accessories of escape in exchange for a petrol station in Chicago. *Destination Unknown.*

MOLLY The "sympathetic waitress" at the Gallant Endeavour and a friend of Mr. Bonnington's, she put Poirot on the trail of the Gascoigne case. "Four and Twenty Blackbirds" from *The Adventure of the Christmas Pudding.*

MONCKTON, COLONEL An old friend of Mr. Satterthwaite's he had been present at the fancy-dress ball at Charnley the night Lord Reggie Charnley apparently shot himself. Although Colonel Monckton rejected spiritualism, he admitted that the house had a "deuced rummy atmosphere." "The Dead Harlequin" from *The Mysterious Mr. Quin.*

MONCRIEFFE, JEAN Dr. Oldfield's pharmaceutical dispenser for three years, she fell in love with Dr. Oldfield and wished to marry him, but she refused his proposal after the death of his wife. She felt they would be supporting the rumours of foul play. Extremely honest and candid in her answers to Poirot, she stated baldly that she would not wish an exhumation and autopsy of Mrs. Oldfield. "The Lernean Hydra" from *The Labours of Hercules.*

MONRO, FLOSSIE Once an intimate friend of Claud Darrell's, she was, according to Hastings, "a somewhat lurid-looking lady no longer in her first youth. Her hair was of an impossible yellow and was prolific in curls over each ear, her eyelids were heavily blackened and she had by no means forgotten the rouge or the lip salve." Flossie answered Poirot's advertisement, and helped Poirot identify Darrell. But before she could supply Poirot with Darrell's photograph, she was run down by an automobile. *The Big Four.*

MONTRESOR, MISS *See* CLEVELAND, JANE.

MONTRESOR, MARY "A beautiful and popular society girl," Mary Montresor was husband hunting when she saw George Dundas looking "so like an island" in the City of London after having been fired from his job. Eventually, she agreed to marry him after putting him through a series of tests. "The Golden Ball" from *The Golden Ball.*

MONTRESSOR, HELEN *See* GRANT, GERDA.

MOODY, ELIZABETH A resident of the Sunny Ridge Nursing Home, she had been a dresser in the theatre where Julia Charrington had danced. She claimed to have recognized a well-known criminal and was soon dead from morphine poisoning. *By the Pricking of My Thumbs.*

MOORHOUSE, HANNAH *See* RYMER, AMELIA.

MORALES, PEDRO *See* DRAKE, VICTOR.

MORELLI, TONY *See* BROWNE, ANTHONY.

MORISOT, ANNE AKA Anne Morisot Leman; Madeleine; Anne Richards. She was the twenty-four-year-old daughter of Madame Giselle and George Leman. As Anne Morisot Leman, which was the name on her birth certificate, she established her identity as Madame Giselle's daughter and heiress. As Madeleine, she was maid to Lady Cicely Horbury and was on board the *Prometheus* when her mother, who did not recognize her, was killed. As the chic and well-dressed Anne Richards, she was married to James Richards, alias Norman Gale. Under this name she was discovered dead in a train holding an empty bottle of prussic acid. *Death in the Clouds.*

MORISOT, MARIE ANGELIQUE *See* GISELLE, MADAME.

MORLEY, GEORGINA Spinster sister of the murdered Henry Morley, she "was a large woman rather like a female grenadier." Poirot casually included her in his list of suspects, since she was heiress to her brother's small estate. She suspected Mr. Reilly, her brother's partner in the dental clinic because he drank and she hated drinkers. *One, Two, Buckle My Shoe.*

MORLEY, HENRY A dentist, he was the brother of Georgina Morley and the partner of Mr. Reilly. "A small man with a decided jaw and a pugnacious chin," he was shot while on the job. *One, Two, Buckle My Shoe.*

MORRIS, DR. On close examination he discovered that, contrary to the appearance of suicide by hanging, Mabelle Annesley had been strangled with a wire before she had been strung up in her bedroom. "The Bird with the Broken Wing" from *The Mysterious Mr. Quin.*

MORRIS, DR. Luther Crackenthorpe's former physician, Dr. Morris was interviewed by Detective Inspector Craddock after the murder of Alfred Crackenthorpe, and informed him of Luther's mother's neuroses. *4.50 from Paddington.*

MORRIS, ISAAC Generously said to be "not a very savoury gentleman," he made all the arrangements for Mr. U.N. Owen regarding the purchase of Indian Island: hiring the guide, stocking the food and drink on the island and inviting some of the guests to the party. Although not a guest, Morris was actually the first victim of the Indian Island murderer, dying most opportunely the day the Island party began, ostensibly from an overdose of barbiturates. *And Then There Were None.*

MORTON, INSPECTOR Inspector working on the Cora Lansquenet murder case, "he was a quiet middle-aged man with a soft country burr in his voice. His manner was quiet and unhurried, but his eyes were shrewd." Accompanied by Superintendent Parwell, he was present at Poirot's denouement of the murderer. *After the Funeral.*

MORY, ANGELE AKA Mademoiselle Geneviève Brun; Countess Varaga Popoleffsky; Queen Varaga of Herzoslavakia; and Virginia Revel. She was a clever young actress dancing with the Folies Bérgères in Paris. She was approached by the Comrades of the Red Hand to help them trap the woman-crazy King Nicholas V of Herzoslavakia, but on winning his heart, decided he would be better as a live husband than a dead monarch and, after a suitable but fraudulent introduction at court as Countess Varaga Popoleffsky, married him and became Queen Varaga of Herzoslavakia. As Mademoiselle Geneviève Brun she was governess to Lord Caterham's two youngest daughters, Daisy and Dulcie Brent. As Virginia Revel she penned the ostensibly adulterous love-letters to Captain O'Neill, an alias belonging to King Victor. *The Secret of Chimneys.*

MOSGOROVSKY, MR. AKA Number Six, Six O'clock, he was a Russian who ran the Seven Dials Club, a legitimate dancing and drinking establishment which also featured illegal gambling. That the Seven Dials Club had been raided only twice was a tribute to its clever manager. He aroused Bundle Brent's suspicions after she learned he had enticed Alfred, the footman at Chimneys, with one hundred pounds and three times his previous salary to work at the Seven Dials Club. *The Seven Dials Mystery.*

MOSS, EDWIN Mary Moss' brother, he stole Bunch Harmon's suitcase at the Chipping Cleghorn station "in mistake" for his own. "Sanctuary" from *Double Sin.*

MOSS, MARY AKA Zobeida. The wife of Walter St. John and the mother of Jewel St. John, she had died three years before. As the exotic dancer Zobeida, she had received a necklace from an Eastern potentate who was in love with her. She made a replica of the necklace and sewed the real emeralds into her costume, which was hidden in a bag at Paddington Station by her husband. "Sanctuary" from *Double Sin.*

MOUNTFORD, MRS. The sister of Edith Pagett, she was married to Mr. Mountford, Dillmouth's confectioner, and was interviewed by Gwenda Reed in an attempt to uncover information about Helen Halliday. *Sleeping Murder.*

MUGG, CHARLES *See* **CARTWRIGHT, SIR CHARLES.**

MULLINS, IRIS AKA Dodo. She was hired by Tuppence Beresford to tend her garden. The Beresford's Manchester terrier Hannibal, whose judgement was usually more reliable that Tuppence's, hated Iris Mullins. *Postern of Fate.*

MURCHISON, BIANCA The wife of research scientist Simon Murchison, she was a stocky, dark Italian who spoke with a strong accent. Mrs. Murchison had studied economics and commercial law before joining Aristides' Brain Trust, where she sometimes gave lectures. *Destination Unknown.*

MURCHISON, DR. SIMON The husband of Bianca Murchison, the "thin, anaemic-looking man of about twenty-six" was a research scientist at Mr. Aristides' Brain Trust complex, whose "conversation seemed always to come out of an old-fashioned novel." *Destination Unknown.*

MURDOCH, CYNTHIA A protegé of Emily Inglethorp's, Cynthia lived at Styles Court and worked in the Red Cross Hospital in Tadminster, where she had mixed Mrs. Inglethorp's bromide powders. When he wasn't imagining himself to be in love with Mary Cavendish, Hastings believed he was in love with Cynthia. *The Mysterious Affair at Styles.*

MURGATROYD, MRS. The old retainer at the ruined Kingsdean House, Mrs. Murgatroyd was given a pension by Harry Laxton when he decided to tear down the old house and rebuild. Excessively upset at being turned out of Kingsdean, which she considered her home, she hurled curses at Louise Laxton: "It's the black sorrow will be upon you! ... May your fair face rot." Shortly afterwards, Louise died following a fall from her horse. "The Case of the Caretaker" from *Three Blind Mice and Other Stories.*

MURGATROYD, AMY A feather-brained and excitable woman, Amy Murgatroyd was "fat and amiable" with a "curly bird's nest of grey hair in a good deal of disorder." She talked her friend Miss Hinchcliffe into going to Little Paddocks to witness the murder announced in Rudi Scherz' advertisement in the *Chipping Cleghorn Gazette.* She became one of the victims. *A Murder is Announced.*

MURRAY, DR. Physician at the Sunny Ridge Nursing Home, he was suspicious about Elizabeth Moody's death, performed an autopsy and discovered morphine poisoning as the cause. *By the Pricking of My Thumbs.*

"N" *See* **HAYDOCK, COMMANDER.**

NADINA *See* **GRÜNBERG, ANITA.**

NANCY The gold-digging typist who worked in George Packington's office, she managed to attract his attention; Maria Packington, George's neglected wife, thought she was "a nasty, made-up little minx, all lipstick and stockings and curls . . . sly little cat!" "The Case of the Middle-Aged Wife" from *Parker Pyne Investigates.*

NARRACOTT, INSPECTOR The efficient police Inspector of Sittaford assigned to the Trevelyan murder case, "he had a quiet persistence, a logical mind and a keen attention to detail." He arrested James Pearson for the murder, but in his "careful and suspicious" manner, he continued to investigate. *The Sittaford Mystery.*

NARRACOTT, FRED The guide to Indian Island, he operated the boat which took the party-goers to the site. Inspector Blore found him "curiously ill-informed, or perhaps unwilling to talk." *And Then There Were None.*

NASBY, LORD The millionaire owner of the *Daily Budget,* Lord Nasby, according to Anne Beddingfeld, was "A big man. Big head. Big face. Big moustache. Big stomach." Anne interviewed Lord Nasby and was successful in getting a job as Special Correspondent investigating the "Man in the Brown Suit" mystery. *The Man in the Brown Suit.*

NASH, SUPERINTENDENT A man of easy confidence and efficiency, "he was the best type of C.I.D. county Superintendent. Tall, soldierly, with quiet reflective eyes and a straightforward, unassuming manner," he was in charge of the poison pen murder cases in Lymstock. *The Moving Finger.*

NAYLOR, CAPTAIN HUMPHREY Lily Margrave's brother, Naylor had discovered a gold mine in Africa, but had been swindled out of his claim by Sir Reuben Astwell. He was staying at the Mitre Hotel the night that Sir Astwell was killed. "The Under Dog" from *The Under Dog.*

NAYLOR, LILY *See* **MARGRAVE, LILY.**

NAZORKOFF, PAULA *See* CAPELLI, BIANCA.

NEEDHEIM, HELGA A prominent endocrinologist, the fanatically pagan Helga Needheim was ironically dressed as Sister Marie on Alcadi's flight to Mr. Aristides' Brain Trust. This militant Fascist had a simple view of the world: "There are those that rule, the few; and there are the many that serve." Helga Needheim hoped to find allies of her world vision at Aristides' Brain Trust. *Destination Unknown.*

NEELE, CHIEF INSPECTOR An old friend of Poirot's, he handled the Scotland Yard investigation into the Restarick concerns and took over the David Baker murder case. He affectionately addressed Poirot as a "secretive old devil" and compared him to "an old mouser." *Third Girl.*

NEELE, INSPECTOR In charge of the Fortescue murder case, he was "a highly imaginative thinker, and one of his methods of investigation was to propound to himself fantastic theories of guilt which he applied to such persons as he was interrogating at the time." *A Pocket Full of Rye.*

NEILSON, DR. The Deputy Director of Mr. Aristides' Brain Trust complex, he was in charge of administration and orientation interviews. *Destination Unknown.*

NEUMANN, LISA Robert Shoreham's faithful employee since his days at the Leveson Foundation, she was a woman who "had loved him, worked with him and now lived beside him, ministering to him with her intellect, giving him devotion in its purest form without pity." *Passenger to Frankfurt.*

NEVILLE, GLADYS The well-behaved, morally upright secretary for Messrs. Morley and Reilly, she was engaged to Frank Carter. She received a spurious telegram that called her away from the office on the day of the murders. Her absence facilitated the murders and the alteration of certain dental records. *One, Two, Buckle My Shoe.*

NEWMAN, JOHN He was an acquaintance of Raymond West, who found him: "a man of intelligence and independent means . . . possessed of a romantic imagination." Newman's hobby was the search for a treasure of gold that was wrecked off the Cornwall coast on the famous Serpent Rocks. Newman was not all what he seemed, and Raymond West's judgement was slightly, but significantly, in error. "Ingots of Gold" from *The Thirteen Problems.*

NICHOLAS V, PRINCE *See* CADE, ANTHONY.

NICOLETIS, MRS. "Mrs. Nick" was the mother of Valerie Hobhouse and the owner of the student hostel on Hickory Road. She was involved in a smuggling operation with her daughter and Nigel Chapman, and was slain by a dose of morphine in her brandy. She was arrested for public drunkenness by Police Constable Bott while she was dying of poisoning. *Hickory Dickory Dock.*

NICHOLSON, DR. JASPER The husband of Moira Nicholson, he ran the Grange, a clinic for people with nervous conditions and drug habits. Among the "little things" that interested him was the fact that Dr. Arbuthnot's car was pointing in the wrong direction for him to have been travelling where he said he was when he stopped at Lady Frances' accident. *Why Didn't They Ask Evans?*

NICHOLSON, MOIRA AKA Rose Emily Templeton, she was the wife of Dr. Nicholson. As Rose Emily Templeton, she was the wife of Edgar Templeton, present at Tudor Cottage at the time of John Savage's death and beneficiary to the will forged by Roger Bassington-ffrench. *Why Didn't They Ask Evans?*

NOFRET The nineteen-year-old concubine that Imhotep brought into his house when he returned from his northern estates, she triggered a wave of hate and violence within the family. Sobek, Imhotep's second son and something of a ladies' man, exclaimed: "May a crocodile devour that woman!" Ultimately, Nofret fell from a cliff to her death. *Death Comes as the End.*

NORRIS, INSPECTOR Although he was portraying a local police officer in Hollowquay, he was actually a member of Intelligence detailed to the Laurels assignment. He said to Tommy, "women are always difficult." *Postern of Fate.*

NORTON, STEPHEN Resident at the Styles Court guesthouse, he was an amateur naturalist who was always hurrying about with a pair of field glasses. He was pronounced a victim of suicide when discovered shot through the centre of his forehead. *Curtain.*

NOSYSTEIN *See* **ISAACSTEIN, HERMAN.**

NUNN, ROSINA The wife of Henry Judd, she was an actress who was among the party that included Mr. Satterthwaite, the Duchess of Leith, Naomi Carlton-Smith, Mr. Tomlinson and Harley Quin at Coti Chiaveeri. Mr. Satterthwaite observed: "For twenty-five years of her life she had been a blond. After a tour in the States, she had returned with the locks of the raven, and she had taken up tragedy in earnest." "The World's End" from *The Mysterious Mr. Quin.*

NYE, SIR STAFFORD The grand-nephew of Lady Matilda Cleckheaton and the uncle of Sybil, Sir Stafford was a member of the Foreign Office who had "singularly failed to fulfil his early promise." Because of the striking resemblance she bore to his dead sister, Pamela, he allowed the international espionage agent Mary Ann to steal his passport and escape. *Passenger to Frankfurt.*

OBOLOVITCH, NICHOLAS SERGIUS ALEXANDER FERDINAND *See* **CADE, ANTHONY.**

OBOLOVITCH, PRINCE MICHAEL AKA Count Stanislaus and Mr. Holmes, he was the heir to the throne of Herzoslavakia. As Count Stanislaus, he roamed incognito at Chimneys; as Mr. Holmes, "a small, fair man with a quiet manner," he purported to represent the publishers Messrs. Balderson and Hodgkins in an attempt to intercept the potentially ruinous memoirs of Count Stylptitch. Superintendent Battle reported: "He was, if I may say so, inclined to be a rather—er—dissipated young man." He was murdered at Chimneys. *The Secret of Chimneys.*

O'CONNOR, SERGEANT A Scotland Yard detective, he was nicknamed by his colleagues as "The Maidservant's Prayer" because of his ability to extract information from parlourmaids. He enticed evidence regarding Mrs. Craddock's private life from Elsie Batt. *Cards on the Table.*

OGLANDER, MISS The daughter of Mr. and Mrs. John Oglander, she was sister to John Oglander, Jr. and to Valerie Sainclair. Hastings remarked: "I began to think that the elements of drama were wasted on Miss Oglander, that her lack of imagination rose superior to any tragedy." "The King of Clubs" from *The Under Dog.*

OGLANDER, MR. AND MRS. They were dining at the table next to Una Drake and Jimmy le Marchant at the Savoy the night of the bet. The Oglanders verified this for Tuppence Beresford in her attempt to aid Montgomery Jones in breaking one of Una's alibis. "The Unbreakable Alibi" from *Partners in Crime.*

O'HARA, EILEEN AKA Cecily March. Eileen O'Hara was the woman who was ill outside Ambassador Randolph Wilmott's cabin. As Cecily March, she claimed having seen O'Hara hiding a slip of paper in the Ambassador's boot. "The Ambassador's Boots" from *Partners in Crime.*

OHLSSON, GRETA A Swedish matron in a missionary school near Stamboul, she had once been the murdered Daisy Armstrong's nurse. She was the last person to see Samuel Edward Ratchet alive and shared a sleeping cabin with Mary Debenham. *Murder on the Orient Express.*

OLDFIELD, DR. CHARLES Haggard physician at Market Loughborough in Berkshire, he consulted Poirot as "a last resort" when rumours that his wife had been poisoned began to circulate. He and his dispenser Jean Moncrieffe were in love, but would not marry until the gossip ceased. "The Lernean Hydra" from *The Labours of Hercules.*

OLGA, GRAND DUCHESS *See* **DE SARA, MADELEINE.**

OLIVER, ARIADNE The godmother of Celia Ravenscroft, she was a celebrated detective novelist and the creator of the famous Finnish detective Sven Hjerson. When she worked for Mr. Parker Pyne, she had already authored "forty-six successful works of fiction, all best sellers in England and America, and freely translated into French, German, Italian, Hungarian, Finnish, Japanese and Abyssinian." She was addicted to apples, and they were her trademark until Joyce Reynolds was drowned in an apple-bobbing bucket in *Hallowe'en Party.* In *Cards on the Table,* she was one of the four sleuths invited to Mr. Shaitana's bridge party, where she formed an association with Hercule Poirot which spanned six novels. She was "handsome in a rather untidy fashion, with fine eyes, substantial shoulders, and a large quantity of rebellious grey hair with which she was continually experimenting." She was a "hot-headed feminist" who often voiced the opinion that a woman should be the head of Scotland Yard because of the female power of intuition. On the whole, she thought that life was "badly constructed," and said that she "could invent a better murder any day than anything *real.*" Just as Christie tired of Poirot, Mrs. Oliver soon detested Sven Hjerson: "If I ever met that bony, gangling vegetable-eating Finn in real life, I'd do a better murder than any I've ever invented. One of her novels was titled *The Body in the Library.* (*See* Bibliography.)

OLIVERA, JANE The American daughter of Julia Olivera and the niece of Alistair Blunt, she "appeared to consist chiefly of arms and legs." Young and politically leftist, she was the girlfriend of Howard Raikes, both of whom were suspicious not only because they disapproved of her Uncle Alistair's financial activities, but also because Jane stood to inherit a large fortune. *One, Two, Buckle My Shoe.*

OLIVERA, JULIA An American, she was the mother of Jane Olivera and the niece by marriage of the murdered Alistair Blunt. She was patronizing and rude to Poirot and fell briefly under suspicion when her voice was mimicked in a threatening call to the detective. She expected to gain a sizeable inheritance from her uncle. *One, Two, Buckle My Shoe.*

OLIVIER, MADAME "Number Three" of the Big Four gang, Madame Olivier was "a famous French chemist who had eclipsed even Madame Curie in the brilliance of her achievements. She had been decorated by the French government, and was one of the most prominent personalities of the day." *The Big Four.*

O'MURPHY As Prime Minister David MacAdam's chauffeur, O'Murphy was a Criminal Investigation Department man from Scotland Yard who hailed from County Clare, Ireland. By 1918 under MacAdam's government, the British abandoned the idea of Home Rule for Ireland, and this cast O'Murphy as a possible suspect in the kidnapping of the Prime Minister. "The Kidnapped Prime Minister" from *Poirot Investigates.*

O'NEELE, MOIRA *See* **HOBHOUSE, VALERIE.**

O'NEILL, CAPTAIN *See* **VICTOR, KING.**

OPALSEN, MRS. The wife of Ed Opalsen, a rich stockbroker, who Hastings knew "slightly," she hired Poirot to recover her pearl necklace, which had been stolen from her room in the hotel. "Jewel Robbery at the 'Grand Metropolitan'" from *Poirot Investigates.*

ORANOFF, PRINCE SERGIUS AKA Sergius Ivanovitch, he and two other professional dancers came to perform in Lady Roscheimer's semi-amateur production of a Harlequinade. Prince Sergius claimed to have loved Anne Denman for the ten years of her absence, and vowed never to be without her again. "Harlequin's Lane" from *The Mysterious Mr. Quin.*

O'ROURKE, FLIGHT LIEUTENANT One of the many admirers of Netta Pryce, he was among the twelve people travelling from Damascus to Baghdad. He suggested that a bump to Captain Smethurst's head might have been responsible for the man's death. "The Gate of Baghdad" from *Parker Pyne Investigates.*

O'ROURKE, MRS. A guest at the Sans Souci in Leahampton, "she was rather like an ogress dimly remembered from early fairy tales." She also resembled a gigantic Buddha, or an obese Chinese mandarin. Little occurred at the hotel without her knowledge, and she discovered the hammer which had been used to cosh Tommy Beresford in the driveway of the Sans Souci. *N or M?*

O'ROURKE, TERENCE The secretary to the Air Minister, he accompanied Sir Stanley Digby to the negotiations for Herr Eberhard's secret metal formula at Wyvern Abbey. He was drugged and the papers were stolen. *The Seven Dials Mystery.*

ORWELL, ROBERT He and Andrew Restarick had been prospecting partners in Kenya some fifteen years before. When Restarick died, Orwell assumed his identity, and with Frances Cary, contrived a scheme to defraud Norma Restarick of her family's money. *Third Girl.*

OSBORNE, ZACHARIAH "A small, middle-aged man with a bald domed head, a round, ingenuous face and glasses," he seemed "a respectably dapper little chemist, old-fashioned, quite a character and a great observer of people." Mr. Osborne was also owner of Customer's Reactions Classified, the market research firm for which Jesse Davis and Eileen Brandon worked. *The Pale Horse.*

OSRIC, PRINCE The uncle of the Grand Duchess Anastasia, Prince Osric had been asked by Sturm, the chancellor of Catonia, to prevent Anastasia's marriage to Lord Roland Gaigh and to engineer a match between Anastasia and her pimply-faced cousin Prince Karl. "The Girl in the Train" from *The Golden Ball.*

OSSINGTON, SIR WILLIAM A Scotland Yard official, he was "known to the cronies of earlier days as Billy Bones." When Luke Fitzwilliam had a suspect for the murders firmly in mind, Billy Bones sent Superintendent Battle and some other officers to Wychwood to aid Fitzwilliam in the case. *Murder is Easy.*

OTTERBOURNE, ROSALIE Bitter, unhappy daughter of Salome Otterbourne, she was vacationing with her mother on the S.S. *Karnak* when Linnet Doyle was murdered. The source of her misery was her mother, who was a closet alcoholic and authoress of many embarrassingly sexually "realistic" novels. Of Linnet Doyle she said: "I'd like to tear the clothes off her back and stamp on her lovely, arrogant, self-confident face." She managed to find some measure of happiness, after the death of her mother, when she and Tim Allerton fell in love. *Death on the Nile.*

OTTERBOURNE, SALOME The mother of Rosalie Otterbourne, she described herself as "practically a teatotaller" who could not "bear the taste of spirits," but was secretly a chronic alcoholic. She was driven to drink following a decline in the sales of her novels, which contained explicit and candid sex scenes. She was slain moments before she could reveal the murderer of Louise Bourget. *Death on the Nile.*

OWEN, ULICK NORMAN *See* **WARGRAVE, MR. JUSTICE LAWRENCE JOHN.**

OWEN, UNA NANCY *See* **WARGRAVE, MR. JUSTICE LAWRENCE JOHN.**

OXLEY, LOUISE A niece of Joan West, she edited Nathaniel Greenshaw's diaries, and witnessed what appeared to be the murder of Miss Greenshaw while she was locked in the library. "Greenshaw's Folly" from *The Adventure of the Christmas Pudding.*

PACE, HARRINGTON The uncle of Roger Havering, he was "a small, spare, clean-shaven man, typically American in appearance." For three years he had lived with his nephew and his nephew's wife Zoe, and after his death they inherited his wealthy estate. "The Mystery of Hunter's Lodge" from *Poirot Investigates.*

PACKARD, MISS Superintendent and manageress of the Sunny Ridge Nursing Home, after Ada Fanshaw's death, "her manner was suitably not quite so brisk as usual. It was grave, and had a kind of semi-mourning about it—not too much—that might have been embarrassing. She was an expert in the exact amount of condolence which would be acceptable." *By the Pricking of My Thumbs.*

PACKINGTON, GEORGE Stout, bald, and middle-aged, he was the husband of Maria Packington and the lover of young Nancy, a typist at his office. After Maria began her soulful affair with Mr. Pyne's gigolo, Claude Luttrell, she pitied her husband: "Poor old George! . . . How terribly he bounced on his feet! He danced in the style of twenty years ago. Poor George, how terribly he wanted to be young!"

George soon had a change of heart: "How could you enjoy taking a girl about when your wife fairly urged you on? Dash it all, it wasn't decent!" "The Case of the Middle-Aged Wife" from *Parker Pyne Investigates.*

PACKINGTON, MARIA The wife of George Packington. George was in for a shock when Maria, "that model of economy," began spending lavish amounts in various beauty parlours and dressmakers' shops. Maria emerged from her affair with Claude Luttrell, Parker Pyne's agent, looking "smart, modish, up-to-date." She felt a "secret splendour" in herself and pity for her foolish husband. "The Case of the Middle-Aged Wife" from *Parker Pyne Investigates.*

PAGETT, EDITH The sister of Mrs. Mountford, she was interviewed by Gwenda Reed for information about Helen Halliday. *Sleeping Murder.*

PAGETT, GUY For six years he worked for Sir Eustace Pedler, MP, who said: "Guy Pagett is my secretary, a zealous, painstaking, hard-working fellow, admirable in every respect. I know no one who annoys me more. For a long time I have been racking my brains as to how to get rid of him. But you cannot very well dismiss a secretary because he prefers work to play, likes getting up early in the morning and has positively no vices." Anne Beddingfeld was under the mistaken impression that Pagett assaulted her on board the *Kilmorden Castle*, and in return, she blackened his eye. Pagett had a wife and four children whose existence he had kept secret from Sir Pedler. *The Man in the Brown Suit.*

PALGRAVE, MAJOR Elderly guest at the Golden Palm Hotel, Miss Marple found that he was "an elderly man who needed a listener so that he could, in memory, relive days in which he had been happy. Days when his back had been straight, his eyesight keen, his hearing acute." He was "purple of face, with a glass eye, and the general appearance of a stuffed frog." He related a story and showed Miss Marple a photograph of a wife-murderer he had once known. Very shortly thereafter he died, ostensibly from a mistaken dose of heart medicine. *A Caribbean Mystery.*

PALGRAVE, EDWARD (TED) Dorothy Pratt's boyfriend and an office clerk, he purchased a fourth-hand Baby Austin for twenty pounds. Of his Sunday outing with Dorothy, he said: "Tea later, petrol—this Sunday motoring business wasn't what you'd call *cheap*. That was the worst of taking girls out! They always wanted everything they saw." Edward also bought Dorothy a small basket of cherries in which was concealed a necklace. Dorothy was convinced it was the ruby necklace, worth fifty thousand pounds, which had recently been reported missing in the newspapers. "A Fruitful Sunday" from *The Golden Ball.*

PALK, CONSTABLE His "habit of giving in to the gentry was life-long," and so he let Miss Marple and Dolly Bantry view the body of Pamela Reeves before his superiors arrived on the scene. *The Body in the Library.*

PALLISER, SIR EDWARD Nearly seventy years old, he had been "one of the most eminent criminal barristers of his day" but no longer practised law and instead amused himself by amassing a very fine criminological library. Magdalen Vaughan came to him to ask his help in solving the mystery of the death of her great-aunt Lily Crabtree, remembering that he had offered his aid unconditionally when they met on board the *Siluric.* "Sing a Song of Sixpence" from *The Listerdale Mystery.*

PALMER, MABEL "A pleasant-faced woman of middle-age," she appeared to be a nurse with the Lark Sisterhood. Suspected to be an agent of the Big Four gang, she brought the insidious Templeton case to Poirot. *The Big Four.*

PAPOPOLOUS, ARISTIDE "A lean Mephistopheles," he was the headwaiter at Hell and had invested some of his own money in the lounge. The police suspected him from being part of the drug ring. "The Capture of Cerberus" from *The Labours of Hercules.*

PAPOPOLOUS, DEMETRIUS The father of Zia Papopolous, he was saved by Poirot from "the worst moment in his career" and in return, gave Poirot a clue leading to the identity of le Marquis. He was suspected by the police for receiving stolen goods, particularly jewels, and was an expert at recutting and resetting gems. He received the stolen Heart of Fire rubies from Ada Beatrice Mason (AKA Kitty Kidd) in Nice. *The Mystery of the Blue Train.*

PAPOPOLOUS, ZIA The daughter of Demetrius Papopolous, she helped Poirot in the Kettering case, and told him that the Heart of Fire rubies were handed over to her father by a woman. *The Mystery of the Blue Train.*

PARAVICINI, MR. He had a wallet crammed with banknotes and was cynical and highly amused at being at the site of a murder, Monkswell Manor. Molly

Davis was struck by the juxtaposition of his age and his springing step, and noticed with some alarm that Mr. Paravicini's face was cleverly but decidedly made-up. Mr. Paravicini leered at Molly like an elderly satyr and said: "If you should receive a case—with a good say, a turkey, some tins of *foie gras*, a ham—some nylon stockings, yes? Well, you understand, it will be with my compliments to a very charming lady." "Three Blind Mice" from *Three Blind Mice and Other Stories.*

PARDOE, WILLIAM REUBEN A cousin of Ellie Guteman's, he was "Uncle Reuben" to her. He visited Michael Rogers to express his shock and grief at his young cousin's death. *Endless Night.*

PARDONSTENGER, AMY *See* **WALLACE, BELLA.**

PARFITT, CANON The Canon of Bradchester's "scientific sermons" were popular with the news media. The Canon disagreed on theological grounds with Dr. Clark's theory of two souls inhabiting the same body, and discussed the relative interrelationships of soul, mind and body with the doctor. "The Fourth Man" from *Witness for the Prosecution.*

PARKER The butler at Roger Ackroyd's Fernly Park, he had worked for Ackroyd for just over a year. Previously he had been employed by Major Ellerby whose indiscreet habits provided ample material for blackmail. James Sheppard remarked that Parker had "a fat, smug, oily face and a shifty eye." *The Murder of Roger Ackroyd.*

PARKER, MR. AND MRS. They intended to blackmail Walter Prothero for blowing up a cruiser when he was a lieutenant in the Royal Navy. "The Market Basing Mystery" from *The Under Dog.*

PARKER, BERNARD Hastings immediately disliked "this particular young man with his white, effeminate face and affected lisping speech." Parker was employed as a go-between for Marcus Hardman, and became a suspect in the theft of the Medici necklace. He sought help from the Countess Vera Rossakoff. "The Double Clue" from *Double Sin.*

PARKER, GEORGE *See* **JONES, ROBERT.**

PARKER, GERALD An old friend of Hastings, he gave a party where Stella Robinson told the tale of the cheap flat in Montagu Mansions that led to the arrest of Elsa Hardt. "The Adventure of the Cheap Flat" from *Poirot Investigates.*

PARKER, HARRY *See* **RAYBURN, HARRY.**

PARKER PYNE, CHRISTOPHER The son of Charles and Harriet Parker Pyne, Mr. Parker Pyne could be contacted through the following advertisement which ran in the Personal column of the daily *Times*: "ARE YOU HAPPY? IF NOT, CONSULT MR. PARKER PYNE, 17 Richmond Street." For thirty-five years, Mr. Parker Pyne had been engaged in compiling statistics in a government office. When he retired he decided to put his experience to use by setting up a detective agency. "The mere sight of Mr. Parker Pyne," it was said, "brought a feeling of reassurance. He was large, not to say fat; he had a bald head of noble proportions, strong glasses, and little twinkling eyes." He told his clients that he "stood in the place of a doctor," and that if he undertook a case the cure was practically guaranteed. He employed the "lounge lizard" Claude Luttrell, the vampish Madeleine de Sara, the efficient Miss Felicity Lemon (who later worked for Hercule Poirot) and the dishevelled detective novelist Mrs. Ariadne Oliver (who subsequently played a major role in a number of Poirot novels). Marriage, he thought, was one of the great causes of unhappiness: "It is a fundamental axiom of married life that you *must* lie to a woman." *Parker Pyne Investigates;* "The Regatta Mystery" and "Problem at Pollensa Bay" from *The Regatta Mystery.*

PARSONS The butler in the Sir Reuben Astwell household, he testified to Inspector Miller that Charles Leverson had been fighting with Sir Astwell the night before Sir Astwell was found dead. Hastings called him "a very well-trained servant, with a manner suitably devoid of emotion," but Victor Astwell said Parsons was "a blithering old idiot." "The Under Dog" from *The Under Dog.*

PARSONS, OLIVE The culprit in the thefts at Miss Amphrey's school, she had "fair hair, rather fuzzy, with pink cheeks and a spot on her chin, blue eyes far apart." Superintendent Battle immediately noted the "calm smug look" that he'd seen many times in police courts. *Towards Zero.*

PARTRIDGE, MR. JAMES Partridge was the last person to see Alice Ascher alive. On first meeting Hercule Poirot, "Mr. Partridge placed his fingertips together and looked at Poirot as though he were a doubtful cheque." *The A.B.C. Murders.*

PATON, CAPTAIN RALPH The son of Roger Ackroyd's first wife, he was married to Ursala Bourne and engaged to Flora Ackroyd. Poirot remarked that Paton was "unusually good-looking for an Englishman—what your lady novelists would call a Greek God." Having quarrelled with his step-father, he had been absent from Fernly Park for about six months. He was staying at the Three Boars in King's Abbot the night Roger Ackroyd died. *The Murder of Roger Ackroyd.*

PATON, MRS. RALPH *See* **BOURNE, URSALA.**

PATTERSON, ELSIE She had a low opinion of her sister Gerda but nevertheless came to take over her household after the death of her brother-in-law John. Her family always maintained that she was wonderful in a crisis. *The Hollow.*

PATTERSON, PHYLLIS She was engaged to Andrew Carmichael, and lived at Wolden, the Carmichael home, while her fiancé was possessed by the spirit of a grey Persian cat. She called Andrew back from the dead after he appeared to have drowned in a pond near Wolden. "The Strange Case of Sir Andrew Carmichael" from *The Golden Ball.*

PAUL, PRINCE OF MAURANIA AKA Count Feodor. Enamoured of Valerie Saintclair, Prince Paul believed her to be the scion of a noble Russian family and wanted to marry her. He was responsible for bringing Poirot into the case. "The King of Clubs" from *The Under Dog.*

PAULINE, GRAND DUCHESS Living in fear of being assassinated, she hired Jane Cleveland to impersonate her at a number of public functions. However, the real Grand Duchess Pauline had eloped with a chauffeur in Paris and the one that hired Jane was an imposter. "Jane in Search of a Job" from *The Golden Ball.*

PAULOVITCH, COUNT SERGIUS *See* **MINKS, ARTHUR.**

PAUNCEFOOT JONES, DR. JOHN (PUSSYFOOT JONES) Married to Elsie, he was a learned and respected archaeologist who was working a dig at the ancient city of Murik. As the senior member at Expedition House, he was Richard Baker's employer. Victoria Jones passed herself off as his niece, Veronica, for a while, posing as an anthropologist from Cambridge University. *They Came to Baghdad.*

PAVLOVITCH, COUNT ALEXIS An old friend of Poirot's, Count Alexis prided himself on knowing all that went on in the artistic world. Poirot, murmuring his questions "with his most flattering intonation," extracted information on Katrina Samoushenka from the Count. "The Arcadian Deer" from *The Labours of Hercules.*

PAYNTER, MR. The uncle of Gerald Paynter, he was "a man of fifty-five, rich, cultured and somewhat of a globe-trotter." He was found dead at Croftlands, his face in a gas fire. At the time of his death he was writing a book called *The Hidden Hand in China.* The manuscript disappeared. *The Big Four.*

PAYNTER, GERALD Mr. Paynter's nephew, he was an impecunious young artist and claimed to have been dining with the Wycherlys on the night of his uncle's death. *The Big Four.*

PEABODY, CAROLINE A friend of Emily Arundell's for over fifty years, she was a vast storehouse of information on the Arundell family, which she freely gave, although Poirot's assumed identity as "Parotti," biographer of the Arundell family did not fool her one iota. She upheld the Victorian sentiments concerning "family dignity, family solidarity and complete reticence on family matters." *Dumb Witness.*

PEARSON, MR One of the directors of the company wishing to purchase documents revealing the location of the Burmese mine, he hired Poirot to recover the papers after the death of Wu Ling. Poirot said: "He talked of disguising himself—he even suggested that I—I should—I hesitate to say it—should shave off my moustache! Yes, *rien que ca*! I pointed out to him that it was an idea ridiculous and absurd. One destroys not a thing of

beauty wantonly." While at an opium den, he and Poirot overheard a conversation implicating Charles Lester in the murder of Wu Ling. "The Lost Mine" from *Poirot's Early Cases.*

PEARSON, MRS. Hercule Poirot's landlady at 14 Farraway Street, she was referred to as "Mrs. Funnyface" by Dr. Ridgeway. *The Big Four.*

PEARSON, BRIAN The nephew of Captain Trevelyan, the younger brother of James Pearson and Sylvia Dering and the son of Mary Pearson, he was supposedly residing in Australia, but was actually near Exhampton at the time of his uncle's murder. *The Sittaford Mystery.*

PEARSON, JAMES A nephew of the murdered Captain Trevelyn, he was the son of Mary Pearson, the brother of Sylvia and Brian Pearson and the fiancé of Emily Trefusis. Mr. Dacres, his solicitor, told Emily that James did not have a "very high standard of commercial honesty." Emily and Charles Enderby eventually freed him from suspicion of his uncle's murder. *The Sittaford Mystery.*

PEBMARSH, MILLICENT The blind grade-school teacher in whose flat the first murder victim was found, she was the mother of Sheila Webb and the sister of Mrs. Lawton. Neither Miss Pebmarsh nor Sheila knew of their relation to each other. *The Clocks.*

PEDLER, SIR EUSTACE AKA the "Colonel," and easily one of the most likeable rogues in the Christie canon, Sir Eustace Pedler was also the most flamboyant and calculating. As the "Colonel," he "organized crime as another man might organize a boot factory." As Sir Eustace Pedler, MP, he had blandly stated: "My only object in life is to be thoroughly comfortable." He said: "There are many fools in the world. One praises God for their existence and keeps out of their way." Anne Beddingfeld could only think of him as a lovable Long John Silver sort of character, and he asked Anne to marry him, but she turned him down. *The Man in the Brown Suit.*

PENDAR, DR. The elderly parish clergyman in St. Mary Mead, he maintained that men of the cloth "hear things. . . . know a side of human character which is a sealed book to the outside world." He was a member of the Tuesday Night Club. *The Thirteen Problems.*

PENN, ELIZABETH Mary Durrant's aunt and the proprietress of an antique shop in Ebermouth, she wore "a cape of priceless old lace," and owned the miniatures that Mary Durrant was taking to J. Baker Wood. "Double Sin" from *Double Sin.*

PENN, MAJOR GENERAL SIR JOSIAH (OLD JOSH) A member of the International Union of Associated Security, he was described by Tommy Beresford as "extremely deaf, half-blind, crippled with rheumatism—and you'd be surprised at the things that don't get past him." He knew and loved Tommy's Aunt Ada as a girl and would have married her had he not gone to India. Tommy had trouble envisioning either of them in the role of a lover, especially Sir Josh, with his "double chin, his bald head, his bushy eyebrows and his enormous paunch." *By the Pricking of My Thumbs.*

PENNINGTON, ANDREW "Uncle" Andrew to Linnet Doyle, he was her American trustee. He was hoping to defraud her of a great deal of money by tricking her into signing certain documents. For this purpose, he arrived "by accident" in Egypt. His gun was used to kill Salome Otterbourne. *Death on the Nile.*

PENNYFATHER, CANON The priest who disappeared, he was a scholar of Hebrew and Aramaic and was on his way to Lucerne to attend a conference on the Dead Sea Scrolls. Unfortunately, he had confused the dates and missed the conference. Returning unexpectedly, he discovered his double in the hotel room just before he was knocked unconscious. The Wheelings found him on the side of a road and nursed him back to health. *At Bertram's Hotel.*

PENNYMAN, MAJOR An elderly man who lived in Baghdad, and a friend of Mrs. Kelsey's, he offered his opinion of the expedition at Tell Yarimjah: "Yes, individually they are all pleasant people. But somehow or other, I may have been fanciful, but the last time I went to see them I got a queer impression of something being wrong. I don't know what it was exactly. Nobody seemed quite natural. There was a queer atmosphere of tension. I can explain best what I mean by saying that they all passed the butter to each other too politely." *Murder in Mesopotamia.*

PENROSE, DR. The Superintendent of the Saltmarsh House nursing home, he had been Major Kelvin Halliday's psychiatrist. Gwenda Reed, Halliday's daughter, consulted Dr. Penrose about her father's suicide; she noticed that he "looked a little mad himself." He gave Gwenda her father's diary. *Sleeping Murder.*

PERCEHOUSE, CAROLINE The invalid aunt of Ronnie Garfield, she had "a thin wrinkled face and one of the sharpest and most interrogative noses" Emily Trefusis had ever seen. Her spineless nephew Ronnie did all he could to stay on her good side, when he could find it: "Every year, I wonder how I can stick it—but there it is. If one doesn't rally round the old bird for Xmas, why, she's quite capable of leaving her money to a cat's home. She's got five of them, you know." *The Sittaford Mystery.*

PERENNA, EILEEN The proprietress of the Sans Souci guest house in Leahampton, she was the mother of Sheila Perenna and the widow of the IRA agitator Patrick Maguire. Mrs. Blenkensop searched Mrs. Perenna's room for evidence to incriminate her in Fifth Column activities, and discovered that Mrs. Perenna had like-wise searched Mrs. Blenkensop's room. *N or M?*

PERENNA, SHEILA Bored, beautiful and bitter daughter of Eileen Perenna and Patrick Maguire, she despised patriotic propaganda because the war had robbed her of her father, an IRA agent who was shot for treachery. Her lover, Carl von Deinim, was arrested for possession of sabotage plans. *N or M?*

PERROT, JULES Booking clerk at the Paris office of Universal Air Lines, he accepted a bribe from Silas Harper to delay Madame Giselle's departure until the noon flight, and booked the seat next to her for Harper. However, that seat stayed empty during the flight. His face broke out in a sweat under Poirot's gaze, and he fell apart completely under Poirot's questioning. *Death in the Clouds.*

PERRY, ALICE AND AMOS For three years they had rented part of Watermead, the house in William Boscowan's painting. Mrs. Perry resembled a "friendly witch": she "had long, straggly hair which when caught up by the wind, flew out behind her" and "a kind of steeple hat perched on her head and her nose and chin came up towards each other." The vicar said that Mr. Perry was "not completely *compos mentis*—but no harm in him." The Perrys were the last people to take care of Julia Lancaster. *By the Pricking of My Thumbs.*

PERRY, PERCY He was the oily-voiced editor of the *X-Ray News,* a newspaper which spread rumours of ex-Prime Minister John Hammet's corrupt government. He claimed to be a reformer who wished to cleanse the "Augean Stables" of Parliament with the "purifying flood of public opinion." Poirot tricked him into printing scandalous but phoney photographs which destroyed the paper's credibility. "The Augean Stables" from *The Labours of Hercules.*

PETERS, ANDREW *See* **GLYDR, MAJOR BORIS ANDREI PAVLOV.**

PETERS, WILLARD J., JR. The eighteen-year-old son of Mrs. Willard J. Peters, he was "her boy, her pet, her delicate, serious Willard," with whom she toured Greece. She described her son to Parker Pyne: "Culture might be said to be his middle name." He was kidnapped by a gang of Greek jewel thieves for his mother's diamond necklace, valued at a hundred thousand pounds. "The Oracle at Delphi" from *Parker Pyne Investigates.*

PETERS, MRS. WILLARD J. A widow, she was on vacation with her son Willard rambling through the ruins of Greece, although her "spiritual homes were Paris, London and the Riviera." She received notes from Demetrius the Black Browed who demanded diamonds for the return of her beloved son. "The Oracle at Delphi" from *Parker Pyne Investigates.*

PETHERICK, MR. A member of the Tuesday Night Club, he was Miss Marple's solicitor, and like Charles Dickens' Thomas Gradgrind from *Hard Times,* he thought that facts were all that mattered, and where there were no facts there was nothing worthy of concern. After his death, his son took over Miss Marple's affairs. "Motive *v* Opportunity" from *The Thirteen Problems.*

PETTIGREW, MISS *See* **MINKS, ARTHUR.**

PHELPS, HAYWARD AKA Number Four, Four o'clock, he was observed by Bundle Brent, at the Seven Dials meeting. He was an American journalist. *The Seven Dials Mystery.*

PHILLPOT, MAJOR The husband of Gervase Phillpot, and a friend to Michael and Ellie Rogers and Claudia Hardcastle, he "was God locally" in the village of Kingston Bishop. He had a particular fondness for old Mother Lee, the gipsy. *Endless Night.*

PHILLPOT, GERVASE The wife of Major Phillpot, she was known to her friends as an invalid. However, Michael Rogers found that, even though she asked him who he knew, "she wasn't a real snob and didn't really want to know." *Endless Night.*

PIERCE, CONSTABLE "Nervous-looking young constable," he had referred Edna Brent for an interview with his boss, Inspector Hardcastle. She became the second murder victim shortly afterward. *The Clocks.*

PIERCE, MRS. Voluble aunt of Louisa Maud, she was the woman who did for Miss Plenderleith and Mrs. Allen. "An elderly woman of ample proportions" who panted as she talked, she was supposed to arrive daily at 9 A.M. but usually got there at noon or not at all. "Murder in the Mews" from *Murder in the Mews.*

PIERCE, MRS. The wife of Mr. Pierce was the mother of eight children and kept the tobacco and paper shop in Wychwood's High Street. She provided Luke Fitzwilliam with the story of her son Tommy's death. *Murder is Easy.*

PIERCE, AMABEL A long-time nursery governess, she toured Jerusalem with, among others, the Boynton family. She experienced some difficulty during the tour: "The unfortunate Miss Pierce had to be almost carried over the precipitous places, her eyes shut, her face green, while her voice rose in a perpetual wail: 'I never could look down places'." *Appointment with Death.*

PIERCE, TOMMY The son of Mr. and Mrs. Pierce, this young ne'er-do-well was disliked by almost everyone in Wychwood. The young miscreant was a red-

cassocked acolyte at Mr. Ellsworthy's satanic coven. In his last job as a window-washer, he had a fatal fall from the third-storey window of Wych Hall. *Murder is Easy.*

PIERRE A nephew of Charles, the Luxembourg's head waiter, Pierre was "a frightened white rabbit of sixteen." Harried by Monsieur Robert, Pierre picked up Iris Marle's dropped handbag while she was dancing, and returned it to the wrong place setting, shifting all the members of the party one seat over. *Sparkling Cyanide.*

PIKE, ALBERT AND JESSIE They witnessed Andrew Marsh's only valid will. "The Case of the Missing Will" from *Poirot Investigates.*

PIKEAWAY, COLONEL EPHRAIM As the head of the Special Branch in England, Colonel Pikeaway was perpetually covered in a layer of cigar ash. He "seldom raised his head. Somebody had said that he looked like a cross between an ancient Buddha and a large blue frog, with perhaps, as some impudent youngster had added, just a touch of a bar sinister from hippopotamus in his ancestry." *Cat Among the Pigeons; Passenger to Frankfurt; Postern of Fate.*

PLENDERLEITH, JANE Barbara Allen's intelligent and clever roommate, she distorted the evidence of Mrs. Allen's suicide to make it appear as though she had been murdered by Major Eustace. She had a great affection for Mrs. Allen, disliked Charles Laverton-West and thoroughly hated Major Eustace. "Murder in the Mews" from *Murder in the Mews.*

POINTZ, ISAAC The rich Hatton Garden diamond merchant, he was the partner of Leo Stein, owner of the yacht Merrimaid and of the diamond mascot Morning Star, valued at over thirty thousand pounds. During the festivities of the Regatta in Dartmouth Harbour, he accepted Eve Leathern's dare that she could steal the Morning Star; the terms of the wager were six pairs of nylon hose and a tobacco pouch. The benign Mr. Pointz was not only unable to detect the theft of the gem, but discovered later that the diamond was completely lost in the end. "The Regatta Mystery" from *The Regatta Mystery.*

POIROT, ACHILLE The existence of Achille Poirot, Hercule Poirot's twin brother, has often been the subject of debate. Hercule was secretive about his family, and the first mention of Achille Poirot was in *The Big Four*, when Hercule remarked that he would have to bring his brother into the case. Hastings expressed a good deal of surprise, and Poirot, with a clear dig at Sir Arthur Conan Doyle, the creator of Sherlock Holmes and his reclusive brother Mycroft, replied: "You surprise me, Hastings. Do you not know that all celebrated detectives have brothers who would be even more celebrated than they are were it not for constitutional indolence?" According to Poirot, Achille lived near Spa in Belgium where "He does nothing. He is, as I tell you, of a singularly indolent disposition. But his abilities are hardly less than my own—which is saying a great deal. . . . He is not nearly so handsome and he wears no moustaches." In a scene from *The Big Four* that took place in Felsenlabyrynth, Hastings and the Countess Vera Rossakoff came face to face with Achille Poirot, who was disguised to look like his famous brother: "The man beside me," said Hastings, "was not Hercule Poirot. He was very like him, extraordinarily like him. There was the same egg-shaped head, the same strutting figure, delicately plump. But the voice was different, and the eyes instead of being green were dark." Just then, Vera Rossakoff, the woman who knew Hercule Poirot more intimately than any other, "leaned forward and snatched at Poirot's moustaches. They came off in her hand, and then, indeed, the truth was plain. For this man's upper lip was disfigured by a small scar which completely altered the expression of the face." But just as Hastings, Vera Rossakoff and

Achille prepared to leave Felsenlabyrynth, the mountain exploded. Hastings awoke in a strange bed to find himself in the company of Hercule Poirot, who told him a strange story: "But yes, my friend, it is I. Brother Achille has gone home again—to the land of myths. It was I all the time. . . . Belladonna in the eyes, the sacrifice of the moustaches and a real scar the inflicting of which caused me much pain two months ago."

Did Achille exist? And if so, what became of him and why did Poirot tell Hastings that Achille had been really Hercule in disguise? If Achille did not exist, Hastings and the Countess Vera Rossakoff were unable to penetrate Hercule's disguise in Felsenlabyrynth, something which, though possible, was very unlikely. A more significant piece of evidence is the scarred upper lip. The nature and magnitude of the scar would have severely impaired any attempt on the part of Poirot to regrow his luxuriant moustaches.

A possible solution to the mystery of Achille Poirot is that Achille died in the explosion at Felsenlabyrynth. Poirot invented the story denying his brother's existence to save Hastings any added grief at the thought that he might in any way have been responsible for the death of his great friend's brother. Hastings had already survived two explosions, one of which he thought had claimed the life of Hercule; he had attended Hercule's supposed funeral; and had been under the impression that his wife had been kidnapped in the Argentine by agents of the Big Four. Solicitous of Hastings' state of mind, Poirot elected to glaze over the Achilles episode with a deception.

The last reference to Achille Poirot appeared in the "Foreword" to *The Labours of Hercules.* Dr. Burton, a classics scholar and a Fellow of All Souls, speculated on what might have prompted Madame Poirot to name her celebrated son Hercule: "If I remember rightly—though my memory isn't what it was—you had a brother called Achille, did you not?" Poirot quietly recalled the details of his brother's career before replying: "Only for a short space of time." Burton sensed the great detective's reticence to discuss his brother, and "passed tactfully from the subject of Achille Poirot." *The Big Four.*

POIROT, HERCULE The brother of Achille Poirot, Hercule Poirot was born in nineteenth-century Belgium to parents of a decidedly classical turn of mind. After growing up near Spa, Poirot moved to Brussels where he became a member of the Belgian police and quickly rose through the ranks until he retired in 1904 as their most illustrious detective. While he was with the Belgian police, Poirot first met Inspector James Japp, the Scotland Yard detective with whom he enjoyed a long though occasionally frustrating friendship, when they were both investigating the Abercrombie forgery case in Brussels. After 1904, Poirot established himself as a private inquiry agent and rapidly became one of the most celebrated sleuths in Europe, and he again encountered Japp in the Baron Altara case, which concluded in Antwerp. Prior to the outbreak of World War I, Poirot met Arthur Hastings, the man who became his Watson and his valued and trusted friend, when both were involved in an investigation for Lloyd's of London (by whom Hastings was employed).

The year 1916 found Poirot a Belgian refugee living at Leastways, a small cottage in Styles St. Mary owned by Emily Inglethorp, the woman whose death launched the Poirot saga. Here Poirot again met Hastings and Japp, and in his account of the case, *The Mysterious Affair at Styles*, Hastings gave us our first description of the great Belgian: "Poirot was an extraordinary-looking little man. He was hardly more than five feet four inches, but carried himself with great dignity. His head was exactly the shape of an egg, and he always perched it a little on one side. His moustache was very stiff and military. The neatness of his attire was almost incredible; I believe a speck of dust would have caused him more pain than a bullet wound." Later, in *Murder on the Links*, Hastings observed Poirot's technique: " 'Order' and 'Method' were his gods. He had a certain disdain for tangible evidence, such as footprints and cigarette ash, and would maintain that, taken by themselves, they would never enable a detective to solve a problem. Then he would tap his egg-shaped head with absurd complacency, and remark with great satisfaction, 'the true work, it is always done from *within*. The little grey cells—* remember always the little grey cells, *mon ami'*."

After the Styles case, Poirot and Hastings took rooms together in London at 14 Farraway Street, where Poirot established himself as a private inquiry agent of considerable renown. A few years later, after Hastings had married and moved to the Argentine, Poirot began investigating the Big Four, which he called "the great case" of his life. During *The Big Four*, Achille Poirot was killed while impersonating his esteemed brother. Later Poirot retired to The Larches in King's Abbot, where he solved the murder of Roger Ackroyd. Retirement, however, did not suit Poirot and he soon returned to London. He resided at Whitehaven Mansions, a new block of flats chosen for its symmetry and exact proportions, and was back in business as a private investigator. At this time George, the imperturbable valet, came to work for him, and Poirot later employed Miss Felicity Lemon, who had worked for Parker Pyne, as his secretary.

Possessed of sharp bird-like eyes which developed a greenish hue when he was deep in concentration. "Papa Poirot," as he liked to call himself, became the darling of London society. His struggle with a bout of the flu was recorded in the pages of *Society Gossip*, and he could be seen in the best restaurants and the finest hotels, immaculately groomed, with pointed black patent leather shoes, striped trousers, jacket and waistcoat and his "big turnip-faced watch," a family heirloom that he always carried. The quaintness of his speech, liberally sprinkled with French phrases and tangled English, and his beguiling lack of modesty were his trademarks. The one great romance of his life was with the Countess Vera Rossakoff, an affair of the heart that spanned three decades.

Death came at Styles Court, which was now a guest house. Hampered by severe arthritis, Poirot had returned to the scene of his first great triumph to conduct what would be his final and most psychologically intriguing case, *Curtain*. Hastings had rejoined him, and it was to his friend that Poirot wrote his last words in a letter explaining the salient points of the case: "They have been good days." *See* Bibliography and Appendix A.

POLI, SIGNOR An Italian, he had met Mr. Parker Pyne on the boat from Brindisi to Beirut, and had difficulty understanding his travelling companion: "He never knew how far the English were serious." Flight Lieutenant O'Rourke thought that the murderer must have been "the Italian fellow." "The Gate of Baghdad" from *Parker Pyne Investigates.*

POLLOCK, SERGEANT A police officer of Exhampton, he was "a cautious man, unwilling to advance further than necessary" in his theories on the Trevelyan murder. Narracott made a reference to " 'Someone who wishes to throw dust in our eyes—and hasn't succeeded.' Sergeant Pollock was grateful for the 'our.' In such small ways did Inspector Narracott endear himself to his subordinates." *The Sittaford Mystery.*

POLLOCK, ALFRED Lazy and obstinate yard worker at Greenshaw's Folly, he was the illegitimate half-cousin of Miss Greenshaw. Because Alfred was a crack shot with a bow and arrow, he came under suspicion of being the murderer, but his laziness provided him with an alibi:

he had left work early that day to eat lunch at the local pub, an act which Miss Marple considered to be "morally wrong." "Greenshaw's Folly" from *The Adventure of the Christmas Pudding.*

POLONSKA, VANDA The mother of the infant Betty, she was a Polish refugee who came to England after the start of World War II; penniless, she had sold her child to Millicent Sprot. However, overcome with maternal remorse at her act, she attempted to kidnap her child, but was apprehended and shot through the head. *N or M?*

POPE, LAVINIA The awe-inspiring mistress of her own school for young girls in Neuilly, France, she ran such a tight establishment that "no speck of dust, one felt, would have the temerity to deposit itself in such a shrine." With her aid, Poirot discovered both the means and reason for Winnie King's kidnapping, and uncovered the stolen Rubens. "The Girdle of Hippolyta" from *The Labours of Hercules.*

POPOLEFFSKY, COUNTESS VARAGA *See* **MORY, ANGELE.**

POPORENSKY, PRINCESS ANNA MICHAELOVNA The lady-in-waiting to the supposed Grand Duchess Pauline, she was a member of the gang involved in the theft at Orion House. "Jane in Search of a Job" from *The Golden Ball.*

PORTAL, ALEC The husband of Eleanor Portal, he was, "like all the Portals, fond of sport, good at games, devoid of imagination. Nothing unusual about Alec Portal. The usual good, sound English stock." Alec Portal suspected that his wife murdered her first husband, Mr. Appleton, but Harley Quin convinced him that his wife was innocent. "The Coming of Mr. Quin" from *The Mysterious Mr. Quin.*

PORTAL, ELEANOR The wife of Alec Portal, she had previously been married to the late Mr. Appleton. Shortly after

Appleton's death, her lover, Derek Capel, shot himself. Appleton's body was subsequently exhumed and it was discovered that he had died from strychnine poisoning. Eleanor stood trial for murder but "was acquitted more through the lack of evidence against her than from any overwhelming proof of innocence." She was saved from committing suicide by the results of Harley Quin's "court of inquiry" into the death of Derek Capel. "The Coming of Mr. Quin" from *The Mysterious Mr. Quin*.

PORTER, MAJOR GEORGE DOUGLAS "A bore," said Gian Vincenzo Lavina, "is a person who deprives you of solitude without providing you with company." At the Coronation Club, "the club bore" was Major George Douglas Porter. At the club he recited a story about Rosaleen Cloade, Gordon Cloade's wife, and her first husband, Robert Underhay. Porter had known Underhay in Nigeria. Rowley Cloade bribed Porter to identify the body of "Enoch Arden" as that of Robert Underhay at the inquest. Porter subsequently committed suicide, unable to bear the guilt of his false testimony. *Taken at the Flood*.

PORTER, MAJOR JOHN D.S.O. A good friend of Richard Scott's, he was a house guest at Greenways House when Jimmy Allenson and Moira Scott were shot. During an African safari, both Porter and Richard Scott had fallen in love with Iris Staverton, and when Iris turned up at Greenways House, where Porter, Scott and Scott's wife Moira were staying, Porter remarked: "She ought not to have come." However, as Harley Quin pointed out, Iris was in love with Porter and not Richard Scott. "The Shadow on the Glass" from *The Mysterious Mr. Quin*.

POWER, EMERY Financial wizard who enjoyed collecting antiquities with personal histories attached, he consulted Poirot about retrieving a chalice which had once belonged to the Borgias and depicted a scene from the Isle of the Blest, where golden apples grew. Poirot recovered the goblet for him, but convinced him to donate it to a convent, where the nuns, he pointed out, would say masses for the man's soul. "The Apples of the Hesperides" from *The Labours of Hercules*.

PRATT, DOROTHY JANE Edward Palgrove's girlfriend, she was employed by Mrs. Mackenzie Jones. With Edward, she accidentally found a ruby necklace: "The belief that she had jewels around her neck worth fifty thousand pounds had made of Dorothy Pratt a new woman. She looked insolently serene, a kind of Cleopatra, Semiramis and Zenobia rolled into one." "A Fruitful Sunday" from *The Golden Ball*.

PRATT, ROSE See **CHUDLEIGH, ROSE**.

PRESCOTT, JOAN Sister and travelling companion to Canon Jeremy Prescott, she was an incurable gossip and told Miss Marple about Molly Kendall's mentally unbalanced family. *A Caribbean Mystery*.

PRESTON, HAILEY Performing the duties of public relations man, personal assistant and private secretary to Jason Rudd, he was "a willowy young man with long wavy hair" whom Margot Bence alluded to as "the elegant Hailey Preston." From all reports, "He talked. He talked freely and at length without much modulation and managing miraculously not to repeat himself too often." Chief Inspector Dermot Craddock thought him to be "an efficient and voluble gas bag." *The Mirror Crack'd from Side to Side*.

PRICE, EMLYN "A young man, possibly nineteen or twenty," he was travelling on the Famous Houses and Gardens of Great Britain excursion. "He wore the appropriate clothes for his age and sex: tight black jeans, a polo-necked purple sweater and his head was an outsize rich mop of non-disciplined black hair." He and Joanna Crawford developed a friendship, and together they saw the unidentifiable figure who pushed the boulder down upon Elizabeth Temple. *Nemesis.*

PRICE, LILY She was the first seen by Miss Marple with her fiancé, Harry, with whom she was inspecting a partially completed house in Carrisbrook Close. When Lily almost fell from a first floor window, and Harry did nothing to prevent her fall, Miss Marple gave the pregnant Lily the "gipsy's warning": "If I were you, my dear, I shouldn't marry that young man. You want someone whom you can rely upon if you're in danger." Lily subsequently broke off the engagement. *The Mirror Crack'd from Side to Side.*

PRICE RIDLEY, MARTHA A village busy-body in St. Mary Mead, she was a self-righteous, pompous, nasty gossip who amused herself by making life unpleasant for anyone who was vulnerable. *Murder at the Vicarage; The Body in the Library.*

PRIMER, DETECTIVE INSPECTOR He investigated the Lily Kimble murder case and had a "deceptively mild manner and a mild apologetic voice." The Detective Inspector was quietly impressed by Miss Marple: "She's a celebrated lady, is Miss Marple. Got the Chief Constables of at least three countries in her pocket. She's not got my Chief yet, but I dare say that will come. So Miss Marple's got her finger in the pie." *Sleeping Murder.*

PRITCHARD, ALEX *See* **CARSTAIRS, ALAN.**

PRITCHARD, GEORGE The poor beleaguered husband of the indomitable Mary Pritchard, George patiently put up with all of his wife's grumblings and tantrums. He was loved by Nurse Copling and in love with Jean Instow. "The Blue Geranium" from *The Thirteen Problems.*

PRITCHARD, MARY The deceased wife of George Pritchard, Mary Pritchard was, according to Colonel Bantry, "one of those semi-invalids—I believe she had really something wrong with her, but whatever it was, she played it for all it was worth. She was capricious, exacting, unreasonable. She complained from morning to night. George was expected to wait on her hand and foot, and everything he did was always wrong and he got cursed for it." Dolly Bantry added, "If George Pritchard had brained her with a hatchet and there had been any women in the jury, he would have been triumphantly acquitted." "The Blue Geranium" from *The Thirteen Problems.*

PROCTOR, DR. Called to examine Miss Gilchrist, "the doctor had had the air of one keeping his temper in leash and who has had some experience of being called out unnecessarily on more than one occasion." *After the Funeral.*

PROTHERO, WALTER AKA Wendover. A recluse, Prothero had lived in Market Basing for eight years and was the target of a blackmail scheme designed by Mr. and Mrs. Parker. He had once been a lieutenant in the Royal Navy, and his real name was Wendover. "The Market Basing Mystery" from *The Under Dog.*

PROTHEROE, ANNE The young wife of Colonel Lucius Protheroe, she was hated by her step-daughter, Lettice Protheroe. Leonard Clement, the vicar of St. Mary Mead, thought that there was "a suggestion of Caesar's wife about Mrs. Protheroe—a quiet, self-contained woman whom one would not suspect of any great depth of feeling." She openly admitted to Clement that she and Lawrence Redding were in love with each other after he surprised them in an intimate moment. *Murder at the Vicarage.*

PROTHEROE, LETTICE The daughter of Colonel Lucius Protheroe by his first wife and the step-daughter of Anne Protheroe, Lettice attempted to implicate her step-mother in the death of her father, and was preparing to go abroad with her natural mother, Mrs. Lestrange. *Murder at the Vicarage.*

PROTHEROE, COLONEL LUCIUS The husband of Anne Protheroe and the father of Lettice Protheroe by his first wife, Mrs. Lestrange, he was the fussy old village Magistrate of St. Mary Mead and the pompous proprietor of Old Hall. He was found dead at the Vicarage. *Murder at the Vicarage.*

PRYCE, NETTA The popular niece of Miss Pryce, she travelled with her aunt and ten other persons, including Mr. Parker Pyne, from Damascus to Baghdad. "Miss Netta Pryce, youngest and most charming of the tourist race . . . managed to enjoy herself in many frivolous ways of which the elder Miss Pryce might possibly have not approved." "The Gate of Baghdad" from *Parker Pyne Investigates.*

PUGH, ERIC Sir Stafford and Eric Pugh were friends: "He had known Eric Pugh for a good many years. They had not been close friends. Old Eric, or so Sir Stafford thought, was rather a boring friend. He was, on the other hand, faithful. And he was the type of man who, though not amusing, had a knack of knowing things. People said things to him and he remembered what they said and stored them up. Sometimes he could push out a useful bit of information." *Passenger to Frankfurt.*

PURDY, PROFESSOR Elderly scholar of archaeology, he hired Sheila Webb through the Cavendish Secretarial and Typing Bureau to work for him. Absent-minded, he often lost sight of time and kept Sheila past working hours, but just as often gave her tea or dinner to make up for it. *The Clocks.*

PURVIS, WILLIAM Emily Arundell's solicitor, of the firm Messrs. Purvis, Purvis, Charlesworth and Purvis, a firm "as respectable and impeccable as the Bank of England." He failed in his attempt to talk Miss Arundell out of revising her will. *Dumb Witness.*

PYE, MR. The rich, dilettantish resident of Prior's End in Lymstock, he was "an extremely lady-like plump little man" who was devoted to his antiques. "A middle-aged spinster" with a falsetto voice, he also received a poison pen letter, and was a source of information on the various habitants of the village. *The Moving Finger.*

"PYNE, MR. PARKER" *See* **DEMETRIUS THE BLACK BROWED.**

QUENTIN Lord Listerdale's butler, he had been with the Listerdale family since he was twenty-one. Lord Listerdale retired Quentin to a little village near King's Cheviot, and then assumed Quentin's identity and served as butler in his own London house at 7 Cheviot Place, which had been let to Mrs. St. Vincent. Quentin was found by Rupert St. Vincent and brought to Cheviot Place, where Lord Listerdale was unmasked. "The Listerdale Mystery" from *The Golden Ball.*

QUENTIN *See* **LISTERDALE, LORD.**

QUENTIN, DR. *See* **DARRELL, CLAUD.**

QUIMPER, DR. Husband of Anna and family physician to the Crackenthorpes, he had "a casual off-hand, cynical manner that his patients found very stimulating. . . ." The body found in the sarcophagous on the grounds of Rutherford Hall was identified as that of his wife, Anna. However, he was totally unmoved by looking at her three-week-old dead form, and was in love with Emma Crackenthorpe. *4.50 from Paddington.*

QUIN, HARLEY One of the strangest associations between characters in Agatha Christie's fiction is the relationship between Mr. Satterthwaite and Harley Quin. Based on the figure of the harlequin from the *commedia dell'arte* of the Renaissance and like the harlequin of the English theatre, Harley Quin had magical powers. Throughout the fourteen stories in which they appear together Harley Quin acted the part of an unobtrusive guide, slowly directing Mr. Satterthwaite towards the prevention of some evil. Satterthwaite said that Quin had "a power—an almost uncanny power—of showing you what you have seen with your own eyes, of making clear to you what you have heard with your own ears." He appeared for the last time in "The Harlequin Tea Set" and delivered his last message via his dog Hermes: "Congratulations! To our next meeting. H.Q." *The Mysterious Mr. Quin;* "The Love Detectives" from *Three Blind Mice and Other Stories;* "The Harlequin Tea Set" from *Winter's Crimes 3.*

RACE, COLONEL JOHNNY A Secret Service agent, Colonel Race aged just over forty years in the four novels in which he appeared. He was the heir of Sir Laurence Eardsley, and proposed to Anne Beddingfeld, but she turned him down and he remained single. Race was "usually to be found in one of the outposts of the Empire where trouble was brewing." In *The Man in the Brown Suit,* he was on the trail of the arch villain the "Colonel," and Sir Eustace Pedler referred to him as: "that long-legged, pompous ass, Race." He first met Poirot when he was one of the four sleuths invited to Mr. Shaitana's bridge party in *Cards on the Table.* Race and Poirot again joined forces in *Death on the Nile* and his last appearance was in *Sparkling Cyanide.*

RADCLYFFE, DENNIS Cousin of Lois Hargreaves and nephew of the deceased Lady Radclyffe's husband, he lived at Thurnley Grange. Having had an argument with him over some debts, Lady Radclyffe disinherited Dennis and left her money to Lois Hargreaves; Lois, distressed at this circumstance, made Dennis the beneficiary of her own will. Dennis was the third poison victim; Ricin was found in his cocktail. "The House of Lurking Death" from *Partners in Crime.*

RADLEY, GENERAL Ancient and very deaf resident of Bertram's Hotel, this gruff General was asleep in his chair, covered by the *Times,* when Chief Inspector Davy went to interview him about the disappearance of Canon Pennyfather. *At Bertram's Hotel.*

RADNOR, JACOB Described as a "friend" of Mrs. Pengelley's, Radnor was in fact making love to her and to her niece, Freda Stanton. His engagement to Freda Stanton was calculated to acquire the money that she was destined to inherit from Edward Pengelley. "The Cornish Mystery" from *The Under Dog.*

RADZKY, COUNTESS ANNA *See* **ST. MAUR, BABE.**

RAFIEL, JASON "The principal thing known about Mr. Rafiel was that he was incredibly rich, he came every year to the West Indies, he was semi-paralyzed and looked like a wrinkled old bird of prey. . . . His principal pleasure in life was denying robustly anything that anyone else said." Rafiel and Miss Marple met in St. Honore and together solved the murders at the Golden Palm Hotel. His son, Michael, was never out of trouble with the law, and when he was arrested for the murder of Nora Broad, Rafiel set about to bring him justice in the form of Miss Marple, whom he called Nemesis. *A Caribbean Mystery; Nemesis.*

RAFIEL, MICHAEL The son of Jason Rafiel, he was convicted and imprisoned for the murder of Verity Hunt, his fiancée. Professor Wanstead thought that "he was a son who would be any father's despair." In spite of this, Jason Rafiel commissioned Miss Marple to investigate the matter. *Nemesis.*

RAGG, GORDON *See* **EASTERFIELD, LORD.**

RAGLAN, INSPECTOR The police inspector from Cranchester, the large town near the village of King's Abbot, he participated in the investigation into the murder of Roger Ackroyd. Flora Ackroyd had described Raglan as "a horrid, weaselly little man," and James Sheppard said that he looked "black as thunder" when he was introduced to Poirot. *The Murder of Roger Ackroyd.*

RAGLAN, INSPECTOR HENRY TIMOTHY A local inspector in Woodleigh Common, Raglan was thought to have a very good reputation locally, and recommended that Poirot, a recent acquaintance, be brought into the Joyce Reynolds murder case. *Hallowe'en Party.*

RAIKES, MRS. The wife of farmer Raikes, she was, according to Hastings, "a pretty young woman of gipsy type [with] a vivid wicked little face," with whom Alfred Inglethorp, the husband of the murdered Emily Inglethorp, met often. *The Mysterious Affair at Styles.*

RAIKES, HOWARD An American who shared leftist sympathies with his girlfriend, Jane Olivera. he was deprived of

her company when her mother intentionally brought her to live with Alistair Blunt. He was suspected of attempting to murder Alistair Blunt because they had strong disagreements about economic policy. *One, Two, Buckle My Shoe.*

RAMONE, DELORES *See* **DE SARA, MADELEINE.**

RAMSAY, TED Son of Mr. and Mrs. Michael Ramsay and younger brother of Bill, he and his brother found the Czechoslovakian coin in Miss Pebmarsh's garden which put Colin Lamb on the trail of Communist intrigue at Wilbraham Crescent. *The Clocks.*

RAMSBOTTOM, EFFIE Sister of Rex Fortescue's first wife Elvira, she still lived at Yewtree Lodge in her own room on the second floor, where she did all her own cooking and cleaning. A Victorian eccentric, she was also a religious maniac, and thought Rex had been "struck down at last in his arrogance and sinful pride." She urged Miss Marple to stay at the house rather than the nearby hotel, which she called "a wicked nest of profiteers." *A Pocket Full of Rye.*

RANSOME, NICHOLAS (NICKY) With his friend Desmond Holland, he prepared the Hallowe'en party. He suggested as a possible murderer either Miss Whittaker, whom he considered a lesbian, or perhaps the vicar who "exposed himself first. . . . I mean, there's always got to be a sex background to all these things." He and his friend were commissioned by Poirot to protect Miranda Butler. *Hallowe'en Party.*

RATCHETT, SAMUEL EDWARD The assumed identity of the murderer-kidnapper Cassetti, he was a rich American businessman who collected pottery. He failed in his attempt to hire Poirot as a bodyguard for twenty thousand dollars. As Cassetti, kidnapping, ransoming and murdering young children was his *modus operandi.* Six months after the discovery of Daisy Armstrong's body, he was arrested, but was acquitted on a technicality. He left America under the name Ratchett and lived abroad off his ill-gotten gains until his "execution" on the *Orient Express. Murder on the Orient Express.*

RATHBONE, DR. According to his employee Edward Goring, Dr. Rathbone was "terrifically keen on uplift and spreading it far and wide. He opens bookshops in remote places—he's starting one in Baghdad." The centre of Rathbone's book distribution operation was the Olive Branch coffee house in Baghdad. Goring, however, blackmailed him and procured the Olive Branch as a base for subversive activities. Dr. Rathbone had been taking a percentage of the donations and grants that he received for books and Goring knew about it. *They Came to Baghdad.*

RATHBONE, DENNIS Conventional boyfriend of Ann Shapland, he was continually rebuffed: "Faithful Dennis returning from Malaya, from Burma, from various parts of the world, always the same, asking her once again to marry him. Dear Dennis! But it would be very dull to be married to Dennis." *Cat Among the Pigeons.*

RATTERY, JOHN He was engaged to Carla Lemarchant, who wished Poirot to clear her mother of the murder of her father. She mused: "Supposing we were married and we'd quarrelled—and I saw him look at me and—and *wonder?*" *Five Little Pigs.*

RAVEL, ANNETTE AKA Annette Ravelli, she was the famous singer who grew up with Raoul Letardeau and Felicie Bault at Miss Slater's English Home for desti-

tute children. Letardeau considered her the *sine qua non* to understanding Felicie Bault's multiple personalities. "The Fourth Man" from *Witness for the Prosecution.*

RAVELLI, ANNETTE *See* **RAVEL, ANNETTE.**

RAVENSCROFT, GENERAL ALISTAIR The husband of Lady Molly Ravenscroft and the father of Celia and Edward Ravenscroft, he had first been in love with Dolly Jarrow, Molly's twin sister, but later transferred his affections to Molly. After his wife's death, he had agreed to protect Dolly and disguised her as his wife. They continued to live at Overcroft, the family home. *Elephants Can Remember.*

RAVENSCROFT, CELIA She was the daughter of General Alistair Ravenscroft and Lady Molly Ravenscroft, the sister of Edward Ravenscroft, the god-daughter of Ariadne Oliver, and the fiancée of Desmond Burton-Cox. Mrs. Oliver told Celia of Mrs. Burton-Cox's strange request regarding the deaths of General and Lady Ravenscroft but Celia, who was away at school when the tragedy occurred, could only supply a few possible sources of information. *Elephants Can Remember.*

RAVENSCROFT, LADY MARGARET (MOLLY) *Née* Preston-Grey. The wife of General Alistair Ravenscroft, the mother of Celia and Edward Ravenscroft and the twin sister of Dolly Jarrow, she had gone to school in Paris with Ariadne Oliver. *Elephants Can Remember.*

RAWLINSON, DR. The Denman family doctor who had tended Geoffrey Denman, he was described by Miss Marple: "to put it in perfectly plain language he was what I would describe as an old dodderer . . . a nice old man, kindly, vague and so short-sighted as to be pitiful, slightly deaf and, withal, touchy and sensitive to the last degree." "The Thumb Mark of St. Peter" from *The Thirteen Problems.*

RAWLINSON, SQUADRON LEADER BOB The brother of Joan Sutcliffe and uncle of Jennifer Sutcliffe, he was a schoolfriend of Prince Ali Yusuf and the Prince's private pilot. Prince Ali entrusted Rawlinson to smuggle over half a million pounds worth of jewels out of the country. He subsequently died in a plane crash in the mountains while attempting to convey the Prince out of the revolution-torn country of Ramat. *Cat Among the Pigeons.*

RAYBURN, HARRY AKA John Eardsley; Harry Lucas; Harry Parker; and the "Man in the Brown Suit." Eardsley had left Cambridge with his friend Harry Lucas, whose name he later assumed for a brief period, and discovered a rich diamond deposit in British Guiana. He and Lucas went to Kimberly where they were conned out of their diamonds by Anita Grünberg and tried for possessing diamonds which had been stolen from De Beers, the famous diamond merchants. Owing to the immense influence of his father Sir Laurence Eardsley, neither Rayburn nor Lucas went to prison. When Lucas was killed in the war, he was wearing Eardsley's identification tag, and Sir Laurence was informed that his son had been killed. Eardsley took the name of Harry Parker and went into seclusion on an island upstream from Victoria Falls. Rayburn wanted to clear his own name, and to that end he traced the movements of Anita Grünberg and her husband, L.B. Carton. Anne Beddingfeld saw him as the "Man in the Brown Suit" in a London tube station, and when she met him again in South Africa, she said to him: "You make my flesh creep." However, she eventually married Rayburn. *The Man in the Brown Suit.*

RAYMOND, GEOFFREY Roger Ackroyd's secretary at Fernly Park for the past two years, Raymond was left five hundred pounds in Ackroyd's will. *The Murder of Roger Ackroyd.*

REDCLIFFE, HERMIA Mark Easterbrook had considered marrying her, but after he met Katherine Corrigan, Hermia looked "damnably dull." *The Pale Horse.*

REDDING, LAWRENCE According to Leonard Clement, the vicar of St. Mary Mead, Lawrence Redding was "not at all one's idea of the typical artist. Yet I believe he is a clever painter in the modern style." Redding initially seemed to be pursuing Lettice Protheroe but was in fact quite involved with Lettice's step-mother, Anne Protheroe. *Murder at the Vicarage.*

REDFERN, CHRISTINE The wife and partner of Patrick Redfern, Christine Redfern was a guest at the Jolly Roger Hotel when Arlena Marshall died. In the midst of all the sunbathers she looked, according to Major Barry, "a bit uncooked." Emily Brewster told her that she had earned Poirot's good opinion: "He doesn't like the sun-tanning crowd. Says they're like joints of butcher's meat or words to that effect." *Evil Under the Sun.*

REDFERN, PATRICK The husband and partner of Christine Redfern, Patrick Redfern was a guest at the Jolly Roger Hotel when Arlena Marshall died. Poirot remarked that he was an "adventurer who makes his living one way or another, out of women." Arlena Marshall was fascinated by him. *Evil Under the Sun.*

REECE-HOLLAND, CLAUDIA The first girl at 67 Borodene Mansions, she was the daughter of Emlyn Reece-Holland and secretary to Andrew Restarick, at whose suggestion she invited Norma Restarick to share the flat with her and Frances Cary. *Third Girl.*

REED *See* **LAVINGTON, MR.**

REED, GILES The newlywed husband of Gwenda Reed, this distant relation of Joan West's had been orphaned young and worked at a job which involved a great deal of travel for indeterminate periods of time. With a life-long love of detective stories, he eagerly assisted his wife when she discovered a mystery in their own home. *Sleeping Murder.*

REED, GWENDA A twenty-one-year-old New Zealander, she was the daughter of Major Kelvin Halliday and Megan Danby Halliday, and the wife of three months to Giles Reed. Miss Marple urged the girl to investigate after Gwenda received strange psychic impressions in her new house, Hillside. Her step-mother, seemingly man-mad, had disappeared some eighteen years before and her father died of suicide in an insane asylum. With her husband Giles, she tried to find her step-mother, Helen Spenlove Kennedy. *Sleeping Murder.*

REEDBURN, HENRY The resident of the villa Mon Desir and a famous impresario, he was found lying in the library of his villa "with the back of his head cracked open like an eggshell." "The King of Clubs" from *The Under Dog.*

REES-TALBOT, MARY An old friend of Colonel Race's, she hired Betty Archdale, the parlourmaid who had left the Barton household. *Sparkling Cyanide.*

REEVES The butler to Colonel Lucius Protheroe at Old Hall who possessed, according to Inspector Slack, "a soapy, oily manner," he was also endowed with an emotionless, deadpan face. He had often quarrelled with the Colonel, and just before Protheroe's death he had given his notice. *Murder at the Vicarage.*

REEVES, INSPECTOR A "stalwart inspector," he considered the death of Hubert Lytcham Roche was such a "perfectly straightforward" case of suicide that it didn't require Poirot's expertise. "The Second Gong" from *Witness for the Prosecution.*

REEVES, PAMELA (PAMIE) A resident of Daneleigh Vale, Pamela Reeves had gone to a Girl Guide rally on Danebury Downs when she was approached by a stranger and asked if she would like to be interviewed for a film. Later, her body, disguised as the flamboyant Ruby Keene, was found in Arthur Bantry's library. *The Body in the Library.*

REICHARDT, DR. A psychologist, he specialized in the mental disorder of megalomania, and was the director of a large institution near Karlsruhe. He was of the opinion that Hitler had escaped retribution by switching places with one of the many "Hitler" megalomaniacs at his institution. *Passenger to Frankfurt.*

REILLY, MR. Partner to Mr. Morley, he was in the house when the murder took place and was the last person to see Morley alive but, aside from his generally untrustworthy character, he had no real motive for the crime. *One, Two, Buckle My Shoe.*

REILLY, DR. GILES Father of Sheila Reilly, he persuaded Nurse Amy Leatheran to write her memoirs of the affair at Tell Yarimjah. He and Captain Maitland decided to ask Poirot to investigate the murder of Louise Leidner. *Murder in Mesopotamia.*

REILLY, JAMES The former lover of Gilda Glen, he was arrested for her murder. A "young man with flaming red hair, a pugnacious jaw and appallingly shabby clothes," he muttered to himself and was a man of violent and indiscreet words. "The Man in the Mist" from *Partners in Crime.*

REILLY, SHEILA "Damned attractive" daughter of Dr. Giles Reilly, she was an outspoken, determined, "cocksure little minx" who received lots of attention from the single Western males in Iraq, and enjoyed it thoroughly. She ultimately married David Emmott, who alone among the men in love with her at Tell Yarimjah, would be able to keep her in her place. *Murder in Mesopotamia.*

REITER, CARL German-American photographer with the American archaeological expedition at Tell Yarimjah, he was probably a lovely baby but grew up looking "just a little like a pig." Clumsy and socially inept, he fell for Louise Leidner's charm; she amused herself by deliberately embarrassing him almost every night at the dinner table in front of the rest of the members of the expedition. *Murder in Mesopotamia.*

RENAULD, MADAME The wife of Paul Renauld and the mother of Jack Renauld, she was described by Hastings: "You knew at once that you were in the presence of what the French call *une maitresse femme.*" *Murder on the Links.*

RENAULD, JACK The son of Paul and Madame Renauld, Jack Renauld had been educated and spent most of his holidays in England before enlisting in the English Flying Corps. After the war he went to work in his father's business. The evening of his father's murder, Jack had violently quarrelled with him over his plan to marry Marthe Daubreuil. A prime suspect, he was eventually cleared by Poirot and, after asking Bella Duveen to marry him, moved to the Argentine. *Murder on the Links.*

RENAULD, PAUL T. AKA Georges Conneau. The husband of Madame Renauld and the father of Jack Renauld, he was a well-known millionaire who had amassed his fortune in South America where he continued to maintain large business and ranching interests. In fear of his life, he sent for Poirot; but before Poirot could arrive Renauld had been murdered at his Villa Genevieve. Poirot learned that Renauld was a French-Canadian who had been involved in a *crime passionelle* with the infamous Jeanne Beroldy. *Murder on the Links.*

RENDELL, DR. Husband of Shelagh Rendell, he had employed Mrs. McGinty and moved to Broadhinny when a series of anonymous letters insinuated that he had murdered his first wife for insurance money. Poirot was extremely gratified that Rendell recognized his name. *Mrs. McGinty's Dead.*

RENDELL, SHELAGH Second wife of Dr. Rendell, she thought Poirot was using the McGinty murder as a cover and that the real object of his investigations was the death of her husband's first wife. *Mrs. McGinty's Dead.*

RENISENB The daughter of Imhotep and the sister of Yahmose, Sobek and Ipy, Renisenb was the mother of the young Teti and the widow of Khay. Renisenb agreed to wed Kameni, who was the beloved of Nofret, but afterwards reconsidered and decided to share her life with Hori who, she intoned, was "a song in my heart forever." *Death Comes as the End.*

RENNIE, MR. Universally disliked by all at The Laurels for his leftist political stance, he and Beatrice concealed their romance from Colonel Kingston Bruce. "The Affair of the Pink Pearl" from *Partners in Crime.*

RESTARICK, ALEXIS The step-son of Carrie Louise Serrocold by her second husband Johnnie Restarick, and the brother of Stephen Restarick, Alexis Restarick was a highly successful playwright and actor. Having taken a very good guess at the identity of Christian Gulbrandsen's murderer, Restarick became one of the three victims. *They Do It with Mirrors.*

RESTARICK, ANDREW The deceased father of Norma Restarick and lover of Louise Birell, his identity was assumed by his partner, Robert Orwell. Orwell was in collusion with Frances Cary to defraud the Restarick family of their fortune. *Third Girl.*

RESTARICK, MARY The assumed identity of Frances Cary, who met Robert Orwell in Africa and conspired with him to divert the Restarick fortune to their own ends. *Third Girl.*

RESTARICK, NORMA AKA Norma West. The "third girl," she shared 67 Borodene Mansions with Frances Cary and Claudia Reece-Holland. Thinking she was responsible for the death of Louise Birell, she asked Mrs. Oliver to recommend a detective. When she met Poirot, she decided he was too old. She was prevented from throwing herself before a speeding Jaguar by Dr. Stillingfleet, whom she later married. *Third Girl.*

REVEL, THE HONOURABLE MRS. TIMOTHY See **REVEL, VIRGINIA.**

REVEL, VIRGINIA *Née* Cawthorn, the widow of Timothy Revel, the daughter of Lord Edgbaston and the cousin of George Lomax, she possessed an "exquisite slimness ... and a delicious and quite indescribable mouth that tilted ever so slightly at one corner in what is known as 'the signature of Venus'." Her ponderous cousin George Lomax invited her for the weekend at Chimneys as an added inducement for Jimmy McGrath (played by Anthony Cade) to hand over Count Stylptitch's memoirs. *The Secret of Chimneys.*

REYNOLDS, MRS. Wife to Mr. Reynolds, she was the mother of Ann and

the murdered Joyce and Leopold Reynolds. *Hallowe'en Party.*

REYNOLDS, ANN Tall and superior, she was the sixteen-year-old daughter of Mr. and Mrs. Reynolds and eldest sister of the murder victims Joyce and Leopold Reynolds. *Hallowe'en Party.*

REYNOLDS, JOYCE Universally unpopular daughter of Mr. and Mrs. Reynolds, she was the sister of Ann and of the murdered Leopold Reynolds. On meeting Ariadne Oliver at the party, the sturdy thirteen-year-old loudly proclaimed that she had once been witness to a murder; she herself was killed shortly thereafter by having her head held in the apple-dunking bucket. *Hallowe'en Party.*

REYNOLDS, LEOPOLD Horrific and egotistical son of Mr. and Mrs. Reynolds and brother to Ann and to the murdered Joyce Reynolds, he deduced the identity of his sister's murderer, but was not clever enough to deal with the ramifications of his blackmail plot and was drowned in the village stream. *Hallowe'en Party.*

RHODES, MR. The widower of the murdered Mrs. Rhodes, he asked Miss Marple to clear him of suspicion in his wife's death. Grateful for Miss Marple's aid, he and his new wife asked her to be the godmother of their child. "Miss Marple Tells a Story" from *The Regatta Mystery.*

RICE, INSPECTOR A Scotland Yard Inspector, he arrived at Friar's Mansions with a constable and a doctor to examine the body of Mrs. Ernestine Grant, occupant of the second-floor flat in the building. "Third Floor Flat" from *Three Blind Mice and Other Stories.*

RICE, MR. A drug addict who was the estranged husband of Frederica Rice, he harrassed her to obtain drugs from her "boy-friend" Commander Challenger. He was killed by the police after an unsuccessful attempt to murder his wife. *Peril at End House.*

RICE, MRS. The "resourceful" mother of Elsie Clayton, she was staying at Lake Stempka on holiday and together with her daughter, she conspired in intricate blackmail schemes to defraud large sums of money from Elsie's young paramours. "The Stymphalian Birds" from *The Labours of Hercules.*

RICE, FREDERICA (FREDDIE) The "weary Madonna" who was Nick Buckley's best friend, Freddie introduced Nick to cocaine and was the beneficiary of her will. The killer attempted to frame Freddie by hiding the murder weapon on her person. *Peril at End House.*

RICH, MAJOR CHARLES A friend of Arnold Clayton's and enamoured of Margharita Clayton, he was arrested for the murder of Clayton when the knifed body was discovered in his Spanish chest. Margharita had consulted Poirot in an effort to clear Major Rich of the murder of her husband. "The Mystery of the Spanish Chest" from *The Adventure of the Christmas Pudding.*

RICH, EILEEN Teacher at Meadowbank, she was what Inspector Kelsey called a "sensitive" or psychic. She was an excellent teacher and loved her work. She was forced to leave Meadowbank for one term while she had a baby, illegitimate offspring from a love affair abroad, but the child was born dead. Inspector Kelsey's opinion of her was that she was "ugly as sin," which he soon qualified on noticing "a certain attraction." She was chosen by Miss Bulstrode as successor to the position of Headmistress at Meadowbank. *Cat Among the Pigeons.*

RICHARDS Ambassador Randolph Wilmott's valet, he provided Tuppence and Tommy Beresford with the information about Senator Ralph Westerham's valet and bag, and also about Eileen O'Hara, who took ill outside the Ambassador's cabin. "The Ambassador's Boots" from *Partners in Crime.*

RICHARDS, ANNE See **MORISOT, ANNE.**

RICHARDS, ERNESTINE AKA Daphne St. John, she was formerly the secretary to Lady Naomi Dortheimer. She consulted Mr. Parker Pyne about a case of a stolen ring. Mr. Parker Pyne speculated that as Miss Richards, she had "invested in a La Merveilleuse transformation—Number Seven side parting, I think . . . shade dark brown." "The Case of the Distressed Lady" from *Parker Pyne Investigates.*

RICHARDS, JAMES See **GALE, NORMAN.**

RICHETTI, SIGNOR GUIDO AKA "X." A loquacious, "slightly podgy middle-aged" Italian, he lost no time in presenting his card to Poirot: "Signor Guido Richetti, Archeologo." Poirot, however, suspected the man because "he was almost too word-perfect in his role; he was all archaeologist, not enough human being." Richetti's real identity was unwittingly revealed by Dr. Bessner, who opened a telegram by mistake and was totally confused by the list of potatoes, artichokes and other vegetables it mentioned. *Death on the Nile.*

RIDDELL, ALBERT Riddell was the first person who entered the tobacco shop after Alice Ascher's murder, thus fixing the time of death. *The A.B.C. Murders.*

RIDDLE, MAJOR Chief Constable in Westshire, he resented Poirot's intrusion in the Chevinix-Gore case, particularly when Poirot insisted that what appeared to be a clear-cut case of suicide was murder. "Dead Man's Mirror" from *Murder in the Mews.*

RIDGEWAY, DR. He was a friend of Poirot's and Hastings' whose house and surgery were just around the corner from Poirot's own rooms at 14 Farraway Street. Ridgeway attended Mayerling and again attended both Hastings and Poirot when the latter was supposedly killed in an explosion. *The Big Four.*

RIDGEWAY, LINNET *See* **DOYLE, LINNET.**

RIDGEWAY, CHARLES AKA Patrick Harter, he was the nephew of Mary Harter and beneficiary of her will after her niece, Miriam, was disinherited: "Charles was a thoughtful young man. He was also a young man who believed in furthering his own inclinations whenever possible . . . Charles was a patient young man. He was also persistent." "Where There's a Will" from *Witness for the Prosecution.*

RIDGEWAY, PHILIP The fiancé of Esmée Farquhar and the nephew of Mr. Vavasour, Ridgeway was carrying one million dollars worth of Liberty Bonds aboard the *Olympia* for the London and Scottish Bank. The documents disappeared. "The Million Dollar Bond Robbery" from *Poirot Investigates.*

RIEGER, KATRINA The half-Russian nurse and companion to Miss Amelia Jane Barrowby, she was suspected of murdering her mistress when a packet of strychnine was discovered under her mattress. Poirot noted a rodent-like cast to her character: "a miserable little cornered rat . . . with courage." "How Does Your Garden Grow?" from *The Regatta Mystery.*

RILEY, MARY *See* **DRAPER, MARY.**

RIVAL, MERLINA A friend to Miss Martindale, she identified the murdered "Mr. R.H. Curry" as her husband Harry Castleton, who had deserted her fifteen years before. She was soon after stabbed to death in Victoria Station during the rush hour. *The Clocks.*

RIVERS, MR. The chauffeur to Lord Easterfield, he was the Wychwood killer's seventh victim. *Murder is Easy.*

RIVINGTON, MRS. The wife of Colonel Hubert Rivington. According to Bobby Jones, who interviewed her concerning John Savage's death, she was "clearly a woman of more looks than brains." *Why Didn't They Ask Evans?*

ROBERT Inefficient waiter at Rochers Neige resort in Switzerland, he was Inspector Drouet in disguise and was imprisoned and murdered by Marrascaud. "The Erymanthian Boar" from *The Labours of Hercules.*

ROBERTS, DR. "His manner was cheerful and confident. You felt that his diagnosis would be correct and his treatments agreeable and practical—'a little champagne in convalescence perhaps'." Of himself he said, "I make a good income and I only kill a reasonable number of my patients." *Cards on the Table.*

ROBERTS, MR. The husband of Mary Roberts and father of her two children, he consulted Mr. Parker Pyne, who thought he wanted "to live gloriously for ten minutes." He became involved with international espionage, secret plans, Russian Crown Jewels and an exotic Grand Duchess and during his adventure he "felt more and more as though he were in the middle of one of his favourite novels." The case of Mr. Roberts was only one in which Mr. Parker Pyne lost, rather than made, money. "The Case of the City Clerk" from *Parker Pyne Investigates.*

ROBERTS, GLADYS *Née* Evans and formerly the parlourmaid at Tudor Cottage, she had since married a Mr. Roberts and with him ran Reverend Thomas Jones' vicarage at Marchbolt. She was the "Evans" referred to in Alan Carstairs' dying words. *Why Didn't They Ask Evans?*

ROBINSON, MR. He appeared in the Poirot, Marple and Tuppence and Tommy books. He was a member of a mysterious syndicate called The Arrangers which dealt with matters relating to the financial world. Just about everyone who met him speculated on exactly what he did, but Robinson summed himself up best when he said: "I'm just a man who knows about money . . . and the things that branch off from money, you know. People and their idiosyncracies and their practices in life." He was of indeterminate nationality. "He was fat and well-dressed, with a yellow face, melancholy dark eyes, a broad forehead, and a generous mouth that displayed rather over-large very white teeth." Colonel Pikeaway called him "that yellow whale of a fellow," and noted that Robinson had been offered a peerage but had turned it down. *Cat Among the Pigeons; Passenger to Frankfurt; Postern of Fate.*

ROBINSON, EDWARD He bought a sportscar, which "stood to him for Romance, for Adventure, for all the things that he had longed for and that he had never had." He then took a stroll in the Devil's Punch Bowl, and inadvertently drove off in a car which, though it looked like his, actually belonged to Gerald Champneys. This led to the discovery of a diamond necklace and an evening of adventure with Lady Noreen Elliott. "The Manhood of Edward Robinson" from *The Golden Ball.*

ROBINSON, JOHN *See* **GALE, NORMAN.**

ROBINSON, STELLA Mrs. Robinson's story about her incredible good luck when she acquired a very under-priced flat in Montagu Mansions in Knightsbridge put Poirot on the trail of Elsa Hardt. "The Adventure of the Cheap Flat" from *Poirot Investigates.*

ROBSON, CORNELIA RUTH Ingenuous but poor American relation of Miss Van Schuyler, she accompanied her cousin to Egypt and was present on board the S.S. *Karnak* when Linnet Doyle was murdered, where she inspired the passion of Dr. Bessner and agreed to marry him. *Death on the Nile.*

ROCKFORD, STERNDALE The American business partner of Andrew Pennington, he was in collusion with Pennington to defraud their client, Linnet Doyle. *Death on the Nile.*

ROGERS, MRS. The mother of Michael Rogers, she was "tall and angular, grey hair parted in the middle, mouth like a rattletrap and eyes that were eternally suspicious." *Endless Night.*

ROGERS, ELLIE AKA Ellie Guteman, Fenella Goodman, and Mrs. Michael Rogers, she was the American grand-daughter of Herman Guteman and the stepdaughter of Cora van Stuyvesant. She met Michael Rogers on Gipsy's Acre, and fell in love with him; they eloped to avoid her family's interference with the marriage. She died after falling from her horse, Conquer, and Michael inherited her vast estate. *Endless Night.*

ROGERS, ETHEL AND THOMAS The Rogers had been hired by the Owens to serve as butler and cook to the house party on Indian Island. When they were accused of contributing to the death of Jennifer Brady, they became the second and fourth victims of the Indian Island murderer. Ethel died while under the influence of a sleeping draught, and Thomas was hatcheted to death while chopping kindling, thus fulfilling the parts of the rhyme: "Nine little Indian boys sat up very late; One overslept himself and then there were eight;" and "Seven little Indian boys chopping up sticks; One chopped himself in halves and then there were six." *And Then There Were None.*

ROGERS, MICHAEL A "rolling stone" possessed of gipsy blood, Rogers said of himself: "I'd rather be myself, Michael Rogers, seeing the world, and getting off with good-looking girls." He went through women like he went through jobs, and when he met Ellie Guteman on one of her escapes from her wealthy sequestered life they soon wed. After Ellie died from a fall from her horse, Rogers became the sole beneficiary of her fortune. *Endless Night.*

ROLF, GREGORY B. The American film-star husband of Mary Marvell, Rolf, according to Hastings, was "a splendid-looking man. From his crisp curling black head, to the tips of his patent-leather boots, he was a hero fit for romance." Three years previously, Rolf had had an affair with Lady Yardly in California and had been given Lady Yardly's Star of the East diamond which he then re-christened the Western Star and gave to Mary Marvell as a wedding present. "The Adventure of the 'Western Star' " from *Poirot Investigates.*

RONNIE *See* **GOODMAN, ADAM.**

ROSALIE Seven-year-old daughter of Deborah and grand-daughter of Tuppence and Tommy Beresford, she was the sister of Andrew and Janet. *Postern of Fate.*

ROSCARI, SIGNOR The famous Italian baritone, Roscari was to have sung "Scarpia" in the performance of *Tosca* at Rustonbury Castle, but he was poisoned, though not fatally, before the performance, and his place was taken by Edouard Bréon. It was to be Bréon's last role. "Swan Song" from *The Golden Ball.*

ROSCHEIMER, LADY The determinedly philanthropical wife of Sir Leopole Roscheimer, she was the village patroness of the arts who maintained many aspiring and talented village girls and young men of the town. Lady Roscheimer had imported the famous dancer Prince Sergius Oranoff and two other professional dancers to lend polish to her amateur Harlequinade, in which Molly Stanwell, one of her protegées, was to make her debut.

"Harlequin's Lane" from *The Mysterious Mr. Quin.*

ROSE, DR. The nephew of Mr. Rose, who died in rather mysterious circumstances when he was apparently hit with a bolt of lightning that left a curious shape in the form of a hound on his body, Dr. Rose was the village doctor in Folbridge, Cornwall. Dr. Rose began to learn the secrets of the House of the Crystal from Sister Marie Angelique and had begun to exercise the power that this knowledge gave him. He and Sister Marie were both killed when an avalanche flung his small cliff cottage down on the beach. "The Hound of Death" from *The Golden Ball.*

ROSEN, DR. The uncle of Greta Rosen, "he was a big man with a fine head, and a very deep voice, with only a slight guttural intonation to tell of his nationality." The Schwartze Hand had been broken up through his efforts and he had moved to King's Gnaton to lay low. "The Four Suspects" from *The Thirteen Problems.*

ROSEN, GRETA The niece of Dr. Rosen, Greta was "a very pretty girl" who had been a member of the Schwartze Hand, a blackmail and terrorist organization that her uncle had helped to uncover. "The Four Suspects" from *The Thirteen Problems.*

ROSENTELLE, MADAME She made the four wigs purchased by Dolly Barrow to aid her disguise as Molly Ravenscroft, her twin sister. At the time of the Overcliffe tragedy, she owned a fashionable hairdressing shop called Eugene and Rosentelle in London's Bond Street. *Elephants Can Remember.*

ROSS, MISS Secretary and dental assistant to Norman Gale, she was described by her employer as "big, lots of bones, nose rather like a rocking-horse, frightfully competent" in order to prevent Jane Grey's jealousy. In reality, "Miss Ross' bones were not really quite as formidable as stated and she had an extremely attractive head of red hair." *Death in the Clouds.*

ROSS, DONALD A friend of Sir Montagu Corner's and the thirteenth guest at Sir Montagu's dinner party, he was an actor with "a characteristic lack of interest in any one else's performance but his own." On hearing the real Jane Wilkinson confuse Paris the city with Paris the son of Priam and Hecuba, he knew she was not the Jane Wilkinson with whom he had dined at Sir Montagu Corner's party. Before he could tell Poirot, he was murdered. *Lord Edgware Dies.*

ROSSAKOFF, COUNTESS VERA AKA Inez Veroneau. The mother of Niki Rossakoff, she was the only woman to capture the mind, imagination, appreciation and heart of Hercule Poirot. Vera Rossakoff first came to Poirot's office in an effort to clear Bernard Parker from a charge of theft. Hastings described her entrance: "Without the least warning the door flew open, and a whirlwind in human form invaded our privacy, bringing with her a swirl of sables (it was as cold as only an English June day can be) and a hat rampant with slaughtered ospreys. Countess Vera Rossakoff was a somewhat disturbing personality." Poirot was immediately taken with her, calling her "a remarkable woman," and expressed a decided opinion that he would meet her again. In *The Big Four,* the Countess, as Inez Veroneau, was Madame Olivier's secretary in the Big Four gang. Poirot returned her lost young son to her; there has been speculation that this child, Niki, was fathered by Poirot. Poirot knew the Countess for what she was—a jewel thief and a member of the underworld—but that knowledge did not cause his affection for her to wane. At the conclusion of *The Big Four,* there was a subtle suggestion that he and the Countess might marry. The marriage, however, did not take place, and twenty years passed before Poirot again encountered Vera Rossakoff. By then, she was as flamboyant as ever, and was the proprietress of Hell, a new and

fashionable lounge in London which she operated with Paul Varesco. Unknown to her, Hell was being used as the front for a dope ring, and only Poirot's efforts on her behalf prevented her from being incriminated. Hastings once remarked that "crimson roses express her temperament," and the last reference to the Countess was when Poirot sent her an arrangement of roses when the engagement of her son was announced. "Small men," said Hastings, "always admire big, flamboyant women." "The Double Cure" from *Double Sin; The Big Four;* "The Capture of Cerberus" from *The Labours of Hercules.*

ROSSITER, EDWARD This "fair-haired amiable young giant" and his fiancée and cousin Charmain Stroud expected to receive all Mathew Stroud's estate, since they were his only living relatives, his great-great-nephew and -niece. After his death, they discovered that he was penniless. They approached Miss Marple through their mutual friend, Jane Helier, in hopes that the elderly sleuth could help them solve the puzzle their old uncle had left them. "Strange Jest" from *Three Blind Mice and Other Stories.*

ROUSELLE, MADAMOISELLE (MADDY) Celia Ravenscroft's childhood governess, she told Poirot that Dolly Jarrow was a jealous woman. *Elephants Can Remember.*

ROWAN, MISS "Thin and dark and intense" mistress at Meadowbank, she was a psychology graduate and as such looked for psychological explanations of Miss Springer's death. She concluded that it was a case of suicide caused by a persecution complex despite the fact that Miss Springer had been shot from at least four feet away. *Cat Among the Pigeons.*

ROWE, JANET The Nannie to the Leonides household, Janet was "a good old Black Protestant" who felt that the murder of Aristide Leonides was the work of either the Communists or the Catholics.

She died after drinking a cup of cocoa which had been adulterated with Edith de Haviland's digitalin and had been meant for Josephine Leonides. *Crooked House.*

ROWLAND, GEORGE The nephew of William Rowland, George Rowland resembled P.G. Wodehouse's Bertie Wooster. A slight misunderstanding one morning had led to his being fired by his uncle: "In the course of a brief ten minutes, from being the apple of his uncle's eye, the heir to his wealth and a young man with a promising career in front of him, George had suddenly become one of the vast army of the unemployed . . . George embodied a veritable triumph of the tailor's art. He was exquisitely and beautifully arrayed. Solomon and the lilies of the field were simply not in it with George." George decided that his fate lay in the little village of Rowland's Castle and like Dick Whittington, minus the cat, he set off to discover if Rowland's Castle would bestow upon the last remaining member of the Rowland family the office of mayor. On his way he met Lady Elizabeth Gaigh, disguised as the Grand Duchess Anastasia. He succeeded in concealing her from Prince Osric and Prince Karl, and was eventually rewarded with her acceptance of his idea that she should marry him. George eventually helped Detective Inspector Jarrold of Scotland Yard retrieve the plans of the Portsmouth harbour defences from Mardenberg, a German spy. "My best dream," he told Elizabeth, "was one where King George borrowed half a crown from me to see him over the weekend." "The Girl in the Train" from *The Golden Ball.*

ROYDE, THOMAS The son of Mrs. Royde, brother of the deceased Adrian Royde, cousin of Audrey Strange, and a family friend of the Tressalians, he was partner to Allen Drake in their Malaysian plantation. "He walked a little sideways, crablike. This, the result of being jammed in a door during an earthquake, had contributed towards his nickname of the Hermit Crab." His silence, perhaps, was the most characteristic thing about him, and he was known as Silent Thomas, Taciturn Thomas and, in reference to Audrey Strange, True Thomas. *Towards Zero.*

RUBEC, DR. The psychologist at Mr. Aristides' Brain Trust complex, he was "a tall, melancholy Swiss of about forty years of age" who gave Hilary Craven, disguised as Olive Betterton, psychology tests upon arrival. He said to her: "It is a pleasure . . . to deal with someone who is not in any way a genius." *Destination Unknown.*

RUDD, JASON (JINKS) Marina Gregg's fifth and final husband, he was a very influential and successful film director. At first sight, Dolly Bantry thought that Jason Rudd was "the ugliest man she had ever seen." *The Mirror Crack'd from Side to Side.*

RUDGE, FRANKLIN According to Mr. Satterthwaite, Franklin Rudge "was a young American, a typical product of one of the Middle West states, eager to register impressions, crude, but lovable, a curious mixture of native shrewdness and idealism." After he heard Pierre Vaucher's story he admitted to being at a loss to understand Europeans, and realizing the delightful Americanness of Elizabeth Martin, went off into the night with her. "The Soul of the Croupier" from *The Mysterious Mr. Quin.*

RUSSELL, MISS Roger Ackroyd's housekeeper at Fernly Park, Miss Russell, according to James Sheppard, was "a redoubtable lady who had reigned undisputed for five years at Fernly" who went about "with pinched lips and an acid smile." She was left one thousand pounds by Roger Ackroyd. *The Murder of Roger Ackroyd.*

RUSSELL, BARTON The American millionaire, he was the widower of Iris Russell and the brother-in-law and guardian of Iris' sister, Pauline Weatherby. He invited the same guests who had been present at the dinner party where Iris died to a memorial dinner exactly four years after her death. He greatly resented Poirot's presence at the memorial dinner, and called Poirot "an interfering little Belgian jackanapes." "Yellow Iris" from *The Regatta Mystery.*

RUSSELL, IRIS Deceased wife of Barton Russell and sister to Pauline Weatherby, she had died from a dose of poison at a dinner party given exactly four years before the memorial celebration at the Jardin des Cygnes. "Yellow Iris" from *The Regatta Mystery.*

RUSSINGTON, JANET A guest of Isaac Pointz' at the Regatta, she was a writer who "didn't ram her writing down your throat. High-brow sort of stuff she wrote, but you'd never think it to hear her talk." Evan Llewellyn was in love with her, but powerless to pursue the lady until his name was cleared of any connection with Pointz' missing gem. "The Regatta Mystery" from *The Regatta Mystery.*

RUSTONBURY, LADY "Lady Rustonbury was both an ambitious and an artistic woman; she ran the two qualities in harness with complete success. She had the good fortune to have a husband who cared for neither ambition nor art and who therefore did not hamper her in any way." Lady Rustonbury arranged for Paula Nazorkoff to sing at Rustonbury Castle. Although she was hoping to stage *Madame Butterfly,* she willingly gave way

to Madame Nazorkoff's demand that it be *Tosca* or nothing. During the performance, Edouard Bréon, singing the role of "Scarpia," was killed. "Swan Song" from *The Golden Ball.*

RYAN, WILLIAM P. An American newspaper correspondent who was "unbelievably long-winded" when it came to recalling his experiences in World War I, William Ryan first acquainted Mr. Anstruther with the story of Sister Marie Angèlique and informed him that the Sister had been sent as a Belgian refugee to Trearne, the house that belonged to Mr. Anstruther's sister Kitty. "The House of Death" from *The Golden Ball.*

RYCROFT, MR. Ornithologist and amateur criminologist, Mr. Rycroft was a precise, "little elderly, dried-up man" who lived in one of the bungalows on the Sittaford estate. A member of the Psychical Research Society, he was an ardent believer in spiritualism and was present at the séance the night of Captain Trevelyan's murder. *The Sittaford Mystery.*

RYDER, HANK P. The extremely wealthy Alabamian admirer of Marguerite Laidlaw, he came over to "Yurrop" to see life. He soon befriended Tommy Beresford and told him of Marguerite's financial difficulties. "The Crackler" from *Partners in Crime.*

RYDER, JAMES BELL Managing director of the Ellis Vale Cement Company, currently in severe financial trouble, he was in Paris to negotiate a loan, although not from Madame Giselle. Seated immediately in front of the murdered woman, he made enough money from reporters for his eyewitness account to support his business. *Death in the Clouds.*

RYLAND, ABE The American Soap King, Ryland was described by Poirot as "the richest man in the world, richer even than Rockefeller." Ryland commissioned Poirot to travel to Rio de Janeiro in South America and look after some business for him. In reality, Ryland was "Number Two" of the Big Four gang; his symbol was a dollar sign and a star and two stripes indicating his wealth and nationality. *The Big Four.*

RYMER, AMELIA AKA Hannah Moorhouse. The wealthy widow of Abner Rymer the button-shank king, she literally did not know what to do with her money, so she consulted Mr. Parker Pyne. She related how she had been a farm hand, courted for eight years by Abner before they wed and that none of their four children had survived into adulthood. Mr. Parker Pyne treated her case in a somewhat high-handed fashion: his agent Dr. Constantine drugged the woman with cannabinol, a hemp extract, and then with other drugs; when she awoke in Mrs. Gardner's Cornish farmhouse she was told that she was Hannah Moorhouse, a farm servant. There she worked and fell in love with Joe Walsh, another farmhand. "The Case of the Rich Woman" from *Parker Pyne Investigates.*

SAINSBURY SEALE, MABELLE The third murder victim, she was a harmless, slightly vacuous woman who began her career as an actress, later moving to India to teach and to do missionary work. *One, Two, Buckle My Shoe.*

SAINTCLAIR, VALERIE The stage name of Valerie Oglander, she was the daughter of John Oglander, Sr., and Mrs. Oglander. Hastings remarked, "not a look, not a gesture of Valerie Saintclair's but expressed drama. She seemed to exhale an atmosphere of romance." A famous dancer, Miss Saintclair was blackmailed by Henry Reedburn when she refused to dispense the sexual favours he demanded. She was engaged to Prince Paul of Maurania, who thought her to be the scion of a noble Russian family. "The King of Clubs" from *The Under Dog.*

SALMON, SIR JOSEPH AKA Sir Herman Cohen, the name Jane Helier gave to Sir Salmon in her description of her plot to expose the true nature of "Mary Kerr," the wife of Jane's ex-husband Claud Averbury. "The Affair at the Bungalow" from *The Thirteen Problems.*

SAMOUSHENKA, KATRINA World-famous Russian ballet artist admired by Poirot when he saw her dance with Michael Novgin, she had developed tuberculosis and retired suddenly from the stage. Poirot found her in a sanatorium in Vagray les Alpes, Switzerland where, according to Count Alexis Pavlovitch, she had gone to die. Although she claimed to be a White Russian, offspring of "a Prince or Grand Duke," she was really only the daughter of a lorrydriver in Leningrad. With her aid, Poirot discovered the identities of "Nita," "Juanita" and "Incognita." "The Arcadian Deer" from *The Labours of Hercules.*

SAMPSON, MR. Mr. Sampson was the oldest man in St. Mary Mead. While "he boasted proudly of being ninety-six . . . his relations insisted firmly that he was only eighty-eight." He gave the fête being held on the grounds of Gossington Hall for the benefit of the St. John's Ambulance Association his highest praise: "There'll be a lot of wickedness." *The Mirror Crack'd from Side to Side.*

SAMUELSON, MRS. The wife of Jacob Samuelson and the mistress of the kid napped Pekinese Nanki Poo, she sent three hundred pounds ransom money to Commander Blackleigh at the Harrington Hotel. After the return of Nanki Poo, she went to the hotel to get the money back, but when she opened the parcel it contained only blank sheets of paper. "The Nemean Lion" from *The Labours of Hercules*.

SANCHIA *See* **DE SARA, MADELEINE.**

SANDBOURNE, MRS. The efficient and competent guide on Tour 37 of the Famous Houses and Gardens of Great Britain, she "did her part very well, creating little groups by adding anyone who looked as if they were left out to one or other of them, saying 'You *must* make Colonel Walker describe his garden to you.' . . . With such little sentences she drew people together." *Nemesis*.

SANDBOURNE, WILLIAM The name the Eccles gave to the dying man in the church at Chipping Cleghorn, identifying him as Pam's brother. The Eccles' said that "Sandbourne" had been in a low state of health and nerves for some time and was lately getting worse, and that they suspected him of committing suicide. "Sanctuary" from *Double Sin*.

SANDEMAN, SIR EDWIN The Harley Street doctor summoned by Miss Griffith to relieve Rex Fortescue's fatal fit, he arrived at the same time as Dr. Isaacs, but both physicians were too late to save the poisoned man. *A Pocket Full of Rye*.

SANDERFIELD, SIR GEORGE The "dark horse" described by Ambrose Vandel, he was a "nasty fellow." He was having an affair with Katrina Samoushenka at the time Ted Williamson met the maid "Nita," and Poirot consulted him to try to discover Nita's whereabouts. "The Arcadian Deer" from *The Labours of Hercules*.

SANDERS, GLADYS She and her husband Jack Sanders lived off her income which derived from the interest of a cap-

ital sum which, although she could not touch, she was free to will to whomever she pleased. She had not been married very long before she died at the Keston Spa Hydro after being hit over the head with a sandbag. "A Christmas Tragedy" from *The Thirteen Problems*.

SANDERS, JACK AKA Mr. Littleworth. The husband of the murdered Gladys Sanders, Jack Sanders was "a big, good-looking, florid-faced man, very hearty in his manners and popular with all. And nobody could have been pleasanter to his wife than he was." Mr. Littleworth was a name that Sanders assumed when he had telephoned his wife one day. "A Christmas Tragedy" from *The Thirteen Problems*.

SANDFORD, DR. He was Dr. Haydock's young partner in St. Mary Mead. Miss Marple said: "The younger doctors are all the same. . . . They take your blood pressure, and whatever's the matter with you, you get some kind of mass-produced variety of new pills. Pink ones, yellow ones, brown ones. Medicine nowadays is just like a supermarket—all packaged up." *The Mirror Crack'd from Side to Side*.

SANDFORD, REX A young architect, according to Colonel Melchett, he "built peculiar houses . . . full of new-fangled stuff." The murdered Rose Emmott was pregnant with his child, but he claimed that he had not taken unfair advantage of her. "Death by Drowning" from *The Thirteen Problems*.

SANSEVERATO, REBECCA. *See* **BLUNT, ALISTAIR.**

SANTONIX, RUDOLF The half-brother of Claudia Hardcastle, he was a famous architect and designer whose talents were in demand by many more wealthy patrons than he could handle. Michael Rogers had commissioned Santonix to build the house on Gipsy's Acre, which the architect claimed was his best work. Before his death, Santonix warned Rogers,

"I want the house I built purged of evil."
Endless Night.

SARAH An aspiring young spiritualist, she and her friends John and Evelyn were contacted by the Ouijah spirit Ada Spiers. During their session, Ada's communication was broken into by Harley Quin, who spelled out the message "PABZL... QUIN.... LAIDELL," which convinced Mr. Satterthwaite to accept an invitation to Laidell. "The Bird with the Broken Wing" from *The Mysterious Mr. Quin.*

SATIPY The wife of Yahmose and the mother of two young boys, Satipy, thought Renisenb, was "a tall, energetic, loud-tongued woman, handsome in a hard, commanding kind of way. She was eternally laying down the law, hectoring the servants, finding fault with everything, getting impossible things done by sheer force of vituperation and personality. Everyone dreaded her tongue and ran to obey her orders." She became the second victim in the series of deaths that plagued Imhotep's household. *Death Comes as the End.*

SATTERTHWAITE, MR. The godfather of Lilly Gilliat, Mr. Satterthwaite was an old friend of Hercule Poirot's and the longtime associate of the mysterious Harley Quin. Mr. Satterthwaite was a snob and his friends were those who counted in the social world. "His role was that of the looker on, and he knew it, but sometimes, when in the company of Mr. Quin, he had the illusion of being an actor— and the principal actor at that." An appreciator and a connoisseur of all the arts, Mr. Satterthwaite was especially fond of good music. One of his hobbies was amateur photography, and he was also the author of *Homes of My Friends.* In *The Mysterious Mr. Quin,* Mr. Satterthwaite aged from sixty-two to sixty-nine and described himself as having "neither chick nor child." Poirot said of him that "he has the playgoer's mind; he observes the characters, he has the sense of atmosphere." In the final Satterthwaite story,

"The Harlequin Tea Set," Mr. Satterthwaite returned to Doverton Kingsbourne, a house he knew as a boy, and with only a very subtle hint from Harley Quin managed to work some magic of his own. *The Mysterious Mr. Quin; Three-Act Tragedy;* "Dead Man's Mirror" from *Murder in the Mews;* "The Love Detectives" from *Three Blind Mice and Other Stories;* "The Harlequin Tea Set" from *Winter's Crimes 3.*

SAUNDERS, DORIS The model for Henrietta Savernake's sculpture of Nausicaa, she was discovered by the artist on a bus. Henrietta thought her "a common mean spiteful little piece—but what eyes.... Lovely lovely lovely eyes." Unfortunately, the spitefulness emerged in the sculpture and Henrietta destroyed the work. *The Hollow.*

SAVAGE, JOHN An enormously wealthy man whose money could not buy him a cure for terminal cancer, he apparently died by committing suicide. His close friend Alan Carstairs, however, not content with the inquest's verdict, began an independent investigation of the man's death. *Why Didn't They Ask Evans?*

SAVARONOFF, DR. *See* **DARRELL, CLAUD.**

SAVERNAKE, HENRIETTA Cousin to Lady Lucy Angkatell, Midge Hardcastle and Edward Angkatell, she was a sculptress who not only did representational work but also *avant garde* pieces. Mistress of John Christow, she relied on her artistic detachment by channelling her grief into a sculpture after he was murdered. *The Hollow.*

SAYERS, MAGGIE *See* **DE SARA, MADELEINE.**

SCHEELE, ANNA The sister of Elsie Pauncefoot Jones, Anna Scheele was Otto Morganthal's confidential secretary. Over a period of time, Anna had compiled information which proved that money, jewels and people were being diverted by a subversive group with evil intentions. She planned to take her information to the special convention in Baghdad, and because her life was in peril she disguised herself as her sister Elsie. *They Came to Baghdad.*

SCHERZ, RUDI According to Mr. Rowlandson, his employer at the Royal Spa Hotel, Rudi was "a very ordinary, pleasant young chap," Swiss by birth, but was suspected of stealing small sums from the hotel. Rudi placed the following advertisement in the *Chipping Cleghorn Gazette*: "*A murder is announced and will take place on Friday, October 29th at Little Paddocks at 6:30 p.m. Friends please accept this, the only intimation.*" Rudi was later found shot at Letitia Blacklock's house, Little Paddocks. *A Murder is Announced.*

SCHLAGAL, HERR A pilot in a Baghdad air service, he related to Mr. Parker Pyne how he had fallen in love with Muriel King, Lady Esther Carr's maid, and fondly recalled her before the report of her death: " 'I have a heart,' said Herr Schlagel. 'I feel. She was, to me, most beautiful, that lady'." "The House at Shiraz" from *Parker Pyne Investigates.*

SCHMIDT, FRAULEIN HILDEGARDE Maid and companion to Princess Dragomiroff, she was formerly the cook for the Armstrong household when Daisy Armstrong was kidnapped and murdered. *Murder on the Orient Express.*

SCHNEIDER, MR. A member of the Menher-Ra expedition, Mr. Schnieder represented the Metropolitan Museum of New York. He died of tetanus at the site of the excavation. "The Adventure of the Egyptian Tomb" from *Poirot Investigates.*

SCHUSTER, MR. Junior partner in the firm of Broadribb and Schuster, Solicitors, he was very curious about Jason Rafiel's will in relation to Miss Marple, thinking Rafiel "an odd cuss" and the whole enterprise a joke. *Nemesis.*

SCHWARTZ, MR. Enthusiastic, brown-eyed American tourist travelling through Europe, he was present at the Rochers Neige resort with Poirot. In a typically American fashion, he saved Poirot from being murdered by members of Marrascaud's gang: "And then, startling in its crisp transatlantic tones, a voice said: 'Stick 'em up'." "The Erymanthian Boar" from *The Labours of Hercules.*

SCOTT, MOIRA O'CONNELL Richard Scott's bride of three months, Moira Scott and her husband were houseguests at Ned Unkerton's Greenways House. Moira had "a slender figure, big wistful brown eyes, and golden red hair that stood out round her small face like a saint's halo." She was shot dead in the Privy Garden at Greenways. "The Shadow on the Glass" from *The Mysterious Mr. Quin.*

SCOTT, RICHARD The husband of Moira Scott, he was a guest at Ned Unkerton's Greenways House where his young bride was murdered. Scott had been to Greenways before as a guest of the previous owners, the Elliots, and knew the story of the Watching Cavalier. "The Shadow on the Glass" from *The Mysterious Mr. Quin.*

SCUTTLE, MR. Head of Messrs. Breather and Scuttle, house-agents, he had once employed James Bentley. Before Poirot revealed his reason for interviewing Mr. Scuttle, the latter speculated that Poirot was either a restaurant proprietor, a hotel manager or in films. *Mrs. McGinty's Dead.*

SEDGWICK, LADY BESS An internationally famous adventuress and the mother of Elvira Blake by her second marriage to Lord Coniston, she was also married, the first and only legitimate time, to Michael Gorman (the marriage was never dissolved), and subsequently to Johnnie Sedgwick—whom she truly loved but who broke his neck steeple-chasing—and Ridgeway Becker. For decades her exploits had astounded, shocked and delighted the world, and she made a dramatic exit when she drove her car at ninety miles an hour into the park railings by the side of a highway shortly after offering a confession to the murder of Micky Gorman. *At Bertram's Hotel.*

SEDLEY, AMELIA MARY One of the witnesses at Elinor Carlisle's trial for the murder of Mary Gerrard, she identified Nurse Jessie Hopkins as being Mary Draper, *née* Riley. *Sad Cypress.*

SELKIRK, EVE *See* **CARPENTER, EVE.**

SEMINOFF, OLGA Formerly the "opera" (*au pair*) girl to Mrs. Llewellyn-Smythe, she steadfastly maintained that she was beneficiary to her deceased employer's will, even in the face of evidence that the codicil in question was an obvious forgery. *Hallowe'en Party.*

SERAKIS, CATHERINE The secretary at the Olive Branch in Baghdad, the centre of Dr. Rathbone's enterprises, and Edward Goring's lover, she had "a melancholy Levantine face with great sad eyes and a heavy nose." *They Came to Baghdad.*

SERROCOLD, CARRIE LOUISE Married three times, Carrie Louise Serrocold had been the wife of Eric Gulbrandsen (with whom she adopted Pippa San Saveriano and bore Mildred Gulbrandsen Strete), Johnnie Restarick and Lewis Serrocold. She was also the grandmother of Gina

Hudd, the daughter of Pippa and Guido San Severiano, and the sister of Ruth Van Rydock. As the mistress of Stoneygates, it was said that: "she sees no evil, hears no evil and speaks no evil." *They Do It with Mirrors.*

SERROCOLD, LEWIS The third husband of Carrie Louise Serrocold and the father of Edgar Lawson, Lewis Serrocold was a man who "always put causes before people," he conducted the day-to-day affairs of Stoneygates, his large home for delinquent boys near Market Kimble. Serrocold died attempting to save his son Edgar from drowning. *They Do It with Mirrors.*

SESSLE, CAPTAIN ANTHONY An ex-soldier, he inherited some money and went into partnership with Mr. Hollaby and Hollaby's son in the Porcupine Assurance Company. After an afternoon of golf with Holloby, Sr., Sessle was discovered dead on the seventh tee of the Sunningdale Golf Course with a woman's hatpin thrust through his heart. The typist Doris Evans was arrested for his murder. "The Sunningdale Mystery" from *Partners in Crime.*

SETTLE, DR. Andrew Carmichael's doctor, Dr. Settle invited his good friend Dr. Edward Carstairs, the eminent psychologist, to Wolden to see if he could understand his patient's strange behaviour. "The Strange Case of Sir Andrew Carmichael" from *The Golden Ball.*

SHAISTA, PRINCESS She professed to be the niece of Emir Ibrahim and the cousin of Prince Ali Yusef, and claimed that she and the Prince would have wed had he not been assassinated. She attended Meadowbank school. Princess Shaista disappeared very shortly before Emir Ibrahim's surprise visit. *Cat Among the Pigeons.*

SHAITANA, MR. He had "a very fine moustache—the only moustache in London, perhaps, that could compete with that of Monsieur Hercule Poirot," although Poirot maintained that his own was superior. It was generally felt that he "knew a little too much about everybody," and he certainly knew something about the lives of Anne Meredith, Dr. Roberts, Mrs. Lorrimer and Major John Despard, for they all in some way feared him. He was killed at his own dinner and bridge party. *Cards on the Table.*

SHANE, MICHAEL Actor and husband of Rosamund Abernethie Shane, he was .considered "something of a dark horse—he's a man with ambition and also a man of overweening vanity." He had been having an affair with an ex-leading lady, Sorrell Dainton, which explained some of his suspicious behaviour. *After the Funeral.*

SHANE, ROSAMUND ABERNETHIE Daughter of Geraldine Abernethie and wife of Michael Shane, although she was called "a lovely nitwit" and was "not conspicuous for brains," she was the only one of the family to see through Poirot's disguise as Monsieur Pontarlier, agent of UNARCO, ostensibly purchasing Enderby Hall. She very happily became pregnant during the course of the novel. *After the Funeral.*

SHANNON, CHRISTINE The 'blond lovely' at the table next to the one where George Barton died at the Luxembourg, she was a gold digger, "dumber than you'd believe possible except where money is concerned," according to Inspector Kemp. *Sparkling Cyanide.*

SHAPLAND, ANN AKA Angelica or Senora Angelica de Toredo, she was a "near-Spanish" cabaret dancer. Although she could have picked any secretarial job she wished, she chose to work for Miss Bulstrode at Meadowbank, ignoring the pleas of her would-be fiancé Dennis Rathbone. *Cat Among the Pigeons.*

SHAW, DR. The physician to the village of Kingston Bishop, he was "an elderly man with a kindly but tired manner" and a friend of Major Phillpot's. "Dr. Shaw was the kind of practitioner that is fairly rare nowadays and was, indeed, known locally as 'Leave-it-to-Nature-Shaw'." He treated Ellie Rogers for a sprained ankle and later established the time of her death. *Endless Night.*

SHAW, MR. AKA Mr. Ventnor. Along with Mr. Vavasour, Mr. Shaw was a joint general manager of the London and Scottish Bank. As Mr. Ventnor, an invalid, he booked passage on the *Olympia*, the same boat on which Philip Ridgeway was carrying one million dollars in Liberty Bonds to New York. "The Million Dollar Bond Robbery" from *Poirot Investigates.*

SHELDON, ROSE Once an actress, she was working as a maid at Bertram's Hotel when she was questioned by Chief Inspector Davy about the disappearance of Canon Pennyfather. The "calm and competent" woman gave a "straightforward coherent account" of the matter which unfortunately, for the most part, was fabrication. *At Bertram's Hotel.*

SHEPPARD, CAROLINE The sister of James Sheppard, she and her brother shared a cottage in King's Abbot next to the one occupied by Poirot. She made it her business to know everything about everybody, and had an "intelligence corps" made up of servants and tradesmen. James suggested that "somebody like Caroline must have invented the questions on passports, I think." *The Murder of Roger Ackroyd.*

SHEPPARD, DR. JAMES The brother of Caroline Sheppard, the physician of Mrs. Ferrars and the friend and physician of Roger Ackroyd, he was acquainted with some of the work of Arthur Hastings, played Watson to Poirot's Sherlock and narrated the Ackroyd case just as Hastings had chronicled the adventures of Poirot before he moved to the Argentine. Sheppard initially thought that Poirot's profession must have been that of a hairdresser, citing the evidence of his large and carefully groomed moustaches. *The Murder of Roger Ackroyd.*

SHOREHAM, ROBERT (ROBBIE) Professor Gottlieb said that this distinguished physicist was "one of the greatest geniuses of our age." With Lisa Neumann, who had been his lab assistant and later was his secretary, he had discovered Project Benvo, a gas which, when used on humans, left them permanently benevolent and passive. He made a free gift of his research to the British government. *Passenger to Frankfurt.*

SHRIVENHAM, LIONEL A junior member of the British Embassy, Lionel Shrivenham had made a number of unfortunate errors in the past and was therefore insecure about his job. "Since his arrival three months ago in Baghdad he felt he had been consistently unlucky. One more raspberry, he felt, would finally blight what might have been a promising career." *They Came to Baghdad.*

SIMMONS, ARCHDEACON "A confident cleric," the Archdeacon was a friend of Canon Pennyfather's. Simmons discovered that the Canon had really disappeared, and not merely mislaid himself, as was his custom, and brought the police into the matter. *At Bertram's Hotel.*

SIMMONS, JULIA *See* **STAMFORDIS, EMMA JOCELYN.**

SIMMONS, PATRICK The brother to Julia Simmons and the cousin to Letitia and Charlotte Blacklock, Patrick was tall with "a handsome devil-may-care face." He lived at Little Paddocks while studying for an engineering degree at Milchester University. *A Murder is Announced.*

SIMONE, MADAME The most successful psychic of her generation and the subject of studies by numerous researchers, she was fiancée of Raoul Daubreuil. Lately, her materializations had become increasingly spectacular and had taken a heavy

toll on her health. She agreed to give one last séance for Madame Exe, where she succeeded for the second time in materializing Madame Exe's dead daughter, Amelie. Madame Simone died soon after. "The Last Séance" from *Double Sin.*

SIMPSON, MR. AKA Mr. Crotchet. A bank clerk by profession, Simpson was a paying guest at the home of Mr. and Mrs. Todd. "The Adventure of the Clapham Cook" from *The Under Dog.*

SIMPSON, LIEUTENANT ALEC, R.N. A young officer with the Royal Navy, Alec Simpson discovered the body of The Honourable Mrs. Rupert Carrington under his seat while travelling on the *Plymouth Express.* "The Plymouth Express" from *The Under Dog.*

SIMPSON, ALEXANDER A friend of Poirot's, he sent for the detective after a valuable Rubens was stolen from his art gallery. He knew who had contrived the theft and for whom the painting was destined in France. Poirot accepted the task without enthusiasm. "He was not very interested in his quest, but because of it, he was introduced to the case of the Missing Schoolgirl, which interested him very much indeed." "The Girdle of Hippolyta" from *The Labours of Hercules.*

SIMS, INSPECTOR The "too amiable" police inspector in Charman's Green, he sympathized with Katrina Rieger's position in the Barrowby case: "Fetch this, fetch that, fetch the other, rub my back, pour out my medicine, run round to the chemist—all that sort of thing. You know how it is with these old women—they mean to be kind, but what they need is a sort of black slave!" "How Does Your Garden Grow?" from *The Regatta Mystery.*

SIMS, MR. Hired by Gwenda Giles to refurbish her newly-purchased Hillside house, he was "the builder and decorator, a persuasive middle-aged man with a husky voice and a little notebook, which he always held at the ready, to jot down any expensive idea that might occur to his patrons." *Sleeping Murder.*

SIMS, DORIS One of the mannequins at Cynthia Dacre's dressmaking establishment, Ambrosine, Ltd., she was accosted on her lunch hour by Egg Lytton Gore who wanted information about Mrs. Dacres. *Three-Act Tragedy.*

SKINNER, EMILY AKA Mary Higgins. The younger sister of Lavinia Skinner, she lived comfortably in a flat in Old Hall (the former home of Colonel Lucius Protheroe), a bed-bound hypochondriacal recluse with hair that looked "like a bird's nest of which no self-respecting bird could be proud." As Mary Higgins, she was a paragon of domestic virtue, the perfect maid to replace the adenoidal Gladdie Holmes, who had been fired for having supposedly stolen a brooch. "The Case of the Perfect Maid" from *Three Blind Mice and Other Stories.*

SKINNER, LAVINIA (LAVVIE) The elder sister of Emily Skinner, she hired Mary Higgins as a maid after she had fired Gladdie Holmes when one of Emily's brooches went missing and some crockery had been broken. "The Case of the Perfect Maid" from *Three Blind Mice and Other Stories.*

SLACK, INSPECTOR "Rude and overbearing in the extreme," Inspector Slack was attached to the Much Benham police headquarters and was a man who "determinedly strove to contradict his name." He had no more than a grudging toleration of Miss Marple, but it was her description of him that hit the mark: "Inspector Slack—well, he's exactly like the young lady in the boot shop who wants to sell you patent leather because she's got it in your size, and doesn't take any notice of the fact that you want brown calf." Slack was in charge of the investigation into the death of Lucius Protheroe and assisted Melchett in the Ruby Keene case. *Murder at the Vicarage; The Body in the Library;* "Tape-Measure Murder" and "The Case of the Perfect Maid" from *Three Blind Mice and Other Stories.*

SLICKER, MR. A "tweed-suited young man in horsy checks," he was a partner of Messrs. Lovebody and Slicker, estate agents in Market Basing, whom Tuppence Beresford asked about the house in William Boscowan's painting, "House by a Canal." *By the Pricking of My Thumbs.*

SMETHURST, CAPTAIN A traveller with a group going from Damascus to Baghdad, he was not popular with the others and was murdered on the trip. "The Gate of Baghdad" from *Parker Pyne Investigates.*

SMITH, IVOR An investigator and a friend of Tommy Beresford's, Smith conveyed numerous facts about Mr. Eccles and his activities to Tommy. He also possessed a pair of eyebrows that would have rivalled the great moustaches of Hercule Poirot. *By the Pricking of My Thumbs.*

SMITH, NURSE JANET A friend of Tuppence Beresford's, she worked at Madame Violette's hat shop. She wished to encourage that "weak-kneed" Vincent St. Lawrence to propose marriage to her, and to this end, she and Tuppence contrived a successful scheme whereby her sudden disappearance would shock the young man into realizing how much he wanted to marry her. "A Pot of Tea" from *Partners in Crime.*

SOBEK The second eldest son of Imhotep and the brother of Yahmose, Renisenb and Ipy, Sobek was married to the dull but single-minded Kait by whom he had three children. After his death from drinking poisoned wine, his wife felt no remorse: "A handsome braggart—a man who was always going to other women. . . . What love and respect should I have for a man like that? And what are men anyway? They are necessary to breed children, that is all." *Death Comes as the End.*

SOLOMON, MR. He owned the bookstore which was the front for Colonel Beck's Special Branch: "On a stool in a corner, hemmed in by books, was an old man in a pork-pie hat with a large flat face like a stuffed fish. He had the air of one who has given up an unequal struggle. He had attempted to master the books, but the books had obviously succeeded in mastering him." *The Clocks.*

SOMERS, MISS Newest and most inefficient of the typists at Rex Fortescue's Consolidated Investments Trust, she was "no longer young and had a mild worried face like a sheep." *A Pocket Full of Rye.*

SONIA Secretary to Sir Roderick Horsefield, she was helping him write his memoirs and had inspired an infatuation in him. Although she had been passing important Word War II documents from Sir Roderick's archives to the Hertzogovinian Embassy, she finally chose to marry Sir Roderick and live a life of ease, discarding her romantic thoughts of political intrigue. *Third Girl.*

SOPWORTH, CLAUD The brother of Alice, Clara and Dorothy Sopworth, with whom he was vacationing at Kimpton-on-Sea, Claud Sopworth, according to James Bond, was "a poisonous idiot . . . a man . . . of no moral worth whatsoever." He was pursuing Grace, James Bond's girlfriend. "The Rajah's Emerald" from *The Golden Ball.*

SOUTHWOOD, THE HONOURABLE JOANNA Cousin to Tim Allerton, she was a "tall thin young woman of twenty-seven, with a long clever face and freakishly plucked eyebrows." She was once involved in a series of society robberies investigated by Inspector Japp. "If any misfortune happens to my friends," she said, "I always drop them at once. . . . They always want to borrow money off you, or else they start a dressmaking business and you have to get the most terrible clothes from them. Or they paint lampshades, or do batik scarves." *Death on the Nile.*

SPALDING, CAROLINE *See* **CRALE, CAROLINE.**

SPENCE, MRS. With Mr. Spence, she was a guest at Major Jack Rich's card party the night Edward Clayton was slain. She loved dancing to the latest records and "displayed a slight acidity concerning Major Rich's luck at cards" when questioned by Hercule Poirot. "The Mystery of the Baghdad Chest" from *The Regatta Mystery.*

SPENCE, SUPERINTENDENT The head of the Oatshire police and in charge of the investigation into the death of "Enoch Arden," he knew of Poirot through Inspector Japp, who told him that Poirot had a torturous mind. *Taken at the Flood.*

SPENCE, SUPERINTENDENT BERT The brother of Elspeth McKay, Superintendent Spence was the head of the Kilchester police and an old friend of Poirot's, having worked with him on a number of unrecorded cases in the past. He asked for Poirot's assistance in clearing James Bentley, who had been convicted of the murder of Mrs. McGinty. Spence was "the bull-dog breed. Good honest police officer of the old type. No graft. No violence. Not stupid either. Straight as a die." After his retirement, he went to live with his sister in Woodleigh Common. *Mrs. McGinty's Dead; Hallowe'en Party; Elephants Can Remember.*

SPENCE, JEREMY (JIM) Husband of Linda Spence and friend of the Clayton family's, he was a member of the party at Major Rich's the night Arnold Clayton was slain. "The Mystery of the Spanish Chest" from *The Adventure of the Christmas Pudding.*

SPENCE, LINDA Wife of Jeremy Spence and friend of the Clayton's, she was a member of the party at Major Rich's the night Arnold Clayton was murdered.

Poirot "decided grudgingly that she was attractive in the modern style (which at that moment resembled an underfed orphan child). It was not a type he admired. The artistically disorderd hair fluffed out round her head, a pair of shrewd eyes watched him from a slightly dirty face devoid of make-up save for a vivid cerise mouth. She wore an enormous pale-yellow sweater hanging almost to her knees, and tight black trousers." This woman, to whom Commander McLaren referred as a "hell-cat," was extremely candid with Poirot: she thought that Rich and Margharita were having an affair, and in her allusion to *Othello*, she gave Poirot the "little idea" with which he ultimately solved the case. "The Mystery of the Spanish Chest" from *The Adventure of the Christmas Pudding.*

SPENDER, MR. He and Mr. Hitchcock gave Jack Sanders an alibi for the time of the death of his wife, Gladys Sanders. "A Christmas Tragedy" from *The Thirteen Problems.*

SPENLOW, MRS. The active wife of Arthur Spenlow, Mrs. Spenlow had sold her successful London flower shop to retire to the country where murder intruded into her gregarious life. "Tape-Measure Murder" from *Three Blind Mice and Other Stories.*

SPENLOW, ARTHUR The husband of the murdered Mrs. Spenlow, Arthur Spenlow was a middle-aged jeweller who had come to live in St. Mary Mead, a choice which Miss Marple thought odd as he had so obviously lived in towns all his life. Spenlow said that his choice was motivated by his love for gardening, but it quickly became apparent that he knew nothing about the subject. "Tape-Measure Murder" from *Three Blind Mice and Other Stories.*

SPENSER, MISS An employee of St. Guildric's Agency, Miss Spenser was Victoria Jones' employment counsellor. Miss Spenser recognized Victoria "as one of those who were destined to pass through the office with reasonable frequency." *They Came to Baghdad.*

SPIESS, HERR HEINRICH The Chancellor of Germany, he met with British officials in their attempt to resolve the international youth crisis. *Passenger to Frankfurt.*

SPRAGG, EURYDICE The wife of Absalom Spragg, Mrs. Spragg "was a stout woman of middle-age, dressed in a flamboyant style. Very full of cant phrases about 'Our dear ones who have passed over,' and other things of the kind." As a spiritualist, she was well-established as an honoured and friendly guest in the household of Simon Clode. By holding séances she attempted to contact Simon Clode's dead grand-daughter Christobel, and Clode reciprocated by making her his heiress, much to the chagrin of his family, two months before his death. Motive *v* Opportunity" from *The Thirteen Problems.*

SPRAGGE, FREDERICK The senior partner in Messrs. Spragge, Spragge, Jenkinson and Spragge, he was Lady Frances Derwent's solicitor. Mr. Spragge, rumoured to know more discreditable secrets of noble families than any other lawyer in London, had a strong, almost hypnotic power of extracting confidential information from his clients. Lady Frankie decided it would facilitate their amateur investigation of Alex Pritchard's death if Bobby Jones assumed the lawyer's identity in his interview with Mrs. Rivington. *Why Didn't They Ask Evans?*

SPRIG, MR. An "elderly man of apparently despondent disposition," he was a house agent in Market Basing whom Tuppence Beresford consulted about Watermead House and who masked as best he could an expression of "the foolishness of women is incredible." *By the Pricking of My Thumbs.*

SPRINGER, GRACE The games mistress at Meadowbank, she was thought by her students to be "a female Gorgon with freckles, red hair and a voice like a corncake" or, in a more graphic adolescent terminology, "ginger hair and smells when she's hot." Possessed of "the manners of a pig," she enjoyed exposing anything slightly off-colour in her colleagues' past lives. She was shot in the Sports Pavillion, the first of a series of murder victims at Meadowbank school. *Cat Among the Pigeons.*

SPROT, BETTY *See* **BERESFORD, BETTY.**

SPROT, MILLICENT AKA "M." As Millicent Sprot, she had been in Leahampton for the duration of the war with her adopted daughter Betty. With "pale gooseberry eyes" and "a slightly adenoidal voice," she seemed to be a passionately maternal woman, but as "M," she was the female head of Fifth Column activities in Britain. *N or M?*

STAMFORDIS, EMMA JOCELYN AKA Julia Simmons. The sister of Phillipa Haymes and the niece of Randall Goedler, Emma was to inherit half of Randall Goedler's fortune if Letitia Blacklock died before Emma's grandmother Belle Goedler. Emma passed herself off as Julia Simmons, a cousin of Letitia and Charlotte Blacklock. *A Murder is Announced.*

STAMFORDIS, PIP *See* **HAYMES, PHILLIPA.**

STAMFORDIS, SYBIL DIANA HELEN Sybil Stamfordis "was a tall willowy

woman with dark, rather greasy hair, a simpering expression, and a fish-like mouth" who lived with Thyrza Grey and Bella Webb at The Pale Horse. She was a psychic medium of some repute. *The Pale Horse.*

STANISLAUS, COUNT *See* **OBOLOVITCH, PRINCE MICHAEL.**

STANLEY, NIGEL Son of Sir Arthur Stanley, he lived in Mrs. Nicoletis' youth hostel under the assumed identity of Nigel Chapman, a student of Bronze Age, Mediaeval and Italian history. He poisoned his mother with an overdose of medinal, but his father, a famous research chemist, concealed this fact out of loyalty to his dead wife until his death. *Hickory Dickory Dock.*

STANTON, FREDA The niece of Mr. and Mrs. Edward Pengelley (the latter through marriage), she was dating Jacob Radnor. She left her aunt and uncle when Mrs. Pengelley, herself enamoured with the affections of Radnor, became incensed at the suggestion the young man was interested only in Freda. "The Cornish Mystery" from *The Under Dog.*

STANWELL, MOLLY The beloved of John Denman, she was to dance Pierette in Lady Roscheimer's amateur Harlequinade, but Anna Denman thought she had clumsy feet. "Harlequin's Lane" from *The Mysterious Mr. Quin.*

STARKE, SIR PHILIP A botanist, author and industrialist, Sir Starke was the seventy-year-old husband of Lady Julia Starke who might have come, Tuppence Beresford thought, "straight out of an El Greco canvas." Although he loved children, Mrs. Copleigh thought that he was responsible for the rash of child murders in the area. Sir Starke reported that his wife had died in southern France in 1938. *By the Pricking of My Thumbs.*

STARR, RAYMOND A male professional dancer at the Majestic Hotel in Danemouth, he also taught tennis to the daughters of rich patrons at the hotel. As a dancer he was partner to both Josephine Turner and Ruby Keene. He composed a story about his name being Thomas Ramon Starr and that his ancestors were really an ancient, well-bred Devonshire family who had come to grief and lost everything, including the family estates. His pedigree was invented to impress Adelaide Jefferson, whose hand he was hoping to win in marriage. *The Body in the Library.*

STAVANSSON, GABRIEL When this well-known explorer returned unexpectedly from a two-year sojourn at the North Pole, his fiancée Hermione Crane was missing, and he consulted Tuppence and Tommy Beresford to find her. This otherwise praiseworthy gentleman had one peculiarity—he could not abide fat women: "Fat woman and fat dogs are an abomination unto the Lord." "The Case of the Missing Lady" from *Partners in Crime.*

STAVERTON, IRIS Iris Staverton was invited by the Ned Unkertons to be their houseguest at Greenways House at the same time as Richard Scott, her former lover, and his new wife Moira. Cynthia Drage said of her: "She's what I call a dangerous woman—the sort of woman who'd stick at nothing." When the bodies of Jimmy Allenson and Moira Scott were discovered, she was found in the Privy Garden holding the murder weapon. "The Shadow on the Glass" from *The Mysterious Mr. Quin.*

STEIN, LEO Partner to Isaac Pointz and one of the guests at the Regatta, Stein was a Hatton Garden diamond merchant. "The Regatta Mystery" from *The Regatta Mystery.*

STELLA Betty Gregg's sister, she and her husband were Betty's hosts during her holiday at Pollensa Bay. Mrs. Chester maintained that Betty's relatives were part of an arty set: "Her sister lived out there—

was married to an artist—a Dutchman. The whole set was most undesirable. Half of them were living together without being married." "Problem at Pollensa Bay" from *The Regatta Mystery.*

STENGELBERG, NURSE *See* **OHLSSON, GRETA.**

STEPANOV, COUNT *See* **IVANOVITCH, BORIS.**

STEPANYI, COUNT PAUL An employee of Mr. Parker Pyne, he assumed the identity of Count Paul to present Mr. Roberts with the Order of St. Stanislaus, tenth class, with laurels. "The Case of the City Clerk" from *Parker Pyne Investigates.*

STEPHENS *See* **HEMMINGWAY, GERALD.**

STEVENS, MR. The wonderful and efficient manservant to Jimmy Thesiger, he was married to Mrs. Stevens, Thesiger's cook. His employer said: "Brain, you know. Sheer brain," and was impressed by all the correspondence courses, including French, that Stevens took. *The Seven Dials Mystery.*

STILLINGFLEET, DR. JOHN He called his friend Poirot into the Farley "suicide" case after police found a letter from Benedict Farley to Poirot in Farley's possession, and later cared for Norma Restarick, whom he eventually married and took to Australia. He speculated on whether Poirot would ever take to crime: "I bet you could get away with it all right. As a matter of fact, it would be *too* easy for you—I mean the thing would be off as definitely too unsporting." " 'That,' said Poirot, 'is a typical English idea'." "The Dream" from *The Adventure of the Christmas Pudding; Third Girl.*

STIRLING, PAMELA (POPPY) According to Mark Easterbrook, Poppy was "a very pretty girl, with a fashionable hair-do, all ends, bits and pieces, sticking out at improbable angles on the crown of her head. Strange to say, it suited her. She had enormous blue eyes and a mouth that was usually half-open. She was as all [David Ardingly's] girls were known to be, extremely silly." She mentioned The Pale Horse during a conversation that Easterbrook and Hermia Redcliffe were having with her and Ardingly at the Fantasie, but when Easterbrook went to see her at her shop to ask what she knew about The Pale Horse, she retreated in fear. *The Pale Horse.*

St. John, Jewel (Jill) The daughter of Walter St. John and Mary Moss, she was living with Mrs. Mundy in Chipping Cleghorn. It was for her that Walter St. John escaped to Chipping Cleghorn a few months before he was due to be released from Charrington Prison. She ultimately obtained possession of her mother's jewels. "Sanctuary" from *Double Sin.*

St. John, Walter Edmund The dying man Bunch Harmon found in her husband's church at Chipping Cleghorn, Walter St. John was the husband of the deceased Mary Moss and the father of Jewel St. John. St. John had been sent to jail for a jewel theft, and had recently escaped from Charrington Prison when Bunch Harmon found him. He had hidden his wife's jewels (which were stitched into her dancing costume) in a suitcase at the baggage check at Paddington Station, and asked Bunch to see that his daughter inherited them. "Sanctuary" from *Double Sin.*

St. Lawrence, Vincent Nephew and heir of the Earl of Cheriton, Vincent consulted the International Detective Agency about his missing girlfriend, Janet Smith. Tuppence Beresford assured him of the Agency's special twenty-four-hour service, much to Tommy Beresford's dismay. "A Pot of Tea" from *Partners in Crime.*

St. Maur, Babe AKA Countess Anna Radzky; Number One; One o'clock (an alias she assumed after the death of Gerald Wade). An actress whose motto was:

"If you want to live, be high-handed," she was, according to Bill Eversleigh, "a Yankee girl—a perfect stunner." As the Countess Radzky and Number One, she was a member of the Seven Dials Group. *The Seven Dials Mystery.*

Stoddart, Dr. Michael This young physician was well-liked by Poirot, who was attracted to "the shy friendliness of his grin, was amused by his naive interest in crime and respected him as a hard-working and shrewd man in his chosen profession." Called in to administer medical aid to a man mistakenly shot at Patience Grace's cocaine party, he became enamoured of one of the guests, Sheila Grant. "The Horses of Diomedes" from *The Labours of Hercules.*

Stoddart-West, James Young son of Lord Robert and Lady Stoddart-West, he and his friend Alexander Eastley were allowed to view the three-week old dead body in the sarcophagous, and aided the investigation by finding the letter Emma Crackenthorpe received from "Martine Crackenthorpe" on the grounds of Rutherford Hall. *4.50 from Paddington.*

Stoddart-West, Lady Martine *Née* Martine Dubois, she was the wife of Sir Robert Stoddart-West and mother of James. As Martine Dubois she fell in love with Edmund Crackenthorpe, but he was slain at Dunkirk before they could wed. She met her future husband, an air force officer, while she was a Resistance fighter, and aided his passage to France for a special assignment. At first, it was thought that the body of the woman in the sarcophagous at Rutherford Hall was hers. *4.50 from Paddington.*

Stokes, Dr. An embittered physician, he was "struck off" for performing illegal abortions, and was no longer a licensed doctor when the Wheelings brought the wounded Canon Pennyfather to him. Mrs. Wheeling thought it "was only his kind heart, really, helping a lot of girls who were no better than they should be." *At Bertram's Hotel.*

STONE, DR. The alias assumed by a well-known cracksman. Raymond West, Miss Marple's nephew, knew the real Dr. Stone, an archaeologist, and informed his aunt and Leonard Clement that the man was an imposter. *Murder at the Vicarage.*

STONOR, GABRIEL Paul Renauld's secretary for the previous two years, Stonor was one of Christie's archetypal Englishmen: "He had knocked about all over the world. He had shot big game in Africa, ranched in California and traded in the South Sea Islands. He had been secretary to a New York railway magnate, and had spent a year encamped in the desert with a friendly tribe of Arabs." *Murder on the Links.*

STRANGE, AUDREY Nevile Strange's first wife for eight years, she had grown up with her cousin Thomas Royde who had been in love with her ever since. Evidence implicating her in the murder of Lady Tressilian began to augment: the fatal blow to Lady Tressilian's head was dealt by a left-handed person; a blood-stained glove was found shoved in the ivy outside her window and its mate was discovered in the pocket of her coat; the murder weapon came from her room. It was fortunate for Audrey Strange that Diana Brinton's wire-haired terrier Don had a fondness for the odour of dead fish, and that Mr. MacWhirter once tried to commit suicide. *Towards Zero.*

STRANGE, SIR BARTHOLOMEW (TOL-LIE) Big, grey-haired, intelligent, kindly and middle-aged physician, he was a life-long friend of Sir Charles Cartwright's whom he treated for nervous disorders. He was present at Sir Charles' home when the Reverend Babbington was murdered, and his sudden death from nicotine poisoning came as a shock to his friends. *Three-Act Tragedy.*

STRANGE, KAY Nevile Strange's second wife, she had fairly manipulated him into divorcing his first wife, Audrey, to marry her. Lady Tressilian thought her: "New and vulgar! . . . that scarlet-toed creature. . . . I do not like her—she's quite a wrong wife for Nevile—no background, no roots!" When Nevile asked her for a divorce while both were visiting Lady Tressilian at Gull's Point, where Audrey Strange was also a guest, she showed her true form: "a tartar—devil of a temper. Brains as well as temper, though." *Towards Zero.*

STRANGE, NEVILE Divorced from Audrey Strange and married to Kay Strange, he had been the ward of the deceased Sir Matthew Tressilian, who had left Nevile's money in trust to Lady Tressilian during her lifetime. Well-known to the British public as a sports figure, his main game was tennis. He wrote to Lady Tressilian, arranging that he and his bride visit Gull's Point at the same time as Audrey's yearly visit, so that his two wives could become friends. Lady Tressilian thought he was "like Henry the Eighth. . . . Conscience, you know! Henry was always trying to get Catherine to agree that the divorce was the right thing. Nevile knows that he had behaved badly—he wants to feel *comfortable* about it all. So he had been trying to bully Audrey into saying everything is all right and that she'll come and meet Kay and that she doesn't mind at all." Superintendent Battle thought him "a Bluebeard." *Towards Zero.*

STRANLEIGH, LADY The mother of Margery Gale by her deceased husband Charles Gale, Lady Stranleigh was born Barbara (Babs) Barron, the sister of Beatrice Barron. Her strong suit was getting married: "If entries in *Who's Who* were strictly truthful, the entry concerning Lady Stranleigh might have ended as follows: *hobbies: getting married.* She had floated through life shedding husbands as she went. She had lost three by divorce and one by death." She asked Mr. Satterthwaite to go to Abbot's Mead, the family pile, and look into her daughter Margery's claims that she was being haunted by ghostly voices. Lady Stranleigh was subsequently discovered murdered in her bath. "The Voice in the Dark" from *The Mysterious Mr. Quin.*

STRAVINSKA, ANNA AKA Anna Quimper, she was formerly a ballet dancer with Madame Joliet's Ballet Maritski, but she had left the troupe in London. A devout Catholic, she would not countenance the divorce her husband wanted. Her strangulation on board a train was observed by Mrs. McGillicuddy; her body was hidden in the sarcophagous on the grounds of Rutherford Hall and was finally discovered three weeks after her death by Lucy Eyelesbarrow. The body was identified as Martine Dubois' until Lady Stoddart-West resolved the misunderstanding. *4.50 from Paddington.*

STREPTITCH, COUNT FEODOR ALEXANDROVITCH As a member of the gang that burglarized Lady Anchester's Orion House during the bazaar for the Ostrovian refugees, Feodor Alexandrovitch acted as the Grand Duchess Pauline's secretary. "Jane in Search of a Job" from *The Golden Ball.*

STRETE, MILDRED The wife of the deceased Canon Strete, the younger daughter of Carrie Louise Serrocold and her first husband Eric Gulbrandsen, Mildred was a bitter woman who as a child resented her beautiful sister Pippa and later was envious of Pippa's equally beautiful daughter Gina. She was offended that Stoneygates, the family pile, had been transformed into a home for delinquent boys under Lewis Serrocold's direction. *They Do It with Mirrors.*

STROUD, CHARMIAN The niece of the late Mathew Stroud, she and her fiancé . . . Edward Rossiter . . . had expected to receive all of Mathew Stroud's estate. Shocked when they discovered that he had only left them a puzzle, they con-

sulted Miss Marple in the hope that she could solve it for them. "Strange Jest" from *Three Blind Mice and Other Stories.*

STROUD, MATHEW The deceased great-great uncle to Charmian Stroud and to her fiancé, Edward Rossiter, he bequeathed them only this dying message: "*You'll* be all right, my pretty pair of doves." Luckily for the young lovers, Miss Marple's Uncle Henry had also been a bachelor with a fondness for puns. "Strange Jest" from *Three Blind Mice and Other Stories.*

STUART, ARLENA *See* **MARSHALL, ARLENA.**

STUART, HELEN *See* **MARSHALL, ARLENA.**

STUBBS, SIR GEORGE Assumed name of James Folliat. As Sir George, husband of Lady Hattie Stubbs, he owned Nasse House, the Folliat ancestral home. Sir George was "a big man with a rather florid red face and a slightly unexpected beard. It gave a rather disconcerting effect of an actor who had not quite made up his mind whether he was playing the part of a country squire, or of a 'rough diamond' from the Dominions." *Dead Man's Folly.*

STUBBS, LADY HATTIE The assumed name of Elsa, the Italian wife of Sir George Stubbs (alias James Folliat), who was twenty years his junior. Some members of the household at Nasse House were beginning to guess that she was not as subnormal in intelligence as she appeared. She vanished and was presumed drowned during the fête at Nasse House. *Dead Man's Folly.*

ST. VINCENT, MRS. The mother of Barbara and Rupert St. Vincent, Mrs. St. Vincent had been the mistress of Ansteys and was now a member of the "poor gentlefolk." She agreed to take tenancy of Lord Listerdale's London townhouse, and she came to know Listerdale in his disguise of Quentin, the butler. When Listerdale was unmasked, he asked Mrs. St. Vincent to marry him, an offer which she could not, in all honesty, turn down. "The Listerdale Mystery" from *The Golden Ball.*

ST. VINCENT, BARBARA (BABS) The daughter of Mrs. St. Vincent, Barbara and her family were very hard up, a condition she deplored: "Frowsy landladies, dirty children on the stairs, haddocks for breakfast that aren't quite-quite and so on." On a vacation she had taken in Egypt as her cousin Amy's companion, she had met the wealthy young Jim Masterton. After the St. Vincents moved into 7 Cheviot Place, where Barbara was in her "proper setting," Masterton asked her to marry him, a proposal which was quickly accepted. "The Listerdale Mystery" from *The Golden Ball.*

ST. VINCENT, RUPERT The son of Mrs. St. Vincent and the brother of Barbara St. Vincent, Rupert was "a son starting on the bottom rung of office life." His suspicions were aroused when the family moved into Lord Listerdale's vacant London townhouse and, after a bit of sleuthing, he managed to unmask Lord Listerdale, who had been disguised as the butler Quentin. "The Listerdale Mystery" from *The Golden Ball.*

STYLPTITCH, COUNT A Herzoslavakian nobleman, he was for a time Prime Minister of that country. "The Grand Old Man of the Balkans. The Greatest Statesman of Modern Times. The biggest villain unhung. . . . Every move and countermove in the Near-East for the last twenty years had had Count Stylptitch at the bottom of it. He's been a dictator and a patriot and a statesman—and nobody knows exactly what he has been, except that he's been a perfect king of intrigue." While Prime Minister, he learned the truth of the scoundrel Queen Varaga and her connections with King Victor; although he did not reveal any of this information while he lived, he included it in his memoirs. In thanks to Jimmy McGrath who had once saved his life, Stylptitch directed in his will that McGrath was to have his memoirs, which included all the details of his colourful and controversial activities. *The Secret of Chimneys.*

SUBAYSKA, MADAME The name given by Mr. Parker Pyne to a woman who stopped the train on which Mrs. Elsie Jeffries was travelling by means of a smoke bomb. She was discovered in Mrs. Jeffries' compartment, concurrent with the disappearance of the jewels. "Have You Got Everything You Want?" from *Parker Pyne Investigates.*

SUGDEN, SUPERINTENDENT The Superintendent of the Middleshire police and a bastard son of Simeon Lee's, Sugden was "a tall man with square shoulders and a military bearing who had an aquiline nose, a pugnacious jaw and a large flourishing chestnut-coloured moustache." Colonel Johnson, Sugden's superior, said that Sugden was without excessive imagination and for this reason asked Poirot to help in the investigation of the death of Simeon Lee. *Hercule Poirot's Christmas.*

SUMMERHAYES, MAJOR JOHN (JOHNNIE) Husband of Maureen, and Poirot's host (at seven guineas a week) in Broadhinny, he was of late in the India service and had returned to take over the decaying family estate. He tried his hand at farming but was unsuccessful, so he converted the house into something of a guest house that specialized in "roughing it." He had a terrible temper, which Poirot experienced first-hand almost to his cost. He thought his wife found Hercule Poirot's name familiar, but he thought she had confused it with "Home Perm." *Mrs. McGinty's Dead.*

SUMMERHAYES, MAUREEN Wife of Major John Summerhayes, she was manageress of the guest house in which Poirot "decidedly suffered" during the investigation of the McGinty murder case. Used to life in India where everything was done by servants, she was incapable of cleaning, or cooking anything edible. She thought that Poirot looked like a hairdresser. *Mrs. McGinty's Dead.*

SUTCLIFFE, ANGELA (ANGIE) "A very fascinating woman, mainly owing to the fact that she seldom took anything seriously," she was an actress who once had an affair with Sir Charles Cartwright and was self-acclaimed as "appallingly indiscreet." She also thought, on the whole, that it was a compliment to be suspected as a murderess. *Three-Act Tragedy.*

SUTCLIFFE, JOAN Wife of Henry and mother of Jennifer Sutcliffe, she was Bob Rawlinson's elder sister. Rawlinson chose her to convey the jewels entrusted to him by Prince Ali Yusuf out of the country, but because he also knew that she could not keep a secret, he hid them in Jennifer's tennis racquet without telling anyone. *Cat Among the Pigeons.*

SWARTZ, GERTRUDE The housekeeper to Dr. Rosen, she was an old German servant who had been with Rosen for forty years, and was one of the four suspects in the death of the doctor. "The Four Suspects" from *The Thirteen Problems.*

SWEENY, MRS. A "clean, wholesome-looking woman," this hearty lady was the keeper of the keys of Moat House to which Tommy Beresford and Julius Hersheimmer had been falsely led in their search for Tuppence Cowley. *The Secret Adversary.*

SWEETIMAN, MRS. Owner and proprietress of the post office and the sweetshop, she remembered that Mrs. McGinty bought a bottle of ink the day before her murder. Poirot described Mrs. Sweetiman: "undoubtedly the brains of the village of Broadhinny." *Mrs. McGinty's Dead.*

SWETTENHAM, EDMUND The son of the redoubtable Mrs. Swettenham and an aspiring writer, Edmund was "a tall rather solemn young man with an anxious face and large spectacles [and] sandy hair." He was dragged by his mother to Little Paddocks to see the murder that had been advertised by Rudi Scherz in the *Chipping Cleghorn Gazette.* He was also in love with Phillipa Haymes, whom he eventually married. *A Murder is Announced.*

SYMMINGTON, BRIAN Elder son of Richard and Mona Symmington and half-brother of Megan Hunter, along with his brother Colin, he was much more loved by their mother than was Megan. *The Moving Finger.*

SYMMINGTON, MONA "Querulous, bridge-playing" wife of Richard Symmington, she was mother of his sons Colin and Brian and the mother of Megan Hunter by her former husband, Captain Hunter. She had an "anaemic middle-aged prettiness" concealing "a selfish, grasping nature." A woman "ailing in health . . . neurotic, hysterical," she was ill-treated by her first husband and disliked her daughter by that marriage, Megan. Her death by poison was pronounced to be suicide. *The Moving Finger.*

SYMMINGTON, RICHARD Partner in the solicitors' firm of Messrs. Galbraith, Galbraith and Symmington, he was the husband of Mona Symmington, father of Colin and Brian and the stepfather of Megan Hunter. "Not one to set the pulses madly racing," he and his clerk Miss Ginch were the subject of one of the anonymous letters in Lymstock, which suggested illicit relations between them, and which was the cause of her leaving the firm. *The Moving Finger.*

TAMPLIN, THE HONOURABLE LEN-OX The daughter of Lady Rosalie Tamplin and second cousin of Katherine Grey, she was described "a daughter such as Lenox was a sad thorn in Lady Tamplin's side, a girl with no kind of tact, who actually looked older than her age, and whose peculiar sardonic form of humour was, to say the least of it, uncomfortable." Lenox fell in love with Derek Kettering and was complimented by Poirot: "It was you who gave me the first inkling of the truth when you said that the person who committed the crime need not have been on the train at all. Before that, I could not see how the thing had been done." *The Mystery of the Blue Train.*

TAMPLIN, LADY ROSALIE The mother of Lenox Tamplin and the cousin of Katherine Grey, Lady Rosalie had been married several times—the first husband was "merely an indiscretion," and was seldom mentioned; the second, a button manufacturer, died after three years; the third was Viscount Tamplin; and the fourth husband, Charles "Chubby" Evans, she married for "pure pleasure." A well-known figure on the Riviera, Lady Tamplin owned the Villa Marguerite,

which had once been the residence of Madame Daubreuil. (See *Murder on the Links*.) *The Mystery of the Blue Train.*

TANIOS, BELLA Daughter of Emily Arundell's sister Arabella, cousin of Charles and Theresa Arundell, wife of Dr. Jacob Tanios and mother of Edward and Mary, she had a "pathetic eagerness to assimilate and memorize" her cousin Theresa's exotic clothes. Miss Peabody called her a "miserable kind of woman—always wanting what she hadn't got." She died from an overdose of a sleeping medication. *Dumb Witness.*

TANIOS, DR. JACOB Husband to Bella, he was the father of Edward and Mary Tanios. Despite his personal charm, Miss Arundell disapproved of him on the grounds of his Greek nationality. He doted on his wife, but speculated with the money she inherited and lost it. *Dumb Witness.*

TANNER, INSPECTOR A Scotland Yard Inspector, he was known as Major Metcalf during his incognito investigation of matters at Monkswell Manor. "Three Blind Mice" from *Three Blind Mice and Other Stories.*

TAVENER, CHIEF INSPECTOR The Scotland Yard man in charge of the investigation of Aristide Leonides' death, he said to Charles, "Of course you realize, I expect, that these questions I'm asking are a lot of hooey! Doesn't matter a hoot who was in the house or who wasn't, or where they all were on a particular day. . . . Because it at least gives me a chance to look at them all, and size them up, and hear what they've got to say, and to hope that, quite by chance, somebody might give me a useful pointer." He and Detective Sergeant Lamb arrested Brenda Leonides and her platonic lover Laurence Brown for the murder. *Crooked House.*

TEEVES, DR. The physician to Mr. Templeton, Teeves was an agent for the Big Four gang. *The Big Four.*

TEMPLE, MISS Because she was the maid who served the fatal cocktails to the Reverend Stephen Babbington, Poirot asked her to repeat the scene for his benefit. *Three-Act Tragedy.*

TEMPLE, ELIZABETH A mutual friend with Miss Marple to Henry Clithering, she was travelling on the Famous Houses and Gardens of Great Britain tour. Someone—observed but not identified by Joanna Crawford and Emlyn Price—pushed a boulder down upon her, causing her to lapse into a coma from which she awoke only sporadically, calling for Miss Marple, with whom she had previously discussed Verity Hunt. She thought love "one of the most frightening words there is in the world." Miss Marple thought she radiated integrity. *Nemesis.*

TEMPLETON, MR. AND MRS. They were agents of the Big Four. Mr. Templeton posed as a dying man whose circumstances were investigated by Poirot when Mabel Palmer persuaded him to take interest in the case. *The Big Four.*

TEMPLETON, CHARLES The secretary to Dr. Rosen, Templeton was also an undercover agent working for Sir Henry Clithering. "The Four Suspects" from *The Thirteen Problems.*

TEMPLETON EDGAR *See* **CAYMAN, LEO.**

TEMPLETON, MICKY *See* **DARRELL, CLAUD.**

TEMPLETON, ROSE EMILY *See* **NICHOLSON, MOIRA.**

THEODOFANOUS, DAPHNE *See* **ZERKOWSKI, COUNTESS RENATA.**

THÉRÈSE, SISTER A member of Edward Goring's group, she accompanied Victoria Jones, alias Sister Marie des Anges, on the flight to Baghdad. *They Came to Baghdad.*

THESIGER, JIMMY The employer of Mr. and Mrs. Stevens, Thesiger appeared to be no more than a wealthy, young, high-society rake who had nothing weightier on his mind than the business of living off his inheritance. He was the best friend of the murdered Gerald Wade. *The Seven Dials Mystery.*

THIBAULT, MAITRE ALEXANDRE Genial and courteous lawyer for Madame Giselle, he identified Madame Giselle's body as that of Marie Angèlique Morisot, and explained the nature of his client's business at the court of inquest. *Death in the Clouds.*

THOMAS, DR. He examined the man, later identified as Alex Pritchard, when he and his companion Bobby Jones discovered his body at the bottom of a cliff near the golf course. *Why Didn't They Ask Evans?*

THOMAS, DR. GEOFFREY Dr. John Humbleby's partner and Rose Humbleby's lover, he catered to the more modern-minded persons of the village with his innovative methods, in contrast to the traditional techniques of Dr. Humbleby. Luke Fitzwilliam considered Thomas as a suspect for the killings in Wychwood. *Murder is Easy.*

THOMAS, GLADYS See HOBHOUSE, VALERIE.

THOMPSON, DR. "The famous alienest" present at the first "conference of powers" on the A.B.C. murders case, Dr. Thompson suggested that an "alphabetical complex" linked the murders, although he did not rule out coincidence in the case. He discussed the psychological implications of the murders. *The A.B.C. Murders.*

THOMPSON, MRS. The "rather notorious medium," she conducted a séance after the Trent's party. While in a trance, Mrs. Thompson said to Jack Trent, Dermot West and Sir Alington West: "Danger! Blood! Not very much blood—quite enough." This augmented Dermot West's apprehension of foul play. "The Red Signal" from *Witness for the Prosecution.*

TIDDLER, DETECTIVE SERGEANT WILLIAM (TOM) Tiddler was the competent assistant requested by Chief Inspector Dermot Craddock to accompany him to St. Mary Mead to look into the death of Heather Badcock: "He's a good man, and what's more, he's a film star. That might come in useful." *The Mirror Crack'd from Side to Side.*

TIO, MARCUS Victoria Jones reflected that the proprietor of the Hotel Tio was "a charming person in his child-like enthusiasm for life, but conversation with him reminded her of Alice in Wonderland's endeavours to find a path that led to the hill. Every topic found them returning to the point of departure." *They Came to Baghdad.*

TODD, MR. AND MRS. Mrs. Todd convinced Poirot to undertake the search for Eliza Dunn, her missing cook, but when Mr. Todd convinced her to terminate the investigation, she signalled her change of mind by sending Poirot a one-guinea consultation fee. Poirot framed the guinea and hung it on the wall. "The Adventure of the Clapham Cook" from *The Under Dog.*

TOMLINSON, MR. A retired Indian judge, he took the Duchess of Leith and Mr. Satterthwaite on a picnic to the World's End at Coti Chiaveeri, where he opened Rosina Nunn's Indian box and discovered the opal that Alec Gerard had been convicted of stealing. "The World's End" from *The Mysterious Mr. Quin.*

TOMLINSON, JEAN A physiotherapist at St. Catherine's Hospital, she lived in Mrs. Nicoletis' student hostel and thought that anyone straying from the straight and narrow should be punished. *Hickory, Dickory, Dock.*

TOSSWILL, DR. A minor official connected with the British Museum, Tosswill was a member of the Men-her-Ra expedition and thought that Poirot's lecture on magic and superstition was a "hotch-potch of ignorance and credulity." "The Adventure of the Egyptian Tomb" from *Poirot Investigates.*

TREDWELL "A butler like an archbishop," he served Lord Caterham at Chimneys. *The Secret of Chimneys; The Seven Dials Mystery.*

TREFUSIS, EMILY This determined and ingenious woman set out to investigate the murder of Captain Trevelyan in an attempt to clear her fiancé and the Captain's nephew, James Pearson, of suspicion. She enlisted Charles Enderby, a reporter on the *Daily Wire*, to aid her in the case. She knew that she was in complete control of James, and thought she could "run him and make something of him." She saw a striking similarity of nature and attitude between herself and the shrewd old invalid, Caroline Percehouse. *The Sittaford Mystery.*

TREFUSIS, OWEN Sir Reuben Astwell's secretary, he was "a prim, proper young man, disarmingly meek, the type of man who can be, and is, systematically bullied. One could feel quite sure that he would never display resentment." "The Under Dog" from *The Under Dog.*

TRELAWNY, MR A partner in the firm Askwith and Trelawny of St. Loo, he was Lady Tressilian's solicitor. He informed Superintendent Battle that Nevile Strange's trust was to be divided not between Nevile and his wife, as Kay Strange thought, but between Nevile and his first wife, Audrey. *Towards Zero.*

TRENT, CLAIRE The wife of Jack Trent, in Dermot West's eyes she was: "A statue, a beautiful statue, a thing of gold and ivory and pale-pink coral—a toy for a king, not a real woman." Dermot feared for her sanity. "The Red Signal" from *Witness for the Prosecution.*

TRENT, HUGO Son of Reggie Trent and Pamela Chevenix-Gore, he was described by his fiancée Susan Cardwell: "Hugo, poor sweet, is a perfect pet, but he's got absolutely no brains." He was present when his uncle Sir Gervase was killed. "Dead Man's Mirror" from *Murder in the Mews.*

TRENT, JACK The husband of Claire Trent and the best friend of Dermot West, Jack invited Sir Alington, a prominent mental specialist, to the party, and Dermot feared his motives to certify Claire Trent's insanity. "The Red Signal" from *Witness for the Prosecution.*

TRENTON, CHARLES AKA "Enoch Arden." Charles Trenton was Frances Cloade's ne'er-do-well cousin. He was involved in a scandal and sent off by the Trenton family to the Colonies, but arrived back in England in time to help

Frances gain ten thousand pounds from David Hunter and Rosaleen Cloade. As, "Enoch Arden" in Warmsley Vale, he intimated that he knew something about Robert Underhay that he could be paid to conceal. He was later found dead in room 5 at the Stag. *Taken at the Flood.*

TRESSILIAN The butler at Gorston Hall, Tressilian had been with Simeon Lee for forty years. Lydia Lee said: "He's like the faithful old retainers of fiction. I believe he'd lie himself blue in the face if it was necessary to protect one of the family!" *Hercule Poirot's Christmas.*

TRESSILIAN, LADY CAMILLA A friend to Aubrey Strange and to Thomas Royce, and widow to Sir Matthew Tressilian, she was a self-confessed enthusiast of scandal and gossip. She admitted that Gull's Point was the perfect locale for observing the eternal triangle. She often proclaimed: "It seems I am one of those creaking gates—those perpetual invalids who never die." The poignantly defiant but helpless old woman was found murdered in her bed, her skull crushed. *Towards Zero.*

TREVELYAN, CAPTAIN JOSEPH ARTHUR A retired Royal Navy officer and the owner of Sittaford House, he was inordinately fond of money. He was the brother of the deceased Mary Pearson, whose marriage he had always resented, Brian Pearson, Sylvia Dering and James Pearson. His best friend and crony was Major Burnaby. A misogynist, he was "not the sort of man who had any knowledge of what literature meant . . . he was a regular philistine in every way—devoted to sport." He was found dead and his head crushed with one of the sandbags with which he kept out the winter cold from under his study door. *The Sittaford Mystery.*

TREVES, MR. An old friend of Lady Tressilian's, "he was said to know more of backstairs history than any man in England and he was a specialist on criminology. Unthinking people said Mr. Treves ought to write his memoirs. Mr. Treves knew better. He knew that he knew too much." Mr. Treves thought the standard belief that a murder mystery began with the act of killing was erroneous: "The story begins long before that—years before sometimes—with all the causes and events that bring certain people to a certain place at a certain time on a certain day." He agreed with Inspector Battle, who said: "The murder itself is the *end* of the story. It's Zero Hour." After climbing the stairs at Balmoral Court, obeying an out-of-order sign on the lift, Mr. Treves died of a heart attack. The sign had been unauthorized. *Zero Hour.*

TRIPP, ISABEL AND JULIA The sisters were considered "appalling women." As far as Hastings could tell, they were "vegetarians, theosophists, British Israelites, Christian Scientists, spiritualists and enthusiastic amateur photographers." They held a séance at which Miss Arundell was wrapped in a "luminous haze." It was later proved to be a sign of phosphorus poisoning. *Dumb Witness.*

TUCKER, MARLENE Daughter of Mr. and Mrs. Jim Tucker, sister to Gary and Marilyn, and grand-daughter to the murdered Merdell, she was named the pretend "victim" in Mrs. Oliver's Murder Hunt at the fête at Nasse House. She became a real murder victim during the course of the Hunt, and was garotted with a piece of clothesline. *Dead Man's Folly.*

TUCKERTON, THOMASINA ANN (TOMMY) The daughter of the deceased Thomas Tuckerton and the step-daughter of Mrs. Tuckerton, Tommy was a member of the "Chelsea crowd." Mark Easterbrook first saw her when she was engaged in a fight with Lou Ellis over Gene Pleydon in Luigi's espresso bar off King's Road in Chelsea. A week later he read her obituary in *The Times*; she supposedly died of encephalitis. *The Pale Horse.*

TURNER, MRS. Felise Marchaud dreamt that Mrs. Turner had been murdered by her husband who had then left Heather Cottage for parts unknown. Felise attributed the cries of "Murder—help! Murder!" that Jack Hartington heard at 7:25 every morning to Mrs. Turner's spirit. "The Blue Jar" from *Witness for the Prosecution.*

TURNER, JOSEPHINE (JOSIE) The secret wife of Mark Gaskell, she procured a job for her cousin Ruby Keene as a dancer with her at the Majestic Hotel in Danemouth. Miss Marple remarked: "She's got one of those shrewd, limited practical minds that never do foresee the future and are usually astonished by it." *The Body in the Library.*

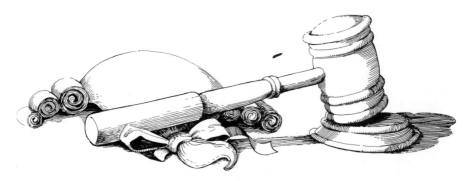

UNDERHAY, CAPTAIN ROBERT
Rosaleen Cloade's first husband, he was
known by Major Porter when they were
in Nigeria. Underhay married Rosaleen,
but she could not abide life in the bush
so he sent her home and agreed to give
her a divorce. He had confided to Porter
about pretending to be dead and assuming another identity, such as "Enoch Arden." Porter related Underhay's story in
the presence of Jermey Cloade at the Coronation Club. *Taken at the Flood.*

UNKERTON, MRS. The wife of Ned Unkerton and the hostess of Greenways
House, she was bothered about the ghostly
visage of the Elliot ancestor in the west
window at Greenways and decided to have
the window pane replaced without in-
forming her husband. "The Shadow on
the Glass" from *The Mysterious Mr. Quin.*

UNKERTON, NED The *nouveau riche*
owner of Greenways House and the husband of Mrs. Unkerton, he hosted the
party at which Jimmy Allenson and Moira
Scott were killed. The house contained
the legendary Elliot family ghost that was
connected with a window pane on the

west wall of the house. Unkerton made
the mistake of inviting Richard Scott,
Scott's wife Moira and Scott's former lover
Iris Staverton to the same party. "The
Shadow on the Glass" from *The Myste-
rious Mr. Quin.*

UPJOHN, MRS. Agreeable mother of
Julia Upjohn, she was in Intelligence work
during the war and loved it, but her present thirst for excitement was quenched
by bus travel to exotic places. Mrs. Upjohn recognized the identity of "Angelica" as a dangerous freelance agent she
had known in the war. *Cat Among the
Pigeons.*

UPJOHN, JULIA Daughter of Mrs. Upjohn and a great friend of Jennifer Sutcliffe's, she discovered gems in her friend
Jennifer's tennis racquet and took them
to Poirot. Poirot told her: "I have formed
a high opinion of your courage and your
resource." *Cat Among the Pigeons.*

UPWARD, LAURA The former famed
actress Laura Hargraves and "madre" of
Robin Upward, she adopted him, thinking his mother was a ballerina who died

in Paris. She employed Mrs. McGinty to aid Janet Groom. An invalid tied to her chair, she was also a snob, who had been made a protegé of one Alex Roscoff but dropped him when she discovered that he was not a Russian emigré but the son of a tailor. On the night that Robin Upward and Ariadne Oliver went to Cullenquay, she was found strangled in her chair with the scent of perfume in the air and lipstick on a cup on the table. *Mrs. McGinty's Dead.*

UPWARD, ROBIN The identity of Evelyn Hope after his adoption by Laura Upward. He was a talented playwright, and was collaborating with Ariadne Oliver on an adaptation of one of her detective novels for the stage. *Mrs. McGinty's Dead.*

Van Aldin, Rufus An American millionaire and the father of Ruth Kettering, he was determined to divorce her from her husband, Derek Kettering, and hired Mr. Goby to provide information on Kettering's infidelities. He purchased the Heart of Fire rubies for his daughter, and after her death hired Poirot to investigate the murder. *The Mystery of the Blue Train.*

Valdez, Lola The famous Peruvian dancer, she responded to Poirot's excuse that he was too much the antique to dance with her: " 'Ah, it ees nonsense that you talk there! You are steel young! Your hair, it is steel black!' Poirot winced slightly." After Poirot solved the double mystery of Iris Russell's death and the attempted murder at the Jardin des Cygnes, he said: " 'Senora, as the evening advances I become more brave. If you would dance with me now—' 'Oh, yes, indeed. You are the cat's whiskers, M. Poirot. I inseest on dancing with you'." "Yellow Iris" from *The Regatta Mystery.*

Vandemeyer, Janet *See* Finn, Jane.

Vandemeyer, Marguerite AKA Rita, she was an international Bolshevist agent who shadowed Danvers, saw him giving the Draft Treaty plans to Jane Finn and followed Jane by pretending to be her aunt. She had once had an affair with Sir James Peel Edgerton. Tuppence Cowley, who applied for the post of her parlourmaid, found Mrs. Vandemeyer dead of an overdose of chloral. *The Secret Adversary.*

Vanderlyn, Mrs. The employer of Leonie and with her a guest at Lord Mayfield's country house when the bomber plans were stolen, Mrs. Vanderlyn had had three husbands, an Italian, a German, and a Russian, and through them had made some very valuable contacts for her espionage work in those countries. This "Vulture Number One," as Lord Mayfield called her, "was usually at a disadvantage when left alone with members of her own sex. That charming sympathetic manner of hers, so much appreciated by members of the male sex, did not for some reason or other commend itself to women." Lady Julia Carrington felt the woman laid "it on with a palette knife." Luckily, the scent with which she doused herself was expensive. "The Incredible Theft" from *Murder in the Mews.*

VANE, CLARICE Dr. Haydock's niece, she was attracted to Harry Laxton but chose instead to befriend Laxton's young bride, Louise, and was indignant at the gossip about Harry circulating in the village. "The Case of the Caretaker" from *Three Blind Mice and Other Stories.*

VAN HEIDEM, PAUL (VAN) A Dutchman, he was the official spokesman for Mr. Aristides at the Brain Trust complex. He appeared genial but "had a smile which didn't touch his cold pale eyes." He thought using a leper colony as a front for the complex was "a very good joke." *Destination Unknown.*

VAN RYDOCK, RUTH With her sister Carrie Louise Serrocold, Ruth had been a schoolgirl friend of Miss Marple's. Like her sister, she was American, rich and had been married three times, "each time to an extremely wealthy man, and the resultant divorces had increased her bank balance without in the least souring her disposition." Worried about her sister, Carrie Louise, Ruth sent Miss Marple to Stoneygates to find out if anything was amiss. *They Do It with Mirrors.*

VAN SCHUYLER, MARIE Thought by Mr. Ferguson to be a "vicious old harridan," she was cousin to Cornelia Robson and employed Nurse Bowers. Miss Van Schuyler was somewhat distressed when Mr. Ferguson, her cousin's suitor whom she had dismissed for having no social position, was revealed to be Lord Dawlish. On learning that her shawl had been used to muffle the shot that killed Linnet Doyle, she snapped: "Impertinence!" Despite her eminent social position and prestige, Miss Van Schuyler had one "little idiosyncrasy": as explained by Nurse Bowers, "She can't help it, you know, but she does—er—take things. Especially jewellery." *Death on the Nile.*

VANSITTART, ELEANOR Impeccably dressed mistress at Meadowbank, she had "every hair in place." She was killed by a blow to the head with a sandbag. *Cat Among the Pigeons.*

VAN SNYDER, MRS. COURTLAND An alias used by Prince Vladiroffsky, Mrs. Van Snyder was "a middle-aged fashionably-dressed woman" from Detroit. She claimed to have been drugged by a man accompanied by a similarly doped girl, who was thought to have been Prince Vladiroffsky and Marise (Tuppence Beresford). She was not expecting the second entrance of Tommy Beresford and Secret Service agent Evans into her suite. "The Man Who Was No. 16" from *Partners in Crime.*

VANSTONE, COMMANDER See CARTWRIGHT, SIR CHARLES.

VAN STUYVESANT, CORA Before Herman Guteman's death, she had been provided with an allowance from the estate which could be stopped at any time by her step-daughter, Ellie Guteman Rogers. For this reason, she pretended to like Michael Rogers, her son-in-law, even though he sensed that she hated him *Endless Night.*

VARAGA, QUEEN OF HERZOSLAVAKIA See MORY, ANGÈLE.

VARESCO, PAUL "A nasty bit of work," he was the silent partner of Countess Vera Rossakoff in the fashionable lounge, Hell. The Countess Vera, on learning of his failed attempt to implicate her in the cocaine and jewel gang, described him as "that lizard, that monster, that double-faced, double-crossing, squirming adder of a pig's son, Paul Varesco!" "The Capture of Cerberus" from *The Labours of Hercules.*

VAREZ, PAUL DE A French invalid leaving the Blitz Hotel accompanied by a hospital nurse, he was thought to be No. 16 but was really an accomplice who allowed the real No. 16 time to escape. "The Man Who Was No. 16" from *Partners in Crime.*

VASSILIEVITCH The dastardly Bolshevist agent threatened Mr. Roberts during his European adventure. The Grand Duchess Olga commented that locked doors meant nothing to Vassilievitch. "The Case of the City Clerk" from *Parker Pyne Investigates.*

VASSILOVNA, OLGA *See* **DEMIROFF, OLGA.**

VAUCHER, JEANNE AKA the Countess Czarnova. She was a Parisian guttersnipe when she met Vaucher, who was then a jeweller. Vaucher took her off the streets, and married her, but she eventually left him and began drinking absinthe. As the Countess Czarnova she claimed to be descended from the Radzynski family. She had been the *cher amie* of the King of Bosnia in days gone by and had once smuggled papers out of the kingdom for him. "Mr. Satterthwaite had seen the Countess at Monte Carlo for many seasons now," on each occasion with a different man. When she was about to lose the last of her money at the roulette table at the Casino in Monte Carlo, the croupier, who happened to be her estranged husband Pierre Vaucher, took pity on her and assigned her Mr. Satterthwaite's winnings. She and Vaucher were then reunited. "The Soul of the Croupier" from *The Mysterious Mr. Quin.*

VAUCHER, PIERRE The estranged husband of Jeanne Vaucher, Pierre Vaucher

was Harley Quin's guest at the "Hedges and Highways" party and was there reunited with his wife after saving her at the gambling table. *See* **VAUCHER, JEANNE.** "The Soul of the Croupier" from *The Mysterious Mr. Quin.*

VAUGHAN, GWENDA The secretary of some years to Leo Argyle, she was in love with her employer; Chief Constable Major Finney remarked that "these women secretaries always seem to be in love with their boss." Gwenda and Leo had planned to marry, but Dr. Calgary's investigation of the murder of Leo's wife Rachel caused them to postpone their plans for the future. *Ordeal by Innocence.*

VAUGHAN, MAGDALEN The twin sister of Matthew Vaughan and the great-niece of Lily Crabtree, Magdalen Vaughan had first met Sir Edward Palliser nine years before on board the *Saluric,* returning from America. Then she had been no more than "a charming child," but now, a tall dark girl of twenty-six, appealing to him for help in solving the mystery of the death of her great-aunt Lily Crabtree, "she was still a very good-looking girl, but had lost. . . that look of dewy untouched youth." Sir Palliser thought that "she was of the type that can only see one thing at a time and what she was seeing at this moment was her own need." "Sing a Song of Sixpence" from *The Listerdale Mystery.*

VAUGHAN, MATTHEW The twin brother of Magdalen Vaughan and the great-nephew of Lily Crabtree, Matthew owed a great deal of money, and his only income seemed to come from the little bit of journalism that he pounded out on a typewriter that made "a nasty, irritating tap-tapping noise" according to Martha. "Sing a Song of Sixpence" from *The Listerdale Mystery.*

VAUGHN, LADY MILLICENT CASTLE The name assumed by Gertie when she came to consult Poirot. Daughter of an impecunious Irish peer, she was engaged to wed the Duke of Southshire in one of the best matches in England. However, his jealous and suspicious nature would have signalled the end of the engagement should an indiscreet but innocent letter she wrote to a soldier, long since dead, fall into his hands. "The Veiled Lady" from *Poirot's Early Cases.*

VAVASOUR, ROLEY The son of Lady Stranleigh's first cousin and second in line to the Stranleigh title after Margery Gale, Roley Vavasour had asked Margery to marry him but she refused; she felt that he had "always been out for what he can get." He participated at Mrs. Lloyd's séance. "The Voice in the Dark" from *The Mysterious Mr. Quin.*

VENABLES, MR. An acquaintance of Rhoda Despard's, Mr. Venables was a "been everywhere and done everything" kind of Englishman before he became confined to a wheelchair after contracting polio. Mark Easterbrook said: "He had I was sure, first-class brains. And there was something about him—what word could I use?—the word vulpine came to me. Predatory—destructive. A man, perhaps, too clever to be a killer himself—but a man who could organize killing very well if he wanted to." Zachariah Osborne had identified him as the man that he saw following Father Gorman the night that the priest was killed. *The Pale Horse.*

VENTNOR, MR. *See* **SHAW, MR.**

VERA The twin sister of Una Drake, she helped establish the double alibi which was the subject of Una's bet with Montgomery Jones. "The Unbreakable Alibi" from *Partners in Crime.*

VERONEAU, INEZ *See* **ROSSAKOFF, COUNTESS VERA.**

VERRALL, DETECTIVE ISPECTOR JOE "For a detective," said Anthony Eastwood, "he was a singularly human person." Verrall, however, was a member

of the Patterson gang in the plot to con Eastwood out of his collection of old enamels. "Mr. Eastwood's Adventure" from *The Listerdale Mystery.*

VERRIER, MONSIEUR French archaeologist and friend of Dr. Leidner, he arrived at the dig shortly after the death of Mrs. Leidner. He exuded cheer and bonhomie until informed of Mrs. Leidner's death: "He was profuse in condolences and apologies, finally striding over to Dr. Leidner and clasping him warmly by both hands. 'What a tragedy! My God, what a tragedy! I have no words. *Mon pauvre collegue.'* And shaking his head in one last ineffectual effort to express his feelings, the little man climbed into his car and left us." *Murder in Mesopotamia.*

VICAR The vicar at St. Mary Mead, he came to the village after Leonard Clement died. According to Miss Marple, "one of the great mysteries of St. Mary Mead was what made the vicar remember certain things—only outstripped by the greater mystery of what the vicar could manage to forget." He attended the special reception held by Marina Gregg at Gossington Hall for the St. John's Ambulance Association fête, and heard Heather Badcock tell Miss Gregg that she had been suffering from the German measles the time that they had met in Bermuda. *The Mirror Crack'd from Side to Side.*

VICTOR, KING AKA Monsieur Chelles; Captain O'Neill; Prince Nicholas; Monsieur Lemoine. He was, according to Superintendent Battle, "one of the most celebrated jewel thieves in the world." He was known as King Victor to his gang in Paris, and was a confederate of Angele Mory's before his capture and incarceration on a minor charge for seven years. After Mory's accession as Queen Varaga of Herzoslavakia, the two corresponded under the names Captain O'Neill and Virginia Revel which appeared to be letters from an adulterous wife to her lover, but which were actually coded messages concerning the crown jewels of Herzoslavakia and other *sub rosa* matters. As Prince Nicholas, he conned a great deal of money from American businessmen by promising them oil concessions when he took the throne of Herzoslavakia but, being unmasked, he was forced to flee the country. As Monsieur Lemoine of the Sûreté, "he was tall, wore a light-coloured overcoat and glasses, and for the rest, had a short pointed black beard and slightly foppish manner." As Monsieur Chelles, he was staying at the Jolly Cricketers in Market Basing, purporting to be a traveller in silk. *The Secret of Chimneys.*

VINEGAR, MRS. The name Miss Marple gave to the postmistress in Carristown, "a middle-aged woman with rather a vinegar face." Miss Marple flummoxed her into revealing the destination of a package of used clothes she claimed to have mailed, an act which shocked the Home Secretary. The postmistress thought Miss Marple as "scatty as they make them, poor old creature." *Nemesis.*

VINER, AMELIA A friend of the late Jane Harfield's, she was delighted at having outlived Jane and attributed her longevity to eating a slice of brown bread every night and taking a "little stimulant with her meals." Her main concerns were with the shortness of skirts, the absence of good, woolen stockings among the younger women of the village and the High Church ways of the new curate in St. Mary Mead. She provided Poirot with a newspaper clipping about a jewel robbery that took place at the Villa Margeurite during World War I while Major Knighton was a patient in the villa hospital. *The Mystery of the Blue Train.*

VITELLI, SIGNOR An Italian official, he represented his country at Monsieur le President Grosjean's conference on the problems of student unrest. He compared the student riots in his country to a "swarm of bees. A disaster of nature intensified." Signor Vitelli suggested that corruption in high places was another factor in the problem. *Passenger to Frankfurt.*

VLADIROFFSKY, PRINCE AKA No. 16 and Mrs. Courtland Van Snyder, was sent to investigate why other Russian agents failed to report their activities. As Prince Vladiroffsky, he contacted his alleged agents Blunt and Marise (Tommy and Tuppence Beresford) and kidnapped Tuppence; as Mrs. Van Courtland he portrayed a drugged woman terrorized by a Russian agent; and as No. 16 he was, in Mr. Carter's estimation, "a man who gave us great trouble in the war, an ubiquitous kind of fellow who turned up all over the place where we least wanted him. He is a Russian by birth, and an accomplished linguist—so much so that he can pass as half a dozen other nationalities, including our own. He is also a past master in the art of disguise. And he has brains. It was he who devised the No. 16 code." "The Man Who Was No. 16" from *Partners in Crime.*

VOLE, LEONARD The husband of Romaine Vole, he had become the friend, financial manager and heir to Emily French, the murder victim. She was discovered dead following an evening spent in Vole's company at her home, and he was then arrested and charged with her murder. However, his wife refused to verify his alibi, but when she broke down on the witness stand, her damning testimony was disqualified and Vole was acquitted. "Witness for the Prosecution" from *Witness for the Prosecution.*

VOLE, ROMAINE AKA Romaine Heilger and Mrs. Mogson, she was married to Leonard Vole, but had been an actress in Vienna and maintained that her real husband was still alive in an Austrian insane asylum. As Romaine Heilger, she was an Austrian subject and the mistress of the defendant at the trial for the murder of Miss French. As Mrs. Mogson, she was a semi-literate woman with an acid-scarred face who wrote to Mr. Mayherne offering to sell him evidence which would disprove Romaine Vole's testimony. "Witness for the Prosecution" from *Witness for the Prosecution.*

VON DEINIM, CARL A German refugee, von Deinim was a chemist researching immunization from and contamination of certain gases. The real Carl von Deinim committed suicide and a British Intelligence agent who had assumed his identity was in Leahampton to track down the fifth columnists "M" and "N." The agent fell in love with Sheila Perenna, but was arrested as a spy after documents of sabotage schemes written in invisible ink were found in his possession. *N or M?*

VON WALDSAUSEN, the GRÄFIN CHARLOTTE AKA Big Charlotte; Charlotte Krapp. She was an old schoolfriend of Lady Matilda Checkheaton's. "A whale of a woman, Stafford Nye thought, there really was no other word to describe her. A great, big, cheesy-looking woman, wallowing in fat. Double, treble, almost quadruple chins. . . . A great, white, creased, globbering mass of fat was her face. And set in it, rather like currants in a vast currant bun, where two small black eyes." A woman of unbelievable wealth, The Gräfin Charlotte was the financier behind the Youth Movement figureheaded by Franz Joseph. When she smiled, she looked like a crocodile to Sir Stafford. The Countess Renata Zerkowski told Sir Stafford: "That is her mode of power. To control youth." *Passenger to Frankfurt.*

VYSE, MR. Rosina Nunn's producer, Mr. Vyse had considered producing Alec Gerard's play, *Rachel's Children,* but decided against it when Gerard was convicted of stealing Rosina Nunn's prize opal. He was a member of Miss Nunn's party at World's End at Coti Chiaveeri. "The World's End" from *The Mysterious Mr. Quin.*

VYSE, CHARLES Cousin to Nick Buckley, he was a lawyer with the firm of Messrs. Vyse, Trevannion and Wynnard. Poirot's opinion was that "he has the good poker-face, Mr. Vyse, besides looking as though he had swallowed one." *Peril at End House.*

WADE, GERALD (GERRY) AKA Number One; One o'clock. He was one of the young men working in an apparently ornamental capacity at the Foreign Office. Wade had an unfortunate inability to get up in the morning, which a group of his associates sought to remedy with the prank of hiding a number of alarm clocks in his room. He was killed with a sleeping potion the night before the prank was scheduled. *The Seven Dials Mystery.*

WADE, IRIS The estranged wife of Reginald Wade, she had agreed to a six-month moratorium before moving out to marry her lover, Sinclair Jordan. After Mr. Parker Pyne undertook Reggie's cause, Iris discovered hitherto unsuspected strains of jealousy in her attitude towards her husband. "The Case of the Discontented Husband" from *Parker Pyne Investigates.*

WADE, LORAINE Gerald Wade's stepsister and also the object of his affection, "she had a supremely natural manner and, as she looked up smiling, the faint wild rose flush deepened in her cheeks. Her eyes were a very dark blue—like cornflowers." *The Seven Dials Mystery.*

WADE, REGINALD The uxorious husband of Iris Wade, he was "the inarticulate type. The type that finds it hard to put into words anything connected with the emotions." He asked Mr. Parker Pyne to save his marriage before Iris moved out to join her lover, Sinclair Jordan. Aided by the seductively lovely Madeleine de Sara, Parker Pyne undertook Reggie Wade's almost hopeless case. "The Case of the Discontented Husband" from *Parker Pyne Investigates.*

WAGSTAFF, INSPECTOR He was consulted concerning the recent history of the Borgia goblet theft and said to Poirot: "I speak a bit of Italiano, you know, and I went over and had a pow-wow with the Macaronis." "The Apples of the Hesperides" from *The Labours of Hercules.*

WAINWRIGHT, DEREK A friend of Sylvia Carslake's, he managed to arouse an almost insane pitch of jealousy in the anonymous narrator: "He had everything that I hadn't. He had brains and a witty tongue. He was good-looking, too, and—I'm forced to admit it—a thoroughly good chap." The narrator was convinced that his jealousy had driven Sylvia into Wainwright's consoling arms. "In a Glass Darkly" from *The Regatta Mystery*.

WAKE, ALFRED An "elderly antiquarian clergyman," he was the vicar of Wychwood and interested in the Roman ruins near the village. He provided Luke Fitzwilliam with numerous facts, gossip and hearsay on the deaths and personalities in Wychwood. *Murder is Easy*.

WALES, EMMA A housemaid of Lady Tressilian's, she was referred to as "the tall thin bit of vinegar" by Superintendent Battle. She overheard the argument between her employer and Nevile Strange the night of Lady Tressilian's death. *Towards Zero*.

WALLACE, BELLA AND RUBE They aided Mary Montresor's husband hunting scheme by playing Mrs. Pardonstenger, "a big florid lady with peroxide hair" and a gun-toting thug respectively. "The Golden Ball" from *The Golden Ball*.

WALTERS, ESTHER AKA Esther Anderson. She was secretary to Mr. Rafiel for five years and was extremely competent and efficient at her work. Esther was in love with Tim Kendall, who would have gone to any lengths to make her—or the money he discovered would be hers on Mr. Rafiel's death—his own. She later married Edmund Anderson, and Miss Marple remembered that the last time they met, "Esther had looked as though she hated her and probably she had hated her at that moment. But now, well now, perhaps, she might feel slightly grateful. She might have realized that she, herself, might even have been under a stone slab in a respectable churchyard, instead of living a presumably happy life with Mr. Anderson." *A Caribbean Mystery; Nemesis*.

WANSTEAD, PROFESSOR A traveller on the garden tour with Miss Marple, he had been commissioned by Jason Rafiel to keep an eye on her. He looked as though he had been "carelessly assembled by an ambitious child out of chunky bricks." In his official capacity he was acting as confidential advisor to the Home Office, attempting to prove the theory he shared with Sir Andrew McNeil, that Michael Rafiel was innocent of the murder of Verity Hunt. *Nemesis*.

WARBURTON, CAPTAIN JIM Agent for the Mastertons, he insisted on calling himself "Captain" although he had "never been within miles of a German." *Dead Man's Folly*.

WARGRAVE, ALFRED JAMES Rosegrower living at Emsworth, Berkshire, he testified that the type of rose grown around Hunterbury Hall was in fact a thornless variety, invalidating Jessie Hopkins' testimony that she pricked herself with a rose. *Sad Cypress*.

WARGRAVE, MR. JUSTICE LAWRENCE JOHN AKA Ulick Norman Owen and Una Nancy Owen, which formed the anagram "unknown." Mr. Justice Wargrave recognized his personal desire to commit murder, and for that reason had chosen a profession which allowed him to do so legally. He was reputed to be "a hanging judge." As U.N. Owen, he commissioned Isaac Morris to purchase Indian Island and make all the arrangements for the house party. His death complied with this verse of the nursery rhyme: "Five little Indian boys going in for law; One got in Chancery and then there were four." *And Then There Were None*.

WARING, HAROLD Patriotic and somewhat provincial Undersecretary to the Prime Minister, he was a man with a future in politics. On holiday at Lake Stempka in Herzoslavakia, he became acquainted with Mrs. Rice and not only fell in love with her daughter, Elsie Clayton, but witnessed what appeared to be manslaughter. Luckily for his reputation, Poirot managed to relieve him from alarm by means of a well-placed telegram. "The Stymphalian Birds" from *The Labours of Hercules.*

WARREN, DR. The physician in Sittaford, he lived in a house near the police station, and was not pleased at being roused by Constable Graves and Major Burnaby to accompany them in breaking into Captain Trevelyan's bungalow. The grudging doctor established the time and cause of Trevelyan's death. *The Sittaford Mystery.*

WARREN, ANGELA Aunt of Carla Lemarchant and sister-in-law of Amyas Crale, she was a half-sister to Caroline Crale. Poirot accurately pinpointed the day she jokingly put valerian—an herb whose smell can unfavourably be compared to that of old socks—in Amyas' beer, which became an important key to unlocking the sixteen-year-old mystery. *Five Little Pigs.*

WATERHOUSE, EDITH Sister of James Waterhouse, who was terrified of her, she was the kind of woman with "no nonsense about her who is extremely intolerant of nonsense in others." *The Clocks.*

WATERHOUSE, JAMES Henpecked brother of Edith Waterhouse, he lived with his sister in the neighbourhood where the first murder victim was discovered. "He had to look apologetic so often that it was practically his prevailing cast of countenance." *The Clocks.*

WAVERLY, ADA The wife of Marcus Waverly and the mother of Johnnie Waverly, she was described by Poirot: "a love of money warred with the essential mother love of Mrs. Waverly, and the latter was at last gaining the day." "The Adventure of Johnnie Waverly" from *Three Blind Mice and Other Stories.*

WAVERLY, MARCUS The husband of Ada Waverly and the father of Johnnie

Waverly, he was the only member of the household who liked Tredwell the butler. Mr. Waverly approached Hercule Poirot with an interesting kidnapping case: he had received ransom notes for his son, Johnnie, before the boy had been kidnapped; the notes described when the kidnapping would take place and demanded money for *not* kidnapping the boy. Just as the notes had promised, the boy disappeared at the appointed time. "The Adventure of Johnnie Waverly" from *Three Blind Mice and Other Stories.*

WAYNFLETE, HONORIA She acted as librarian and museum caretaker at Wych Hall, formerly her family's home, and attempted to aid Luke Fitzwilliam in his investigation of the deaths at Wychwood. *Murder is Easy.*

WEARDALE, SIR HARRY An Admiral and the First Sea Lord, Sir Harry was the husband of Lady Juliet Weardale and the father of Leonard Weardale. He was Lord Alloway's guest the night the submarine plans were stolen. "The Submarine Plans" from *The Under Dog.*

WEARDALE, LADY JULIET The wife of Sir Harry Weardale and the mother of Leonard Weardale, she believed that her son stole the submarine plans. "The Submarine Plans" from *The Under Dog.*

WEARDALE, LEONARD The son of Lady Juliet and Sir Harry Weardale, he was "rather an effeminate-looking young man" who came under suspicion in the theft of the submarine plans. "The Submarine Plans" from *The Under Dog.*

WEATHERBY, PAULINE Sister of the deceased Iris Russell, ward and sister-in-law to Russell Barton, and beloved of the whimsical Tony Chappell, she attended the memorial dinner held by Russell on the fourth anniversary of his wife's death at the Jardin des Cygnes. She was in the midst of a lover's spat with Tony the night of the dinner, and collapsed during the dinner in much the same way as her sister had four years before. Potassium cyanide was discovered in Stephen Carter's pocket. "Yellow Iris" from *The Regatta Mystery.*

WEBB, BELLA Bella Webb was the cook at The Pale Horse where she lived with Sybil Stamfordis and Thyrza Grey. It was rumoured that she, like her mother, was a witch. During the séance at The Pale Horse, Mark Easterbrook remarked: "Bella's hand was cold and boneless—it felt like a slug in mine and I shivered in revulsion." She had "a queer, rather formless face, like something made in putty by a child who had strayed in to play in a sculptor's studio. It was the kind of face . . . that you sometimes see amongst a crowd in an Italian or Flemish painting." *The Pale Horse.*

WEBB, SHEILA ROSEMARY Employee at the Cavendish Secretarial and Typing Bureau, daughter of Miss Millicent Pebmarsh, niece and adopted daughter of Mrs. Lawton, she was sent by her employer, Katherine Martindale, to the residence of the blind Miss Pebmarsh; there she discovered a murdered man who was surrounded by four rather disparate-looking clocks, all set at 4:13. Included among the clocks was one bearing her own middle name. She rushed out of the flat after discovering the body and flew into the arms of Colin Lamb, whom she eventually married. *The Clocks.*

"WEEPING LADY WITH THE SILVER EWER" *See* **GLEN, ASPASIA; CHARNLEY, LADY ALIX.**

WELMAN, LAURA Aunt to Elinor Carlisle and Roderick Welman, wife of Henry Welman and, once the mistress of Sir Lewis Rycroft, she was the natural mother of Mary Gerrard by Sir Lewis and understandably devoted to her, a fact which bothered virtually everyone else at the Hall. She stated: "I've had one besetting sin always, Mary: I'm proud. Pride can be the devil. It runs in our family." Her health was deteriorating owing to a stroke, but her death was caused by morphine poisoning. *Sad Cypress.*

WELMAN, RODERICK (RODDY) Nephew of Laura Welman, he fell in love with Mary Gerrard and broke his engagement with Elinor Carlisle, who nevertheless made him the sole beneficiary of her newly written will. A romantic, he identified Mary Gerrard with "Atalanta" and admiringly called Elinor Carlisle "la Princesse Lointaine." Roddy's pride, stung by Mary's rejection, would not allow him to admit that he had come back to England to be near her. Poirot cleared him of suspicion and revealed the real perpetrator of the murder. *Sad Cypress.*

WELSH, JOE A farmhand on the Gardners' Cornwall farm, he fell in love with Hannah Moorhouse, alias Amelia Rymer, who told Parker Pyne: "Joe's good enough for me and I'm good enough for him. We suit each other and we're going to be happy. . . . Joe's a dear, good fellow, but he's weak. Give him money and you'd ruin him. I've got him off the drink now, and I'll keep him off it." "The Case of the Rich Woman" from *Parker Pyne Investigates.*

WELWYN, DAVID A young man who was in love with Sarah Lacey, he was invited to Kings Lacey by Em Lacey as a match for Diana Middleton. He was "rather obviously addicted to soap and water." When Sarah rejected him, he turned to Diana. "The Theft of the Royal Ruby" from *Double Sin.*

WENDOVER, MR. *See* **PROTHERO, WALTER.**

WEST, SIR ALINGTON The uncle of Dermot West, he was a famous Harley Street authority on mental disease who, with his nephew, was a guest at the Trents' party. In an argument, which was overheard by Sir Alington's butler, Johnson, Sir Alington threatened to exclude Dermot from his will and Dermot responded by threatening to shoot him. Five minutes later, Johnson found the body of his master shot through the heart. "The Red Signal" from *Witness for the Prosecution.*

WEST, BASIL The private secretary to Sir George Grayle, he was having an affair with Pamela Grayle and absolutely delighted Lady Ariadne Grayle. Although Lady Ariadne plagued everyone within complaining distance, she "did not snap at Basil West . . . because nobody ever snapped at Basil. His smile disarmed you before you began." "Death on the Nile" from *Parker Pyne Investigates.*

WEST, CHLOE ELIZABETH An actress, she was hired by George Barton to impersonate his dead wife Rosemary, at the Luxembourg. She received a phone call purporting to be from Barton cancelling her appearance. "Her voice was rather conscious of its diction." *Sparkling Cyanide.*

WEST, DAVID Second son of Raymond and Joan West and the affectionate grandnephew of Miss Marple, he worked with British Railways and provided schedules of those trains on which Mrs. McGillicuddy might have observed the murder. *4.50 from Paddington.*

WEST, DERMOT AKA Milson, he was Sir Alington West's nephew and Jack Trent's best friend. Even though he loved Claire Trent, he thought that she was insane, and learned that his uncle had been invited to the party to certify her madness. During his life Dermot occasionally experienced a psychic phenomena which he termed "the Red Signal." It warned him of danger once in Mesopotamia and saved his life and he received the same signal at the Trents' party. After quarrelling with Sir Alington West, Dermot passed himself off as Milson, his absent

manservant, and escaped. Cawley discovered a discharged revolver, the murder weapon, in Dermot's dresser. "The Red Signal" from *Witness for the Prosecution.*

WEST, GILLIAN The beloved of Charlie Burns and Phil Eastney, and musical protegé of the latter, she was the "Helen" observed by Mr. Satterthwaite and Harley Quin at *I Pagliacci.* In spite of her incredible beauty, "there was nothing of the conscious siren about her." However, she had a history of tragedies caused by her beauty. "The Face of Helen" from *The Mysterious Mr. Quin.*

WEST, JOAN The wife of Raymond West, mother of two sons, the aunt of Louise Oxley and the cousin of Giles Reed, she was originally Joyce Lemprière, an artist and a member of the Tuesday Night Club. Miss Marple described her paintings as "remarkable pictures of square people with curious bulges on them." By the time of *Sleeping Murder,* she and her husband were leading a very highbrow life in London. *The Thirteen Problems;* "Miss Marple Tells a Story" from *The Regatta Mystery;* "Greenshaw's Folly" from *The Adventure of the Christmas Pudding; Sleeping Murder.*

WEST, MAGDA *See* **LEONIDES, MAGDA.**

WEST, MAUREEN An employee at Katherine Martindale's Cavendish Secretarial and Typing Bureau, she thought her boss "mean as hell." She was "a rather rakish-looking brunette with the kind of hair-do that suggested she'd been out in a blizzard lately." *The Clocks.*

WEST, NORMA *See* **RESTARICK, NORMA.**

WEST, RAYMOND The husband of Joan West and the father of two sons, Raymond West was Miss Marple's celebrated nephew, of whom Leonard Clement said: "He is, I know, supposed to be a brilliant novelist, and has made quite a name as a poet. His poems have no capital letters in them, which is, I believe, the essence of modernity. His books are about unpleasant people leading lives of surpassing dullness." West was quite fond of his Aunt Jane, but like his wife Joan, he remained a background figure in the Marple books, often referred to but seldom seen. *Murder at the Vicarage; The Thirteen Problems;* "Miss Marple Tells a Story" from *The Regatta Mystery;* "Greenshaw's Folly" from *The Adventure of the Christmas Pudding; Sleeping Murder.*

WESTCHESTER, BISHOP OF This "handsome and well-gaitered" cleric was "dear Robbie" to Miss Marple, who knew him when he was a child. He responded affectionately to his "Aunt Jane." *At Bertram's Hotel.*

WESTHOLME, LADY "A big masterful woman with a rocking-horse face," she was an American who married an English country squire. Elected as an MP by a sizeable majority, it was rumoured that she was soon to become Undersecretary when her party came back into power. "She was much respected and almost universally disliked." Dr. Gerard responded to Lord Westholme's statement of pride in his wife's political activities: "Because they take her away from home? That is understandable." Dr. Gerard's remark— "that woman should be poisoned. . . . It is incredible to me that she has had a husband for many years and that he has not already done so"—recalls the famous exchange that took place in the House of Commons between Lady Astor and Winston Churchill: "Winston, if you were my husband I should flavour your coffee with poison" followed by "Madam, if I were your husband, I should drink it." *Appointment with Death.*

WESTON, COLONEL The Chief Constable presiding over the investigation of the death of Arlena Marshall. Workmanlike and unremarkable in every way, he was a perfect foil for Poirot's more suc-

cessful sleuthing. Weston first met Poirot when both were investigating a case in St. Loo (*Peril at End House*). He asked Poirot to lend a hand in the Marshall case. *Evil Under the Sun.*

WETHERBY, MISS A post-mistress in St. Mary Mead, she was appalled that the Skinners had given Gladys Holmes a reference which said she was willing, sober and respectable but did not mention her honesty: "That seems to me most significant! . . . You'll see the Skinners won't find anyone else, and then, perhaps that dreadful hypochrondriac sister will have to get up and do something!" "The Case of the Perfect Maid" from *Three Blind Mice and Other Stories.*

WETHERBY, MR. Step-father to Diedre Henderson and husband of Mrs. Wetherby, he resented his own failure and the fact that his step-daughter, through inheritance, had control of all the money in the family. He looked at her with "cold dislike." *Mrs. McGinty's Dead.*

WETHERBY, MRS. Invalid mother of Diedre Henderson and wife of Mr. Wetherby, she was a former employer of Mrs. McGinty. She had a fear of open windows which saved her daughter from incrimination as the murderess of Laura Upward, and she was convinced that James Bentley murdered Mrs. McGinty. *Mrs. McGinty's Dead.*

WETHERBY, CAROLINE One of the old village gossips in St. Mary Mead, she lived two doors away from Miss Marple. According to Leonard Clement, Caroline was "a mixture of vinegar and gush." *Murder at the Vicarage; The Body in the Library.*

WEYMAN, MICHAEL Architect hired by Sir George Stubbs to design a tennis pavilion and repair the "Folly," he was an old friend and admirer of Sally Legge, and escaped with her when her husband's moody preoccupation with the state of the world was more than she could bear. *Dead Man's Folly.*

WHALLEY, JONATHAN He wrote a letter to John Ingles in which he stated that he was being chased by the Big Four gang. Ingles gave this information to Poirot, but when the latter went to see Whalley, he found the man dead. *The Big Four.*

WHARTON, COLONEL A colleague of Jessop's, he spoke "with a kind of machine-gun volley abruptness." The pressures of Intelligence bureaucracy appeared to have affected him: "he was pacing up and down, from time to time throwing off a remark in a jerky manner." *Destination Unknown.*

WHEELING, EMMA She and her husband found Canon Pennyfather unconscious on the road near Milton St. John and thought the Canon was merely drunk until they saw his collar. She referred to the Canon as "ducks," and fed him broth instead of the sausage and mash he wanted. *At Bertram's Hotel.*

WHISTLER, DR. JAMES Police-surgeon for Croydon, he examined Madame Giselle's body and set the time of death as one hour previous, but was unable to identify the particular poison as the cause of death. *Death in the Clouds.*

WHITFIELD, DR. Lawyer with Messrs. Whitfield, Pargiter and Whitfield, he was Captain Michael Seton's solicitor. He told Poirot about the provisions of the wills left by both Sir Matthew Seton and Captain Michael Seton. *Peril at End House.*

WHITTAKER, ELIZABETH A teacher at The Elms, where Joyce Reynolds was murdered, she helped arrange the fatal Hallowe'en party. She showed "a kind of academic contempt" for the "quite happy giggling" at the party. Desmond Holland and Nicky Ransome tendered her among their incredible but unique list of murder suspects, speculating that she was either a sex-starved old maid or a lesbian. *Hallowe'en Party.*

WHITTINGTON, EDWARD Inept member of the Bolshevist revolutionary gang, he triggered the interest of both Tuppence Cowley and Tommy Beresford in the Draft Treaty case. Julius Hersheimmer called him "the skunk, with his big sleek fat face." For Tuppence, it was child's play to deceive him. *The Secret Adversary.*

WICKHAM, CLAUDE He had been commissioned by Lady Roscheimer to write the music for her amateur Harlequinade. Mr. Satterthwaite thought that "Wickham was an unutterable ass, but he could write music—delicate gossamer stuff, intangible as a fairy web—yet with nothing of the pretty-pretty about it." "Harlequin's Lane" from *The Mysterious Mr. Quin.*

WIDBURN, MRS. Wife of Archie Widburn and a friend of Jane Wilkinson's, she held the dinner party where Jane confused the Trojan prince Paris with the city of Paris. This incident aroused Donald Ross' suspicions about the identity of the Jane Wilkinson he met at Sir Montagu Corner's dinner. *Lord Edgware Dies.*

WILBRAHAM, MAJOR CHARLIE A soldier recently returned from East Africa, he consulted Mr. Parker Pyne to free him from the boredom of his tame English life. Mr. Parker Pyne proceeded to entangle him in an adventure which involved rescuing the short, fair-haired, blue-eyed, slightly anaemic Freda Clegg from the clutches of two enormous Negroes, which involved a secret message written in Swahili, one of the Major's languages. Freda thought he was just like someone from a book. "The Case of the Discontented Soldier" from *Parker Pyne Investigates.*

WILKINSON, JANE The estranged wife of George Alfred St. Vincent Marsh, the step-mother of Geraldine Marsh and the aunt by marriage of Captain Ronald Marsh, she was a beautiful and talented young American actress. She wished to divorce her husband and marry the Duke of Merton, whom she called her "dreamy monk," and attempted to enlist Poirot's aid in her plan. *Lord Edgware Dies.*

WILLARD, SIR GUY The son of Sir John Willard and Lady Willard, Guy Willard was twenty-two years old and had just lately come down from Oxford. Hastings remarked that there was "a certain impulsiveness about his manner that reminded one of his mother." Guy Willard took over the Men-her-Ra excavation after the death of his father. "The Adventure of the Egyptian Tomb" from *Poirot Investigates.*

WILLARD, SIR JOHN The husband of Lady Willard and the father of Guy Willard, he was a devoted Egyptologist. Not long after the discovery of the tomb of the legendary Egyptian King Tutank-Amen by Lord Carnarvon and Howard Carter, Sir John and Mr. Bleibner discovered the tomb of King Men-her-Ra, who was "one of the shadowy kings of the eighth Dynasty." Sir John died quite suddenly at the excavation site, apparently from heart failure. "The Adventure of the Egyptian Tomb" from *Poirot Investigates.*

WILLETT, MRS. AKA Mrs. Johnson, she was the mother of Violet Willett. She and her daughter hosted get-togethers at Sittaford House, and it was at one of their séances that the spirits announced the murder of her landlord, Captain Trevelyan. Mr. Rycroft thought both mother and daughter "Colonial, of course. No real poise," but Inspector Narracott held that Mrs. Willett was "an exceedingly clever woman." *The Sittaford Mystery.*

WILLETT, VIOLET AKA Miss Johnson, she was the daughter of Mrs. Willett and in love with Brian Pearson. She was present at the séance where Captain Trevelyan's murder was announced on the planchette. Major Burnaby said she was

"scraggy, of course, they all were nowadays." As Miss Johnson, she booked passage from Melbourne to London. *The Sittaford Mystery.*

WILLIAMS, CONSTABLE A young police officer working in the investigation of Lady Tressilian's murder, he found a bloody bundle of clothes at the bottom of Nevile Strange's closet. *Towards Zero.*

WILLIAMS, INSPECTOR An old acquaintance of Lady Frances Derwent's, he liked the young aristocrat: "He enjoyed this friendly conversation with an Earl's daughter. Nothing stuck-up or snobbishy about Lady Frances." He supplied her with the information that only one photograph had been found on the body discovered by Bobby Jones. *Why Didn't They Ask Evans?*

WILLIAMS, CECILIA "Thin, frail and indomitable," she was the governess of Angela Warren and was resident at the home of the Crales at the time Amyas Crale was murdered. Sixteen years later, she was an ancient, poverty-stricken spinster when Poirot interviewed her and she made Poirot feel like "a meek and apprehensive little boy." Somewhat of a man-hater, she witnessed Caroline wiping fingerprints off her husband's beer bottle and was thus convinced of Caroline's guilt, although she never testified to that effect because she thought Caroline was justified. *Five Little Pigs.*

WILLIAMS, MAUDE The daughter of Alfred Craig's murdered wife, she was "a very healthy young woman, with a full buxom figure that Poirot approved. About thirty-three or -four, he judged. and by nature dark-haired, but not one to be dictated to by nature." When Poirot met her, she had "determinedly golden hair" and "enough confidence for two." To aid Poirot, she took a job at Wetherbys. She also visited Laura Upward the night of that lady's death and was thus the light-haired lady whom Edna saw. *Mrs. McGinty's Dead.*

WILLIAMSON, FLIGHT LIEUTENANT
An Air Force officer travelling with the group of twelve between Damascus and Baghdad, he overheard Smethurst, the murder victim, speaking to an unidentified person in the dark. "The Gate of Baghdad" from *Parker Pyne Investigates*.

WILLIAMSON, TED A mechanic, he met Poirot when the detective's expensive Messarro Gratz broke down. He was "one of the handsomest specimens of humanity" Poirot had ever seen, "a simple young man with the outward semblance of a Greek God." Poirot approved of Williamson's looks: "There were, he considered, too many rats in spectacles about." In an effort to find his lost love, "Nita," Williamson asked Mr. "Pwarrit" to help him. "The Arcadian Deer" from *The Labours of Hercules*.

WILLOUGHBY, DR. Poirot consulted him about Dolly Jarrow. His late father, who was also a doctor, had known Dolly Jarrow at two distinct times in her life: once when she was a child and he was doing a study of twins; and shortly after her son was killed in a tragic accident when he assessed her degree of convalescence from the terrible emotional shock. *Elephants Can Remember*.

WILLS, MURIEL "Rabbit-faced" spinster who, under the name Anthony Astor, was the successful author of such witty and daring plays as *One Way Street* and *Little Dog Laughed*, she witnessed the deaths of both the Reverend Babbington and Sir Bartholomew Strange. Behind a nondescript appearance, this clever, observant woman was merciless with her pen. Only she and Sir Bartholomew Strange recognized that the butler John Ellis was actually Sir Charles Cartwright in disguise. *Three-Act Tragedy*.

WILMOTT, AMBASSADOR RANDOLPH
The U.S. ambassador to the Court of St. James, he consulted Tuppence and Tommy Beresford at Blunt's International Detective Agency about a mistaken exchange of his bag for Senator Westerham's. "The Ambassador's Boots" from *Partners in Crime*.

WILSON, DETECTIVE SERGEANT "A very large, blue-clad, impassive-looking policeman," he accompanied Inspector Japp in the investigation of the Madame Giselle murder. He discovered a blowgun behind Poirot's seat on the aeroplane, which led the inquest jury to lay a verdict of wilful murder against Poirot, but it was dismissed immediately by the Coroner. The incident greatly amused Japp. *Death in the Clouds*.

WILSON, ELLEN The wife of William Wilson and the mother of Alfred, she was the housekeeper at End House. "Completely uninterested" in the events surrounding her, she and her husband witnessed the will of their employer, Nick Buckley. *Peril at End House*.

WILSON, JOHN "A regular John Bull Englishman, middle-aged and burly," he was a friend of Paul Deroulard's, and was with him at the time of Deroulard's death. Wilson suffered from angina, and his trinitrine was used to murder Deroulard. His account of Deroulard's death is that the man "went very red in the face, and down he fell." "The Chocolate Box" from *Poirot's Early Cases*.

WINBURN, MR. The father of Mrs. Lancaster and the grandfather of Geoffrey Lancaster, he heard two sets of footsteps walking away forever in the haunted Lancaster home. "The Lamp" from *The Golden Ball*.

WINDYFORD, DICK The jealous former lover of Alix Martin (*née* King), he was alarmed when Alix inherited a small fortune. "She had become a woman of means. Delicacy and pride stood in the way of Dick's asking her to be his wife." After he called her unexpectedly one day, Alix very fortunately put off Dick's visit until the following night. "Philomel Cottage" from *Witness for the Prosecution.*

WINTERSPOON, HENRY "A large, dreamy-looking man with a benignant expression. He looked kindly but stupid. It came as something of a shock to learn that he was the chief government analyst and an authority on rare poisons." He analyzed the toxin that killed Madame Giselle, identifying it as the venom of *Dispholidus Typus*, "better known as the boomslang, or tree snake." He had never before heard of using this particular poison to murder a human being and provided Inspector Japp with the list of poison specialists with which to confront Dr. Bryant. *Death in the Clouds.*

WITHERS, JESSIE The nurse of Johnnie Waverly, she, along with most of the domestic staff, had been fired by Mr. Waverly when he discovered yet another ransom note pinned to his pillow. "The Adventure of Johnnie Waverly" from *Three Blind Mice and Other Stories.*

WODDELL, AGNES A maid in the Symmington household, she often consulted Miss Partridge for advice but was murdered one day before they could converse. *The Moving Finger.*

"WOMAN WITH THE SCARF" *See* **GLEN, ASPASIA.**

WOOD, J. BAKER An American millionaire, he was a connoisseur and collector of miniatures staying at the Seaside Hotel in Charlock Bay. Hastings reported that "he was a large vulgar man, very much overdressed and wearing a diamond solitaire ring. He was blustering and noisy." The Cosway miniatures that Mary Durrant was meant to deliver to him were stolen. "Double Sin" from *Double Sin.*

WOODWORTH, GENERAL LORD "A choleric gentleman," he was the father of the Honourable Patricia Brice-Woodworth who was present at the Luxembourg the night George Barton was killed. The general was outraged: "If a girl couldn't go out with her fiancé to dine in a restaurant without being subjected to annoyance by detectives of Scotland Yard, what was England coming to?" *Sparkling Cyanide.*

WREN, CHRISTOPHER This student of architecture, appropriately named, was almost universally disliked by the residents of Monkswell Manor. He had a perspicacity that others found disconcerting, and a shrill laugh that irritated them. He wore checked ties of a particularly virulent green. He also threatened to strangle Mrs. Boyle on numerous occasions. "Three Blind Mice" from *Three Blind Mice and Other Stories.*

WRIGHT, GERALD The "disgruntled young schoolmaster," he was Elaine Fortescue's lover but much more interested in her money than in her. Her father attempted to separate them after discovering the young man's leftist sympathies. He "scatted" when Rex Fortescue confronted the pair "like a ton of bricks." *A Pocket Full of Rye.*

WU LING His family had records of the Lost Mine in Burma, and he voyaged on the S.S. *Assuta* to England to sell the documents. The party attempting to obtain Wu Ling's documents had hired another Chinese to impersonate him, but the imposter found it easier merely to murder the unfortunate merchant. Charles Lester was arrested for his murder. "The Lost Mine" from *Poirot's Early Cases.*

WYATT, CAPTAIN A surly, rather unsociable invalid, he and his native servant Abdul lived in one of the bungalows on the Sittaford estate. Miss Percehouse was of the opinion that he was an opium smoker. He maintained that he didn't "mind seeing people when I am in the mood—but it has to be my mood, not theirs. . . . Nobody understands the art of living nowadays. . . . I could teach people how to live if they would listen to me." *The Sittaford Mystery*.

WYE, MAUD According to Dolly Bantry, Maud Wye, a friend of Sylvia Keene's, was "one of those dark ugly girls who manage to make an effect somehow." Mrs. Bantry saw Maud kissing Jerry Lorimer, Sylvia's fiancé. "The Herb of Death" from *The Thirteen Problems*.

WYLDE, MARTIN In love with the loyal but slightly stupid Sylvia Dale, he was arrested, tried, convicted and sentenced to hang for the murder of Lady Barnaby. Harley Quin and Mr. Satterthwaite took an interest in his plight and managed to identify the real murderer. "The Sign in the Sky" from *The Mysterious Mr. Quin*.

WYNWOOD, PROFESSOR A specialist in code-breaking, he was called in to examine the Revel-O'Neill correspondence by Superintendent Battle. It took him no time at all to break the code in the letters. Invited to stay to lunch, he replied: "Bad habit, lunch. A banana and a water biscuit is all any sane and healthy man should need in the middle of the day." *The Secret of Chimneys*.

YAHMOSE Imhotep's eldest son and the brother of Sobek, Renisenb and Ipy, Yahmose was the husband of Satipy and "was always in a state of anxiety over something or other." Satipy was constantly goading him to stand up to his father and demand a partnership in the family business. Yahmose was a typical hen-pecked husband, and comments from the mouth of his wife like: "Sometimes I feel that I am married to a worm" did nothing to improve his disposition. He was killed by an arrow. *Death Comes as the End.*

YARDLY, LORD The Tenth Viscount Yardly was the husband of Lady Yardly and the father of their two daughters. He had served in the Boer War and had "a good humoured bonhomie about him that was distinctly attractive and made up for any lack of mentality." In need of cash, Yardly had to make a painful decision. He could sell the Star of the East diamond, which he had obtained in China for his wife, unaware that she had given it to Gregory Rolf and substituted the diamond with a paste replica. Or he could lease the family pile, Yardly Chase, which Hastings called "one of the show places of England," for a film. "The Adventure of 'The Western Star' " from *Poirot Investigates.*

YARDLY, LADY MAUDE *Née* Stopperton, she and Lord Yardly were one of Christie's aristocratic couples who spent at least part of the World War I years in the United States. In California, she had given Gregory Rolf her famous diamond, the Star of the East, which he then rechristened the Western Star and gave to Mary Marvell as a wedding present, "The Adventure of 'The Western Star' " from *Poirot Investigates.*

YOASCHBIM Said to have an operatic voice equal to Caruso's, he was rumoured by the news media to be "a Yugoslav, a Czech, an Albanian, a Magyar and a Bulgarian, with a beautiful impartiality." Like Caruso's, Yoaschbim's voice could shatter glass. "The Face of Helen" from *The Mysterious Mr. Quin.*

Z

ZARA The crystal gazer at the Primrose League Fête, she told retired Inspector

Evans that he would "very shortly—very shortly indeed—be engaged on a matter of life or death—life or death to one person. . . . You must be very careful—very, very careful. If you were to make a mistake—the smallest mistake—" the result, she recounted in her sing-song, droning voice, would be death. "Accident" from *Witness for the Prosecution.*

ZARIDA *See* COPLING, NURSE.

ZERKOWSKI, COUNTESS RENATA AKA Mary Ann; Daphne Theodofanous. She was the daughter of an English nobleman and a Greek woman, and was the granddaughter of an Austrian. Sir Stafford Nye first met her in Frankfurt, where her strong resemblance to both himself and his dead sister intrigued him. As the agent Mary Ann, she convinced Sir Stafford to allow her to drug him and steal his passport so that she could make use of the extraordinary physical similarity between them to escape the city. He met her as the Countess Renata Zerkowski at the American Embassy dinner, but she did not acknowledge their previous acquaintance. As Daphne Theodofanous, she met him secretly at a performance of Wagnerian music. She and Sir Stafford Nye combined their espionage abilities and worked on dismantling the Youth Movement which was headed by Renata's old protector, the Gräfin Charlotte von Waldsausen. *Passenger to Frankfurt.*

ZEROPOULOS, MONSIEUR A Greek antique dealer, he was interviewed by Poirot regarding a blowpipe and dart, which he sold three days before the murder of Madame Giselle. He described the purchaser of the pipe as an American: "His voice was in his nose. He could not speak French. He was chewing the gum.

He had tortoise-shell glasses. He was tall and, I think, not very old." His shop on Rue St. Honore was a high-class antique store, but he was unable to charge Americans the prices he once did: "Alas! They have had the depression over there!" *Death in the Clouds.*

ZIELINSKY, ELLA Marina Gregg's social secretary, she suffered from a number of allergies, for relief from which she would resort to the use of an atomizer. She died by inhaling prussic acid. *The Mirror Crack'd from Side to Side.*

ZIYARA, SHEIK HUSSEIN EL Sheik Hussein was renowned "throughout the Moslem world, both as a Holy Man and a poet. . . . He was considered by many to be a Saint." He had been a life-long friend to Henry Carmichael, who passed on microfilms of the Asian weapon site to the Sheik. Carmichael also left coded messages in the form of a red knitted scarf and a letter of reference (*See* JONES, VICTORIA AND BAKER, RICHARD) which directed Mr. Dakin to the Sheik. *They Came to Baghdad.*

ZOBEIDA *See* MOSS, MARY.

ZULEIKA, MADAME Sally Legge assumed the identity of a fortune-teller at the fête. "Madame Zuleika was wearing flowing black robes, a gold tinsel scarf wound round her head and a veil across the lower half of her face which slightly muffled her remarks. A gold bracelet hung with lucky charms tinkled as she took Poirot's hand and gave him a rapid reading, agreeably full of money to come, success with a dark beauty and a miraculous escape from an accident." To her chagrin, Poirot saw through her disguise. *Dead Man's Folly.*

Bibliography

The following Bibliography is a chronological listing of Agatha Christie's mystery novels and short stories. The main title entry refers to the U.K. title, and the alternate titles are to U.S. editions. The date indicates the date of publication in England. The short stories contained in collections not published in the U.S. are cross-referenced to their subsequent appearance in U.S. collections. An alphabetical Index of the novels and short story collections of Agatha Christie follows the Bibliography for easy reference. Separate chronologies for Hercule Poirot, Miss Marple and Ariadne Oliver are contained in Appendix A; Appendix B lists other works by Agatha Christie.

1. *The Mysterious Affair at Styles* 1920
2. *The Secret Adversary* 1922
3. *Murder on the Links* 1923
4. *The Man in the Brown Suit* 1924
5. *Poirot Investigates* 1924
   "The Adventure of 'The Western Star' "; "The Tragedy at Marsdon Manor"; "The Adventure of the Cheap Flat"; "The Mystery of Hunter's Lodge"; "The Million Dollar Bond Robbery" ("The Million Dollar Bank Robbery" U.S. title); "The Adventure of the Egyptian Tomb"; "The Jewel Robbery at the 'Grand Metropolitan' "; "The Kidnapped Prime Minister"; "The Disappearance of Mr. Davenheim"; "The Adventure of the Italian Nobleman"; "The Case of the Missing Will"; "The Veiled Lady"*; "The Lost Mine"*; "The Chocolate Box"*
   *available in U.S. collection only; reprinted in *Poirot's Early Cases*
6. *The Secret of Chimneys* 1925
7. *The Murder of Roger Ackroyd* 1926
8. *The Big Four* 1927
9. *The Mystery of the Blue Train* 1928
10. *The Seven Dials Mystery* 1929
11. *Partners in Crime* 1929
    "A Fairy in the Flat"/"A Pot of Tea"*; "The Affair of the Pink Pearl" ("Blunt's Brilliant Detectives" U.S. title); "The Affair of the Sinister Stranger"; "Finessing the King"/"The Gentleman Dressed in Newspaper"*; "The Case of the Missing Lady"; "Blindman's Bluff"; "The Man in the Mist"; "The Crackler"; "The Sunningdale Mystery"; "The House of Lurking Death"; "The Unbreakable Alibi"; "The Clergyman's Daughter"/"The Red House"*; "The Ambassador's Boots"; "The Man Who Was No. 16"
    (*two parts of the same story)
12. *The Mysterious Mr. Quin* 1930 *(The Passing of Mr. Quin U.S. title)*
    "The Coming of Mr. Quin"; "The Shadow on the Glass"; "At the Bells and Motley"; "The Sign in the Sky"; "The Soul of the Croupier"; "The World's End"; "The Voice in the Dark"; "The Face of Helen"; "The Dead Harlequin"; "The Bird with the Broken Wing"; "The Man from the Sea"; "Harlequin's Lane"
13. *Murder at the Vicarage* 1930
14. *The Sittaford Mystery* 1931 *(Murder at Hazelmoor U.S. title)*
15. *Peril at End House* 1932
16. *The Thirteen Problems* 1932 *(The Tuesday Club Murders U.S. title)*
    "The Tuesday Night Club"; "The Idol House of Astarte"; "Ingots of Gold"; "The Blood-Stained Pavement"; "Motive *v* Opportunity"; "The Thumb Mark of St. Peter"; "The Blue Geranium"; "The Companion"; "The Four Suspects"; "A Christmas Tragedy"; "The Herb of Death"; "The Affair at the Bungalow"; "Death by Drowning"

17. *Lord Edgware Dies*   1933   *(Thirteen at Dinner* U.S. title*)*
18. *Hound of Death*   (not published in the U.S.)   1933
    "The Hound of Death"*; "The Red Signal"†; "The Fourth Man"†; "The Gypsy"*; "The Lamp"*; "Wireless"† ("Where There's a Will" U.S. title); "The Witness for the Prosecution"†; "The Mystery of the Blue Jar"†; "The Strange Case of Sir Andrew Carmichael"*; "The Call of Wings"*; "The Last Séance"‡; "S.O.S."†; (*reprinted in *The Golden Ball*; †reprinted in *Witness for the Prosecution*; ‡reprinted in *Double Sin*)
19. *Murder on the Orient Express*   1934   *(Murder in the Calais Coach* U.S. title*)*
20. *The Listerdale Mystery* (not published in the U.S.)   1934
    "The Listerdale Mystery"*; "Philomel Cottage"†; "The Girl in the Train"*; "Sing a Song of Sixpence"‡; "The Manhood of Edward Robinson"*; "Accident"†; "Jane in Search of a Job"*; "A Fruitful Sunday"*; "Mr. Eastwood's Adventure"‡‡ ("The Mystery of the Spanish Shawl U.S. title); "The Golden Ball"*; "The Rajah's Emerald"*; "Swan Song"*
    (*reprinted in *The Golden Ball*; † reprinted in *Witness for the Prosecution*; ‡appeared in the U.S. in *Ellery Queen's Mystery Magazine*, February, 1947; ‡‡reprinted under its alternate title in the Christie short story anthology *Surprise! Surprise!*)
21. *Why Didn't They Ask Evans?*   1934   *(The Boomerang Clue* U.S. title*)*
22. *Parker Pyne Investigates*   1934   *(Mr. Parker Pyne, Detective* U.S. title*)*
    "The Case of the Middle-Aged Wife"; "The Case of the Discontented Soldier"; "The Case of the Distressed Lady"; "The Case of the Discontented Husband"; "The Case of the City Clerk"; "The Case of the Rich Woman"; "Have You Got Everything You Want?"; "The Gate of Baghdad"; "The House at Shiraz"; "The Pearl of Price"; "Death on the Nile"*; "The Oracle at Delphi"
    (*In no way similar to the 1937 novel with the same title)
23. *Three-Act Tragedy*   1935   *(Murder in Three Acts* U.S. title*)*
24. *The A.B.C. Murders*   1935
25. *Death in the Clouds*   1935   *(Death in the Air* U.S. title*)*
26. *Murder in Mesopotamia*   1936
27. *Cards on the Table*   1936
28. *Dumb Witness*   1937   *(Poirot Loses a Client* U.S. title*)*
29. *Death on the Nile*   1937
30. *Murder in the Mews*   1937   *(Dead Man's Mirror* U.S. title*)*
    "Murder in the Mews"; "The Incredible Theft"*; "Dead Man's Mirror"; "Triangle at Rhodes"
    (*Not included in the U.S. edition; appeared in *Ellery Queen's Mystery Magazine*, March, 1972)
31. *Appointment with Death*   1938
32. *Hercule Poirot's Christmas*   1938   *(Murder for Christmas* U.S. title*)*
33. *Murder is Easy*   1939   *(Easy to Kill* U.S. title*)*
34. *Ten Little Niggers*   1939   *(And Then There Were None; Ten Little Indians* U.S. title*)*
35. *The Regatta Mystery* (published in the U.S. only)   1939
    "The Regatta Mystery"; "The Mystery of the Baghdad Chest"; "How Does Your Garden Grow?"; "Problem at Pollensa Bay"; "Yellow Iris"; "Miss Marple Tells a Story"; "The Dream"; "In a Glass Darkly"; "Problem at Sea"
36. *Sad Cypress*   1940
37. *One, Two, Buckle My Shoe*   1940   *(The Patriotic Murders* U.S. title*)*
38. *Evil Under the Sun*   1941
39. *N or M?*   1941
40. *The Body in the Library*   1942
41. *Five Little Pigs*   1943   *(Murder in Retrospect* U.S. title*)*

42. *The Moving Finger* 1943
43. *Towards Zero* 1944 *(Come and Be Hanged* U.S. title*)*
44. *Death Comes as the End* 1944
45. *Sparkling Cyanide* 1945 *(Remembered Death* U.S. title*)*
46. *The Hollow* 1946 *(Murder After Hours* U.S. title*)*
47. *The Labours of Hercules* 1947
    "Foreword"; "The Nemean Lion"; "The Lernean Hydra"; "The Arcadian Deer"; "The Erymanthian Boar"; "The Augean Stables"; "The Stymphalian Birds"; "The Cretan Bull"; "The Horses of Diomedes"; "The Girdle of Hippolyta"; "The Flock of Geryon"; "The Apples of the Hesperides"; "The Capture of Cerberus"
48. *Taken at the Flood* 1948 *(There is a Tide* U.S. title*)*
49. *Witness for the Prosecution* (published in the U.S. only) 1948
    "Witness for the Prosecution"; "The Red Signal"; "The Fourth Man"; "S.O.S."; "Where There's a Will"; "The Mystery of the Blue Jar"; "Philomel Cottage"; "Accident"; "The Second Gong"
50. *Crooked House* 1949
51. *A Murder is Announced* 1950
52. *Three Blind Mice and Other Stories* (published in the U.S. only) 1950 *(The Mousetrap and Other Stories* U.S. title*)*
    "Three Blind Mice"; "Strange Jest"; "The Tape-Measure Murder"; "The Case of the Perfect Maid"; "The Case of the Caretaker"; "The Third-Floor Flat"; "The Adventure of Johnnie Waverly"; "Four and Twenty Blackbirds"; "The Love Detectives"
53. *They Came to Baghdad* 1951
54. *The Under Dog* (published in the U.S. only) 1951
    "The Under Dog"; "The Plymouth Express"; "The Affair at the Victory Ball"; "The Market Basing Mystery"; "The Lemesurier Inheritance"; "The Cornish Mystery"; "The King of Clubs"; "The Submarine Plans"; "The Adventure of the Clapham Cook"
55. *Mrs. McGinty's Dead* 1952 *(Blood Will Tell* U.S. title*)*
56. *They Do It with Mirrors* 1952 *(Murder with Mirrors* U.S. title*)*
57. *After the Funeral* 1953 *(Funerals are Fatal* U.S. title*)*
58. *A Pocket Full of Rye* 1953
59. *Destination Unknown* 1954 *(So Many Steps to Death* U.S. title*)*
60. *Hickory, Dickory, Dock* 1955 *(Hickory, Dickory, Death* U.S. title*)*
61. *Dead Man's Folly* 1956
62. *4.50 from Paddington* 1957 *(What Mrs. McGillicuddy Saw!* U.S. title*)*
63. *Ordeal by Innocence* 1958
64. *Cat Among the Pigeons* 1959
65. *The Adventure of the Christmas Pudding* (not published in the U.S.) 1960
    "The Adventure of the Christmas Pudding"* ("The Theft of the Royal Ruby" U.S. title); "The Mystery of the Spanish Chest"; "The Under Dog"†; "Four and Twenty Blackbirds"‡; "The Dream"‡‡; "Greenshaw's Folly"††
    (*reprinted under its alternate title in *Double Sin*; †published in *The Under Dog*; ‡published in *Three Blind Mice*; ‡‡published in *The Regatta Mystery*; ††reprinted in *Double Sin*)
66. *The Pale Horse* 1961
67. *Double Sin* 1961
    "Double Sin"; "Wasps' Nest"; "The Theft of the Royal Ruby" ("The Adventure of the Christmas Pudding" U.S. title); "The Dressmaker's Doll"; "Greenshaw's Folly"; "The Double Clue"; "The Last Séance"; "Sanctuary"
68. *The Mirror Crack'd from Side to Side* 1962
69. *The Clocks* 1963
70. *A Caribbean Mystery* 1964

71. *At Bertram's Hotel*   1965
72. *Third Girl*   1966
73. *Endless Night*   1967
74. *By the Pricking of My Thumbs*   1968
75. *Hallowe'en Party*   1969
76. *Passenger to Frankfurt*   1970
77. "The Harlequin Tea Set" (a Harley Quin short story anthologized in *Winter's Crimes 3*, Macmillan London Ltd.)   1971
78. *Nemesis*   1971
79. *The Golden Ball* (published in the U.S. only)   1971
    "The Listerdale Mystery"; "The Girl in the Train"; "The Manhood of Edward Robinson"; "Jane in Search of a Job"; "A Fruitful Sunday"; "The Golden Ball"; "The Rajah's Emerald"; "Swan Song"; "The Hound of Death"; "The Gipsy"; "The Lamp"; "The Strange Case of Sir Andrew Carmichael"; "The Call of Wings"; "Magnolia Blossom"; "Next to a Dog"
80. *Elephants Can Remember*   1972
81. *Postern of Fate*   1973
82. *Poirot's Early Cases*   1974
    "The Affair at the Victory Ball"; "The Adventure of the Clapham Cook"; "The Cornish Mystery"; "The Adventure of Johnnie Waverly"; "The Double Clue"; "The King of Clubs"; "The Lemesurier Inheritance"; "The Lost Mine"; "The Plymouth Express"; "The Chocolate Box"; "The Submarine Plans"; "The Third-Floor Flat"; "Double Sin"; "The Market Basing Mystery"; "Wasps' Nest"; "The Veiled Lady"; "Problem at Sea"; "How Does Your Garden Grow?"
83. *Curtain*   1975
84. *Sleeping Murder*   1976

Index to Bibliography

The following alphabetical listing of Agatha Christie's novels and short story collections is offered as a quick and easy guide to the main entry bibliography. The number following the title below corresponds to the number in the Bibliography where full information about the title may be found.

A.B.C. Murders, The   24
Adventure of the Christmas Pudding, The   65
After the Funeral   57
Appointment with Death   31
At Bertram's Hotel   71
Big Four, The   8
Body in the Library, The   40
By the Pricking of My Thumbs   74
Cards on the Table   27
Caribbean Mystery, A   70
Cat Among the Pigeons   64
Clocks, The   69
Crooked House   50
Curtain   83
Dead Man's Folly   61
Death Comes as the End   44
Death in the Clouds   25
Death on the Nile   29
Destination Unknown   59
Double Sin   67
Dumb Witness   28
Elephants Can Remember   80
Endless Night   73
Evil Under the Sun   38
Five Little Pigs   41
4.50 from Paddington   62
Golden Ball, The   79
Hallowe'en Party   75
"Harlequin Tea Set, The"   77
Hercule Poirot's Christmas   32
Hickory, Dickory, Dock   60
Hollow, The   46
Hound of Death   18
Labours of Hercules, The   47
Listerdale Mystery, The   20
Lord Edgware Dies   17
Man in the Brown Suit, The   4
Mirror Crack'd from Side to Side, The   68
Moving Finger, The   42
Mrs. McGinty's Dead   55
Murder at the Vicarage   13
Murder in Mesopotamia   26

Murder in the Mews   30
Murder is Announced, A   51
Murder is Easy   33
Murder of Roger Ackroyd, The   7
Murder on the Links   3
Murder on the Orient Express   19
Mysterious Affair at Styles, The   1
Mysterious Mr. Quin, The   12
Mystery of the Blue Train, The   9
N or M?   39
Nemesis   78
One, Two, Buckle My Shoe   37
Ordeal by Innocence   63
Pale Horse, The   66
Parker Pyne Investigates   22
Partners in Crime   11
Passenger to Frankfurt   76
Peril at End House   15
Pocket Full of Rye, A   58
Poirot Investigates   5
Poirot's Early Cases   82
Postern of Fate   81
Regatta Mystery, The   35
Sad Cypress   36
Secret Adversary, The   2
Secret of Chimneys, The   6
Seven Dials Mystery, The   10
Sittaford Mystery, The   14
Sleeping Murder   84
Sparkling Cyanide   45
Taken at the Flood   48
Ten Little Niggers   34
Thirteen Problems, The   16
They Came to Baghdad   53
They Do It with Mirrors   56
Third Girl   72
Three-Act Tragedy   23
Three Blind Mice and Other Stories   52
Towards Zero   43
Under Dog, The   54
Why Didn't They Ask Evans?   21
Witness for the Prosecution   49

Appendix A

The following lists are meant as a guide, to be used in conjunction with the main entry bibliography, for those readers who wish to follow the careers of Agatha Christie's different sleuths. The novels and stories in which Mr. Parker Pyne, Tuppence and Tommy Beresford, Superintendent Battle, Harley Quin and Mr. Satterthwaite, Inspector Japp and Colonel Race appear are listed at the end of their individual entries.

HERCULE POIROT

(*denotes those stories in which Captain Arthur Hastings appeared)

The Mysterious Affair at Styles*, 1920; *Murder on the Links**, 1923; *Poirot Investigates* (fourteen short stories)*, 1924; *The Murder of Roger Ackroyd*, 1926; *The Big Four**, 1927; *The Mystery of the Blue Train*, 1928; *Peril at End House**, 1932; *Lord Edgware Dies**, 1933; *Murder on the Orient Express*, 1934; *Three-Act Tragedy*, 1935; *The A.B.C. Murders**, 1935; *Death in the Clouds*, 1935; *Murder in Mesopotamia*, 1936; *Cards on the Table*, 1936; *Dumb Witness**, 1937; *Death on the Nile*, 1937; *Murder in the Mews* (four novellas), 1937; *Appointment with Death*, 1938; *Hercule Poirot's Christmas*, 1938; from *The Regatta Mystery:*, 1939; "The Mystery of the Baghdad Chest"* "How Does Your Garden Grow?" "Yellow Iris" "The Dream" "Problem at Sea", *Sad Cypress*, 1940; *One, Two, Buckle My Shoe*, 1940; *Evil Under the Sun*, 1941; *Five Little Pigs*, 1943; *The Hollow*, 1946; *The Labours of Hercules* ("Foreword" and twelve short stories), 1947; *Taken at the Flood*, 1948; from *Three Blind Mice:*, 1950; "The Third-Floor Flat" "The Adventure of Johnnie Waverly" "Four and Twenty Blackbirds", *The Under Dog* (nine short stories)*, 1951; *Mrs. McGinty's Dead*, 1952; *After the Funeral*, 1953; *Hickory, Dickory, Dock*, 1955; *Dead Man's Folly*, 1956; *Cat Among the Pigeons*, 1959; from *The Adventure of the Christmas Pudding:*, 1960; "The Mystery of the Spanish Chest" (a re-telling of "The Mystery of the Baghdad Chest"), from *Double Sin:*, 1961; "Double Sin"* "Wasps' Nest" "The Double Clue"*, *Third Girl*, 1966; *Hallowe'en Party*, 1969; *Elephants Can Remember*, 1972; *Poirot's Early Cases* (eighteen short stories)*, 1974; *Curtain*, 1975.

MISS JANE MARPLE

Murder at the Vicarage, 1930; *The Thirteen Problems* (thirteen short stories), 1932; from *The Regatta Mystery:*, 1939; "Miss Marple Tells a Story", *The Body in the Library*, 1942; *The Moving Finger*, 1943; *A Murder is Announced*, 1950; from *Three Blind Mice:*, 1950; "Strange Jest" "The Tape-Measure Murder" "The Case of the Perfect Maid" "The Case of the Caretaker", *They Do It with Mirrors*, 1952; *A Pocket Full of Rye*, 1953; *4.50 from Paddington*, 1957; from *The Adventure of the Christmas Pudding:*, 1960; "Greenshaw's Folly", from *Double Sin:*, 1961; "Sanctuary", *The Mirror Crack'd from Side to Side*, 1962; *A Caribbean Mystery*, 1964; *At Bertram's Hotel*, 1965, *Nemesis*, 1971, *Sleeping Murder*, 1976.

ARIADNE OLIVER

(*indicates a Hercule Poirot novel)

from *Parker Pyne Investigates:*, 1934; "The Case of the Discontented Soldier" "The Case of the Rich Woman", *Cards on the Table**, 1936; *Mrs. McGinty's Dead**, 1952; *Dead Man's Folly**, 1956; *The Pale Horse*, 1961; *Third Girl**, 1966; *Hallowe'en Party**, 1969; *Elephants Can Remember**, 1972.

Appendix B

I. Original Mystery Plays by Agatha Christie (title followed by date of the first London production) *Black Coffee*, 1930; *Spider's Web*, 1954; *Verdict*, 1958; *The Unexpected Guest*, 1958; *Rule of Three* (three one-act plays: *Afternoon at the Seaside*; *Patients*; *Rats*), 1962.

II. Romantic Novels published as Mary Westmacott *Giant's Bread*, 1930; *Unfinished Portrait*, 1934; *Absent in the Spring*, 1944; *The Rose and the Yew Tree*, 1947; *A Daughter's a Daughter*, 1952; *The Burden*, 1956.

III. Books published as Agatha Christie Mallowan *Come, Tell Me How You Live*, 1946 (memoir of archaeological expeditions in Syria); *Star Over Bethlehem*, 1965 (poems and children's stories).

IV. Other books by Agatha Christie *The Road of Dreams*, 1924 (a book of poems, republished 1973); *Akhnaton*, written 1937, published 1973 (a play set in ancient Egypt); *An Autobiography*, 1977.